Testing in Language Programs:

A Comprehensive Guide to English Language Assessment

James Dean Brown

Testing in Language Programs: A Comprehensive Guide to English Language Assessment

1 2 3 4 5 6 7 8 9 QPD 09 08 07 06 05

ISBN: 0-07-294836-1

Editorial director: Tina B. Carver
Executive editor: Erik Gundersen
Developmental editor: Linda O'Roke
Production Manager: MaryRose Malley
Cover design: Karolyn Wehner

This book is dedicated with love to my mother, Jeanne Yvonne Brown.

Among many other things, she taught me to love books.

TABLE OF CONTENTS

As is often true in the language teaching field, this volume had its roots in a class that I teach quite regularly—in this case, a graduate-level course in language testing. While many books exist on language testing, none seemed to offer the types of information that I wanted to present in my class. I felt that some books were too technical and complex to be thoroughly covered in one semester, while others were too practical—offering many ideas for different types of language test questions, but very little on test construction, analysis, and improvement. As a result, this language testing book is designed to cover the middle ground. I have tried to provide a balance between the technical and practical aspects of language testing that is neither too complex nor too simplistic.

My overall goal was to provide information about language testing that would not only be immediately useful for making program-level decisions (e.g., admissions and placement decisions), but also information about testing for classroom-level decisions (i.e., assessing what the students have learned through diagnostic or achievement testing). These two categories of decisions and the types of tests that are typically used to make them are quite different.

The category of tests most useful for program-level decisions consists of tests specifically designed to compare the performances of students to each other. These are called norm-referenced tests because interpretation of the scores from this category of tests is linked closely to the notion of the normal curve (also known as the "bell" curve). Such tests are most commonly used to spread students out along a continuum of scores based on some general knowledge or skill area so that the students can be placed, or grouped, into ability levels. The administrator's goal in using this type of test is usually to group students of similar abilities together in order to make the teacher's job easier. In other situations, the administrator may be interested in making comparisons between the average proficiency levels of students in different levels, between different language institutions or among students across the nation. Norm-referenced tests are also appropriate for language proficiency testing. Notice that the purpose of the tests in the norm-referenced family is to make comparisons in performance either between students within an institution (for placement purposes) or between students across courses or institutions (for proficiency assessment purposes). In short, sound norm-referenced tests can help administrators and teachers do their jobs better.

In contrast, the criterion-referenced family of tests is most useful to teachers in the classroom (though administrators should be interested in these tests as well). Criterion-referenced tests are specifically designed to assess how much of the material or set of skills taught in a course is being learned by the students. With criterion-referenced tests, the purpose is not to compare the performances of students to each other, but rather to look at the performance of each individual student vis-à-vis the material or curriculum at hand. They are called criterion-referenced tests because interpretation of the scores is intimately linked to assessing well-defined criteria for what is being taught. Such tests are often used to diagnose the strengths and weaknesses of students with regard to the goals and objectives of a course or program. At other times, criterion-referenced tests may be used to assess achievement, in the sense of "how much has each student learned." Such information may be useful for grading student performance in the course, or for deciding whether to promote the students to the next level of study, as well as for improving the materials, presentation, and sequencing of teaching points. In short, sound criterion-referenced tests can help the teacher do a better job.

My primary motivation in writing this book was to provide practical and useful testing tools that will help language program administrators and teachers do their respective jobs better. The distinction between the norm-referenced and criterion-referenced tests will help administrators and teachers focus on the respective types of tests most appropriate for the kinds of decisions that they make in their work. Hence the topic of each chapter will be approached from both norm-referenced and criterion-referenced perspectives. After all, the decisions made by administrators and teachers affect students' lives, sometimes in dramatic ways, involving a great deal of time and money, other times in more subtle ways, including psychological and attitudinal factors.

I assume that teachers, though most interested in classroom tests, will also take an interest in program-level decisions. Similarly, I assume that administrators, though primarily interested in program-level decisions, will also take an interest in classroom-level tests. Each group is inevitably involved in the other's decision making—perhaps in the form of teachers proctoring and scoring the placement test, or perhaps in the form of an administrator evaluating the effectiveness of teachers' classroom tests. The types of decisions discussed in this book may interact in innumerable ways, and I think that any cooperation between administrators and teachers in making decisions will be healthy for the curriculum in general and test development in particular.

Regardless of whether the reader is a teacher, an administrator, or both, the goal of reading this book should be to learn how to do all types of testing well. Inferior or mediocre testing is common, yet most language professionals recognize that such practices are irresponsible and eventually lead to inferior or mediocre decisions being made about their students' lives. The tools necessary to do high quality testing are provided in this book. Where statistics are involved, they are explained in a straightforward "recipe book" style so that readers can immediately understand and apply what they learn to their teaching or administrative situations. If this book makes a difference in the quality of decision making in even one language program, the time and effort that went into writing it will all have been worthwhile.

This is the second edition of this book. Brown (1996a) was the first edition, and Brown (translated by Wada 1999) provided a Japanese translation. This edition differs in several ways from the first edition. Most prominently, this edition has been updated throughout to reflect the present state of knowledge on all the topics covered, including many new sections and new references. But also of importance, based on the feedback and suggestions of professors using the first edition of the book, the conceptual and computational explanations of the various statistical techniques in the first edition have been expanded to include clear directions for doing the various statistics in a spreadsheet computer program. Judging by feedback from readers, the first edition of this book was found to be useful by many. I hope this new expanded edition will prove even more useful in real language teaching situations like yours.

I would like to thank Kathleen Bailey, John Nelson, and Betsy Parrish for their helpful comments during the reviewing proccess. Also, I would like to thank Mark Nelson and Sophia Wisener for their help in the editing process.

Finally, I would like to thank Microsoft for permission to use their *Excel*™ program.

CHAPTER 1

TYPES AND USES OF LANGUAGE TESTS

INTRODUCTION

Before getting into the nuts and bolts of doing language testing, I need to first lay some groundwork by discussing the differences between the two basic families of tests found in language testing. Then, I will define and discuss the four primary functions that these tests serve in language programs. Next, I will explain how administrators and teachers can best match the four basic types of language tests to the purposes and decision-making needs of their own language programs and courses. I will then explain why it is impossible to create a single test that can fulfill the functions of all four basic types of language tests. Finally, I will give a brief introduction to the Microsoft *Excel*™ spreadsheet program. As in all the chapters of this book, I will end with a series of review questions, that will help to summarize the chapter, and a set of application exercises.

TWO FAMILIES OF LANGUAGE TESTS

The first and most basic distinction in language testing involves two families of tests that perform two very different functions: one family helps administrators and teachers make program level decisions, such as proficiency and placement decisions, and the other family helps teachers make classroom-level decisions, such as diagnostic and achievement decisions. In the technical jargon of testing, these two families are called norm-referenced tests and criterion-referenced tests. The concepts underlying norm-referenced testing have been fully developed in educational measurement circles for most of the twentieth century, and many language teachers have been exposed to this category of testing in one way or another. However, the idea of criterion-referenced testing did not surface in educational measurement circles until 1963 when Glaser first mentioned the idea. The distinction between norm-referenced and criterion-referenced tests has only gradually entered the language testing literature, starting in the sixties (see Cartier 1968), skipping the seventies, reappearing in the early eighties (Cziko 1982, 1983; Brown 1984a; Hudson & Lynch 1984), becoming more prominent in the late eighties (Delamere 1985; Henning 1987; Bachman 1987, 1989; Brown 1988a, 1989a; Hudson 1989a, 1989b), gaining more prominence in the nineties (Bachman 1990; Cook 1990; Davidson & Lynch 1993; Griffee 1995; Brown 1990a, 1990b, 1992, 1993, 1995a, 1995b, 1996a; Lynch & Davidson 1994, 1997), and continuing into the new millennium (Brown & Hudson 2002; Davidson & Lynch 2002).

In recent years, the distinction between norm-referenced and criterion-referenced testing has continued to be important in educational and psychological measurement. I hope this will continue because an understanding of the fundamental differences and similarities between these two types of tests can help language program administrators and language teachers make much better decisions about their students.

Norm-Referenced Tests

In brief, a **norm-referenced test** (NRT) is designed to measure global language abilities (i.e., overall English language proficiency, academic listening ability, reading comprehension, and so on). Each student's score on such a test is interpreted relative to the scores of all other students who took the test. Such comparisons are usually done with reference to the concept of the **normal distribution** (familiarly known as the "bell curve"; for more on this concept, see Chapters 5 and 6). The purpose of an NRT is to spread students out along a continuum of scores so that those with low abilities in a general area such as reading comprehension are at one end of the normal distribution, while those with high abilities are at the other end (with the bulk of the students falling between the extremes). In addition, while students may know the general format of the questions on an NRT (for example, multiple-choice, true-false, dictation, or essay), they will typically not know before the test what specific content or skills will be covered by those questions.

Criterion-Referenced Tests

In contrast, a **criterion-referenced test** (CRT) is usually produced to measure well-defined and fairly specific instructional objectives. Often these objectives are specific to a particular course, program, school district, or state. An example of a very strict instructional objective would be the following: By the end of the course the students will be able to underline the sentence containing the main idea of an academic paragraph of 200–250 words at the eleventh grade readability level with 60 percent accuracy. However, objectives come in many forms. Other objectives might be defined in terms of tasks we would expect the students to be able to perform by the end of the term, or experiences we would expect them to go through. For example: by the end of the term the students will watch at least five English language movies with no subtitles. (For more example objectives, see Chapter 3 of Brown 1995a).

The interpretation of scores on a CRT is considered absolute in the sense that each student's score is meaningful without reference to the other students' scores. In other words, a student's score on a particular objective indicates the percent of the knowledge or skill in that objective that the student has learned. Moreover, the distribution of scores on a CRT need not necessarily be normal. If all the students know 100 percent of the material on all the objectives, then all the students should receive the same score with no variation at all. The purpose of a CRT is to measure the amount of learning that a student has accomplished on each objective. In most cases, the students should know in advance what types of questions, tasks, and content to expect for each objective because the question content should be implied (if not explicitly stated) in the objectives of the course.

A more detailed step-by-step comparison of norm-referenced and criterion-referenced tests will help to clarify the distinction. The six characteristics listed in the first column of Table 1.1 indicate that norm-referenced and criterion-referenced tests contrast in: the ways that scores are interpreted, the kinds of things that they are used to measure, the purposes for testing, the ways that scores are distributed, the structures of the test, and the students' knowledge of test question content.

Table 1.1 Norm-referenced and criterion-referenced test differences

Characteristic	Norm-Referenced	Criterion-Referenced
Type of Interpretation	Relative (A student's performance is compared to those of all other students in percentile terms.)	Absolute (A student's performance is compared only to the amount, or percentage, of material learned.)
Type of Measurement	To measure general language abilities or proficiencies	To measure specific objectives-based language points
Purpose of Testing	Spread students out along a continuum of general abilities or proficiencies	Assess the amount of material known or learned by each student
Distribution of Scores	Normal distribution of scores around the mean	Varies; often non-normal. Students who know the material should score 100%.
Test Structure	A few relatively long subtests with a variety of item contents	A series of short, well-defined subtests with similar item contents
Knowledge of Questions	Students have little or no idea of what content to expect in test items.	Students know exactly what content to expect in test items.

Type of interpretation

In terms of the type of interpretation, one essential difference between these two categories of tests is that each student's performance on a CRT is compared to a particular criterion in absolute terms. Some confusion has developed over the years about what the *criterion* in criterion-referenced testing refers to. This confusion is understandable because two definitions have evolved for criterion. For some authors, the material that the students are supposed to learn in a particular course is the criterion against which they are being measured. For other authors, the term criterion refers to the **standard**, also called a criterion level or cut-point (see Chapter 10), against which each student's performance is judged. For instance, if the cut-point for passing a CRT is set at 70 percent, that is the criterion level.

Regardless of which version of the term is being applied in a given situation, the primary focus in interpreting CRT scores is on how much of the material each student has learned in absolute terms. For example, the following would be a characteristic CRT score interpretation: a student scored 85 percent, which means that the student knew 85 percent of the material. Notice that no reference is made to the performances of other students in that score interpretation.

In contrast, on an NRT, each student's performance is interpreted relative to the performances of the other students in the norm group. In fact, NRT scores are sometimes expressed with no reference to the actual number of test questions answered correctly. For example, the following would be a typical NRT score interpretation: a student scored in the 84th percentile, which means that the student scored better than 84 out of 100 students in the group as a whole (and by extension, worse than 16 out of 100 students). How many questions did the student answer correctly? We have no way of knowing because a percentile score only expresses the student's position relative to the other students.

One key to understanding the difference between NRT and CRT score interpretations is captured in the terms percentage and percentile. On CRTs, teachers are primarily concerned with how much of the material the students know. That is, they focus on the **percentage** of material known, which tells them the proportion that each student has learned without reference to the performances of the other students. In other words, the teachers only care about the percentage of questions the students answered correctly (or percentage of tasks the students correctly completed) in connection with the material at hand and perhaps in relationship to a previously established criterion level. The percentages are interpreted directly without reference to the students' positions vis-à-vis each other. Hence, a high percentage score means that the test was easy for the students, which may in turn mean that the students knew the material being tested very well or that the test questions were written at too low a level. Similarly, a low percentage score means that the test was difficult for the students, which may in turn mean that the students did not know the material being tested or that the test questions were written at too high a level of difficulty.

On NRTs, the concern is entirely different. Teachers focus instead on how each student's performance relates to the performances of all other students. Thus, in one way or another, they are interested in the student's **percentile** score, which tells them the proportion of students who scored above and below the student in question. For instance, a student with a percentile score of 70 performed better than 70 out of 100 students but worse than 30 out of 100. If another NRT were administered to the same students but had much more difficult questions on it, the percentage of correct answers would be lower for all students, but their positions relative to each other in terms of percentile scores could be virtually the same. Similarly, if another NRT had easy questions on it, the percentage of correct answers would be high for all students, but their positions relative to each other in terms of percentile scores could be very similar.

In short, CRTs look at the amount of material known by the students in percentage terms, while NRTs examine the relationship of a given student's performance to those of all other students in percentile terms.

Type of measurement

With regard to type of measurement, NRTs are typically most suitable for measuring general abilities. Examples would include reading ability in French, listening comprehension in Chinese, and overall English language proficiency. The *Test of English as a Foreign Language*, more commonly known as the TOEFL, is a good example of such a test. While the TOEFL paper-and-pencil version does have three subtests measuring listening comprehension, writing and analysis, and reading comprehension and vocabulary (ETS 2002a, 2003), the computer-based TOEFL has four subtests: listening, structure, reading, and writing (ETS 2000)—all of which must necessarily be considered general abilities.

In contrast, CRTs are better suited to providing precise information about each individual's performance on well-defined learning points. For instance, if a language course focuses on a structural syllabus, the CRT for that course might contain four subtests on: subject pronouns, the *a/an* distinction, the third person *-s*, and the use of present tense copula. However, CRTs are not limited to grammar points. Subtests on a CRT for a notional-functional language course might consist of a short interview where ratings are made of the student's abilities to: perform greetings, agree or disagree, express an opinion, and end a conversation. The variety and types of test questions used on a CRT are limited only by the imagination of the test developer(s).

Purpose of the testing

In terms of the purpose of the testing, major differences clearly exist in the way scores are interpreted on NRTs and CRTs. As mentioned above, NRT interpretations are relative, while CRT interpretations are absolute. The purpose of an NRT is, therefore, to generate scores that spread the students out along a continuum of general abilities so that any existing differences among the individuals can be distinguished. However, since the purpose of a CRT is to assess the amount of knowledge or skill learned by each student, the focus is on the individuals' knowledge or skills, not on distributions of scores. As a result, the distributions of scores for NRTs and CRTs can be quite different.

Distributions of scores

Since NRTs must be constructed to spread students out along a continuum or distribution of scores, the manner in which test questions for an NRT are generated, analyzed, selected, and refined (see Chapter 4) will usually lead to a test that produces scores which fall into a normal distribution. Such a distribution is desirable so that any existing differences among the students will be clearly revealed. For instance, if you want your students to be accurately placed into levels of study in your institution, you would want to do so on the basis of tests that reveal clear differences in their abilities. In other words, if there is variation in the group with regard to the knowledge or skill being tested, any differences among students should be reflected in their scores so the students will be placed in a fair and equitable manner.

In contrast, on a criterion-referenced final examination, students who have learned all the course material should all be able to score 100 percent on the final examination. Thus, very homogeneous scores can occur on a CRT. In other words, very similar scores among students on a CRT may be perfectly logical, acceptable, and even desirable if the test is administered at the end of a course. In this situation, a normal distribution of scores may not appear. In fact, a normal distribution in CRT scores may even be a sign that something is wrong with the test, with the curriculum, or with the teaching (see Chapters 4, 5, & 11).

Test structure

Differences also arise in the test structure for the two families of tests. Early on, Popham and Husek (1969) contended that "…it is not possible to tell a NRT from a CRT by looking at it." However, even though you may not be able to tell whether an item is NRT or CRT in orientation by looking at it, I would argue that you can tell an NRT from a CRT in terms of the structure and organization of the test. Typically, an NRT is relatively long and contains a wide variety of question content types. Indeed, the content can be so diverse that students find it difficult to know exactly what is being tested. Such a test is usually made up of a few subtests on rather general language skills like reading comprehension, listening comprehension, grammar, writing, and so forth. Each of these subtests is relatively long (30–50 questions) and covers a wide variety of different contents.

In contrast, CRTs usually consist of numerous shorter subtests. Each subtest will typically represent a different instructional objective. If a course has twelve instructional objectives, the associated CRT will usually have twelve subtests. Sometimes, in courses with many objectives, for reasons of practicality, only a sub-sample of the objectives will be tested. For example, in a course with 30 objectives, it might be necessary due to time constraints to randomly select 15 of the objectives for testing, or to pick the 15 most important objectives (as judged by the teachers). Because of the number of subtests involved in most CRTs, the subtests are usually kept short (i.e., three to ten test items).

For reasons of economy of time and effort, the subtests on a CRT will sometimes be collapsed together, which makes it difficult for an outsider to identify the subtests. For example, on a reading comprehension test, the students might be required to read five passages and answer four multiple-choice questions on each passage. If on each passage there is one fact question, one vocabulary question, one cohesive device question, and one inference question, the teachers will most likely consider the five fact questions (across the five passages) together as one subtest, the five vocabulary questions together as another subtest, the five cohesive device questions together as yet another subtest, and the five inference questions together as the last subtest. In other words, the teachers will be focusing on the question types as subtests, not the passages, and this fact might not be obvious to an outside observer.

Finally, the two families of tests differ in the *knowledge of the questions* that students are expected to have. Students rarely know in any detail what content to expect on an NRT. In general, they might know what question formats to expect (for example, multiple-choice, true-false, and so forth), but seldom would the actual language points be predictable. This unpredictability of the question content results from the general nature of what NRTs are measuring and the wide variety of question content types that are typically used.

On a CRT, good teaching practice is more likely to lead to a situation in which the students can predict not only the question formats on the test, but also the language points that will be tested. If the instructional objectives for a course are clearly stated, if the students are given those objectives, if the objectives are addressed by the teacher, and if the language points involved are adequately practiced and learned, then the students should know exactly what to expect on the test, unless for some reason the criterion-referenced test is not properly referenced to the criteria (i.e., the instructional objectives).

This can often lead to complaints that the development of CRTs will cause teachers to "teach to the test" to the exclusion of other more important ways of spending classroom time. While I acknowledge that not all elements of the teaching and learning process can be tested, I argue that teaching to the test should nevertheless be a major part of what teachers do. If the objectives of a language course are worthwhile and have been properly constructed to reflect the needs of the students, then tests based on those objectives should reflect the important language points that are being taught. Teaching to such a test should help teachers and students stay on track, and the test results should provide useful feedback to both groups on the effectiveness of the teaching and learning processes. In short, teaching to the test, if the test is a well-developed CRT, should help the teacher and students rather than constrain them.

A very useful side effect of teaching to the test is that the information gained can have what Oller (1979, p. 52) termed **instructional value**, that is, the test-derived information can "enhance the delivery of instruction in student populations." In other words, such CRTs can provide useful information for evaluating the effectiveness of the needs analysis, the objectives, the tests themselves, the materials, the teaching, the students study habits, and so forth. In short, CRTs will prove enlightening in the never-ending evaluation process (see Brown 1995a).

I am not arguing that teachers should only address a very restricted set of objectives in a language course. Flexibility and time must be allowed in any curriculum for the teachers to address problems and learning points that arise along the way.

Nevertheless, if a common core of objectives can be developed for a course, a CRT can then be developed to test those objectives, and a number of benefits will accrue to the teachers, the students, and the curriculum developers alike (see Brown 1995a).

CRTs are not better than NRTs. Both categories of tests are very important for the decision-making processes in a language program, but for different types of decisions. Understanding the distinction between NRTs and CRTs can help teachers to match the correct type of test with any decision purpose.

MATCHING TESTS TO DECISION PURPOSES

A variety of decisions are made in almost any language program, and language tests of various kinds can help in making such decisions (e.g., placement decisions, pass/fail decisions, etc.). In order to test appropriately, administrators and teachers must be very clear about their purpose for making a given decision and then match the correct type of test to that purpose. In this section, I will summarize the main points that administrators and teachers must keep in mind when matching the appropriate measuring tool (NRT or CRT) with the types of decisions they must make about their students. The main points to consider are shown in Table 1.2. As the discussion develops, I will briefly cover each point as it applies to four types of decisions.

Table 1.2 Matching tests to decision purposes

Test Qualities	Type of Decision			
	Norm-Referenced		Criterion-Referenced	
	Proficiency	Placement	Achievement	Diagnostic
Detail of Information	Very general	General	Specific	Very specific
Focus	Usually general skills prerequisite to entry	Learning points from all levels & skills of program	Terminal objectives of course or program	Terminal and enabling objectives of courses
Purpose of Decision	To compare an individual's overall ability with other individuals	To find each student's appropriate level	To determine the degree of learning for advancement or graduation	To inform students and teachers of objectives needing more work
Relationship to Program	Comparisons with other institutions or programs	Comparisons within program	Directly related to objectives	Directly related to objectives still needing work
When Administered	Before entry and sometimes at exit	Beginning of program	End of courses	Beginning and/or middle of courses
Interpretation of Scores	Spread of wide range of scores	Spread of narrower, program-specific range of scores	Overall number and percentage of objectives learned	Percentage of each objective in terms of strengths and weaknesses

In administering and teaching in language programs, I have found myself making four basic kinds of decisions: proficiency, placement, achievement, and diagnostic. Since these are also the four types of tests identified in Alderson, Krahnke, and Stansfield (1987) as the most commonly used types of tests in our field, I will call them the primary **language testing functions** and focus on them in the remainder of this chapter. These testing functions correspond neatly to the NRT and CRT categories as follows: NRTs help in making program-level decisions (proficiency and placement), and CRTs are useful in making classroom-level decisions (diagnostic and achievement). They provide a useful framework for thinking about decision making in language programs.

Generally speaking, the program-level proficiency decisions (usually for admissions) and placement decisions are the prerogative of administrators. That is, administrators are most interested in and usually responsible for seeing to it that students are properly admitted to their institutions, and then that students are properly placed in the correct level of study. In contrast, the classroom-level decisions for diagnosis and achievement are the prerogative of classroom teachers. That is, teachers are usually most interested in and responsible for determining the individual student's strengths and weaknesses through diagnostic testing and the individual student's level of attainment through achievement testing.

Of course, other categories of tests do exist. For instance, aptitude tests, intelligence tests, learning strategy tests, and attitude tests do not fit neatly into these four language testing functions. However, those other types of tests are not generally administered in language programs, and so are not relevant to the topic of this book.

Program-level proficiency decisions

Sometimes, administrators need to make decisions based on the students' general levels of language proficiency. The focus of such decisions is usually on the general knowledge or skills prerequisite to entry or exit from some type of institution, for example, American universities. Such **proficiency decisions** are necessary in setting up entrance and exit standards for a curriculum, in adjusting the level of program objectives to the students' abilities, or in making comparisons between programs. Proficiency decisions are often based on proficiency tests specifically designed for such decisions. By definition, then, **proficiency tests** assess the general knowledge or skills commonly required or prerequisite to entry into (or exemption from) a group of similar institutions. One example is the *Test of English as a Foreign Language* (TOEFL), which is used by many American universities that have English language proficiency prerequisites in common (see ETS 1997, 2000, 2001, and 2002a). Understandably, such tests are very general in nature and cannot be related to the goals and objectives of any particular language program. Another example of the general nature of proficiency tests is the *ACTFL Proficiency Guidelines* from the American Council on the Teaching of Foreign Languages (ACTFL 1986, 2004). Though proficiency tests may contain subtests for different language skills, the testing of those skills remains very general, and the resulting scores can only serve as overall indicators of proficiency.

Since proficiency decisions require knowing the general level of proficiency of language students in comparison to other students, the test must provide scores that form a wide distribution so that interpretations of the differences among students will be as fair as possible. Thus, proficiency decisions should be made on the basis of norm-referenced proficiency tests, because NRTs have all the qualities desirable for such decisions (see Table 1.1, p. 3).

Proficiency decisions based on large scale standardized tests may sometimes seem unfair to teachers and administrators because of the arbitrary way that they are handled in some settings. However, such proficiency decisions are often necessary: to protect the integrity of the institutions involved, to keep students from getting in over their heads, and to prevent students from entering programs that they really do not need.

Proficiency decisions most often occur when a program must relate to the external world in some way. The students are arriving. How will they fit into the program? And when the students leave the program. Is their level of proficiency high enough so they can succeed linguistically in other institutions?

Sometimes, comparisons are also made among different language programs. For instance, since proficiency tests, by definition, are general in nature, rather than geared to any particular program, they could serve to compare regional branches of a particular language teaching system. Consider what would happen if the central office for a nationwide chain of ESL business English schools wanted to compare the effectiveness of all its centers. To make such decisions about the relative merit of the various centers, the administrators in charge would probably want to use some form of business English proficiency test.

Because such tests are not geared to any particular language program, extreme care must be exercised in making comparisons among different language programs. By chance, the test could fit the teaching and content of one program relatively closely, and as a consequence, the students in that program might score high on average. By chance, the test might not match the curriculum of another program quite so well, and consequently, the students would score low on that particular proficiency test. The question is: Should one program be judged less effective than another simply because the teaching and learning that is going on in that program (though perfectly effective and useful) is not adequately assessed by the test? Of course not. Hence, **program fair tests** (after Baretta 1986) must be used in such comparisons. That is, great care must be used in making such comparisons to make sure the test(s) involved appropriately match the curriculum goals and objectives of the programs involved.

Because of the general nature of proficiency decisions, a proficiency test must be designed so that the general abilities or skills of students are reflected in a wide distribution of scores. Only with such a wide distribution can decision-makers make fair comparisons among the students, or groups of students. This need for a wide spread of scores most often leads testers to create tests that produce normal distributions of scores. All of which is to argue that proficiency tests should usually be norm-referenced.

Proficiency decisions should never be undertaken lightly. Instead, these decisions must be based on the best obtainable proficiency test scores as well as other multiple sources of information about the students (for example, other test scores, grade point averages, interviews, recommendation letters, statements of purpose, research papers written by the students, etc.). Proficiency decisions can dramatically affect students' lives, so slipshod decision making in this area would be particularly unprofessional.

Program-level placement decisions

Placement decisions usually have the goal of grouping students of similar ability levels together. Teachers benefit from placement decisions because they end up with classes that have students with relatively homogeneous ability levels. As a result, teachers can focus on the problems and learning points appropriate for that level of students. To that end, placement tests are designed to help decide what each student's appropriate level will be within a specific program, skill area, or course. The purpose of such tests is to reveal which students have more or less of a particular knowledge or skill so that students with similar levels of ability can be grouped together.

Examining the similarities and differences between proficiency and placement testing will help to clarify the role of placement tests. At first glance, a proficiency test and a placement test might look very similar because they are both testing fairly general material. However, a proficiency test will tend to be very, very general in character because it is designed to assess extremely wide bands of abilities, from say beginning to near-native-speaker levels. In contrast, **placement tests** must be more specifically related to a given program, particularly in terms of the relatively narrow range of abilities assessed and the content of the curriculum, so that it efficiently separates the students into level groupings within that program.

Put another way, a general proficiency test might be useful for determining which language program is most appropriate for a student, but once in that program, a placement test would be necessary to determine the level of study that the student would most benefit from. Both proficiency and placement tests should be norm-referenced instruments because decisions must be made on the students' relative knowledge or skill levels. However, the degree to which a test is effective in spreading students out is directly related to the degree to which that test fits the ability levels of the students.

Consider, for example, the English Language Institute (ELI) at the University of Hawaii at Manoa (UHM). All the international students at UHM have been fully admitted by the time they arrive. In order to have been admitted, they must have taken the TOEFL (a proficiency test) and scored at least 500 on the paper-and-pencil version (or 173 on the computer-based version). From the ELI's point of view, language proficiency test scores are used to determine whether these students are eligible to study in the ELI and follow a few courses at UHM. Those students who score 600 or above on the paper-and-pencil TOEFL (or 250 on the computer-based version) are told that they are completely exempt from ELI training. Thus, I can safely say that most of the ELI students at UHM have scored between 500 and 600 on the paper-and-pencil TOEFL or between 173 and 250 on the computer-based version.

Within the ELI, there are three tracks, each of which is focused on one skill (reading, writing, or listening) with two skill levels in each track. As a result, the placement decisions and the tests upon which they are based must be much more focused than the information provided by TOEFL scores. The placement tests must provide information on each of the three skills involved as well as on the language needed by students in the relatively narrow proficiency range reflected in their TOEFL scores. While the contrasts between proficiency and placement decisions may not be quite so clear in all programs, these definitions and ways of distinguishing between proficiency and placement decisions should help teachers and administrators think about the program level decisions and testing in their own language programs.

If a particular program is designed with levels that include true beginners as well as very advanced learners, a general proficiency test *might* adequately serve as a placement test. However, such a wide range of abilities is not common in most language programs and, even when appropriately measuring such general abilities, each test must be examined in terms of how well it fits the abilities of the students and how well it matches what is actually taught in the classrooms.

If there is a mismatch between the placement test and what is taught in a program (as reported in Brown 1981), the danger is that the groupings of similar ability levels will simply not occur. For instance, consider an elementary school ESL program in which a general grammar test is used for placement. If the focus of the program is on oral communication at three levels and a pencil-and-paper test is used to place the children into those levels, numerous problems may arise. Such a test is placing the children into levels on the basis of their *written grammar* abilities. While grammar ability may be related to oral proficiency, other factors may be more important to successful oral communication. The result of such testing practices might be that the oral abilities of the children in all three of the (grammar-placed) levels could turn out to be about the same on average.

Some form of oral placement procedure, for example, the oral proficiency scale of the American Council on the Teaching of Foreign Languages (ACTFL 1986, 2004), might more accurately separate the children into three ability-level groups for the purposes of teaching them oral communication skills. However, the ACTFL scale was designed for assessing overall language proficiency and, therefore, may be too general for making responsible placement decisions in this particular elementary school program. In addition, the ACTFL scale may only be tangentially related to the goals and purposes of this particular school. Most importantly, the ACTFL scale was designed with adult university students in mind so it may not be at all appropriate for elementary school children. Clearly then, the purpose of a program, the range of abilities within the program, and the type of students involved are all factors that may make a proficiency test inappropriate for purposes of testing placement. Typically, placement decisions should be based on placement tests that have either been designed with a specific program in mind or been seriously examined for their appropriateness for the program in question.

Classroom-level achievement decisions

All language teachers are in the business of fostering achievement in the form of language learning. In fact, the purpose of most language programs is to maximize the possibilities for students to achieve a high degree of language learning. As a result, most language teachers will sooner or later find themselves interested in making achievement decisions. **Achievement decisions** are decisions about the amount of learning that students have accomplished. Such tests are typically administered at the end of the term, and such decisions may take the form of deciding which students will be advanced to the next level of study, determining which students should graduate, or simply for grading the students. Teachers may find themselves wanting to make rational decisions that will help improve their students' achievement. Or they may need to make and justify changes in curriculum design, staffing, facilities, materials, equipment, and so on. Such decisions should most often be made with the help of achievement test scores.

Making decisions about the achievement of students and about ways to improve their achievement will at least partly involve testing to find out how much each person has learned within the program. Thus, **achievement tests** should be designed with very specific reference to a particular course. This link with a specific course usually means that the achievement tests will be directly based on course objectives and will therefore be criterion-referenced. Such tests will typically be administered at the end of a course to determine how effectively students have mastered the instructional objectives.

Achievement tests must not only be very specifically designed to measure the objectives of a given course, but also must be flexible enough to help teachers readily respond to what they learn from the tests about the students' abilities, the students' needs, and the students' learning of the course objectives. In other words, a good achievement test can tell teachers a great deal about their students' achievement *and* about the adequacy of the course. Hence, while achievement tests should definitely be used to make decisions about students' levels of learning, they can also be used to affect curriculum changes.

Classroom-level diagnostic decisions

From time to time, teachers may also take an interest in assessing the strengths and weaknesses of each individual student in terms of the instructional objectives for the purpose of correcting an individual's deficiencies "before it is too late." To that end, **diagnostic decisions** are typically made at the beginning or middle of the term and are aimed at fostering achievement by promoting strengths and eliminating the weaknesses of individual students. Naturally, the primary concern of the teacher must be the entire group of students collectively, but some attention can also be given to each individual student. Clearly, this last category of decision is concerned with diagnosing problems that students may be having in the learning process. While diagnostic decisions are definitely related to achievement, diagnostic testing often requires more detailed information about which specific objectives students can already do well and which they still need to work on. The purpose is to help students and their teachers to focus their efforts where they will be most effective.

As with achievement tests, **diagnostic tests** are designed to determine the degree to which the specific instructional objectives of the course have already been accomplished. Hence, they should be criterion-referenced in nature. While achievement decisions are usually focused on the degree to which the objectives have been accomplished at the end of the program or course, diagnostic decisions are normally made along the way as the students are learning the language. As a result, diagnostic tests are typically administered at the beginning or in the middle of a language course. In fact, if well constructed to reflect the instructional objectives, one CRT in three equivalent forms could serve as a diagnostic tool at the beginning and midpoints in a course and as an achievement test at the end.

Perhaps the most effective use of a diagnostic test is to report the performance level on each objective (in a percentage) to each student so that they can decide how and where to most profitably invest their time and energy. For example, telling a student that she scored 100 percent on the first objective (selecting the main idea of a paragraph) but only 20 percent on the second objective (guessing vocabulary from context) would tell that student that she is good at finding the main idea of a paragraph but needs to focus her energy on guessing vocabulary from context.

It would also be useful to report the average performance level for each class on each objective (in percentage terms) to the teacher(s) along with indications of which students have particular strengths or weaknesses on each objective.

WHY A SINGLE TEST CANNOT FULFILL ALL FOUR FUNCTIONS

In my various contacts with language educators around the world, I have found that what many administrators and teachers would really like would be a proficiency-placement-diagnostic-achievement test that they could use for all kinds of decisions. Wouldn't that be wonderful? Why can't we have such a proficiency-placement-diagnostic-achievement test? Basically, there are at least two reasons why such a test could never be created: differences in ranges of ability and differences in variety of content.

Differences in ranges of ability

First, the ranges of ability tested by the four types of tests are very different. Typically, norm-referenced proficiency tests are designed to measure a very wide range of abilities as represented by the entire width of the outside box in Figure 1.1. In English for instance, the paper-and-pencil TOEFL measures from virtually no English (that is to say "guessing on the test") at 200 to native, or native-like ability at 677. That range is appropriate for passing students from institution to institution for admissions decisions and for comparing different institutions.

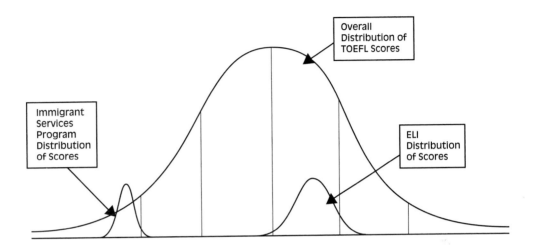

Figure 1.1 Distributions on the TOEFL for various groups of students

Placement tests would normally be very different in the range of abilities they assess, usually limited to the range of abilities handled by the particular institution involved. For example, Figure 1.1 shows the overall distribution of scores on the TOEFL proficiency test, and inside that distribution the distribution of TOEFL scores for two different institutions, one a survival-level ESL immigrant services program and the other a university English language institute (ELI). In both cases, the ranges of abilities within each of the institutions are much narrower than the range of abilities on the overall TOEFL and are very different from each other in terms of the overall abilities of the groups of students. Thus, to make placement decisions within either of these institutions, a much more narrowly focused placement test would be necessary. Also, note that a placement test developed for one institution would not be appropriate in level for the students in the other institution.

In addition, a proficiency test like the TOEFL would not be appropriate for such placement decisions for two reasons. One, because a proficiency test is designed to measure a very wide range of abilities, many of the items would be far too easy or far too difficult, or both, for the students in the particular institution. Two, because only a small subset of items would actually be at the appropriate level for placement decisions; the test items that discriminate at all would probably be too few to provide reliable enough measurement for making responsible decisions (see Chapter 9).

Conversely, a placement test designed for the specific range of abilities in a particular institution would not be of much use in making proficiency decisions between institutions. In other words, a placement test designed for a particular institution would probably not have a wide enough range of item difficulties to be useful for making admissions decisions that must by definition include students with wide spans of abilities from many different institutions.

The criterion-referenced diagnostic and achievement tests in the courses of the immigrant services program or in the courses of the ELI would have to be even more narrowly defined in terms of the ranges of abilities they test because they would typically be developed to measure the very specific levels of material taught in the particular courses within the particular institution. Hence, the range of abilities would be even narrower than that for the placement test used to put the students into that level of study, not to mention the proficiency test that was used to put the students in that institution. It wouldn't make any sense to use a very broad scale inter-institutional proficiency test, or even an inter-course placement test for diagnostic or achievement testing in a particular course. Conversely, such a course diagnostic or achievement test would be far too narrowly defined for placement into different courses, or for proficiency testing across institutions.

Differences in variety of content

The content of a proficiency test is also very broadly defined so that it will not favor one institution or another, but rather will cover the whole range of content types and ability levels covered across many institutions. In contrast, the content of a placement test should be more narrowly defined to meet the needs of the particular program in which it is being used. For instance, if one program has an overall grammar-translation orientation, the placement test should reflect that orientation across the range of abilities of the students within that program; if another program has a task-based orientation, the placement test should reflect that orientation, again across the appropriate range of abilities of the students in that program.

The content of diagnostic or achievement tests for a course should be even more narrowly defined to reflect the exact content of the course, perhaps as expressed in the goals and objectives for that course. For example, if an intermediate reading course has 15 intensive reading objectives and one extensive reading objective, the 15 *intensive reading objectives* (e.g., getting the main idea, reading for facts, reading for inferences, identifying language functions, etc.) should be directly reflected on the diagnostic and achievement tests with perhaps three items for each, while the single *extensive reading objective* (e.g., each student will read at least three books from the library) might take quite a different form (e.g., student summaries of the three books they read), because teachers simply need to check off something as students turn in their summaries in order to verify that each student has accomplished the objective. Thus, simply checking off the students' achievement of the objective can become a part of the testing system.

As with ability ranges, the variety of *contents* in an inter-institutional proficiency test would not be appropriate for placement testing, nor would the *contents* in a proficiency or placement test be appropriate for diagnostic or achievement purposes in most programs or courses. Conversely, a single course diagnostic or achievement test would be far too narrowly defined to use for placement into multiple courses, just as either a course or placement test would be far too narrowly defined to use for proficiency testing across institutions.

All in all, norm-referenced proficiency and placement tests have important, but different roles to play in language education vis-à-vis the ranges of ability and types of contents involved. Criterion-referenced diagnostic and achievement tests also have important roles in language education that are quite different from each other and different from proficiency or placement tests, again vis-à-vis the ranges of ability and types of contents involved. Trying to mix these purposes is likely to simply make a mess. (For example, see what happens when a company attempts to use a proficiency test for achievement testing purposes in Childs 1995.)

To bring this discussion home to you, consider how you would prefer to be tested on the material in this book when you have finished reading it. Would you prefer a test that is designed to spread people out so the results will be a few grades of *F*, some *D*s, many *C*s, some *B*s, and a few *A*s? That would be a norm-referenced approach. Or would you prefer a purely criterion-referenced achievement test that measures your knowledge of the language testing concepts in this book, designed such that anyone who knows the material will score well? If you would prefer the latter approach, you cannot in good conscience advocate the use of a norm-referenced test for assessing your students' achievement.

USING SPREADSHEET PROGRAMS IN LANGUAGE TESTING

The statistical analyses in this book will be explained in conceptual terms such that the reader can do them with a pencil and paper, or a calculator if necessary. However, they will also be described in terms of how they can be done on a spreadsheet program, which is a much easier way to proceed. If you have never worked with a spreadsheet program, you might reasonably ask three questions: What is a spreadsheet program? How will you personally benefit from using a spreadsheet program in this book? How can you get started with your spreadsheet program?

What Is a Spreadsheet Program?

A **spreadsheet program** is a very flexible computer tool that allows you to enter rows and columns of numbers, then manipulate, analyze, and present them in any way you like. *Excel*™ (Microsoft, 2003) is the spreadsheet program that most people use today. Regardless of which computer platform or which version of *Excel* you use, the layout, menus, commands, functions, etc., are generally the same. Thus, because it is ubiquitous and fairly standard, *Excel* is the logical choice to use as the example program in this book. However, if you are using a different spreadsheet program (e.g., *Quattro Pro*™, *Lotus 1-2-3*™, etc.) the processes will be very similar, so you will be able to work by analogy as long as you have a copy of the manual and/or a good book explaining how to use that particular spreadsheet program.

How Will You Personally Benefit from Using a Spreadsheet Program in This Book?

You can use a spreadsheet to enter your students' responses to the items on a test, analyze those responses to see which items are working and which are not (as explained in Chapter 4), calculate the students' total scores and descriptive statistics as well as their standardized scores (see Chapters 5 and 6), work out the correlation between their scores on the test and those from some other measure (see Chapter 7), estimate the reliability or dependability of the test (see Chapters 8 and 9), investigate the **validity** of the test (see Chapter 10), and keep records of their progress through the entire language program (see Chapter 11). All of this will prove relatively easy when using a spreadsheet program and very useful for any language teacher or administrator. While many of the above uses of a spreadsheet program may sound very complicated and difficult, they will all be explained step-by-step in the subsequent chapters so that, before you know it, these concepts will all be clear to you and become tools you can use in your classroom or program-level testing projects.

In the next chapter, you will be asked to get on a computer, actually open such a spreadsheet program, and have a look around. So you might want to begin now to get access both to a computer and a spreadsheet program.[1] I'm sure you will enjoy using a spreadsheet once you learn how. One warning, however, spreadsheets can be so addictive that they have been known to ruin relationships, marriages, and lives. So please use your spreadsheet prudently and only with the utmost restraint.

---

[1]If you don't already have a spreadsheet program at home or at work, you might consider buying *Excel* or downloading a program from the Internet by searching the phrase "free spreadsheet." Naturally, the *Excel* spreadsheet program will better match the instructions in this book.

REVIEW QUESTIONS

1. For which type of test (NRT or CRT) would you expect the interpretation to be absolute? For which type would it be relative?

2. For which type of test (NRT or CRT) would you expect the scores to spread students out along a continuum of general abilities or proficiencies?

3. For which type of test (NRT or CRT) would you expect all the students to be able to score 100 percent if they knew all of what was taught?

4. For which type of test (NRT or CRT) would the students usually have little or no idea what content to expect in questions?

5. For which type of test (NRT or CRT) would you expect to find a series of short, well-defined subtests with fairly similar test questions in each?

6. For which type of decision (proficiency, placement, diagnostic, or achievement) would you use a test that is designed to find each student's appropriate level within a particular program?

7. For which type of decision (proficiency, placement, diagnostic, or achievement) would you use a test that is designed to inform students and teachers of objectives needing attention?

8. For which type of decision (proficiency, placement, diagnostic, or achievement) would you use a test that is designed to determine the degree of learning (with respect to the program objectives) that had taken place by the end of a course or program?

9. For which type of decision (proficiency, placement, diagnostic, or achievement) would you use a test that is designed to compare an individual's overall performance with that of groups/individuals at other institutions?

10. Do you think that the concepts behind CRTs and NRTs can be mixed into one test? In other words, do you think it is possible to create a proficiency-placement-diagnostic-achievement test? If so, why do you think that is desirable? And how on earth would you go about doing it?

APPLICATION EXERCISES

A. Consider a specific language teaching situation in an elementary school, a secondary school, a commercial language center, a university intensive program, or other language teaching setting. Think of one type of decision that administrators and teachers must make in that program. Decide what type of decision it is (proficiency, placement, diagnostic, or achievement).

B. Now describe the test that you would recommend using to make the decision that you selected in Question A. Decide what type of test you would use and what it should be like in terms of overall characteristics, as well as the skills tested, level of difficulty, length, administration time, scoring, and type of report given to teachers and students.

C. Best of all, if you have the opportunity, match a real test to a real decision in some language program; administer, score, interpret, and report the results of the test; and make or help others make the appropriate decisions so that they minimize any potential negative effects on the students' lives.

CHAPTER 2

ADOPTING, ADAPTING, AND DEVELOPING LANGUAGE TESTS

INTRODUCTION

Numerous considerations influence the kinds of choices teachers and administrators must make if they want to develop an effective testing program at their institution. I explore these considerations in this chapter as a series of theoretical and practical testing issues, each of which can be described and thought about separately. The theoretical issues include language teaching methodology issues, the distinction between competence and performance, and the difference between discrete-point and integrative tests. The practical issues include fairness issues, cost issues, and logistical issues.

Though they are discussed separately, all of these issues must be considered simultaneously when addressing the next topic of the chapter: whether you want to adopt, adapt, or develop language tests for your language program. After a brief discussion of the important factors necessary for putting sound tests in place, I will end the chapter by showing how to get started with your spreadsheet program.

THEORETICAL ISSUES

The **theoretical issues** that I will address have to do with what tests should look like and what they should do. These issues have a great deal to do with how a group of teachers feels their course or program fits pedagogically within the overall field of language teaching, and how well they communicate their beliefs about teaching and testing with each other. After all, it is only through communication that teachers can create curriculum and tests that are at least modestly coordinated within and between courses so that students do not face a bewildering array of disconnected teaching and testing methods.

Theoretical issues may include pedagogical beliefs in various language teaching methodologies ranging from grammar-translation to communicative language teaching, or beliefs in the relative importance of the skills that teachers teach and test in their program (written or oral, productive or receptive, and various combinations of the four). Other theoretical issues may range from the linguistic distinction between competence and performance to the purely testing distinction among the various types of tests that are available in language teaching. These test types range from what are called discrete-point to integrative tests and various combinations of the two. I will discuss each of these issues in turn, then, look at some of the ways in which they may interact with each other. Remember, they are theoretical viewpoints on what tests should look like and what they should do.

One problem that arises is that language teaching professionals often disagree on these issues. Since tests are instruments developed by people to make decisions about other people, test development and test administration are inherently political activities. Thus, the policies of a given program on the various testing issues should be decided consciously and purposefully by the teachers and administrators involved, whether by consensus, by majority vote, or by executive decree. Regardless of the strategy used, healthy discussions can help clarify the issues involved whenever new tests are put into place. Recognizing the political nature of testing early in the process can stave off many problems later.

LANGUAGE TEACHING METHODOLOGY ISSUES

Since views of what constitutes good language teaching vary widely throughout the profession, ideas about what constitutes good testing (or a good test) will also differ. Consider how a teacher like the mythical Miss Fiditch (of the granny glasses, hair-in-a-bun, ruler-in-hand, structuralist school of language teaching) might argue with the much more real, and realistic, Sandra Savignon, one of the early advocates of communicative teaching and testing (see Savignon 1972, 1985; Bachman & Savignon 1986). Miss Fiditch would tolerate only strict testing of knowledge of grammar rules, probably having students translate a selection from one of the "great books" of the target language into their mother tongue. In contrast, Savignon (1972) advocated testing "the students' ability to communicate in four different communicative contexts: discussion, information-getting, reporting, and description" (p. 41). How did language testing get from the extreme views of Miss Fiditch to the more modern views of Savignon?

An exceptionally short history of language testing

Spolsky (1978) and Hinofotis (1981) both pointed out early on that language testing can be broken into periods, or trends, of development. Hinofotis labeled them the prescientific period, the psychometric-structuralist period, and the integrative-sociolinguistic period. As shown in Table 2.1, I will use the term **movements** instead of periods to describe them because these movements overlap chronologically and can be said to all co-exist today in different parts of the world. I will also add one movement, which I will label the communicative movement. (For very different takes on the history of language testing, see Spolsky 1995 and Barnwell 1996.)

Table 2.1 Language testing movements

Testing Movement	Linguistic Basis
Prescientific	Ability to translate
Psychometric-structuralist	Ability to manipulate grammatical structures
Integrative-sociolinguistic	Ability to use sociolinguistic aspects of language
Communicative	Ability to communicate functions/notions and perform tasks with language

The **prescientific movement** in language testing is associated with the grammar-translation approaches to language teaching. Since such approaches have existed for ages, the end of this movement is usually delimited rather than its beginning. I infer from Hinofotis's article that the prescientific movement ended with the onset of the psychometric-structuralist movement, but clearly such movements have no end in language teaching because, without a doubt, such teaching and testing practices are going in many places in the world today (e.g., the current grammar-translation tests in the *yakudoku* language teaching tradition found in many of Japan's prestigious high school and university entrance examinations; see Brown & Yamashita 1995a & 1995b; Brown 1996b, 1999a).

The prescientific movement is characterized by translation and essay tests developed exclusively by the classroom teachers, who are on their own when it comes to developing and scoring tests. One problem that arises with these types of tests is that they are relatively difficult to score objectively. Thus, subjectivity becomes an important factor in scoring such tests. Perhaps mercifully, no language testing specialists were involved in the prescientific movement. Hence, there was little concern with the application of statistical techniques such as item analysis, descriptive statistics, reliability coefficients, validity studies, and so forth (see Chapters 4 to 10). Some teachers may think back to such a situation with a certain nostalgia for its simplicity, but along with the lack of concern with statistics came an attendant lack of concern with concepts like objectivity, reliability, and validity, that is, a lack of concern with making fair, consistent, and correct decisions about the lives of the students involved. Most teachers would protect their own students from such unfair testing practices and would complain even more vigorously if such lax practices were applied to themselves as students in a teacher training course. How would you like to have to show your knowledge of the material in this book (after you have read it) by taking a test that is subjective, inconsistent, and based on material unrelated to the book? That would seem unfair, right? Wouldn't any decisions based on such a test be unreliable, arbitrary, and unfair? Those are the types of problems the next movement was designed to rectify.

With the onset of the **psychometric-structuralist movement** of language testing, worries about the objectivity, reliability, and validity of tests began to arise. Psychological and educational measurement specialists interacted with linguists, and language tests were created that were increasingly scientific, reliable, and precise, that is to say, they were state-of-the-art for their day. Psychometric-structuralist tests typically set out to measure the discrete structural points (Carroll 1972) being taught in the audio-lingual and related teaching methods of the time. Like the language teaching methods of the day, these tests were influenced by behavioral psychology. The psychometric-structuralist movement saw the rise of the first carefully designed and standardized tests like the *Test of English as a Foreign Language* (first introduced in 1963), the *Michigan Test of English Language Proficiency: Form A* (University of Michigan 1961), *Modern Language Association Foreign Language Proficiency Tests for Teachers and Advanced Students* (ETS 1968), *Comprehensive English Language Test for Speakers of English as a Second Language* (Harris & Palmer 1970), and others. Such tests, usually in multiple-choice format, are easy to administer and score and are carefully constructed to be objective, reliable, and valid. Thus, they were felt to be an improvement on the test design and scoring practices of the prescientific movement.

The psychometric-structuralist movement is important because, for the first time, language test development follows scientific principles. In addition, psychometric-structuralist test development is squarely in the hands of trained linguists and language testers. As a result, statistical analyses are used for the first time (as described in Lado 1961). Psychometric-structuralist tests are still very much in evidence around the world, but they have been supplemented (and in some cases, supplanted) by what Carroll (1972) labeled integrative tests.

The **integrative movement** has its roots in the argument that language is creative. More precisely, language professionals began to believe that language is more than the sum of the discrete parts being tested during the psychometric-structuralist movement. Beginning with the work of sociolinguists like Hymes (1967a), it was felt that the development of communicative competence depended on more than simple grammar control; communicative competence also hinged on knowledge of the language appropriate for different situations. Tests typical of this movement were the cloze test and dictation, both of which assess the student's ability to manipulate language within a context of extended text rather than in a collection of discrete-point questions. The possibility of testing language in context led to further arguments for the benefits of integrative tests with regard to **pragmatics,** the ways that linguistic and extra-linguistic elements of language are interrelated and relevant to human experience (see Oller 1979). The integrative-sociolinguistic movement is probably most important because it questions the linguistic assumptions of the previous structuralist movement, yet uses the psychometric tools made available by that movement to explore language testing techniques designed to assess contextualized language.

In Hinofotis's discussion of trends for the 1980s, she suggests that the influence of notional-functional syllabuses and English for specific purposes have added new elements to language testing including new attempts to define communicative competence. She refers to Brière (1979) and Canale and Swain (1981). I will include this sort of testing here as the **communicative movement**, and expand her references to include at least Savignon (1972), Canale and Swain (1980), Canale (1983a & b), and Bachman (1990). I will go into more detail on this movement because it is the current bandwagon of choice and because, in my view, it is still developing. (For different perspectives on these issues, see Allison 1999, pp. 42–56; Brown, Hudson, Norris, & Bonk 2002; or the articles in Norris 2002.)

The communicative tests advocated within this movement were new and different in the 1980s, because they promoted certain characteristics that initially proved novel. Tests typical of this movement would include role plays, problem-solving tests, group tests, and task-based tests. Based on my reading and experiences trying to create such communicative tests, I would list their characteristics in two categories as shown in Table 2.2: test-setting requirements and bases for ratings. As for the communicative test-setting requirements, insofar as possible, the communication that is required of the students should be meaningful to the students as individuals, that is, it should include functions of the language that are useful to them. Also, in order for communication to be meaningful, it will probably be necessary to create a situation that is as authentic as possible. Moreover, the students should encounter unpredictable language input and be put in a position where they must produce creative language output (in the same sense that language input in real life is unpredictable and therefore language output must be creative, whether in a first or second language). Finally, just like in real life, students should be using all four language skills, including reading, writing, listening, and speaking.

> **Table 2.2** Characteristics of communicative tests
>
> ### Communicative test-setting requirements:
> *Meaningful* communication
> *Authentic* situation
> *Unpredictable* language input
> *Creative* language output
> *All language skills* (including reading, writing, listening, & speaking)
>
> ### Bases for ratings:
> *Success* in getting meanings across
> *Use* focus rather than usage
> *New components* to be rated

Three characteristics exist for the bases for rating such tests. Because of the need to somehow assign a score or grade for feedback on such productive and oral tests, ratings by teachers or testers become a normal part of the testing process. To begin with, those ratings should also be based, at least to some degree, on students' relative *success* in getting their meanings across. In addition, the ratings should focus on language *use* rather than usage, which means in some cases that the focus is on fluency rather than accuracy. Finally, ratings should perhaps include *new rating components* (in addition to the traditional phonemes/graphemes, vocabulary, and grammar) like suprasegmentals, paralinguistic features, proxemics, pragmatics, strategy use, and so forth. (For more on these topics see the feedback scales in Mendelsohn 1992; Brown (with contributions by LAIRDIL) 1995; or Brown 1996c.) In short, a communicative test would necessarily create a situation involving "…a coming together of organized knowledge structures with a set of procedures for adapting this knowledge to solve new problems of communication that do not have ready-made and tailored solutions" (Candlin 1986, p. 40).

To clarify by counter-example, during a meeting about communicative testing, a language teacher at my university once volunteered that he was already doing communicative testing because he had his students memorize dialogues and perform them in front of the class. Unfortunately, though his dialogue "communicative test" was oral and productive, it did not require any meaningful communication on the part of the students. It was not set in an authentic situation, had no unpredictable or creative elements at all, and was not rated for anything but accuracy. Hence, it clearly does not qualify as a communicative test, at least as that sort of test is defined here.

In addition to the test-setting and rating characteristics of communicative tests, they are sometimes discussed in terms of the components of language that they should assess. For instance Candlin (1986) cites Hymes (1967b; 1972) augmented view of the components of communicative competence (pp. 40-41), which included grammar, semantics, and sociolinguistic components. He also cites Halliday's (1979) model of communicative competence (pp. 42-44), which included textual (linguistic), ideational (semantic), interpersonal (pragmatic), and discoursal "capacity" (psycholinguistic) components.

Probably the best known model of the components of communicative competence is the one offered by Canale and Swain (Canale & Swain 1980; Canale 1983a & b). The version of that model outlined in Table 2.3 (from Canale 1983b) is still relevant today. Notice that under grammatical competence the model covers the elements of language that have traditionally been taught, that is, the ones that even lay people recognize as important aspects of language: phonology, orthography, vocabulary, word formation, sentence formation. Note also that, like Hymes, Canale and Swain include a sociolinguistic component (with two subcomponents: expressing and understanding appropriate social meanings and grammatical forms in different contexts) and, like Halliday, they include a discourse component (with cohesion and coherence subcomponents). However, in addition, they include strategic components (that is, the abilities necessary to overcome grammatical, sociolinguistic, discourse, and performance difficulties).

Table 2.3 The components of communicative competence

A. Grammatical competence
  1. Phonology
  2. Orthography
  3. Vocabulary
  4. Word formation
  5. Sentence formation

B. Sociolinguistic competence: Expressing and understanding *appropriate:*
  1. Social meanings
  2. Grammatical forms in different sociolinguistic contexts

C. Discourse competence
  1. Cohesion in different genres
  2. Coherence in different genres

D. Strategic competence for
  1. Grammatical difficulties
  2. Sociolinguistic difficulties
  3. Discourse difficulties
  4. Performance factors

Because of the need to address both the characteristics of communicative testing (listed in Table 2.2) and the components of communicative competence as just discussed (and summarized in Table 2.3), a natural part of this communicative movement has been the development of performance assessment and task-based assessment, which, in my view, are both ways of designing communicative tests, or assessment procedures. **Performance assessment**, according to Norris, Brown, Hudson, and Yoshioka (1998, p. 8), is distinguished from other types of testing in that: "(a) examinees must perform tasks, (b) the tasks should be as authentic as possible, and (c) success or failure in the outcome of the tasks, because they are performances, must usually be rated by qualified judges." They then point out that, "These three characteristics might just as well serve as a working definition…that will help us to distinguish already existing performance assessments, such as essays, interviews, extensive reading tasks, and so forth from integrative tests like dictations and cloze tests which do not fully meet any of the three criteria."

One type of performance assessment, **task-based assessment**, is defined by Brown, Hudson, Norris, and Bonk (2002, p. 9) as follows:

> In task-based language assessment, then, we are interested in eliciting and evaluating students' abilities to accomplish particular tasks or task types in which target language communication is essential. Such assessment is obviously performance assessment because a student's second language performance on the task is that which gets evaluated.

Why knowing about these movements is important

The methodology issue, initially described in terms of language teaching practices ranging from structuralist to communicative, has serious implications in thinking about historical movements within language testing, as well as important ramifications for the decisions that teachers make about which types of tests to use in their language programs.

To begin with, it is important to recognize that different theoretical views on linguistics and language teaching may exist in any program. These views might vary from teachers who still believe in a structural approach to others who passionately argue for communicative language teaching—with the bulk of the teachers falling somewhere in between. The degree to which different teachers believe in various language teaching theories (even if they do not know what they are called) can strongly influence the teaching in a program, and also the choices made in testing. Thus, a program will have to come to grips with such differences before any serious efforts can be made to implement tests of one type or another.

As a result, the content of any given test and the types of test questions used will be determined by the language teaching view(s) that underpin the test. As a result, understanding these movements and their relationships to language teaching is important for understanding the very purpose of your test and the degree to which the test is meeting that purpose, that is, the validity of your test (see Chapter 10).

THE COMPETENCE/PERFORMANCE ISSUE

Much has been made in linguistics of the distinction originally proposed by Chomsky between competence and performance. Chomsky (1965, p. 4) differentiates between the two as follows: "*competence* (the speaker-hearer's knowledge of his language) and *performance* (the actual use of language in concrete situations)." This distinction has some interesting ramifications for language testing. If linguistic performance is viewed as imperfect and full of flaws (even in native speakers), such performances can only be taken to be the outward manifestations of the underlying, but unobservable, linguistic competence. And, if such a difference exists for native speakers of a language, the difference may be even more pronounced in non-native speakers.

This distinction can help teachers to realize that tests are at best fairly artificial observations of a student's performance, and performance is only an imperfect reflection of the underlying competence. Since both competence and performance are of interest to language teachers, teachers must be very careful in their interpretation of test results to remember that performance is only part of the picture—a part that is a second-hand observation of competence.

In testing circles, the underlying competence is more often described in terms of a psychological construct (see Chapter 10). An example of a **psychological construct** in the ESL field is the notion of overall English as a foreign language proficiency. Thus, a student's competence in EFL might more readily be discussed as overall EFL proficiency, which is a psychological construct. However, even a relatively successful attempt to test this construct, as with the TOEFL, only provides an estimate of the student's performance, which is only a reflection of the underlying construct, or competence. The important thing to remember, in my view, is that language testing can provide an estimate of a student's performance (sometimes from various angles as in listening, reading, and grammar subtests), but never provides a direct measure of the actual competence that underlies the performance.

THE DISCRETE-POINT/INTEGRATIVE ISSUE

Another issue which concerns language testers has to do with the different types of tests, which can range from discrete-point tests to integrative tests. Various combinations of these two types are possible as well.

Discrete-point tests are those which measure the small bits and pieces of a language as in a multiple-choice test made up of questions constructed to measure students' knowledge of different structures. One question on such an ESL test might be written to measure whether the students know the distinction between *a* and *an* in English. A major assumption that underlies the use of test questions like this is that a collection of such discrete-point questions covering different structures (or other language learning points), if taken together as a single score, will produce a measure of some global aspect of language ability. In other words, a teacher who believes in discrete-point tests would argue that scores based on the administration of fifty narrowly defined discrete-point multiple-choice questions covering a variety of English grammatical structures will reveal something about the students' overall proficiency in grammar. Anyone holding the psychometric-structuralist view of language teaching and testing would probably be comfortable developing a test along these lines. A corollary to this general view would be that the individual skills (reading, writing, listening, and speaking) can be tested separately, and that different aspects of these skills (like pronunciation, grammar, vocabulary, culture, and so forth) can also be assessed as isolated phenomena.

As noted above, however, not all testers and teachers are so comfortable with the discrete-point view of testing. **Integrative tests** are those designed to use several skills at one time. Consider dictation as a test type. The student is usually asked to listen carefully and write down a short prose passage as it is read aloud three times (with or without pauses) by the teacher, or played on a tape. The skills involved are at least listening comprehension and writing, but different aspects of these two skills come into play as well. Sometimes handwriting is a factor; certainly distinguishing between phonemes is important as are grammar, vocabulary, and spelling knowledge. In short, dictation is testing many different things at the same time and does so in the context of extended text. Advocates of the integrative-sociolinguistic movement would argue that such a test is complex in a similar fashion to the ways actual language use is complex. They would also argue that the language tested in integrative procedures like dictation, cloze test, and writing samples is being tested in the more natural, or at least larger, context of extended text.

Along the continuum between the most discrete-point types of tests and the most integrative tests, other kinds of tests are in a sense both integrative and discrete-point in nature. Consider a typical reading test in which the student is asked to read a passage and then answer multiple-choice fact, vocabulary, and inference questions about the passage. Viewing this task as a combination of reading a passage and integrating that reading into answering questions at different conceptual levels (that is, fact, vocabulary, and inference) might lead a teacher to conclude that reading comprehension is an integrative test. Yet looking at the focused nature of the fact and vocabulary questions, a discrete-point label would come to mind. The point is that the sometimes useful distinction between discrete-point and integrative tests is not always clear.

PRACTICAL ISSUES

The **practical issues** that I will address have to do with physically putting tests into place in a program. Teachers may find themselves concerned with the degree to which tests are fair in terms of objectivity. Or they may have to decide whether to keep the tests cheap or fight for the resources necessary to do a quality job of testing. Teachers may also be concerned about the logistics of testing. For instance, they may be worried about the relative difficulty of constructing, administering, and scoring different types of tests. In discussing each of these practical issues, I will illustrate how each works and how it interrelates with the other practical issues.

THE FAIRNESS ISSUE

Fairness can be defined as the degree to which a test treats every student the same, or the degree to which it is impartial. Teachers would generally like to ensure that their personal feelings do not interfere with fair assessment of the students or bias the assignment of scores. The aim in maximizing objectivity is to give each student an equal chance to do well. Therefore, teachers and testers often do everything in their power to find test questions, administration procedures, scoring methods, and reporting policies that optimize the chances that each student will receive equal and fair treatment. This tendency to seek objectivity has led to the proliferation of "objective" tests, which is to say tests, usually multiple-choice, which minimize the possibility of varying treatment for different students. Since such tests can be and often are scored by machine, the process is maximally dispassionate and therefore viewed as objective.

However, many of the elements of any language course may not be testable in the most objective test types, such as multiple-choice, true-false, and matching. Whether teachers like it or not, one day they will have to recognize that they are not able to measure everything impartially and objectively. Consider what would happen if a group of adult education ESL teachers decide that they want to test their incoming students' communicative abilities. In thinking through such a placement test, they will eventually have to recognize that a multiple-choice format is not appropriate and that, instead, they need to set up situations, probably role plays, in which the students will use the spoken language in interactions with other students (or with native speakers if they can convince some to help out). Having set up the testing situations, they will then have to decide how the performance of each student will be scored and compared to the performances of all other students.

They might begin by designing some sort of scale, which includes descriptions of what they are looking for in the language use of their adult education students, that is, whether they want to score for grammar accuracy, fluency, clear pronunciation, ability to use specific functions, or any of the myriad other possible focuses. The teachers may then have to further analyze and describe each area that they decide to focus on in order to provide descriptive categories that will help them to assign so many points for excellent performance, fewer points for mediocre performance, and no points for poor performance. All this is possible and even admirable if their methodological perspective is communicative. The problem is not with the scale itself, but rather with the person, or rater, who will inevitably assign the scores on such a test. Can any person ever be completely objective when assigning such ratings? Of course not.

There are a number of test types that necessitate rater judgments like that just described. These tend to be toward the integrative end of the discrete-point to integrative continuum and include tests like oral interviews, translations, and compositions. Such tests ultimately require someone to use some scale to rate the written or spoken language that the students produce. Since the results must eventually be rated by some scorer, there is always a threat to objectivity when these types of tests are used. The question is not whether the test is objective, but rather the degree of subjectivity that the teachers are willing to accept. For example, the University of Hawaii ELI placement test mixes relatively objective subtests like multiple-choice reading, multiple-choice proofreading, and multiple-choice academic listening subtests with a fairly judgmental, and therefore relatively subjective, composition subtest. There are also cloze and dictation subtests which cannot be classed as entirely objective (because some judgments must be made) nor completely subjective (because the range of possibilities for those judgments is fairly restricted).

Thus, teachers may find that their thinking about this issue cannot be framed in absolutes, but rather must center on the trade-offs that are sometimes necessary in testing theoretically desirable elements of student production while trying to maintain a relatively high degree of objectivity.

THE COST ISSUES

In the best of all possible worlds, unlimited time and funds would be available for teaching and testing languages. Unfortunately, this is rarely true. Most teachers are underpaid and overworked and must constantly make decisions which are based on how expensive some aspect of teaching, or testing, may turn out to be. This issue affects all the other issues covered in this chapter so it cannot be ignored even if it seems self-evident. Lack of funds can cause the abandonment of otherwise well-thought-out theoretical and practical positions that teachers have taken (and cause them to do things that they would previously have found detestable).

Consider the example of the adult education ESL communicative test that I discussed above. The teachers may have decided, for sound and defensible theoretical reasons, that they want to include a communicative test in their placement battery. They have also agreed that they are willing to tolerate a certain amount of subjectivity in order to achieve their collective theoretical ends. They develop a scale and procedures for administering the test and take them proudly to the department head, who says that it is absolutely impossible to conduct these interviews because of the time (and therefore cost) involved in paying teachers to do the ratings.

Something happens to teachers when they become administrators. I know that this is true because I watched it happen to me. When I first became a language teacher, I staunchly detested multiple-choice tests because I could not see how they represented students' abilities to actually use language in real situations. After all, people rarely communicate in real life with four optional answers provided. However, when I became an administrator I found myself arguing for large-scale placement testing in machine scorable multiple-choice formats—a position based on the fact that such testing is relatively easy and cheap to administer and score. While testing each student individually may sometimes be desirable, teachers must recognize that it is very expensive in terms of both time and money. Nevertheless, if a group of teachers decides that interviews or role plays are worth doing, they must somehow find adequate funding to do such testing well.

EASE OF TEST CONSTRUCTION

Special considerations with regard to test construction can range from deciding how long the test should be to considering what types of questions to use. All things being equal, a long test of 100 questions is likely to be better in terms of the consistency and accuracy of what is being measured than a shorter one. This is logical given that a one-question multiple-choice test is not likely to be as accurate in assessing students' performance as a two-question test, or a ten-question test, or a fifty-question test. Which test should teachers have the most confidence in? The fifty-question test, right? The problem is that this characteristic of tests is in direct conflict with the fact that short tests are easier to write than long ones. One goal of many test development projects is to find the "happy medium," that is, the shortest test length that does a consistent and accurate job of testing the students.

Another test construction issue involves the degree to which different types of tests are easy or difficult to produce. Some test types, for instance a composition test, are relatively easy to construct. A teacher needs only to think of a good topic for the students to write on and make up some test directions that specify how long the students will have to write and perhaps the types of things that the teacher will be looking for in scoring the writing samples. Dictation tests are also easy to construct: just find an appropriate passage, provide paper, read the passage aloud (perhaps once straight through, a second time in phrases with pauses so that students can write, and a third time straight through for proofreading), and have the students write the passage down. Short-answer questions and translations are also relatively easy to construct. Constructing a cloze test is somewhat more difficult: one must find an appropriate passage and type it up replacing every nth word with a numbered blank (for evidence that this process is not quite as easy as it seems, see Brown 2002).

Writing fill-in, matching, true-false and multiple-choice questions, as I will explain in the next chapter, is more difficult. Most language testers find that writing sound multiple-choice questions is the most difficult of these. Anyone who does not find that to be the case might want to look very carefully at their questions to see if they are indeed sound and effective. With these more restricted receptive types of test questions, questions must be carefully constructed so that the correct answers are truly correct and incorrect answers are really wrong. Any teacher who has ever tried this will verify that the process of writing such questions can quickly become time-consuming.

EASE OF TEST ADMINISTRATION

My experience also indicates that ease of administration is a very important issue because testing is a human activity, which is very prone to mix-ups and confusion. Perhaps this problem results from the fact that students are often nervous during a test and teachers are under pressure. The degree to which a test is easy to administer will depend on the amount of time it takes, on the number of subtests involved, on the amount of equipment and materials required to administer it, and on the amount of guidance that the students need during the test. A short 30-question, 15-minute, one-page cloze test with clear directions is relatively easy to administer. A one-hour lecture listening test based on a video tape that requires the students to write an essay will probably be relatively difficult to administer.

EASE OF TEST SCORING

Ease of scoring is an important issue because a test that is easy to score is cheaper and is less likely to result in scorers making simple tallying, counting, and copying mistakes that might affect the students' scores. Most teachers will agree that such scoring mistakes are undesirable because they are not fair to the students, but I am willing to wager that any teacher who has served as a scorer in a pressure-filled testing situation has made such scoring mistakes. In one composition scoring situation, I found that ten language teachers made numerous mistakes resulting in adding five two-digit subscores to find each student's total score. These mistakes affected about 20 percent of the compositions and no teacher (myself included) was immune. The best that teachers can hope to do is to minimize mistakes in scoring by making the processes as simple and clear as humanly possible and by double and triple checking those parts of the process that are error prone.

Ease of scoring seems to be inversely related to the ease of constructing a test type. In other words, the easiest types of tests to construct initially (composition, dictation, translation, and so forth) are usually the most difficult to score and least objective, while those test types which are more difficult to construct initially (multiple-choice, true-false, matching, and so forth) are usually the easiest to score and most objective.

INTERACTIONS OF THEORETICAL ISSUES

While it may seem redundant, I must stress the importance of recognizing that each of the theoretical issues discussed above can and will interact with all the others—sometimes in predictable patterns and at other times in unpredictable ways. For instance, if a group of high school language teachers wants to develop a test that, from a theoretical point of view, is communicative yet integrative and measures productive skills, they may have to accept that the test will be relatively subjective, expensive, and hard to administer and score. Thus, they must be willing to put in the effort to create a test that validly assesses the aspects of language learning they think are important.

If, on the other hand, they decide they want a test that is very objective, easy to administer, and easy to score, they may have to accept the fact that the questions must be relatively discrete-point (and therefore difficult to write) so that the answer sheets can be machine scorable. This decision will naturally result in a test that is not communicative and that focuses mostly on receptive skills. Hence, they may be sacrificing the validity of their test to practical considerations simply because they are not giving testing much priority in terms of resources and energy.

I am not arguing for one type of test or another. I am, however, arguing that all of these trade-offs are inevitably linked to the many testing issues discussed in this chapter as well as to the issues of test reliability and validity that I will discuss in Chapters 8 to 10.

ADOPT, ADAPT, OR DEVELOP?

In adopting, adapting, or developing language tests for a particular situation, teachers may be surprised at the diversity of opinion that exists, even within a specific institution, about what a good test should include. Some teachers may have naive views of what a test should be, while others hold very sophisticated, or idealistic, or impractical views. For instance, those teachers who studied languages in the audio-lingual tradition often think of a language test as a longer and more varied form of the transformation drill, while colleagues who have recently graduated from M.A. or Ph.D. programs may be talking about communicative, task-based procedures, which take two teachers 20 minutes to administer to each student.

The appropriate managerial strategies for developing tests must, of course, be tailored to each situation. But every management strategy falls somewhere along a continuum that ranges from authoritarian to democratic. Since most language teachers of my acquaintance do not take well to dictatorial administrative practices, I find that the best strategies to employ are those which involve the teachers in the process of adopting, adapting, or developing tests. An additional benefit, of course, is that they can usually be drawn into contributing more than just their ideas and opinions. Since testing sometimes involves long hours of work (often with no extra pay), any help colleagues can give will help.

A consensus must first be built about the purpose and type of test to employ. Then a strategy must be worked out that will maximize the quality and effectiveness of the test that will eventually be put into place. In the best of all possible worlds, each program would have a resident testing expert, whose entire job is to develop tests especially tailored for that program. But even in the worst of all possible worlds, rational decisions can be made in selecting commercially available tests if certain guidelines are followed. In many cases, any rational approach to testing will be a vast improvement over the existing conditions. Between these two extremes of developing tests from scratch or adopting them from commercial sources on pure faith is the notion of adapting existing tests and materials so that they better serve the purposes of the program.

The main point here is that many tests are, or should be, situation-specific. That is to say, a test can be very effective in one situation with one particular group of students and be virtually useless in another. In other words, teachers cannot simply go out and buy a test and automatically expect it to work with their students. Any particular commercial test may have been developed for an entirely different type of student and for entirely different purposes. The goal of this section of the chapter is to provide teachers with rational bases for adopting, adapting, or developing language tests so they will be maximally useful in their specific language programs.

ADOPTING LANGUAGE TESTS

The tests that are used in language programs are often adopted from sources outside of the program. This may mean that the tests are bought from commercial publishing houses, adopted from other language programs, or pulled straight from the current textbook. Given differences that exist among the participants in the various language programs around the world (for instance, differences in gender, number of languages previously studied, types of educational background, educational level, levels of proficiency, differences in native languages, and so forth), it is probable that many of the tests which have been acquired from external sources are being used with students quite different from those envisioned when the tests were originally developed and standardized. Using tests with the wrong types of students can result in mismatches between the tests and the abilities of the students as well as between the tests and the purposes of the program. For instance, I have seen situations where a proficiency test like the TOEFL is used for making placement decisions in a program with narrowly defined ability levels. Such practices are irresponsible and should be corrected whenever they are discovered, because the decisions are being based on test questions that are to a large extent too easy or too difficult for the students involved. Thus, the test items are quite unrelated to the needs of the particular students in the given language program or unrelated to the curriculum being taught in that program.

Selecting good tests to match the purposes of a particular language program is therefore very important. However, making these matches properly is often difficult because of the technical aspects of testing that many language teachers find intimidating. In searching for tests that are suitable for a program, teachers and administrators may therefore wish to begin by looking for help from testing experts by reading test reviews. Test reviews are useful in the same way that book reviews are. That is, they provide at least one other person's informed opinion about the test. However, a good reviewer may also explain key concepts for the reader and point to what features of a test are important to consider. Test reviews sometimes appear in the review sections of language teaching journals along with reviews of textbooks and professional volumes. Naturally, testing is not the focus of these journals, so test reviews tend to appear infrequently. *Language Testing* is a journal that specializes in articles on testing and, therefore, is more likely to provide test reviews. These particular reviews are sometimes fairly technical because the intended audience is testing specialists. For those teachers in ESL/EFL, Alderson, Krahnke, and Stansfield (1987), though somewhat dated now, is the only book I know of that provides a collection of practical and useful test reviews specifically designed for them. Most of the major tests available for ESL at that time are reviewed. One other source for language test reviews is available in any full-fledged research library: It is commonly referred to as *Buros Mental Measurements Yearbook*, a book of reviews of all kinds of published tests (including language tests) that comes out every two or three years (for full names, see Plake & Impara 2001; Plake, Impara, & Spies 2003).

Other approaches that teachers might want to use to improve their abilities to select quality tests for their programs would include: informing themselves about language testing through taking a course or reading up on it; hiring a new teacher, who also happens to have an interest in, or already knows about, the subject of testing; and giving one member of the faculty release time to become informed on the topic. In all cases, the checklist provided in Table 2.4 should (with some background in testing) help in selecting tests that match the purposes for which a particular language program needs them.

In using the checklist, teachers should look at the test manual provided by the publisher and begin by considering the general facts about the test. What is the title? Who wrote it? Where and when was it published? As shown in the table, the theoretical orientation of the test should probably be reviewed next. Is it in the correct family of tests (NRT or CRT) for the program's purposes? Is it designed for the type of decisions

Table 2.4 Test evaluation checklist

A. General background information
  1. Title
  2. Author(s)
  3. Publisher and date of publication
  4. Published reviews available
B. Your theoretical orientation
  1. Test family—Norm-referenced or criterion-referenced (see Chapter 1)
  2. Purpose of decision—placement, proficiency, achievement, diagnostic (see Chapter 1)
  3. Language methodology orientation—structural ←→ communicative
  4. Type of test—discrete-point ←→ integrative
C. Your practical orientation
  1. Objective ←→ subjective
  2. Expensive ←→ inexpensive
  3. Logistical issues—easy ←→ difficult
    a. Test construction
    b. Test administration
    c. Test scoring
D. Test characteristics
  1. Item description (see Chapter 3)
    a. Receptive mode (written text, picture, cassette tape, CD, and so on)
    b. Productive mode (marking choice, speaking, writing, and so on)
  2. Norms (see Chapter 6)
    a. Standardization sample (nature, size, method of selection, generalizability of results, availability of established norms for subgroups based on nationality, native language, gender, academic status, and so on)
    b. Number of subtests and separate scores
    c. Type of standardized scores (percentiles, and so on)
  3. Descriptive information (see Chapter 5)
    a. Central tendency (mean, mode, and median)
    b. Dispersion (low-high scores, range, and standard deviation)
    c. Item characteristics (facility and discrimination)
  4. Reliability/dependability (see Chapters 8 & 9)
    a. Types of reliability procedures used (test-retest, equivalent forms, internal consistency, interrater, intrarater, and so on)
    b. Degree of reliability for no. 4.a. above
    c. Standard error of measurement
  5. Validity (see Chapter 10)
    a. Types of validity procedures used (content, construct, and/or predictive/concurrent criterion-related validity)
    b. Degree to which you find convincing the validity statistics and argument(s) referred to above
  6. Actual practicality of the test
    a. Cost of test booklets, audio components, manual, answer sheets, scoring templates, scoring services, and any other necessary test components
    b. Quality of items listed in number 6.a. above (paper, printing, audio clarity, durability, and so on)
    c. Ease of administration (time required, proctor/student ratio, proctor qualifications, equipment necessary, availability and quality of directions for administration, and so on)
    d. Ease of scoring (method of scoring, amount of training necessary, time per test, score conversion information, and so on)
    e. Ease of interpretation (quality of guidelines for the interpretation of scores in terms of norms or other criteria)

involved? Does it match the methodological orientation of the teachers and the goals of the curriculum? What types of subtests are involved? Are they discrete-point or integrative, or some combination of the two?

From a practical point of view, a number of other issues must be considered. For instance, to what degree is the test objective? Will allowances have to be made for subjectivity? What about cost? Is the test too expensive for the program, or just about right? What about logistics? Is the test going to be easy to put together, administer, and score?

In terms of test characteristics, the nature of the test questions must be considered. What are the students confronted with in the receptive mode? And what are they expected to do in the productive mode? If the test is designed for norm-referenced decisions, is information about norms and standardized scores provided? Does the test seem to be aimed at the correct group of students and organized to test the skills that are taught in the program? How many parts and separate scores will there be, and are they all necessary? Do the types of test questions reflect the productive and receptive types of techniques and exercises that are used in the program? Is the test described clearly and does the description make sense? Is the test reliable and valid?

There are other practical considerations that are also important. What are the initial and ongoing costs of the test? How good is the quality of the audio program, test booklets, answer sheets, and so forth? Are there preview booklets or other sorts of preparatory materials available to give out to the students? Is the test easy to administer? Is the scoring reasonably easy relative to the types of test questions being used? Is the interpretation of scores explained with guidelines for reporting and clarifying the scores to the students and teachers involved?

In short, there are many factors that must be considered even in adopting an already published test for a particular program. Many of these issues can be addressed by any thoughtful language teacher, but others, such as examining the degree to which the test is reliable and valid, will take more knowledge and experience with language tests. (For a quick idea of the scope of what a teacher must know to decide about the relative reliability and validity of a test, take a brief glance through Chapters 8 to 10.) However, for commercial test products, it is the publisher's responsibility to convince potential test users that the test is worth adopting. The test users should, therefore, expect to find clearly explained arguments supporting the quality of the test. If such is not the case, then they should probably be suspicious of what the publisher is hiding and seriously ask themselves if they want to adopt such a poorly defended test.

ADAPTING LANGUAGE TESTS

A newly developed test may work fairly well in a program, but perhaps not as well as was originally hoped. Such a situation would call for further adapting of the test so that it better fits the needs and purposes of the particular language program. A number of strategies are described in the next chapter, which will help teachers to use qualitative and statistical analyses of test results to revise and improve tests. Generally, however, the process of adapting a test to a specific situation will involve some variant of the following steps:

1. Administer the test in the particular program, using the appropriate teachers and students;

2. Select those test questions that work well at spreading out the students (for NRTs), or are efficient at measuring the learning of the objectives (for CRTs) in this particular program;

3. Develop a shorter, more efficient revision of the test—one that fits the program's purposes and works well with its students (some new questions may be necessary, ones similar to those which worked well, in order to have a long enough test); and

4. Evaluate the quality of the newly revised test (see Table 2.4, p. 32).

With the basic knowledge provided in this book, any language teacher can accomplish all these steps. In fact, following the guidelines given in Chapter 4 will enable any teacher to adapt a test to a specific set of program goals and decision-making purposes. However, in the interest of fair advertising, I must provide the warning that test development is hard work and can be time-consuming. Nevertheless, in the end, the hard work is worthwhile because of the useful information that is gained and the satisfaction that is derived from making responsible decisions about students' lives. The point is that, before teachers begin a test revision project, they should insure that they will have enough time and help to do the job well.

DEVELOPING LANGUAGE TESTS

In an ideal situation, teachers will have enough resources and expertise available in their program so that proficiency, placement, achievement, and diagnostic tests can be developed and fitted to the goals of the program and to the ability levels and needs of the students enrolled there. The guidelines offered in this book should help with that process.

If a group of teachers decides to develop their own tests, they will need to begin by deciding which tests to develop first. Perhaps those tests which were identified as most program-specific in the previous chapter should have priority. That would mean developing tests of achievement and diagnosis first because they will tend to be based entirely and exclusively on the objectives of the particular program. In the interim, while developing these achievement and diagnostic tests, previously published proficiency and placement tests could be adopted as needed. Later, these teachers may wish to develop their own placement test so that the test questions being used to separate students into levels of study are related to the objectives of the courses and to what the students are learning in the program. However, because of their inter-programmatic nature, proficiency tests may necessarily always be adopted from outside sources so that comparisons between and among various institutions will make sense.

Somewhere in the process of developing tests, teachers may want to stop and evaluate them on the basis of the checklist provided in Table 2.4 (p. 32). Teachers should always be willing to be just as critical of their own tests as they are of commercial tests. The fact that a test is developed by and for a specific program does not necessarily make it a good test. So evaluation of test quality should be an integral part of the test development process.

PUTTING SOUND TESTS IN PLACE

Having decided to adopt, adapt, or develop tests, teachers are in a position to actually put them into place to help with decision making. The checklist shown in Table 2.5 should help successfully put tests into place. To begin with, make sure that the purposes for administering the various tests are clear to the curriculum developers and to the teachers (and eventually to the students). This presupposes that these purposes are already clearly defined in both theoretical and practical terms that are understood and agreed to by a majority of the staff.

The next step is to insure that all the necessary physical conditions for the test have been met. This might entail making sure that there is a well-ventilated and quiet place to give the test with enough time in that space for some flexibility and clear scheduling. Also, make sure that the students have been properly notified and have

Table 2.5 A testing program checklist

A. Establishing purposes of test
   1. Clearly defined (from both theoretical and practical orientations)
   2. Understood and agreed upon by staff
B. Evaluating the test itself (see Table 2.4)
C. Arranging the physical needs
   1. Adequate, well-ventilated, and quiet space
   2. Enough time in that space for some flexibility
   3. Clear scheduling
D. Making pre-administration arrangements
   1. Students properly notified of test
   2. Students signed up for test
   3. Students given precise information (where and when test will be, what they should do to prepare, and what they should bring with them, especially identification if required)
E. Administering the test
   1. Adequate materials in hand (test booklets, answer sheets, audio components, pencils, scoring templates, and so on) plus extras
   2. All necessary equipment in hand and tested (cassette/CD players, microphones, public address system, videotape/DVD players, blackboard, chalk, and so on) with backups where appropriate
   3. Proctors trained in their duties
   4. All necessary information distributed to proctors (test directions, answers to obvious questions, schedule of who is to be where and when, and so on)
F. Scoring
   1. Adequate space for all scoring to take place
   2. Clear scheduling of scoring and notification of results
   3. Sufficient qualified staff for all scoring activities
   4. Staff adequately trained in all scoring procedures
G. Interpreting
   1. Clearly defined purpose for results
   2. Provision for helping teachers use scores and explain them to students
   3. A well-defined place for the results in the overall curriculum
H. Record keeping
   1. All necessary resources for keeping track of scores
   2. Ready access to the records for administrators and staff
   3. Provision for eventual systematic termination of records
I. Test analyses
   1. Item analyses for test revision and improvement for future uses
   2. For reliability and validity
   3. Report the results to interested parties
J. Ongoing research
   1. Test results used to full advantage for research
   2. Test results incorporated into overall program evaluation plan

signed up in advance for the test. Perhaps students should be given precise written information that answers their most pressing questions. Where and when will the test be administered? What should they do to prepare for the test? What should they bring with them? Should they bring picture identification? This type of information prepared in advance in the form of a handout or pamphlet may save answering the same questions hundreds of times.

Before actually administering the test, check that there are adequate materials on hand, perhaps with a few extras of everything. All necessary equipment should be ready and checked to see that it works (with backups if that is appropriate). Proctors must be trained in their duties and have sufficient information to do a professional job of test administration.

After the test has been administered, provision must be made for scoring. Again, adequate space and scheduling are important so that qualified staff can be properly trained and carry out the scoring of the test(s). Equally important is the interpretation of results. The purpose of the results must be clear, and provision must be made for helping teachers use the scores and explain the scores to the students. Ideally, there will be a well-defined purpose for the results of the test in the overall curriculum planning.

Record keeping is often forgotten in the process of test giving. Nevertheless, all necessary resources must be marshaled for keeping track of scores including sufficient clerical staff, computers and software, or just some type of ledger book. In all cases, staff members should have ready access to the records. Provision must also be made for the eventual destruction or long-term storage of these records.

Test analysis is another essential part of test administration. Just as the unexamined life may not be worth living, the unanalyzed test may not be worth administering. As you will see in other chapters of this book, the pertinent analyses will most often include item analyses for purposes of revising and improving the test for future administrations (see Chapter 4), as well as analysis of the reliability and validity of the test (see Chapters 8 to 10). Naturally the results of these analyses should be reported to all interested parties.

Last but not least, an ongoing plan for research should be developed to utilize the information generated by test scores. Such research should take full advantage of the test results so that the new information can be effectively incorporated into the overall curriculum development process (see Chapter 11).

GETTING STARTED WITH YOUR SPREADSHEET PROGRAM

In this chapter, I will be asking you to get on a computer, open a spreadsheet program (preferably *Excel*™ because the directions I give here will be directly applicable), move around the spreadsheet, and enter sample test scores. You will benefit most from what follows if you do it while sitting at the computer. So now is the time to get on a computer and open up the *Excel* spreadsheet program.

Screen 2.1 Opening screen for *Excel*

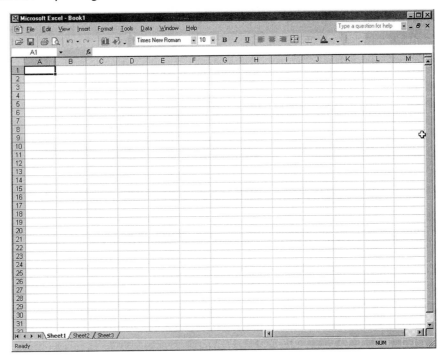

On the opening screen, you will notice the following features when using the *Excel* spreadsheet:

Cells. Your spreadsheet is made up of **cells**, which are squares made by the intersections of the rows and columns in your spreadsheet. Cells are used to store data, such as numbers, names, or dates.

Rows and Columns. Excel stores and calculates data using a row and column format. Rows are labeled with numbers to the left, and columns are labeled with capital letters at the top (A through Z, then, AA, AB, AC, etc.). In a typical *Excel* spreadsheet, there are a total of 65,536 rows and 230 columns. Use your mouse or arrow keys to explore the rows and columns in the spreadsheet.

Cell Addresses. Each cell has an **address**, which is made up of column letter(s) and row numbers. Each cell has its own distinct address that is different from all the other cells' addresses. The cell in the upper left corner of the spreadsheet is labeled A1, and the address of the next cell is B1. The cell at the far right of the spreadsheet is labeled IV1. If you move down the spreadsheet 10 rows, the address is IV10, and if you move to the furthest column to the left, the address is A10.

Moving around the spreadsheet

To move around the spreadsheet, hold down the keys, described below, in quick succession.

END and **RIGHT ARROW** (→) keys will move you to the last column in the spreadsheet. The last column is labeled IV.

END and **DOWN ARROW** (↓) keys will move you to the last row in the spreadsheet. The last row is labeled 65536, which means that there are 65,536 total rows in the spreadsheet.

CTRL (or **CONTROL**) and **HOME** keys will move you to the upper-left hand corner of the spreadsheet, where you originally started when the spreadsheet was opened.

Creating a sample spreadsheet

In the following exercise, you will enter student names and test scores to create a sample spreadsheet. In the steps listed below, items that are in bold type are entered into the cells (i.e. **Name**). You may use the keyboard shortcuts by pressing the ALT key, followed by the underlined letters in the menu choices (i.e., ALT *f* to access the File item in the *Excel* menu, as shown by **File**). Items that are located in a specific menu will appear with a comma between each menu item (i.e., **File**, **Exit** to exit the *Excel* program).

Screen 2.2 Spreadsheet to track student scores

Entering test score data to create a spreadsheet

1. Open the *Excel* program on your computer.
2. Click Cell A1, type **Name**, and then press ENTER.
3. In Cells A2 through A17, type the names of the students, as shown in Screen 2.2.
4. Click Cell B1, type **Score**, and then press ENTER.
5. In Cells B2 through B17, type the student scores in the cells, as shown in Screen 2.2.
6. To align the heading **Score** with the numbers, click Cell B1, and then click the ALIGN RIGHT button on the toolbar, located at the top of your screen. When the data are aligned, the button will have a pushed-down appearance. *Excel* aligns alphabetical data to the left side of the cells by default, and numerical data to the right.
7. To save the spreadsheet, click **File** from the menu bar, and then select **Save**. In the *File name* box, type an appropriate name for the spreadsheet, and then verify that the file will be saved in the correct location by checking the directory name listed in the *Save in* box.
8. Click **Save**, and then click **File**, **Exit** to close the *Excel* program.

You are now able to create spreadsheets to track test scores for students. In the next chapter, you will learn how to use a spreadsheet for analyzing the quality of the questions you use in your tests. But first, a disclaimer: this book is not designed to teach you all the details of using a spreadsheet, but to enhance your understanding of how a spreadsheet can help you perform better language testing. I encourage you to use the manual for your spreadsheet, and to get a good book that explains the ins and outs of your spreadsheet to answer any questions that may arise. Explore the menus and buttons on your spreadsheet to find out their functions, and use the help screens when you run into trouble. Try using your spreadsheet to do different things in your everyday teaching life, like entering and keeping track of your students' attendance and grades, or keeping track of your checks. A spreadsheet is a very useful tool, but it is important for you to establish a playful relationship when using the program. If you fight your spreadsheet and fear it, it will sense your fear and take control. So try playing with it in various ways. I've never known a student to break his or her spreadsheet, and at worst, you might have to reboot, so why not just try some things.

REVIEW QUESTIONS

1. What are the theoretical and practical issues that must be considered in developing language tests? How are the theoretical issues different in general from those classified as practical?

2. On a continuum of methodological choices that ranges from structural language teaching to communicative, where would your philosophy of teaching fit? What about your philosophy of testing? Are you prescientific? Are you a psychometric-structuralist? An integrative-sociolinguist? Or are you part of the communicative wave of the future?

3. How are performance testing and task-based testing related? Different? How are they communicative in nature?

4. What is the difference between competence and performance as discussed by Chomsky? And why might this distinction be important to think about with regard to language testing?

5. What is the fundamental difference between a discrete-point test and an integrative one? Can you think of at least one example of each? Would you prefer to use discrete-point or integrative tests for purposes of placing students into the levels of a language program? Why?

6. What are the five characteristics of a communicative test? What are the three bases for rating communicative language performance? And, what are the four main components of communicative competence (according to Canale 1983b)?

7. Why is objectivity important to language testers? Under what conditions could you justify sacrificing some degree of objectivity? And why?

8. What are some of the logistical conditions that you should consider in any testing project? Which of the three logistical conditions discussed in this book (ease of construction, administration, and scoring) do you think is the most important? How are ease of test construction and ease of scoring inversely related?

9. What are the factors that you must consider in looking at the quality of a test? Which do you think are the most important?

10. What are the factors that you must keep in mind in putting together a successful testing program? Which factors do you think are the most important?

11. What is an address in a spreadsheet? What is a cell? How many columns does your spreadsheet have? How many rows?

APPLICATION EXERCISES

A. Locate a test that you think might be useful in a language program in which you are now working, or if you have never taught, find a test for an elementary, secondary, adult education, commercial, or university language program. Examine the test very carefully using Table 2.5 (p. 35), keeping in mind all the theoretical and practical issues discussed in this chapter. Perhaps you should consult with several colleagues and find out what they think of it. What differences do you now have with your colleagues in your views on testing?

B. What theoretical and practical issues would be of particular importance for implementing the test that you selected for the above application exercise (see Table 2.5, p. 35)?

CHAPTER

3

DEVELOPING GOOD QUALITY LANGUAGE TEST ITEMS

INTRODUCTION

In this chapter, I will begin explaining the elements that make up a good test. The basic unit of any test is the test item, so I will begin the chapter with a broad definition of this crucial concept. Then I will continue with guidelines for item format analysis including four separate sets: general guidelines for all types of test items; guidelines for receptive response items (true-false, multiple-choice, and matching); guidelines for productive response items (fill-in, short-response, and task); and personal response items (self-assessments, conferences, and portfolios). As usual, I will end the chapter with review questions and applications exercises.

WHAT IS A TEST ITEM?

The Multilingual Glossary of Language Testing Terms (ALTE 1998, p. 149) defines an *item* as follows: "Each testing point in a test which is given a separate mark or marks." That is fine as far as it goes, but what is a "testing point" and what is a "separate mark"? I think there is a clearer way to look at test items.

In the same sense that the phoneme is a basic unit in phonology and the morpheme is a basic unit in syntax, an *item* is the basic unit of language testing. Like the linguistic units above, the item is sometimes difficult to define. Some types of items, like multiple-choice or true-false items, are relatively easy to identify because they are the individual test questions that anyone can recognize as discrete units. An item may prove more difficult to identify for the more integrative types of language tests such as dictations, interviews, role plays, and compositions, or for more personal assessments like conferences, self-assessments, or portfolios. To accommodate the variety of discrete-point, integrative, and personal item types found in language testing, I will define the term **item** very broadly as the smallest unit that produces distinctive and meaningful information or feedback on a test when it is scored or rated. This definition will be general enough to work for every type of language test from multiple-choice to portfolio, yet will be specific enough to also prove useful.

Since the *item* is the basic unit, or building block, in testing, one way to improve a test is to examine the individual items and revise the test so that only those items that are performing well remain in the revised version of the test. Teachers often look at the total scores of their students on a test, but careful examination of the individual items that contributed to the total scores can also prove very illuminating. This process of carefully inspecting individual test items is called item analysis.

More formally, **item analysis** is the systematic evaluation of the effectiveness of the individual items on a test. This is usually done for purposes of selecting the "best" items which will remain on a revised and improved version of the test. Sometimes, however, item analysis is performed simply to investigate how well the items on a test are working with a particular group of students. Item analysis can take numerous forms, but when testing for norm-referenced purposes, there are three types of analyses that are typically applied: item format analysis, item facility analysis, and item discrimination analysis. In developing CRTs, three other concerns become paramount: item quality analysis, the item difference index, and the B-index for each item.

GUIDELINES FOR ITEM FORMAT ANALYSIS

In analyzing **item format**, testers focus on the degree to which each item is properly written so that it measures all and only the desired content. Such analyses often involve making judgments about the adequacy of item formats. Consider the following multiple-choice grammar item:

The apple is located somewhere on or around _____.

(A) a table   (C) the table

(B) an table   (D) table

This item has two possible answers (A and C), is wordier than it needs to be ("located somewhere…or around" may be difficult, distracting, and superfluous), and repeats the word "table" inefficiently. Item format analysis could lead us to correct these problems and produce a better item as follows:

Do you see the chair and table? The apple is on _____ table.

(A) a   (C) the

(B) an   (D) (no article)

Now, the first sentence makes "the" the only correct answer; the item has been reworded to avoid difficult, distracting, and superfluous words; and the word *table* is moved up into the main part of the item so it is not repeated four times in the A-D options. The item may still be imperfect because other teachers have not given feedback on it, but it is considerably better than it was when first written.

The guidelines provided in this chapter are designed to help teachers make well-informed and relatively objective judgments about how well items are formatted. The first set of guidelines is a very general set that teachers can apply to virtually all types of items. A second set will help guide teachers to analyze receptive response item formats (true-false, multiple-choice, and matching items). A third set will aid with the different types of productive response item formats (fill-in, short-response, and task), and a fourth set will aid teachers in formatting personal response item formats (conferences, portfolios, self-assessments). In all cases, the purpose is to help teachers improve the formatting of the items that they use in their language tests.

Table 3.1 General guidelines for most item formats

Checklist Questions	Yes	No
1. Is the item format correctly matched to the purpose and content of the item?	☐	☐
2. Is there only one correct answer?	☐	☐
3. Is the item written at the students' level of proficiency?	☐	☐
4. Have ambiguous terms and statements been avoided?	☐	☐
5. Have negatives and double negatives been avoided?	☐	☐
6. Does the item avoid giving clues that could be used in answering other items?	☐	☐
7. Are all parts of the item on the same page?	☐	☐
8. Is only relevant information presented?	☐	☐
9. Have race, gender, and nationality bias been avoided?	☐	☐
10. Has at least one other colleague looked over the items?	☐	☐

GENERAL GUIDELINES

Table 3.1 shows some general guidelines, which are applicable to most language testing formats. They are in the form of questions that teachers can ask themselves when writing or critiquing any type of item format. In most cases, the purpose of asking these questions is to insure that the students score high or low on the item type for the right reasons. In other words, the students should answer the items correctly only if they know the concept or skill being tested or have the skill involved. By extension, the students should answer incorrectly only if they do not know the material or lack the skill being tested. Let's consider each question in Table 3.1.

1. Is the item format correctly matched to the purpose and content of the item?

Teachers will, of course, want their item formats to match the purpose and content of the item. In part, this means matching the right type of item to what is being tested in terms of modes (productive or receptive) and channels (written or oral language). For instance, teachers may want to avoid using a multiple-choice format, which is basically receptive mode (students read and select, but produce nothing), for testing productive skills like writing and speaking. Similarly, it would make little sense to require the students to read aloud (productive) the individual letters of the words in a book in order to test the receptive skill of reading comprehension. Such a task would be senseless, in part because the students would be using both receptive and productive modes mixed with both oral and written channels when the purpose of the test, reading comprehension, is essentially receptive mode and written channel. A second problem would arise because the students would be too narrowly focused in terms of content on reading the letters of the words. To avoid mixing modes and channels and to focus the content at the comprehension level of the reading skill, teachers might more profitably have the students read a written passage and use receptive-response items in the form of multiple-choice comprehension questions. In short, teachers must think about what they are trying to test in terms of all the dimensions discussed in the previous chapter and try to match their purpose with the item format that most closely resembles it.

2. Is there only one correct answer?

The issue of making sure that each question has only one correct answer is not as obvious as it might at first seem. Correctness is often a matter of degrees rather than an absolute. For instance, in the following item there are two possible answers (A or C) depending on how the reader sees the context:

The apple is located on _____ table.

   (A) a   (C) the

   (B) an   (D) (no article)

That problem can be corrected by clarifying the context so that only one answer will work (C):

Do you see the chair and table? The apple is on _____ table.

   (A) a   (C) the

   (B) an   (D) (no article)

Sometimes, an option that is correct to one person may be less so to another, and an option that seems incorrect to the teacher may appear to be correct to many of the students. Such differences may occur due to differing points of view on the world or to differing contexts that people can mentally supply in answering a given question. Every teacher has probably disagreed with the "correct" answer on some test that they have taken or given. Such problems arise because the item writer was unable to take into account every possible point of view. One way that test writers attempt to circumvent this problem is by having the examinees select the *best* answer. Such wording does ultimately leave the judgment as to which is the *best* answer in the hands of the test writer, but how ethical is such a stance? I feel that the *best* course of action is to try to write items for which there is clearly only one correct answer. The statistics discussed in the next chapter under *Item Efficiency Analysis* will help to spot cases where the results indicate that two answers are possible, or that a second answer is very close to correct.

3. Is the item written at the students' level of proficiency?

Each item should be written at approximately the level of proficiency of the students who will take the test. For instance, an item like the following (based on a reading passage not shown here) would obviously contain vocabulary that is far too difficult for most ESL students (and many native speakers of English):

According to the passage, antidisestablishmentarianism diverges fundamentally from the conventional proceedings and traditions of the Church of England.

(T)   (F)

Since a given language program may include students with a wide range of abilities, teachers should think in terms of using items that are at about the *average* ability level for the group. To begin with, teachers may have to gauge this average level by intuition, but later, using the item statistics provided in this chapter, they will be able to more rationally identify which items on average are too difficult, too easy, or at the appropriate level of difficulty for their students.

4. Have ambiguous terms and statements been avoided?

Ambiguous and tricky language should be avoided unless the purpose of the item is to test ambiguity. For instance, a short-answer item like the following (again based on a reading passage that does not appear here) would be ambiguous to some students:

Why are statistical studies inaccessible to language teachers in Brazil according to the reading passage?

If the correct answer was something like "language teachers get very little training in mathematics" and/or "such teachers are naturally averse to numbers," students who answered that "the libraries may be far away" would be wrong because of the ambiguity of the word *inaccessible* (even if that is factually true and mentioned in the passage).

The problem is that ambiguous language may cause students to answer incorrectly even though they know the correct answer. Such an outcome is always undesirable. Getting a colleague or two to proofread the test or having several former students take the test and comment on the items can solve this kind of problem.

5. Have negatives and double negatives been avoided?

Likewise, the use of negatives and double negatives may be needlessly confusing and should be avoided unless the purpose of the item is to test negatives. For example:

One theory that is not unassociated with Noam Chomsky is:
- (A) Transformational generative grammar
- (B) Case grammar
- (C) Non-universal phonology
- (D) Acoustic phonology

Clearly, the three negatives (*not*, *un-*, and *non-*) in this item make the item impossible to process. Whereas the following accomplishes the same thing without confusion (even though it contains the single negative *non-*):

One theory that is associated with Noam Chomsky is:
- (A) Transformational generative grammar
- (B) Case grammar
- (C) Non-universal phonology
- (D) Acoustic phonology

In those rare cases where negatives must be tested, like the example above, wise test writers use only one negative word and emphasize it (by underlining them, typing them in capital letters, or putting them in bold-faced type, as in not, NEVER, *in*consistent, etc.) so the students are sure to notice what is being tested. Students should *not* miss an item because they did *not* notice a negative marker, if indeed they know the answer.

6. Does the item avoid giving clues that could be used in answering other items?

Teachers should also avoid giving clues in one item that will help answer another item. For instance, a clear example of a grammatical structure may appear in one item that will help some students to answer a question about that structure later in the test.

Students should answer the latter item correctly only if they know the concept or skill involved, not because they were clever enough to remember and look back to an example or model of it in a previous item.

7. Are all parts of the item on the same page?

All the parts of each item should be on one page. Students, who know the concept or skill being tested, should not respond incorrectly simply because they did not realize that the correct answer was on the next page. This issue is easily checked, but sometimes forgotten.

8. Is only relevant information presented?

Teachers should also avoid including extra information that is irrelevant to the concept or skill being tested. Since most teachers will probably want their tests to be relatively efficient, any extra information not related to the material being tested should be avoided, because it will just take extra time for the students to read and will add nothing to the test. Such extra information may also inadvertently provide the students with clues they can use in answering other items.

9. Have race, gender, and nationality bias been avoided?

All teachers should also be on the alert for bias that may have crept into their test items. Race, gender, religion, nationality, age, ethnicity, and other biases must be avoided at all costs, not only because they are unethical, morally wrong, and illegal in many countries, but also because they affect the fairness and objectivity of the test. The most famous example of this was the so-called "white picket fence" item on an IQ test. This item apparently required knowledge of what a *white picket fence* is in order to answer it correctly. The item was judged biased against inner city blacks, who seldom, if ever, would see such a suburban lawn fence. The item was meant to test IQ, but instead was testing vocabulary knowledge, vocabulary that one particular group of students was unlikely to know.

The problem is that an item that is biased against one group of people is testing something in addition to what it was originally designed to test, and such an item cannot provide clear and easily interpretable information. The only practical way to avoid bias in most situations is to examine the items carefully and have other language professionals also examine them. Preferably these colleagues will be both male and female and will be drawn from different racial, religious, nationality, age, and ethnic groupings. Since the potential for bias differs from situation to situation, individual teachers will have to determine what is appropriate for avoiding bias in the items administered to their particular populations of students. Statistical techniques can help spot and avoid this bias in items too. However, these bias statistics are well beyond the scope of this book.

10. Has at least one other colleague looked over the items?

Regardless of any problems that teachers may find and correct in their items, they should always have at least one or more colleagues look over and perhaps take the test so that any additional problems may be spotted before the test is actually used to make decisions about students' lives. A related point for teachers who are not native speakers of the language being tested is the possible necessity of having native speakers take the test or at least look it over. As far back as 1961, Lado put it this way, "...if the test is administered to native speakers of the language they should make very high marks on it or we will suspect that factors other than the basic ones of language have been introduced into the items" (p. 323).

Table 3.2 includes other questions that are specifically designed for receptive response items. **Receptive response items** require the student to select a response rather than actually produce one. In other words, the responses involve receptive language in the sense that the item responses from which students must select are heard or read, receptively. Receptive response item formats include true-false, multiple-choice, and matching items.

Table 3.2 Guidelines for receptive response items

Item Format Checklist Questions	Yes	No
True-False		
1. Is the statement worded carefully enough so it can be judged without ambiguity?	☐	☐
2. Have "absoluteness" clues been avoided?	☐	☐
Multiple-Choice		
1. Have all unintentional clues been avoided?	☐	☐
2. Are all of the distracters plausible?	☐	☐
3. Has needless redundancy been avoided in the options?	☐	☐
4. Has the ordering of the options been carefully considered? Or are the correct answers randomly assigned?	☐	☐
5. Have distracters like "none of the above," "A and B only," etc. been avoided?	☐	☐
Matching		
1. Are there more options than premises?	☐	☐
2. Are options shorter than premises to reduce reading?	☐	☐
3. Are the option and premise lists related to one central theme?	☐	☐

TRUE-FALSE

True-false items are typically written as statements, and students must decide whether the statements are true or false. There are two potential problems shown in Table 3.2 that teachers should consider in developing items in this format.

1. Is the statement worded carefully enough so it can be judged without ambiguity?

The statement should be carefully worded to avoid any ambiguities that might cause the students to miss it for the wrong reasons. The wording of true-false items is particularly difficult and important. Teachers are often tempted to make such items "tricky" so that the items will be difficult enough for intermediate or advanced language students. Such trickiness should be avoided: students should miss an item because they do not know the concept or have the skill being tested rather than because the item is tricky.

2. Have "absoluteness" clues been avoided?

Teachers should also avoid absoluteness clues. Absoluteness clues allow students to answer correctly without knowing the correct response. Absoluteness clues include terms like *all, always, absolutely, never, rarely, most often,* and so forth. True-false items that include such terms are very easy to answer regardless of concept or skill being tested because the answer is inevitably *false.* For example:

This book is always crystal clear in all its explanations.

(T)   (F)

MULTIPLE-CHOICE

Multiple-choice items are made up of an **item stem**, or the main part of the item at the top, a **correct answer**, which is obviously the choice (usually, a., b., c., or d.) that will be counted correct, and the **distracters**, which are those choices that will be counted as incorrect. These incorrect choices are called distracters because they should distract, or divert the students' attention away from the correct answer if the students really do not know which is correct. The term **options** refers collectively to all the alternative choices presented to the students including the correct answer and the distracters. All these terms are necessary for understanding how multiple-choice items function. Five potential pitfalls for multiple-choice items appear in Table 3.2 (p. 47).

1. Have all unintentional clues been avoided?

Teachers should avoid unintentional clues (grammatical, phonological, morphological, and so forth) that help students to answer an item without having the knowledge or skill being tested. To avoid such clues, teachers should write multiple-choice items so that they clearly test only one concept or skill at a time. Consider the following item:

The fruit that Adam ate in the Bible was an _____.

   (A) pear   (C) apple

   (B) banana   (D) papaya

The purpose of this item is neither clear nor straightforward. If the purpose of the item is to test cultural or biblical knowledge, an unintentional grammatical clue (in that the article *an* must be followed by a noun that begins with a vowel) is interfering with that purpose. Hence, a student who knows the article system in English can answer the item correctly without ever having heard of Adam. If, on the other hand, the purpose of the item is to test knowledge of this grammatical point, why confuse the issue with the cultural/biblical reference? In short, teachers should avoid items that are not straightforward and clear in intent. Otherwise, unintentional clues may creep into their items.

2. Are all of the distracters plausible?

Teachers should also make sure that all the distracters are plausible. If one distracter is ridiculous, that distracter is not helping to test the students. Instead, those students who are guessing will be able to dismiss that distracter and improve their chances of answering the item correctly without really knowing the correct answer. An example (based again on a reading passage about Eve and Adam not shown here) follows:

Adam ate _____.

- A. an apple
- C. an apricot
- B. a banana
- D. a tire

Clearly, tire is not a plausible answer in this set. Why would any teacher write an item that has ridiculous distracters? Brown's law may help explain this phenomenon. Brown's law: when writing four-option multiple-choice items, the stem and correct option are easy to write, and the next two distracters are relatively easy to make up, as well, but the last distracter is absolutely impossible. The only way to understand Brown's law is to actually try writing a few four-option multiple-choice items. The point is that teachers are often tempted to put something ridiculous for that last distracter, simply because they are having trouble thinking of an effective distracter. Therefore, always check to see that all the distracters in a multiple-choice item are truly distracting.

3. Has needless redundancy been avoided in the options?

In order to make a test reasonably efficient, teachers should double check that items contain no needless redundancy. For example, consider the following item designed to test the past tense of the verb *to fall*:

The boy was on his way to the store, walking down the street, when he stepped on a piece of cold wet ice and _____.

- A. fell flat on his face
- C. felled flat on his face
- B. fall flat on his face
- D. falled flat on his face

In addition to the problem of providing needless words and phrases throughout the stem, the phrase "flat on his face" is repeated four times in the options, when it could just as easily have been written one time in the stem. The item could have been far shorter to read and less redundant, yet equally effective if it had been written as follows:

The boy stepped on a piece of ice and _____ flat on his face.

- A. fell
- C. felled
- B. fall
- D. falled

4. Has the ordering of the options been carefully considered? Or are the correct answers randomly assigned?

Any test writer may unconsciously introduce a pattern into the test that will help the students who are guessing to increase the probability of answering an item correctly. A teacher might decide that the correct answer for the first item should be *C* For the second item, that teacher might decide on *D* and for the third item *A*. Having already picked *C*, *D*, and *A* to be correct answers in the first three items, the teacher will very likely pick *B* to be the correct answer in the next item. Human beings seem to have a need to balance things out like this, and such patterns can be used by clever test takers to help them guess at better than chance levels without actually knowing the answer. Since testers want to maximize the likelihood that students answer items correctly because they know the concepts being tested, they generally avoid patterns that can help students guess.

A number of strategies can be used to avoid creating patterns. If the options are always ordered from the shortest to longest or alphabetically, the choice of which option is correct is out of the test writer's hands. Hence that human tendency to create patterns will be avoided. Another strategy that can be used is to randomly select which option will be correct. Selection can be done with a table of random numbers or with the aces, twos, threes, and fours taken from a deck of cards. In all cases, the purpose is to eliminate patterns that may help students guess the correct answers if they do not know them.

5. Have distracters like "none of the above," "A and B only," etc. been avoided?

Teachers can also be tempted (often due to Brown's law, mentioned above) to use options like "all of the above," "none of the above," and "*A and B*" I normally advise avoiding this type of option unless the specific purpose of the item is to test two things at a time and students' abilities to interpret such combinations. For the reasons discussed in Points 1 and 2 (p. 48), such items are usually inadvisable.

MATCHING ITEMS

Matching items present the students with two columns of information; the students must then find and identify matches between the two sets of information. For the sake of discussion, the information given in the left-hand column will be called the **matching item premise** and that shown in the right-hand column will be labeled **options.** Thus, in a matching test, students must match the correct option to each premise. There are three guidelines that teachers should apply to matching items.

1. Are there more options than premises?

More options should be supplied than premises so that students cannot narrow down the choices as they progress through the test simply by keeping track of the options that they have already used. For example, in matching ten definitions (premises) to a list of ten vocabulary words (options), a student who knows nine will be assured of getting the tenth one correct by the process of elimination without knowing it. If, on the other hand, there are ten premises and 15 options, this problem is minimized.

2. Are options shorter than premises to reduce reading?

The options should usually be shorter than the premises because most students will read a premise then search through the options for the correct match. By controlling the length of the options as described here, the amount of reading will be minimized. Teachers often do exactly the opposite in creating vocabulary matching items by using the vocabulary words as the premises, and using the definitions (which are much longer) as the options.

3. Are the option and premise lists related to one central theme?

The premises and options should be logically related to one central theme that is obvious to the students. Mixing different themes in one set of matching items is not a good idea because it may confuse the students and cause them to miss items that they would otherwise answer correctly. For example, lining up definitions and the related vocabulary items is a good idea, but also mixing in matches between graphemic and phonemic representations of words would only cause confusion. The two different themes could be much more clearly and effectively tested as separate sets of matching items.

Table 3.3 includes additional questions that should be applied to productive response items. **Productive response items** require the students to actually produce responses rather than just select them receptively. In other words, the responses involve productive language in the sense that the answers must either be written or spoken. Productive item formats include fill-in, short-response, and task types of items.

Table 3.3 Guidelines for productive response items

Item Format Checklist Questions	Yes	No
Fill-In		
1. Is the required response concise?	☐	☐
2. Is there sufficient context to convey the intent of the questions to the students?	☐	☐
3. Are the blanks of standard length?	☐	☐
4. Does the main body of the question precede the blank?	☐	☐
5. Has a list of acceptable responses been developed?	☐	☐
Short-Response		
1. Is the item formatted so that only one relatively concise answer is possible?	☐	☐
2. Is the item framed as a clear and direct question?	☐	☐
Task		
1. Is the student's task clearly defined?	☐	☐
2. Is the task sufficiently narrow (and/or broad) for the time available?	☐	☐
3. Have scoring procedures been worked out in advance with regard to the approach that will be used?	☐	☐
4. Have scoring procedures been worked out in advance with regard to the categories of language that will be rated?	☐	☐
5. Have scoring procedures been clearly defined in terms of what each score within each category means?	☐	☐
6. Is scoring to be as anonymous as possible?	☐	☐

FILL-IN ITEMS

Fill-in items are those wherein a word or phrase is replaced by a blank in a sentence or longer text and the student's job is to fill in that missing word or phrase. There are five sets of issues that teachers should consider when using fill-in items.

1. Is the required response concise?

In answering fill-in items, students will often write alternative answers that the teacher did not anticipate when the items were written. For example in the following fill-in item there are many possible answers: John walked down the street _____. Indeed almost any adverb would work, e.g., slowly, quickly, pensively, angrily, carefully, etc.

To guard against this possibility, teachers should check to make sure that each item has one very concise correct answer. For example, a blank with only one acceptable answer (fell) would be the following: John stepped onto the ice and immediately _____ down hard.

Alternatively, the teacher can develop a glossary of acceptable answers for each blank. Obviously, as the number of alternative possibilities rises for each item, the longer and more difficult the scoring becomes. One goal should be to create an answer key that will help make clear-cut decisions as to whether each item is correct. Another goal should be to create an answer key that is so complete that no modifications will be necessary during the scoring process because such modifications necessitate backtracking and rescoring tests that have already been scored.

2. Is there sufficient context to convey the intent of the question to the students?

In deciding how much context to provide for each blank (that is, how many words or phrases each item should contain), teachers should make sure that enough context has been provided so the purpose, or intent, of the item is clear to those students who know the answer. At the same time, avoid giving too much extra context. Extra context will burden students with extraneous material to read (see Table 3.1 no. 8) and may inadvertently provide students with extraneous clues (see Table 3.1 no. 6).

3. Are the blanks of standard length?

Generally speaking, all the blanks in a fill-in test should be the same length, that is, if the first blank is twelve spaces long, then, all the items should have blanks with twelve spaces. Blanks of uniform length do not provide extraneous clues about the relative length of the answers. Obviously, this stricture would not apply if a teacher purposely wants to indicate the length of each word or the number of words in each blank.

4. Does the main body of the question precede the blank?

Teachers should also consider putting the main body of the item before the blank in most of the items so that the students have the information necessary to answer the item when they encounter the blank. For example: Based on the above sentence, teachers should put the main body of the question before the _____. Such a strategy will help to make the test more efficient. Of course, situations do exist in language testing wherein the blank must be early in the item (for instance, when trying to test for the head noun in a sentence), but as a general rule, the blank should occur relatively late in the item.

5. Has a list of acceptable responses been developed?

In situations where the blanks may be very difficult and frustrating for the students, teachers might consider supplying a list of responses from which the students can choose in filling in the blanks. This list will not only make answering the items easier for the students, but will also make the correction of the items easier for the teacher because the students will have a limited set of possible answers to draw on. However, even a minor modification like this one can dramatically change the nature of the items. In this case, the modification would change them from productive response items to selected response items.

SHORT-RESPONSE ITEMS

Short-response items are usually items that the students can answer in a few phrases or sentences. This type of item should conform to at least the following two guidelines.

1. Is the item formatted so that only one relatively concise answer is possible?

Teachers should make sure that the item is formatted so that there is one, and only one, concise answer or set of answers that they are looking for in the responses to each item. The parameters for what will be considered an acceptable answer should be thought through carefully and clearly delineated before correcting such items. As in Point 1 for fill-in items (p. 51), the goal in short-response items is to ensure that the answer key will help the teacher make clear-cut decisions as to whether each item is correct without making modifications as the scoring progresses. Therefore, the teacher's expectations should be thought out in advance, recognizing that subjectivity may become a problem because the teacher will necessarily be making judgments about the relative quality of the students' answers. Thus, partial credit often becomes an issue with this type of item. **Partial credit** entails giving some credit for answers that are not 100 percent correct. For instance, on one short response item, a student might get two points for an answer with correct spelling and correct grammar, but only one point if either grammar or spelling were wrong, and no points if both grammar and spelling were wrong. Like all the other aspects of scoring short-response items, any partial credit scheme must be clearly thought out and delineated before scoring starts so that backtracking and rescoring will not be necessary.

2. Is the item framed as a clear and direct question?

Short-response items should generally be phrased as clear and direct questions. Unnecessary wordiness should particularly be avoided with this type of item so that the range of expected answers will stay narrow enough to be scored with relative ease and objectivity. You may even want to consider giving the students some idea of the shape of the answer you are looking for. For example (based on a reading passage about doing research not supplied here, where the expected answer given in the passage would include some form of the following three steps: gather information, analyze the information, report the results):

> According to the reading passage, what are the three steps in doing research?

Such a question would let the students know that you were looking for three things and that those things are the steps in doing research.

TASK ITEMS

Task items will be defined here as any of a group of fairly open-ended item types that require students to perform a task in the language that is being tested. A task test (or what one colleague accidentally called a *tesk*) might include a series of communicative tasks, a set of problem-solving tasks, and a writing task. In another alternative that has become increasingly popular in the last decade, students are asked to perform a series of writing tasks and revisions during a course and put them together into a portfolio (see discussion of portfolios on p. 62).

While task items are appealing to many language teachers, a number of complications may arise in using them. To avoid such difficulties, consider at least the following six guidelines.

1. Is the student's task clearly defined?

The directions for the task should be so clear that both the tester and the student know exactly what the student must do. The task may be anything that people need to do with language. Thus, task items might require students to solve written word problems, to give oral directions on how to get to the library, to explain to another student how to draw a particular geometric shape, to write a composition on a specific topic, and so forth. The possibilities are only limited by the degree of imagination among the teachers involved. However, the point to remember is that the directions for the task must be concisely explained so the students know exactly what they are expected to do and thus cannot stray too far away from the intended purpose of the item.

2. Is the task sufficiently narrow (and/or broad) for the time available?

The task should be sufficiently narrow in scope so that it fits logistically into the time allotted for its performance. At the same time, since one purpose of task items is to get the students to produce language, the task should be broad enough so that an adequate sample of each student's language is available for proper scoring. For instance, in an essay examination, a topic that requires a yes/no answer (e.g., "Did you have a good summer?") would be far too narrow; a *wh-* question like "What did you do last summer?", though it is a cliché, is much more likely to produce a good language sample. In my high school American Literature class, I will never forget the topic assigned by my teacher for the three-hour in-class essay examination: "Explain American Literature; you have three hours." Even then, I thought that topic was way too broad for the time allowed. I wrote my heart out but only got to Emerson, missing out altogether on the chance to write about my favorite authors from the late nineteenth and twentieth centuries. In other words, I did not have enough time to adequately finish the task.

3. Have the scoring procedures been worked out in advance with regard to the approach that will be used?

Teachers must carefully work out the scoring procedures for task items for the same reasons listed in discussing the other types of productive response items. However, such planning is particularly crucial for task items because teachers have less control over the range of possible responses in such open-ended items.

Two entirely different approaches are possible in scoring tasks. A task can be scored using an **analytic approach**, in which the teachers rate various aspects of each student's language production separately; or a task can be scored using a **holistic approach**, in which the teachers use a single general scale to give a single global rating for each student's language production. The very nature of the item(s) will depend on how the teachers choose to score the task. If teachers choose to use an analytic approach, the task may have three, four, five, or even six individual bits of information, each of which should be treated as a separate item (for example, the rubric shown in Table 3.4 (p. 56) requires raters to judge five different aspects of writing: organization; logical development of ideas; grammar; punctuation, spelling, and mechanics; and style and quality of expression). A decision for a holistic approach will produce results that must be treated differently, that is, more like a single item (see Table 3.5, p. 57). Thus, teachers must decide early as to whether they will score task items using an analytic approach or a holistic one.

4. Have scoring procedures been worked out in advance with regard to the categories of language that will be rated?

If teachers decide to use an analytic approach, they must then decide which categories of language to judge in rating the students' performances. Naturally, these decisions must also occur before the scoring process begins. For example, when I was teaching ESL at UCLA, we felt that compositions should be rated analytically, with separate scores for organization, logic, grammar, mechanics, and style as shown in Table 3.4, p. 56 (see Brown & Bailey 1984). Five categories of language were important to us, but these categories are not the only possible ones. In contrast, when I was director of the English Language Institute at the UHM, we used an analytic scale that helped us rate content, organization, vocabulary, language use, and mechanics (see Jacobs, Zinkgraf, Wormuth, Hartfiel, & Hughey 1981). Thus, the teachers at UHM preferred to rate five categories of language that are different from the five categories used at UCLA. Because such decisions were often very different from course to course and program to program, decisions about which categories of language to rate should most often rest with the teachers who are involved in the teaching process. (For an example of descriptors that are used in a *holistic* six-point scale, see ETS 1996, p. 19.)

5. Have scoring procedures been clearly defined in terms of what each score within each category means?

Having worked out the approach and categories of language to rate, it is still necessary to clearly define the points on the scales for each category. Written descriptions of the kinds of language that would be expected at each score level will help. The descriptors shown in Table 3.4 on page 56 (Brown & Bailey 1984, pp. 39–41) are examples of one way to go about delineating such language behaviors in an analytic scale. Table 3.5 (p. 57) rearranges the same descriptive information to show how it would look as a holistic scale. Regardless of the form that they take, such descriptions will help ensure that the judgments of the scorers are relatively consistent within and across categories and that the scores will be relatively easy to assign and interpret. Sometimes, training workshops will be necessary for the raters so they can agree upon the definitions within each scale and develop consistency in the ways that they assign scores (see Chapter 8 under ***Rater reliabilities***). However, as McNamara (1996, p. 26) points out, rater training may only succeed in making raters more self-consistent and may not resolve average differences in ratings between raters. He goes on to argue that such differences may be the natural state of affairs (pp. 232–239), and that, in any case, such overall differences will be moderated if raters are self-consistent and multiple raters are used.

6. Is scoring to be as anonymous as possible?

Another strategy that can help make the scoring as objective as possible is to assign the scores anonymously. A few changes in testing procedures may be necessary to ensure anonymous ratings. For instance, students may have to put their names on the back of the first page of a writing task so that the raters do not know whose test they are rating. Or, if the task is audio-taped in a face-to-face interview, teachers other than the student's teachers may have to be assigned to rate the tape without knowing who they are hearing on the cassette. Such precautions will differ from task to task and situation to situation. Since they are largely a matter of common sense, teachers can work out the details for themselves. The important thing is that teachers consider using anonymity as a way of increasing objectivity.

Table 3.4 Analytic scale for rating composition tasks

	20-18 Excellent to Good	17-15 Good to Adequate	14-12 Adequate to Fair	11-6 Unacceptable	5-1 Not College-level Work
I. Organization: Introduction, Body & Conclusion	Appropriate title, effective introductory paragraph, topic is stated, leads to body; transitional expressions used; arrangement of material shows plan (could be outlined by reader); supporting evidence given for generalizations; conclusion logical & complete	Adequate title, introduction, & conclusion; body of essay is acceptable but some evidence may be lacking, some ideas aren't fully developed; sequence is logical but transitional expressions may be absent or misused	Mediocre or scant introduction or conclusion; problems with the order of ideas in body; the generalizations may not be fully supported by the evidence given; problems of organization interfere	Shaky or minimally recognizable introduction; organization can barely be seen; severe problems with ordering of ideas; lack of supporting evidence; conclusion weak or illogical; inadequate effort at organization	Absence of introduction or conclusion; no apparent organization of body; severe lack of supporting evidence; writer has not made any effort to organize the composition (could not be outlined by reader)
II. Logical Development of Ideas: Content	Essay addresses the assigned topic; the ideas are concrete and thoroughly developed; no extraneous material; essay reflects thought	Essay addresses the issues but misses some points; ideas could be more fully developed; some extraneous material is present	Development of ideas not complete or essay is somewhat off the topic; paragraphs aren't divided exactly right	Ideas incomplete; essay does not reflect careful thinking or was hurriedly written; inadequate effort in area of content	Essay is completely inadequate and does not reflect college-level work; no apparent effort to consider the topic carefully
III. Grammar	Native-like fluency in English grammar; correct use of relative clauses, prepositions, modals, articles, verb forms, and tense sequencing; no fragments or run-on sentences	Advanced proficiency in English grammar; some grammar problems don't influence communication, although the reader is aware of them; no fragments or run-on sentences	Ideas getting through to the reader, but grammar problems are apparent and have a negative effect on communication; run-on sentences or fragments present	Numerous serious grammar problems interfere with communication of the writer's ideas; grammar review of some areas clearly needed; difficult to read sentences	Severe grammar problems interfere greatly with the message; reader can't understand what the writer is trying to say; unintelligible sentence structure
IV. Punctuation, Spelling, & Mechanics	Correct use of English writing conventions; left & right margins, all needed capitals, paragraphs indented, punctuation & spelling; very neat	Some problems with writing conventions or punctuation; occasional spelling errors; left margin correct; paper is neat and legible	Uses general writing conventions but has errors; spelling problems distract reader; punctuation errors interfere with ideas	Serious problems with format of paper; parts of essay not legible; errors in sentence-final punctuation; unacceptable to educated readers	Complete disregard for English writing conventions; paper illegible; obvious capitals missing, no margins, severe spelling problems
IV. Style & Quality of Expression	Precise vocabulary usage; use of parallel structures; concise; register good	Attempts variety; good vocabulary; not wordy; register OK; style fairly concise	Some vocabulary misused; lacks awareness of register; may be too wordy	Poor expression of ideas; problems in vocabulary; lacks variety of structure	Inappropriate use of vocabulary; no concept of register or sentence variety

Table 3.5 Holistic version of the scale for rating composition tasks

Scores	Descriptors
5	Appropriate title, effective introductory paragraph, topic is stated, leads to body; transitional expressions used; arrangement of material shows plan (could be outlined by reader); supporting evidence given for generalizations; conclusion logical & complete. Essay addresses the assigned topic; the ideas are concrete and thoroughly developed; no extraneous material; essay reflects thought. Native-like fluency in English grammar; correct use of relative clauses, prepositions, modals, articles, verb forms, and tense sequencing; no fragments or run-on sentences. Correct use of English writing conventions; left & right margins, all needed capitals, paragraphs indented, punctuation & spelling; very neat. Precise vocabulary usage; use of parallel structures; concise; register good.
4	Adequate title, introduction, & conclusion; body of essay is acceptable but some evidence may be lacking, some ideas aren't fully developed; sequence is logical but transitional expressions may be absent or misused. Essay addresses the issues but misses some points; ideas could be more fully developed; some extraneous material is present. Advanced proficiency in English grammar; some grammar problems don't influence communication, although the reader is aware of them; no fragments or run-on sentences. Some problems with writing conventions or punctuation; occasional spelling errors; left margin correct; paper is neat and legible. Attempts variety; good vocabulary; not wordy; register OK; style fairly concise.
3	Mediocre or scant introduction or conclusion; problems with the order of ideas in body; the generalizations may not be fully supported by the evidence given; problems of organization interfere. Development of ideas not complete or essay is somewhat off the topic; paragraphs aren't divided exactly right. Ideas getting through to the reader, but grammar problems are apparent and have a negative effect on communication; run-on sentences or fragments present. Uses general writing conventions but has errors; spelling problems distract reader; punctuation errors interfere with ideas. Some vocabulary misused; lacks awareness of register; may be too wordy.
2	Shaky or minimally recognizable introduction; organization can barely be seen; severe problems with ordering of ideas; lack of supporting evidence; conclusion weak or illogical; inadequate effort at organization. Ideas incomplete; essay does not reflect careful thinking or was hurriedly written; inadequate effort in area of content. Numerous serious grammar problems interfere with communication of the writer's ideas; grammar review of some areas clearly needed; difficult to read sentences. Serious problems with format of paper; parts of essay not legible; errors in sentence-final punctuation; unacceptable to educated readers. Poor expression of ideas; problems in vocabulary; lacks variety of structure.
1	Absence of introduction or conclusion; no apparent organization of body; severe lack of supporting evidence; writer has not made any effort to organize the composition (could not be outlined by reader). Essay is completely inadequate and does not reflect college-level work; no apparent effort to consider the topic carefully. Severe grammar problems interfere greatly with the message; reader can't understand what the writer is trying to say; unintelligible sentence structure. Complete disregard for English writing conventions; paper illegible; obvious capitals missing, no margins, severe spelling problems. Inappropriate use of vocabulary; no concept of register or sentence variety.

Table 3.6 (adapted from Brown & Hudson 2002) includes additional questions that should be applied to personal response items. **Personal response items** encourage the students to produce responses that hold personal meaning. In other words, the responses allow students to communicate in ways and about things that are interesting to them personally. Personal response item formats include self-assessments, conferences, and portfolios. (For more on this general class of item formats see Bailey 1998; Genesee & Upshur 1996; O'Malley & Valdez Pierce 1996.)

Table 3.6 Guidelines for personal response items

Item Format Checklist Questions	Yes	No
Self-Assessments		
1. Have you decided on a scoring type (holistic or analytic)?	☐	☐
2. Have you decided in advance what aspect of the students' language performance they will be assessing?	☐	☐
3. Have you developed a written rating scale for the learners to use in scoring?	☐	☐
4. Does the rating scale describe concrete language and behaviors in simple terms?	☐	☐
5. Have you planned the logistics of how the students will score themselves?	☐	☐
6. Have you checked to see if students understand the self-scoring procedures?	☐	☐
7. Have you considered having another student and/or the teacher do the same scoring?	☐	☐
Conferences		
1. Have you introduced and explained conferences to the students?	☐	☐
2. Have you given the students the sense that they are in control of the conference?	☐	☐
3. Have you focused the discussion on the students' views about the learning process?	☐	☐
4. Have you considered working with students on self-image issues?	☐	☐
5. Have you elicited performances on specific skills that need to be reviewed?	☐	☐
6. Are the conferences frequently scheduled at regular intervals?	☐	☐
7. Have you scored conferences by applying Numbers 1-6 under *Task* in Table 3.3 (p. 51)?	☐	☐
Portfolios		
1. Have you introduced and explained portfolios to the students?	☐	☐
2. Have you and the students decided who will take responsibility for what?	☐	☐
3. Have students selected and collected *meaningful* work?	☐	☐
4. Have students periodically reflected in writing on their portfolios?	☐	☐
5. Have other students, teachers, outsiders, etc. periodically examined the portfolios?	☐	☐
6. Have you scored the portfolios by applying Numbers 1-6 under *Task* in Table 3.3 (p. 51)?	☐	☐

SELF-ASSESSMENTS

Self-assessments will be defined here as any items wherein students are asked to rate their own knowledge, skills, or performances. Thus, self-assessments provide the teacher with some idea of how the students view their own language abilities and development. The related concept of **peer assessments** is simply a variation on this theme that requires students to rate each other (see Brown 1998; Gardner 1996; McNamara & Deane 1995; Murphey 1995; Oscarson 1997).

1. Have you decided on a scoring type (holistic or analytic)?

As with the task items in the productive response section, when using self- and peer-assessments, you will need to consider whether you want to use holistic or analytic scoring. In other words, do you want the students to make their judgments holistically (i.e., making a single "gut reaction" judgment on say a scale of one to ten about the students' language performance) or analytically (i.e., making several more-detailed judgments each on its own scale of say one to five about the students' language performance). (For more on this distinction, see Number 3 in the *Task* section of Table 3.3, p. 51).

2. Have you decided in advance what aspect of the students' language performance they will be assessing?

If an analytic approach is to be used, you should next decide what aspects of their language performance the students will be assessing. Since this is an opportunity for the teacher to focus students' attention on particular aspects of the language, these aspects of the language performance should be selected and defined with some care. For example, when developing a self-assessment instrument for students to rate their own video-taped role plays, you could have them rate their fluency, grammar, pronunciation, vocabulary usage, pragmatics, cohesion, repair strategies, turn-taking strategies, error self-correction, body language, facial expressions, hands, etc. There are many possible categories, so the key would seem to be to select those that the teacher thinks are most germane to what and how the students are learning in that particular course. One way to do this would be to discuss the possibilities with the students and decide together (perhaps with considerable guidance from the teacher) which categories should be used and how they should be defined.

3. Have you developed a written rating scale for the learners to use in scoring?

Next, it is important to provide a written rating scale to help guide the students in their ratings. Johnson (1998) shows a scale he used for peer-assessments of speech presentations in his classes in Japan. That scale is shown in Table 3.7 (p. 60). Though simple in form, Johnson's scale would nevertheless be considered analytic because it asks the students to make separate judgments of several subcategories of language performance within the two broader categories of *voice* and *body*. This is a simple, yet effective, written rating scale. If Johnson had decided to use a holistic rating scale instead of an analytic scale, he might, for instance, have asked the students to simply make a single overall judgment of the student performance: was it (1) poor, (2) fair, (3) good, (4) great, or (5) excellent in terms of voice (volume, rate, pitch, & enunciation) and body (posture, gestures, & eye contact)?

Table 3.7 Peer-assessment rating scale

Evaluator: Presenter: _____ Title: _____

Skill	Poor	Fair	Good	Great	Excellent	Comments
			Rating			
VOICE						
Volume	1	2	3	4	5	
Rate	1	2	3	4	5	
Pitch	1	2	3	4	5	
Enunciation	1	2	3	4	5	
BODY						
Posture	1	2	3	4	5	
Gesture	1	2	3	4	5	
Eye-contact	1	2	3	4	5	

General comments:

4. Does the rating scale describe concrete language and behaviors in simple terms?

You will probably want to write the rating scale so it uses concrete language and describes the expected behaviors in simple terms. In many rating rubrics (like the analytic scale from Brown and Bailey shown in Table 3.4, p. 56, or the revised holistic version of that same scale shown in Table 3.5, p. 57), much more detail is given than that given in Table 3.7 above. One goal in any scale should be to describe in the most concrete terms possible, the language and behaviors that the students are to rate at each possible level of performance. That would be an argument for the sort of detailed descriptors found in the scales in Tables 3.4 and 3.5. However, since one goal of such self-assessment or peer-assessment scales is also to explain to students in the clearest possible terms what they should judge, arguments can also be made for the sort of simple, straightforward scale in Table 3.7 above. Both strategies have points to recommend them. You will probably want to decide which way you want to proceed based on the conditions and circumstances in your particular teaching situation.

5. Have you planned the logistics of how the students will score themselves?

It is also probably wise to work out the logistics of the self- or peer-assessments in advance. Who will rate each language performance? How will the students make their judgments? How will those judgments be recorded? How will they be collected? Compiled? Analyzed? And how will they be reported to the students who are being rated? Also, who will do all of the above? These are all questions that should be addressed in advance so that chaos does not ensue during the actual self- or peer-assessment process. As a general rule, the wisest strategy might be for the teacher to involve the students in these responsibilities as much as possible, so that students can not only learn as much as possible from the process, but also so the teacher's roles (and workload) are minimized.

6. Have you checked to see if students understand the self-scoring system?

Naturally, a clear explanation of the self-scoring (or peer-scoring) process and how it will proceed will help the students understand what they are to do and why they are doing it. Therefore, directions and explanations should be developed to include all the aspects of the assessment process explained in Questions 1–5 above.

However, explaining all of the above is not enough. You will also probably want to check to see if students understand the self-scoring procedures, and if necessary, repeat portions of your explanation or explain it more clearly.

7. Have you considered having another student and/or the teacher do the same scoring?

As discussed in our last point, teachers and students have often communicated to me that self- and peer-assessments are fine, but the students often want the teacher to do the same scoring as well. In addition, considerations of reliability (see Chapter 8) indicate that it is probably better to involve more than one student in each rating, which supports the wisdom of having another student and/or the teacher do the scoring in addition to a single self- or peer-assessment.

CONFERENCES

Conferences are defined here as any assessment procedures that involve students visiting the teacher's office alone or in groups for brief meetings. In such conferences, the teacher can assess students' abilities to perform particular language points and/or give students feedback on their work (see O'Malley & Valdez Pierce 1996; Genessee & Upshur 1996; Brown 1998).

1. Have you introduced and explained conferences to the students?

At the outset, you will want to introduce and explain the purpose of the conferences to the students. As pointed out above, those purposes may include assessing students' abilities to perform particular language points or giving students feedback on their work; as you will see below, purposes may also include discussion of students' views of the learning processes, bolstering the students' self-images, reviewing specific language skills, and so forth. Whatever the purposes, you will probably want to clearly explain them in class before setting up the appointments so students don't fear that they have done something wrong or are being singled out for punishment. In order to adequately explain the purpose of the conferences, you will probably need to explain some aspects of the following points.

2. Have you given the students the sense that they are in control of the conference?

You may find it wise to negotiate the purposes of the conferences with the students so they have a sense of control over what will be covered or discussed and how the conference will proceed. The teacher can still guide the students into working on the areas described in Questions 3, 4, and 5 below, but in doing so, advocates of this assessment procedure stress the importance of giving the students the sense that they are in control of the conference.

3. Have you focused the discussion on the students' views about the learning process?

In the process of conducting conferences, you might want to consider focusing the students' attention on their views of the language-learning processes. They may never have thought explicitly about these processes. Hence, conferences give the teacher a chance to encourage students to reflect on what it means to learn a language and on the strategies that work best for them.

4. Have you considered working with students on self-image issues?

Another point often mentioned in the literature on conferences is that they afford the teacher an opportunity to work with students on self-confidence and self-image issues. This is particularly useful for students who lack confidence or have poor self-images when they are in the larger group of the classroom.

5. Have you elicited performances on specific skills that need to be reviewed?

From a language learning point of view, conferences afford the teacher an opportunity to elicit and work on specific language skills. You may want to try to observe which students are having trouble with which language skills in class; then, elicit and work on those skills only with the students who need it. Or it may make more sense to check everyone for the ability to perform certain skills during the conference and then work on it only for those students who need to improve in that particular area.

6. Are the conferences frequently scheduled at regular intervals?

Regardless of what you decide to do in the conferences, they should be held frequently and at regular intervals (say once every week or two). The point is that conferences are not likely to be taken seriously by the students, nor will they do much good, if they are not a regular part of the course curriculum.

7. Have you scored conferences by applying Numbers 1–6 under *Task* in Table 3.3?

Grading conferences may also persuade the students to take the conferences seriously. One way to grade conferences would be to work out (perhaps with the students) a scoring system for the conference. Another way would be to ask the students to reflect in writing on what happened during the conference and then score that. In either case, the principles described in Numbers 3–5 under *Task* in Table 3.3 (p. 51) and the associated prose will be helpful.

PORTFOLIOS

Portfolios are any procedures that require students to collect samples of their second language use (e.g., compositions, audio recording, video clips, etc.) into a box or folder for examination at some time in the future by peers, parents, outsiders, etc. Portfolios were originally developed for professional architects, painters, photographers, dancers, actors, etc. to use as examples of their work to show to prospective employers. However, portfolios have recently been adapted for educational purposes, and specifically for language-learning situations. (For more on portfolios, see Popham 1995; O'Malley & Valdez Pierce 1996; Norris 1996; Genessee & Upshur 1996; Brown 1998.)

1. Have you introduced and explained portfolios to the students?

As with conferences, at the outset, you will want to introduce and explain the purpose of the portfolios to the students. In order to do so, you will probably need to explain Questions 2–6 below.

2. Have you and the students decided who will take responsibility for what?

It is wise to work out who will be responsible for each aspect of the process of assembling the portfolios. Who will organize and keep track of the portfolios? Where will they be stored? Who will collect them and pass them out when students are to work on them? These are all questions that should be addressed in advance so that chaos does not ensue during the portfolio development process. As with the self-assessment procedures, the wisest strategy is for the teacher to involve the students in these responsibilities as much as possible, not only so that students can learn as much as possible from the process, but also so the teacher's roles and workload are minimized.

3. Have students selected and collected meaningful work?

The work that the students collect together into the portfolios should be meaningful to them. This can be accomplished by allowing them to make the selection decisions, at least to some degree. That way they can decide what is meaningful or not to them. For example, if the students will be writing nine compositions during the semester, you might negotiate with them and decide together that they will select one composition from the first set of three, one from the second set of three, and one from the last set of three (including all associated rough, second, and final drafts) to include in their portfolios so their progress in writing ability will be displayed. It may also be a good idea to encourage students to add illustrations, collages, photos, etc. to make the work more personal and meaningful to them.

4. Have students periodically reflected in writing on their portfolios?

Another important component of the portfolio development process is to have students periodically reflect in writing on their portfolios. They might reflect on how much progress they have made in their writing abilities, what they still need to work on, how their attitudes toward writing have changed in the process of developing the portfolio, etc. These reflections need not be lengthy, but they should probably be done on a regular basis, and they should be included in the portfolio.

5. Have other students, teachers, outsiders, etc., periodically examined the portfolios?

Yet another aspect of the portfolio process that is often mentioned in the literature is the importance of having other students, teachers, outsiders, etc. periodically examine the portfolios. Such examination of portfolios can be done at an open house or simply by arranging for classes that are doing portfolios to visit each other and have a look at what the members of the other class did in their portfolios. The purposes for displaying the portfolios in this way are to encourage students to take pride in them, to help students feel ownership in their work, and to make the whole process more meaningful to the students.

6. Have you scored the portfolios by applying Numbers 1–6 under *Task* in Table 3.3?

Grading portfolios may also encourage the students to take them more seriously. The principles described in Numbers 3–5 under *Task* in Table 3.3 (p. 51) and the associated prose will be helpful in setting up a holistic or analytic scoring grid for portfolios. You might find it useful to work out the scoring grid in discussions with the students.

WHY BOTHER WITH ITEM FORMAT ANALYSIS?

In short, item format analysis involves asking those questions in Tables 3.1, 3.2, 3.3, and 3.6, which are appropriate for a specific set of items and making sure that the items conform to the guidelines insofar as they apply to the particular teaching situation. Clearly, this type of item analysis relies heavily on common sense. Nevertheless, item format analysis is important because an item that is badly constructed is not likely to be effective or fair, even if the item looks like it is testing the appropriate content. In other words, good format would seem to be a precondition for effective testing of any content.

REVIEW QUESTIONS

1. What is an item?
2. What is the difference between an item and a test?
3. What is an item on a cloze test? A dictation? A composition?
4. What is item format analysis?
5. Why is item format analysis important?
6. What are the basic differences in item format analysis among receptive response, productive response, and personal response items?

APPLICATION EXERCISES

A. Find a language test that you are now using or have previously used and apply the item format analysis techniques covered in this book to critique the quality of the items on that test.

B. Read the satirical test on page 65. There are gross problems with these items; that is what makes readers laugh. Pick out as many of the violations of the item writing guidelines in this chapter as you can find and jot them down.

MULTIPLE-CHOICE SECTION (Time limit: one month) (2 points each):

1. What dialect of American English is spoken by people in New England?
   a. Southern   **b.** Midwestern   **c.** Hawaiian Creole   **d.** New England

2. Communicative language teaching would be best described as an _____ .
   a. technique
   b. method
   c. type of syllabus
   d. approach

3. Where do foreign students come from?
   a. supermarkets
   b. drug stores
   c. toy stores
   d. other countries
   (please select only one).

4. **Caleb Gattegno's** name is associated with _____ .
   a. Suggestopedia
   b. Total Physical Response
   c. Counseling Language Learning
   d. THE SILENT WAY

SHORT-ANSWER SECTION (Time limit: yes) (1.875 points each):

5. In the space provided, outline the important characteristics of all major language-teaching methodologies with particular reference to grammar-translation, structuralism, audio-lingual approach, communicative language teaching, and the task-based approach, or give Gattegno's first name.

6. Can you explain transformational-generative grammar—Yes or No?

7. True or false - Morphemes are an important class of pain killers.

8. What color is Mike Long's black box?

9. What European language is spoken in French Guyana?

10. Spell Gattegno, Lozanov, Rassias, and Asher.

11. Explain Krashen's monitor model in detail—or spell your name in block letters.

ESSAY SECTION (Time limit: one hour.) (78.875 points):

Explain the history of the English language including its Indo-European, Germanic, and Latin origins. Focus primarily, but not exclusively, on the Great Vowel Shift, Grimm's Law, and the knowledge gained from works like *Beowulf* and Chaucer's *Canterbury Tales*. Be sure to list all words introduced from French since 1066. Also discuss the development of each of the British dialects (which are mostly of historical interest), as well as modern English dialects like American, Australian, Canadian, etc. (Use back of sheet if needed.)

4 ITEM ANALYSIS IN LANGUAGE TESTING

INTRODUCTION

In this chapter, I will explain item analysis techniques for both norm-referenced and criterion-referenced tests. Item analysis techniques include norm-referenced item statistics like item facility and item discrimination analyses. Criterion-referenced item analysis techniques include the difference index and the *B*-index. For both sets of item analyses, certain procedures will be explained for analyzing and selecting items in order to create an improved version of a test from a preliminary version (often a set of piloted items). As usual, the chapter will end with review questions and applications exercises.

NORM-REFERENCED ITEM ANALYSIS

Norm-referenced item analysis involves the use of two statistics: item facility and item discrimination. I will explain each of these in some detail, but I should stress at the outset that these statistical analyses are only useful insofar as they help teachers to understand and improve the effectiveness of their item formats and content. Teachers should be careful to keep these statistical techniques in perspective, remembering that the statistics are only tools for improving actual test items and are not an end in themselves.

ITEM FACILITY ANALYSIS

Item facility (also called item difficulty, item easiness, or simply *IF*) is a statistic used to examine the percentage of students who correctly answer a given item. To calculate *IF,* add up the number of students who correctly answered a particular item and divide that sum by the total number of students who took the test. As an equation, it would look like this:

$$IF = \frac{N_{correct}}{N_{total}}$$

$N_{correct}$ = number of students answering correctly
N_{total} = total number of students taking the test

The equation is just a shorthand way of expressing the same thing that was explained in prose. (Note that this equation assumes that items left blank are incorrect answers.)

The result of this formula is an item facility value that can range from 0.00 to 1.00. By moving the decimal point two places to the right, teachers can interpret this value as the percentage of correct answers for a given item. For example, the correct interpretation for an *IF* index of .27 would be that 27 percent of the students correctly answered the item. In most cases, an item with an *IF* of .27 would be a very difficult question because considerably more students missed it than answered it correctly. In contrast, an *IF* of .96 would indicate that 96 percent of the students answered correctly—a very easy item because almost everyone responded correctly.

Such seemingly simple information can be very useful. For example, consider the item response pattern shown in Table 4.1. As with all testing statistics, the first thing that teachers must do is to arrange the data so that they can easily be examined and manipulated. Notice in Table 4.1 that the students' names have been listed in the left-hand column and the item numbers for the first ten items and the total scores are labeled across the top.

Table 4.1 Norm-referenced item analysis data (first 10 items only)

STUDENTS	ITEMS											TOTAL
	1	2	3	4	5	6	7	8	9	10	etc...	
Shenan	1	1	1	1	1	1	0	1	1	0	...	77
Robert	1	0	1	1	1	1	0	1	0	0	...	75
Mitsuko	1	0	0	1	1	1	0	1	0	0	...	72
Iliana	1	1	0	1	1	1	0	0	0	0	...	72
Millie	1	1	1	1	1	0	0	1	0	0	...	70
Kimi	1	1	0	1	1	0	1	1	1	0	...	70
Kazumoto	1	0	1	1	1	1	0	1	0	0	...	69
Kako	1	1	0	1	1	0	0	1	0	0	...	69
Joji	1	0	1	0	1	0	1	1	0	0	...	69
Jeanne	1	1	0	0	1	1	0	0	1	0	...	69
Issaku	1	0	1	0	1	0	1	0	0	0	...	68
Corky	1	1	0	0	1	1	1	1	1	0	...	68
Dean	1	1	0	0	1	0	1	0	1	0	...	67
Randy	1	1	1	0	1	0	1	0	0	0	...	64
Bill	1	0	0	0	1	0	1	0	1	0	...	64
Archie	0	0	0	0	1	0	1	1	0	0	...	61

The actual responses are recorded with a *1* for each correct answer and *0* for a wrong answer. Notice that Shenan answered the first item correctly—indeed so did everyone else except poor Archie. This item must have been very easy. Note, though, that Item 1 is not the easiest item. Another item was answered correctly by every student. Which one? Item 5, right? And, which item was the most difficult in these data? Item 10 was clearly the most difficult because every student missed it (as indicated by the zeros straight down that column).

The calculation of *IF* for any item will follow a consistent pattern. Consider Item 3. Count up the number of students who answered Item 3 correctly (7); then, count the number of people who took the test (16), fill in the formula, and do the calculations:

$$\text{calculations: } IF = \frac{N_{correct}}{N_{total}} = \frac{7}{16} = .4375 \approx .44$$

With this simple *IF* index in hand, the teacher knows that about 44 percent of the students answered Item 3 correctly. Try calculating the *IF* for a few of the other items shown in Table 4.1. The answers are shown in Screen 4.5 on page 74.

Arranging the data in a matrix like in Table 4.1 can help you to easily calculate *IF*s. As you will soon see next, other item statistics can also be used for ferreting out other kinds of information and patterns from such data.

ITEM DISCRIMINATION ANALYSIS

Item discrimination (*ID*) is a statistic that indicates the degree to which an item separates the students who performed well from those who did poorly on the test as a whole. These two groups are sometimes referred to as the "high" and "low" scorers or "upper" and "lower" proficiency students. The reason for identifying these two groups is that *ID* allows teachers to contrast the performances of the upper students on the test with the performances of the lower students. The process begins by determining which students had scores in the top group on the whole test and which had scores in the bottom group. To do this, you must first line up the students' names, their individual item responses, and total scores in descending order based on the total scores. Notice that the order of the listings in Table 4.1 is from high to low based on total scores. Such a high to low arrangement allows for quickly determining which students fall into the high and low groups.

The upper and lower groups are sometimes defined as the upper and lower third, or 33 percent. Some test developers will use the upper and lower 27 percent. I also know of instances where 25% was used in calculating *ID*. Like so many things in the seemingly "scientific" area of language testing, the decision as to which way to define the upper and lower groups is often a practical matter. In Table 4.1 for instance, where the groups are separated by blank rows, five students each have been assigned to the top and bottom groups and six to the middle group. Rather than using thirds, the groupings here are based on the upper and lower 31.25% (5 ÷ 16 = .3125). Such decisions result from the fact that groups of people do not always come in nice neat numbers that are divisible by three. The solution is often like that found in Table 4.1 (p. 67), that is, the upper and lower groups are defined as some whole number that is roughly 33 percent.

Notice also that Millie and Kimi have exactly the same score of 70, yet Millie ended up in the upper group and Kimi in the middle group. Since these people with the same score occurred at the point where I wanted to make a separation, I decided randomly who should be in the upper group and who in the lower (by flipping a coin in this case). The same thing happened for Issaku and Corky who had the same score of 68.

Once the data are sorted into groups of students, calculation of the discrimination indexes is easy. To do this, calculate the item facility (the same *IF* discussed above) for the upper and lower groups separately for each item. First divide the number of students who answered correctly in the upper group by the total number of students in the upper group; then, divide the number who answered correctly in the lower group by the total number of students in the lower group. Finally, to calculate the *ID* index, the *IF* for the lower group is subtracted from the *IF* for the upper group on each item as follows:

$$ID = IF_{upper} - IF_{lower}$$

ID = item discrimination for an individual item
IF_{upper} = item facility for the upper group on the whole test
IF_{lower} = item facility for the lower group on the whole test

For example, in Table 4.1 (p. 67), the *IF* for the upper group on Item Four is 1.00 because everyone in that group answered it correctly. The *IF* for the lower group on that item is .00 because everyone in the lower group answered it incorrectly. To calculate the item discrimination index for this item, subtract the *IF* for the lower group from the *IF* for the upper group. This will give you an index of the contrasting performance of those students who scored "high" on the whole test with those who scored "low." In this case, it turns out to be 1.00 ($ID = IF_{upper} - IF_{lower} = 1.00 - .00 = 1.00$). An item discrimination index of 1.00 is very high because it indicates the maximum contrast between the upper and lower groups of students, that is, all the high students answered correctly and all the students in the lower group answered incorrectly.

The idea is that the scores on the whole test are the best single estimate of ability for each student. In fact, these whole test scores must be more accurate than any single item because a relatively large number of observations, when taken together, will logically give a better measurement than any of the single observations. Consider, for instance, how accurate one observation of your pulse rate would be as compared to the average of 20 such observations over a period of hours. The average of the multiple observations would clearly be more accurate than any of the single observations. Analogously, since each item is only one observation of the students' performances and the whole test is a collection of such observations, the whole total test scores are more accurate estimates of the students' performances than any given item.

Given the fact that the total test scores best represent students' abilities, those items on a norm-referenced test that are most like the total test scores will be the best items for testing those abilities. In other words, those items that separate students into upper and lower groups in similar manner to the whole test scores are the items that should be kept in any revised versions of the test to make the resulting total scores an even better reflection of the students' abilities. An item with an *ID* of 1.00 is indicating that the item separates the upper and lower groups in the same manner as the whole test scores. Such an item is, therefore, a good candidate for retention in any revised version of the test though the adequacy of the item format and the suitability of the item facility index must also be considered for each and every decision. *ID* indexes can range from 1.00 (if all the upper group students answer correctly and all the lower group students answer incorrectly like Item 4 in Table 4.1) to -1.00 (if all the lower group students answer correctly and all the upper group students answer incorrectly like Item 7 in the table). Naturally, *ID* indexes can also take on all the values between $+1.00$ and -1.00.

Consider several other items in Table 4.1. In Item 6, the students in the upper group have an *IF* of .80 and those in the lower group have an *IF* of .20 so the item discrimination index for Item 6 is .60 (.80 − .20 = .60). This *ID* index indicates that the item is "discriminating" fairly well between the high students and low students on the whole test. On the other hand, an item like Number 9, for which the upper group had an *IF* of .20 and the lower group an *IF* of .60, would have an *ID* of −.40 (.20 − .60 = −.40). This *ID* index indicates that the item is somehow testing something quite different from the rest of the test because those who scored low on the whole test managed to correctly answer this item better than those who scored high on the total test. Since the multiple observations of the whole test are logically a better estimate of the students' actual knowledge or skills than any single item, good reasons exist for doubting the value of the contribution being made to a norm-referenced test by items that have low or negative *ID* indexes.

Another statistic that is often used for the same purpose as the *ID* is the point biserial correlation coefficient. This statistic is usually lower in magnitude when compared directly with the *ID* for a given item but is analogous in interpretation. Because *ID* is easier to calculate and understand conceptually, teachers are much more likely to use it in most language programs. Hence, I can safely delay the discussion of the point biserial correlation coefficient to Chapter 8.

CALCULATING ITEM FACILITY AND DISCRIMINATION WITH YOUR SPREADSHEET

Now that you understand item facility and item discrimination conceptually, let's look at ways to calculate them in a spreadsheet. In the following exercise, you will create a spreadsheet in the *Excel*™ program to analyze norm-referenced items. Using the data in Table 4.1, you will enter student names, test scores, totals, and then you will format the columns. Next, you enter item facility and item discrimination formulas to analyze the test data. After completing the exercise, you will see how a spreadsheet can save enormous amounts of time.

Screen 4.1 Creating a spreadsheet to analyze norm-referenced items

Microsoft Excel - NRTDistEffic3.4.xls

B21 =SUM(B2:B19)/16

	A	I1	I2	I3	I4	I5	I6	I7	I8	I9	I10 etc	......	TOTAL
1	STUDENT	I1	I2	I3	I4	I5	I6	I7	I8	I9	I10 etc	......	TOTAL
2	Shenan	1	1	1	1	1	1	0	1	1	0.	....	77
3	Robert	1	0	1	1	1	1	0	1	0	0.	....	75
4	Mitsuko	1	0	0	1	1	1	0	1	0	0.	....	72
5	Iliana	1	1	0	1	1	1	0	0	0	0.	....	72
6	Millie	1	1	1	1	1	0	0	1	0	0.	....	70
7													
8	Kimi	1	1	0	1	1	0	1	1	1	0.	....	70
9	Kazumoto	1	0	1	1	1	1	0	1	0	0.	....	69
10	Kako	1	1	0	1	0	0	1	0		0.	....	69
11	Joji	1	0	1	0	1	0	1	1	0	0.	....	69
12	Jeanne	1	1	0	0	1	1	0	0	1	0.	....	69
13	Issaku	1	0	1	0	1	0	1	0	0	0.	....	68
14													
15	Corky	1	1	0	0	1	1	1	1	1	0.	....	68
16	Dean	1	1	0	0	1	0	1	0	1	0.	....	67
17	Randy	1	1	1	0	1	0	1	0	0	0.	....	64
18	Bill	1	0	0	0	1	0	1	0	1	0.	....	64
19	Archie	0	0	0	0	1	0	1	1	0	0.	....	61
20													
21	IF	1											
22	IFupper	1											
23	IFlower	1											
24	ID	0											

Sheet1 / Sheet2 / Sheet3

Create the spreadsheet and enter headings and data.

1. Open the *Excel* program on your computer.
2. Using Screen 4.1 as a guide, in Row 1, type in the headings such as **Student**, Items (i.e., I1 for Item number 1), and **Total**.
3. After the data are entered, highlight the headings and data, and then click **Format**, **Column**, **AutoFit Selection** to make the spreadsheet fit in a one-page format. You may use the keyboard shortcuts by pressing the ALT key followed by the underlined letters in the menu choices (i.e., *o*, *c*, and *a*). The columns in the spreadsheet will be changed to a smaller size.

Calculate item facility and item discrimination.[2]

1. To begin calculating Item Facility (*IF*) and Item Discrimination (*ID*), enter the following headings:
   In Cell A21, type **IF**.
   In Cell A22, type **IFupper**.
   In Cell A23, type **IFlower**.
   In Cell A24, type **ID**.
2. To calculate *IF* for Item 1, click Cell B21, type the formula =**SUM(B2:B19)/16**, and then press ENTER. When the equal sign = is typed in a cell, you tell the program that a formula will be used so that the numbers will be calculated to analyze data. The **SUM** function is used to add numbers in a defined range, such as the response to Item 1 for each student, which is held in Cells B2 through B19. The slash / is

---

[2] In these situations in Numbers 2, 3, and 4 where you are summing then dividing by the number of cells, you are really averaging, so you could equally well use the AVERAGE function, as follows:
=**AVERAGE(B2:B19)**, =**AVERAGE(B2:B6)**, and =**AVERAGE(B15:B19)**, respectively.

used to divide the sum by the total number of students, which is 16. Other symbols that are used for calculations can include the plus sign + used for adding (e.g., =B2+B3+B4), the minus sign – used for subtracting (e.g., =(B2+B3)−10), and the asterisk * used for multiplying (e.g., =B2*B3).

3. To calculate IFupper, click Cell B22, and then type =**SUM(B2:B6)/5**. Cells B2 to B6 will be added, and then divided by 5.

4. To calculate IFlower, click Cell B23, and then type =**SUM(B15:B19)/5**. Cells B15 to B19 will be added, and then divided by 5.

5. To calculate *ID*, click Cell B24, and then type =**B22−B23**. Cell B23 will be subtracted from B22.

Adjust spreadsheet formatting.

1. In Cells B21 to B24, you may notice that the result of the formula is three ones and a zero, as shown in Screen 4.1. These figures have been rounded by the program, and do not reflect the true figures calculated by the formula. For example, in Cell B23, the sum of the cells is 4; if you divide 4 by 5, the result is .80. To remove the rounding feature, click Cells B21 to B24, and then select **F̲ormat**, **C̲olumn**, **A̲utoFit Selection**. The numbers in Cells B21 to B24 will change to more accurate figures.

2. In Screen 4.2, the decimal places of numbers in Cells B21 to B24 do not line up, which may make the figures difficult to read. To change the alignment of the decimals so you can view the figures more easily, click Cells B21 to B24, and then select **F̲ormat**, **C̲ells**, and click the **Number** tab.

Screen 4.2 Item analysis spreadsheet before aligning decimal places

	A	B	C	D	E	F	G	H	I	J	K	L	M	N	O	P	Q	R	S	T	U	V	W	X
1	STUDENT		I1	I2	I3	I4	I5	I6	I7	I8	I9	I10	etc	. . . . . .					TOTAL					
2	Shenan		1	1	1	1	1	1	0	1	1	0	.	. . . . . .					77					
3	Robert		1	0	1	1	1	1	0	1	0	0	.	. . . . . .					75					
4	Mitsuko		1	0	0	1	1	1	0	1	0	0	.	. . . . . .					72					
5	Iliana		1	1	0	1	1	1	0	0	0	0	.	. . . . . .					72					
6	Millie		1	1	1	1	1	0	0	1	0	0	.	. . . . . .					70					
7																								
8	Kimi		1	1	0	1	1	0	1	1	1	0	.	. . . . . .					70					
9	Kazumoto		1	0	1	1	1	1	0	1	0	0	.	. . . . . .					69					
10	Kako		1	1	0	1	1	0	0	1	0	0	.	. . . . . .					69					
11	Joji		1	0	1	0	1	0	1	1	0	0	.	. . . . . .					69					
12	Jeanne		1	1	0	0	1	1	0	0	1	0	.	. . . . . .					69					
13	Issaku		1	0	1	0	1	0	1	0	0	0	.	. . . . . .					68					
14																								
15	Corky		1	1	0	0	1	1	1	1	1	0	.	. . . . . .					68					
16	Dean		1	1	0	0	1	0	1	0	1	0	.	. . . . . .					67					
17	Randy		1	1	1	0	1	0	1	0	0	0	.	. . . . . .					64					
18	Bill		1	0	0	0	1	0	1	0	1	0	.	. . . . . .					64					
19	Archie		0	0	0	0	1	0	1	1	0	0	.	. . . . . .					61					
20																								
21	IF	0.9375																						
22	IFupper	1																						
23	IFlower	0.8																						
24	ID	0.2																						
25																								

B21 ▼ *fx* =SUM(B2:B19)/16

Sum=2.9375   NUM

3. Under **Category:** click **Number**, enter or verify that a 2 is in the **Decimal places** box, and then click **OK**. The decimal places of the numbers in Cells B21 to B24 should be lined up, as shown in Screen 4.3.

Screen 4.3 Item analysis spreadsheet after aligning decimal places

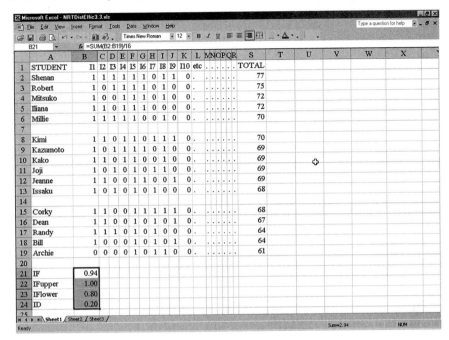

That was a great deal of work just to get four numbers. If you had to do that for every single item, it might seem easier to calculate these statistics by hand, and therefore, the spreadsheet actually wouldn't save you very much effort. However, at this stage you can indeed save time by copying the same calculations to other cells in the spreadsheet with a few simple commands.

Copy formulas to multiple cells.

1. Highlight Cells B21 to B24.
2. Select **Edit**, **Copy**. A moving box will be placed around the highlighted area, signifying that the cells will be copied to another area in the spreadsheet.
3. Click Cells C21 to K24 (i.e., the 36 cells from C21 to K24) and then press **ENTER**. The formulas you created for Item 1 in the previous exercise will be copied to the cells below the other items, as shown in Screen 4.4.

Screen 4.4 Item analysis spreadsheet after copying the formulas from Item 1 to all other items

STUDENT	I1	I2	I3	I4	I5	I6	I7	I8	I9	I10	etc	TOTAL
Shenan	1	1	1	1	1	1	0	1	1	0		77
Robert	1	0	1	1	1	1	0	1	0	0		75
Mitsuko	1	0	0	1	1	1	0	1	0	0		72
Iliana	1	1	0	1	1	1	0	0	0	0		72
Millie	1	1	1	1	1	0	0	1	0	0		70
Kimi	1	1	0	1	1	0	1	1	1	0		70
Kazumoto	1	0	1	1	1	1	0	1	0	0		69
Kako	1	1	0	1	1	0	0	1	0	0		69
Joji	1	0	1	0	1	0	1	1	0	0		69
Jeanne	1	1	0	0	1	1	0	0	1	0		69
Issaku	1	0	1	0	1	0	1	0	0	0		68
Corky	1	1	0	0	1	1	1	1	1	0		68
Dean	1	1	0	0	1	0	1	0	1	0		67
Randy	1	1	1	0	1	0	1	0	0	0		64
Bill	1	0	0	0	1	0	1	0	1	0		64
Archie	0	0	0	0	1	0	1	1	0	0		61
IF	0.94	#	#	#	#	#	#	#	#	##		
IFupper	1.00	#	#	#	#	#	#	#	#	##		
IFlower	0.80	#	#	#	#	#	#	#	#	##		
ID	0.20	#	#	#	#	#	#	#	#	##		

4. The pound # or ## symbols shown in the cells reflect that the columns are not wide enough to display the numbers after the calculation is performed. Highlight Cells C21 to K24, and then select **Format**, **Column**, **AutoFit Selection**. The numbers will display in the cells, and the pound symbols will disappear, as shown in Screen 4.5.

Screen 4.5 Item analysis spreadsheet after adjusting column widths

Screen 4.5 Item analysis spreadsheet after adjusting column widths

STUDENT	I1	I2	I3	I4	I5	I6	I7	I8	I9	I10	etc	TOTAL
Shenan	1	1	1	1	1	1	0	1	1	0		77
Robert	1	0	1	1	1	1	0	1	0	0		75
Mitsuko	1	0	0	1	1	1	0	1	0	0		72
Iliana	1	1	0	1	1	1	0	0	0	0		72
Millie	1	1	1	1	1	0	0	1	0	0		70
Kimi	1	1	0	1	1	0	1	1	1	0		70
Kazumoto	1	0	1	1	1	1	0	1	0	0		69
Kako	1	1	0	1	1	0	0	1	0	0		69
Joji	1	0	1	0	1	0	1	1	0	0		69
Jeanne	1	1	0	0	1	1	0	0	1	0		69
Issaku	1	0	1	0	1	0	1	0	0	0		68
Corky	1	1	0	0	1	1	1	1	1	0		68
Dean	1	1	0	0	1	0	1	0	1	0		67
Randy	1	1	1	0	1	0	1	0	0	0		64
Bill	1	0	0	0	1	0	1	0	1	0		64
Archie	0	0	0	0	1	0	1	1	0	0		61
IF	0.94	0.56	0.44	0.50	1.00	0.44	0.50	0.63	0.38	0.00		
IFupper	1.00	0.60	0.60	1.00	1.00	0.80	0.00	0.80	0.20	0.00		
IFlower	0.80	0.60	0.20	0.00	1.00	0.20	1.00	0.40	0.60	0.00		
ID	0.20	0.00	0.40	1.00	0.00	0.60	-1.00	0.40	-0.40	0.00		

5. To verify that you copied the formulas to the other cells, click **K23**, and =SUM(K15:K19)/5 should display in the entry box above the spreadsheet, as shown in Screen 4.5.

6. Save your spreadsheet, as you will use the data and calculations for exercises in subsequent chapters. Perhaps, you could name your file Screen 4.5 so that you can remember what it represents.

Congratulations! You have now completed your first norm-referenced item analysis. Now, it is just a matter of selecting the items you want to keep and the ones you want to discard as explained in the next section.

NRT Development and Improvement Projects

Like many other aspects of language curriculum development, the development or improvement of a norm-referenced language test is a major undertaking. Such projects are designed to:

1. Pilot a relatively large number of test items on a group of students similar to the group that will ultimately be assessed with the test;
2. Analyze the items using format analysis and statistical techniques; and
3. Select the best items to make up a shorter, more effective revised version of the test.

Ideal items in an NRT development project have an average *IF* of .50 and the highest available *ID*. These ideal items would be considered well-centered, that is, 50 percent answer correctly and 50 percent incorrectly. In reality, however, items rarely have an *IF* of exactly .50, so those that fall in a range between .30 and .70 are usually considered acceptable. Once those items which fall within that allowable range of *IF*s are identified, the items among them which have the highest *ID* indexes would be further selected for retention in the revised test. This process would help the teacher to retain only those items that are well-centered and discriminate well between the low and the high students. Ebel (1979, p. 267) has suggested the following guidelines for making decisions based on *ID*:

.40 and up	Very good items
.30 to .39	Reasonably good, but possibly subject to improvement
.20 to .29	Marginal items, usually needing and being subject to improvement
Below .19	Poor items, to be rejected or improved by revision

Of course, Ebel's guidelines should not be used as hard and fast "rules," but rather as aids in making decisions about which items to keep and which to discard until a sufficient number of items has been found to make up whatever norm-referenced test is under development. This process is usually far less scientific than many novice test developers would like.

Consider the items in Screen 4.5 (p. 74). Which three items from the ten shown in the table would be best to select for a new revised version of the test? Items Four and Six seem like good candidates for retention in a revised version of the test because they both have *IF*s that are close to .50 *and* have the highest *ID*s in this set of items. But which other item should be kept? Items 3 and 8 both seem like possibilities because they have *IF*s within the .30 to .70 range of acceptability and have the highest available *ID*s of those items that remain. But such decisions are not always clear-cut. For instance, a test developer might decide to keep both Items 3 and 8 because they are effective, or to reject both items because they do not discriminate above .40, or to keep both items but revise them to make the distractors more efficient.

CRITERION-REFERENCED ITEM ANALYSIS

Recall that a central difference between NRTs and CRTs is that NRTs (typically designed to spread students out in percentile terms for proficiency or placement testing purposes) are constructed to produce normal distributions, while CRTs (because they are designed to measure what students know or can do in percentage terms for diagnostic or achievement purposes) do not necessarily do so. In addition, the item selection process for developing NRTs is designed to retain items that are well-centered (with *IF*s of .30 to .70) and spread students out efficiently (the highest *ID*s are retained). Such items once selected for a revised version of an NRT will generally work together to provide a normal distribution of scores.

In contrast, CRTs may not necessarily produce scores that are normally distributed. In fact, a CRT that is designed to measure student achievement might produce scores that are predominantly high. Consider an ideal situation in which all the students mastered all the objectives in a particular course because they were highly motivated students, the materials were marvelous, and the teacher was, of course, spectacular. All of those students could reasonably be expected to score 100 percent on the end-of-course criterion-referenced achievement test designed to measure those objectives.

Of course, a teacher could create the same effect (that is, everyone scoring 100 percent) by writing a final examination that is far too easy for the students. To check for this possibility, the teacher may want to administer the test (or an equivalent form of the test) at the beginning of the course as a diagnostic test. If the students perform poorly on the beginning-of-course diagnostic test (**pre-test**) and score well on the end-of-course achievement test (**post-test**), then the teacher can interpret the high scores at the end of the course as legitimate reflections of the students' knowledge or skills, rather than reflections of a test that is too easy for the students.

In fact, the distributions of scores on a CRT may not be normal for either the pre-test or the post-test. On an ideal CRT designed to test course objectives, all the students would score 0 percent at the beginning of the course (indicating that they need to learn the material) and 100 percent at the end of the course (indicating that they have all learned the material). However, in reality, human beings are never perfectly ignorant at the beginning of a course nor are they perfectly knowledgeable at the end. Such distributions are, nonetheless, ideals that teachers can aim for in CRT development in much the same sense that they aim for the normal distribution when they are developing NRTs.

One consequence of this fundamental difference in score distributions between the NRT and CRT categories of tests is that many of the statistics used for analyzing NRTs, which assume that the test scores are normally distributed, do not work very well for analyzing CRTs. Consider the item discrimination statistic. If all the students were to answer all the items wrong at the beginning of a course and answer all the items correctly at the end of the course, the teacher should be delighted from a CRT perspective. However, the *ID* for each and every item would be zero. Statistics that depend on a spread of scores, like the *ID* does in comparing the upper and lower groups of students, become meaningless if the test does not create a spread of scores.

Such a spread occurs naturally in developing NRTs. However, in developing CRTs, other item analysis strategies must be used, especially item quality analysis and attendant item statistics that reflect the degree to which an item is measuring learning.

ITEM QUALITY ANALYSIS

As with NRTs, the quality of a CRT can only be as good as the items that are on it. Remember that the CRT category of tests is commonly used for testing achievement and diagnosis, both of which are fairly specific to a particular program (see Chapter 1). One result of the program-specific nature of CRTs is that the analysis of individual item quality is often crucial. **Item quality analysis** for CRTs ultimately means that judgments must be made about the degree to which the items are valid for the purposes and content of the course or program involved. The first concern in analyzing CRT item quality is with the content of the items. A second consideration is whether the form of the item adequately assesses the desired content.

Because of the program specific nature of CRT items, item quality analysis must often be even more rigorous than it is for NRTs. In developing or revising an NRT, the purposes are general in nature and the test developer's main concern is to find items that discriminate well between students in their overall performances. Hence the tester can rely to some degree on item facility and discrimination statistics to help guide the choices of which items to keep and which to discard in revising the test. In developing CRTs, the test developer must rely less on statistics and more on common sense to create a revised version of the test that measures what the students know, or can do, with regard to the program's objectives.

A criterion-referenced test developer should primarily be concerned with the degree to which a test, and therefore the items within the test, is testing whatever content is desired. This content may turn out to be as narrow, objective, receptive, and discrete-point as a test of each student's ability to distinguish between phonemes, or as broad, subjective, productive, and integrative as a test of the students' overall proficiency in terms of strategic competence. These choices and others are up to the teachers who must develop and use the test. Regardless of what is decided, the goal of **item content analysis** for a CRT is to determine the degree to which each item is measuring the content that it was designed to measure, and the degree to which that content should be measured at all.

In the end, content analysis inevitably involves some "expert" (for example, the language teacher or a colleague) who must judge the items. Typically, even in ideal situations, this involves each teacher looking at the test and having some input as to which items should be kept in the revised version of the test and which should be reworked or thrown out. In some situations, item specifications may prove useful (see Alderson, Clapham, and Wall 1995; Brown and Hudson 2002; or Davidson and Lynch 2002).

Item specifications are clear item descriptions that include a general description, a sample item, stimulus attributes, response attributes, and specification supplements, all of which are defined as follows:

1. **General description**: A brief general description of the knowledge or skills being measured by the item.
2. **Sample item**: An example item that demonstrates the desirable item characteristics (further delimited by the stimulus and response attributes below).

3. **Stimulus attributes**: A clear description of the stimulus material, that is, the material that will be encountered by the student, or the material to which they will be expected to react through the response attributes below.
4. **Response attributes**: A clear description of the types of (a) options from which students will be expected to select their receptive language choices (responses), or (b) standards by which their productive language responses will be judged.
5. **Specification supplement**: For some items, supplemental material will be necessary for clarifying the four previous elements; for example, the specification supplement might include a list of vocabulary items from which the item writer should draw, or a list of grammatical forms, or list of functions of the language.

The goal of such item specifications is to provide a clear enough description so that any trained item writer using them will be able to generate items very similar to those written by any other item writer (for example specifications, see Brown & Hudson 2002, pp. 87–98). Thus, item specifications are particularly useful on large scale projects where numerous item writers are creating items. If there is only a single item writer, or only a few item writers working closely together, it may prove more efficient to create items directly from course objectives. Such a process can lead not only to clear and consistent item creation, but also beneficial revision of the objectives as flaws are spotted in the process of trying to measure those objectives.

Table 4.2 Item content congruence and applicability

DIRECTIONS: Look at the test questions and objectives that they are designed to test. For each item, circle the number of the rating (1 = very poor to 5 = very good) that you give for each criterion described at the left.

Criteria for Judgment	Very Poor	Moderate			Very Good
CONTENT CONGRUENCE Overall match between the item and the objective, which it is meant to test Comment:	1	2	3	4	5
Proficiency level match Comment:	1	2	3	4	5
CONTENT APPLICABILITY Match between the objective and related material that you teach Comment:	1	2	3	4	5
Match between the item and related material that you teach Comment:	1	2	3	4	5

In addition, rating scales may prove helpful in determining the degree to which items reflect the content that they are supposed to be measuring. At the University of Hawaii, when I was director of the ELI, we did not use item specifications. However, we did use rating scales to judge item content in our CRT development projects. An example rating scale is shown in Table 4.2. Notice how the scale is broken into two categories: **content congruence** (to judge the degree to which an item is measuring what it was designed to assess) and **content applicability** (to judge the degree to which the content is appropriate for a given course or program).

From an administrative perspective, certain advantages can be gained from having all the teachers who teach a specific course judge the quality of the items on the test for that course. Consider, for instance, an elementary school ESL program where the children must pass an achievement test at the end of each of three levels of ESL study. If all five of the program's teachers were asked to judge the quality of the items on this achievement test, they would be much more likely to have a vested interest in the tests and would probably be much more cooperative in the testing process. Where conflicting views arise among the teachers in making these quality judgments, compromise will be necessary. However, even this process of compromise can be healthy for the test, because the teachers will have to agree on what test content means and think about the link between what is tested and what is taught in the course. Such teacher activities should probably focus on insuring that each item makes sense for assessing the specific content of the course or program and that the content is worth measuring given the context of language teaching that exists.

Item format analysis is as important in developing CRTs as it was in writing or assessing the quality of NRT items. All the comments made in Tables 3.1, 3.2, 3.3, and 3.6 in Chapter 3 are applicable for CRTs, too. One big difference with CRT item format analysis is that program politics may necessitate drawing all the teachers who will ultimately use and score the tests into the process of doing the item format analysis.

CRT Development and Improvement Projects

The revision process for NRTs was described previously in this chapter as being based on a single administration of the test, which is fine because the purpose of an NRT is usually a one-shot determination of the proficiency or placement of the students in a single population. The piloting of items in a CRT development project is quite different because the purpose of selecting those items is fundamentally different. Since a central purpose of a CRT is to assess how much of an objective or set of objectives has been learned by each student, CRT assessment has to occur before and after instruction in order to determine whether there was any gain in scores. As a result, the piloting of a CRT often involves administering it as a pre-test and post-test and comparing those two sets of results. To limit the practice effect due to taking exactly the same test twice, two forms can be developed with half of the students taking one form on the pre-test then the other form on the post-test, and the other half of the students taking the opposite forms.

Once teachers have selected those items which they judged to have high item quality, the resulting CRTs can be administered and statistical item analysis can proceed. As in NRT item analysis, item facility plays an important role. However, two possible item facilities exist for each item: one for the pre-test and one for the post-test. In CRT development, the goal is to find items that reflect whatever the students have learned, if anything. Hence, an ideal item for CRT purposes is one that has an *IF* (for the whole group) of .00 at the beginning of instruction and another *IF* of 1.00 at the end of instruction. Such pre-test and post-test *IF*s indicate that everyone missed the item at the beginning of instruction (that is, they needed to study the content or skill embodied in the item) and everyone answered it correctly at the end of the instruction (that is, they had completely absorbed whatever was being taught). Of course, this example is an ideal item, in an ideal world, with ideal students, and an infallible teacher.

Reality may be quite a bit different. Students arrive in most teaching situations with differing amounts of knowledge. Thus, an *IF* of .00 for any CRT item that measures a realistic objective seems unlikely, even at the very beginning of instruction. Similarly, students differ in ability and in the speed with which they learn, so they will probably not learn each and every objective to an equal degree. Thus, CRT items with *IF*s of 1.00 are unlikely, even at the end of instruction. Nevertheless, much can be learned about each item on a CRT from comparing the performance on the item of those students who have studied the content (post-test) with those who have not (pre-test). Two different strategies can be used to make such a comparison.

The first approach, called an **intervention strategy**, begins by testing the students before instruction in a pre-test. At this stage, the students are **uninstructed**. The next step is to intervene with whatever instruction is appropriate and then test the **instructed** students on a post-test. This strategy puts the test developer in a position to do an item-by-item comparison of the two sets of *IF* results.

The second approach is the **differential groups strategy**. This strategy begins by finding two groups of students: one group that has the knowledge or skills that are assessed on the test and another group that lacks them. The test developer can then compare the item facility indexes of the first group, sometimes termed **masters**, with the item facility indexes for the second group, called **non-masters**. Whether test developers use the intervention strategy or differential groups strategy depends on what is most convenient and logical in a given teaching situation. (See Chapter 8 in the *Construct Validity* section for other uses of these strategies.) In either case, the item statistic that the tester calculates to estimate the degree of contrast between the two administrations of the test is called the difference index.

DIFFERENCE INDEX

The **difference index** (*DI*, not to be confused with *ID*) indicates the degree to which an item is reflecting gain in knowledge or skill. In contrast to item discrimination, which shows the degree to which an NRT item separates the upper 1/3 of students from the lower 1/3 on a given test administration, the difference index indicates the degree to which a CRT item is distinguishing between the students who know the material or have the skill being taught, and those who do not. These groups of students can be established using either an intervention or differential groups strategy (see previous section). To calculate the difference index, the *IF* for the pre-test results (or non-masters) is subtracted from the *IF* for post-test results (or masters). For example, if the post-test *IF* for Item Ten on a test was .77 and the pre-test *IF* was .22, the teacher would know that only 22% knew the concept or skill at the beginning of instruction while 77% knew it by the end. The relatively high *DI* for that item of .77 − .22 = .55 would indicate a difference of 55%. *DI*s can range from − 1.00, indicating that students knew the material perfectly, but somehow completely unlearned the knowledge or skill in question, to +1.00, showing that the students went from knowing nothing about the knowledge or skill to knowing it completely—and everything in between.

Screen 4.6 Calculating the difference index

Item No.	Posttest IF	minus	Pretest IF	equals	DI
41	0.770	-	0.574	=	0.196
42	0.623	-	0.492	=	0.131
43	0.836	-	0.689	=	0.147
44	0.787	-	0.639	=	0.148
45	0.738	-	0.656	=	0.082
46	0.328	-	0.246	=	0.082
47	0.869	-	0.574	=	0.295
48	0.689	-	0.344	=	0.345
49	0.623	-	0.311	=	0.312
50	0.557	-	0.262	=	0.295
51	0.820	-	0.639	=	0.181
52	0.262	-	0.246	=	0.016
53	0.754	-	0.623	=	0.131
54	0.639	-	0.508	=	0.131
55	0.689	-	0.541	=	0.148
56	0.508	-	0.426	=	0.082
57	0.656	-	0.492	=	0.164
58	0.426	-	0.361	=	0.065
59	0.492	-	0.311	=	0.181
60	0.639	-	0.443	=	0.196

Other examples of calculations for the *DI* are shown in Screen 4.6. The statistics in that screen are derived from pre-test and post-test results in the ESL academic reading course at the University of Hawaii (Brown 1989a). Notice that only the results for Items 41 to 60 are presented. Notice also, in Screen 4.6, that the cursor is on cell F2 as indicated by the highlighted frame around that cell. In the third row of the menus in the formula box, you will see that the formula for the *DI* for Item Number 41 is **=B2-D2**. If you first type that formula into Cell F2 and hit enter, you can then copy it to Cells F3 to F31. The computer will adjust for the differences in the rows and calculate the *DI* for each of your items. Try it for yourself using the data in Screen 4.6, or using your own data.

Clearly, the *DI* is very easy to calculate in a spreadsheet. Yet this simple statistic is also very useful because teachers can use it to identify those items that are most highly related to the material being taught in their courses. The teachers can then keep those items in revised versions of their CRTs and eliminate items that are not related to the curriculum. More importantly, teachers can study those items that have low *DI*s and try to figure out why the material is apparently not being learned by many students. Is it being taught poorly? Are the materials confusing the students? Is the test item poorly constructed? Do the students resist learning the material for some cultural reason? And so forth.

THE *B*-INDEX

One problem that may crop up in using the difference index is that two administrations of the CRT are necessary. To solve this problem, other methods for assessing the sensitivity of CRT items to differences in knowledge or skill have been developed (see Brown & Hudson 2002 for more on these statistics). The most straightforward of these indexes is called the *B*-index. The **B-index** is an item statistic that compares the *IF*s of those students who passed a test with the *IF*s of those who failed it. In other words, the masters and non-masters on the test are identified by whether or not they passed the test, and then the *B*-index indicates the degree to which the masters (students who passed the test in this case) outperformed the non-masters (students who failed the test) on each item. To calculate this statistic, the first step is to determine what the cut-point for passing the test is.

Screen 4.7 Calculating the *B*-index

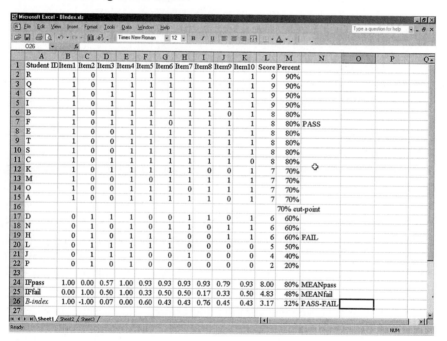

Screen 4.7 shows hypothetical item-by-item performance results on a CRT post-test at the end of a high school ESL course. Notice that the cut-point is 70 percent and that, at the bottom of the table, the *IF*s for those students who passed and those who failed are given separately for each item. To calculate the *B*-index for each item, I subtracted the item facility for those students who failed from that for those who passed. This can be expressed in the following simple formula:

$$\boxed{\begin{array}{c} \textbf{\textit{B}-index = \textit{IF}}_{\textbf{\textit{Pass}}} - \textbf{\textit{IF}}_{\textbf{\textit{Fail}}} \\ \textit{B}\text{-index} = \text{difference in } \textit{IF} \text{ between students who passed and failed a test} \\ \textit{IF}_{\textit{Pass}} \quad = \text{item facility for students who passed the test} \\ \textit{IF}_{\textit{Fail}} \quad = \text{item facility for students who failed the test} \end{array}}$$

Notice in Screen 4.7 that all the students who passed the test answered the first item correctly and all those who failed the test missed Item 1. Hence the B-index, based on an item facility of 1.00 for the students who passed and 0.00 for those who failed, would be:

$$\boxed{\begin{array}{c} \textit{B}\text{-index} = \textit{IF}_{\textit{Pass}} - \textit{IF}_{\textit{Fail}} \\ = 1.00 - 0.00 \\ = 1.00 \end{array}}$$

To calculate the B-index for Item 1 in the spreadsheet shown in Screen 4.7, you would begin by typing the formula =**AVERAGE(B2:B15)**. The result will be the average of the ones and zeros in the range from B2:B15, which in turn is the total number of ones divided by the number of people in the group with passing scores of 70 percent or better on the test. Next, type the same formula in Cell B25 , but for the different range of those students who failed: =**AVERAGE(B17:B22)**. If you got a result of 1.00 in Cell B24 and a result of 0.00 in Cell B25, go ahead and type the formula =**B24−B25** in Cell B26. That last formula should yield a result of 1.00. If so, you are now ready to copy the range of cells from B24 to B26 to the appropriate places in columns C through L. You can then type in the percentages found in column M in Screen 4.7.

Clearly, Item 1 maximally separates the students who passed the test from the students who failed it, and its B-index is as high as the statistic can go. Item 2 shows the opposite situation: all the students who passed the test missed this item and all those who failed the test answered the item correctly. The resulting B-index is -1.00, which is as low as this statistic can go ($0.00 - 1.00 = -1.00$). Item 3 shows the result when the proportion of wrong answers is very nearly the same in the pass and fail groups. Fifty-seven answered Item 3 correctly in the pass group and fifty in the fail group for a DI of 0.07 ($0.57 - 0.50 = 0.07$), indicating that Item 3 does not distinguish very well between students who have passed the test and others who have failed it. Item 4 illustrates what happens if everyone answers an item correctly ($1.00 - 1.00 = 0.00$). The same would be true if everyone answered the item incorrectly. The other items show more realistic results within the extremes just explained.

Interpretation of the B-index is similar to that for the difference index (DI). However, the B-index indicates the degree to which an item distinguishes between the students who passed the test and those who failed rather than contrasting the performances of students before and after instruction, as is the case with the difference index. Nevertheless, the B-index does have the advantage of requiring only one administration of a CRT, and therefore may prove useful.

Having analyzed the items on a CRT, teachers will ultimately want to revise the tests by selecting and keeping those items that are functioning well for achievement or diagnostic decisions. The item quality analysis can help with this selection process by providing information about how well each item fits the objective measured and the degree to which that objective fits the course or program involved. Calculating difference indexes (comparing pre-test and post-test results) would provide additional information about how sensitive each item was to instruction. Calculating B-indexes (for the post-test results) would help teachers understand how effective each item was for deciding who passed the test and who failed.

In other words, teachers can use multiple sources of information, including the *DI*, the *B*-index, as well as item quality analysis and item format analysis, to make decisions about which items to keep and which to discard in the CRT revision process. Consider Screen 4.6 (p. 81) once again. Which of the items should the teacher select if only the five best were needed? Numbers 47 through 50 would be attractive and obvious choices. But what about the fifth item? Should the teacher keep Item 41 or Item 60 (both of which have *DI*s of .196) or should the teacher keep Item 51 or Item 59 (which are not far behind with *DI*s of .181)? This last choice would no doubt involve looking at the items in terms of their other qualities, particularly item quality and item format analyses. Also, consider what you would do if you had the *B*-indexes on the post-test and the one for Number 47 turned out to be only .02.

In short, the difference index and *B*-index can help teachers select that subset of CRT items that are most closely related to the instruction and learning in a course and/or that subset most closely related to the distinction between students who passed or failed the test. With sound CRTs in place, teachers can indeed judge the performance of their students. However, equally important, teachers can also examine the fit between what they think they are teaching and what the students are actually absorbing. Oddly enough, some teachers may be examining this important issue for the first time in their careers.

REVIEW QUESTIONS

1. What is the item facility index? How do you calculate it? How do you interpret the results of your calculations?

2. What is the item discrimination index? How do you calculate it? How do you interpret the results of your calculations?

3. What are basic steps that you should follow in developing an NRT? How are they different and similar to the steps involved in CRT development?

4. What is item quality analysis? Should you be more interested in content congruence or content applicability?

5. What is the item difference index? What role does item facility play in calculating item difference indices?

6. How are the pre-test/post-test strategies used to calculate the difference index different from the pass/fail strategies used to calculate the B-index?

7. Once you have your data using one or the other of these strategies, how do you calculate the difference index and B-index for each of the items? How do you interpret the results of your calculations?

8. How can you use both statistics in combination in selecting CRT items?

9. What are the fundamental differences between the strategies used to revise NRTs and those used for CRTs?

10. Do you now think that careful examination of the items on a test can help you to adapt it for your language program? What general steps would you follow in such a process?

A. Consider the results presented in Screen 4.8 (based on data from Premaratne 1987). Notice that items are coded *1* for correct answers and *0* for incorrect for thirty students (rows labeled with student numbers in the left column) on thirty different items (columns labeled with numbers across the top). Note also that the students' answers are listed in descending order (from high to low) according to their total scores in the right column. These item data are real results of the cloze test performance of a group of high school students in Sri Lanka. The table provides all the information that you will need to go ahead and calculate the *IF* and *ID* for each item in this norm-referenced test. In calculating the *ID*, please use the top ten students for the upper group and the bottom ten for the lower group. [See APPLICATION EXERCISES ANSWER KEY for answers.]

Screen 4.8 Example NRT item data from Sri Lankan High School students on a cloze test

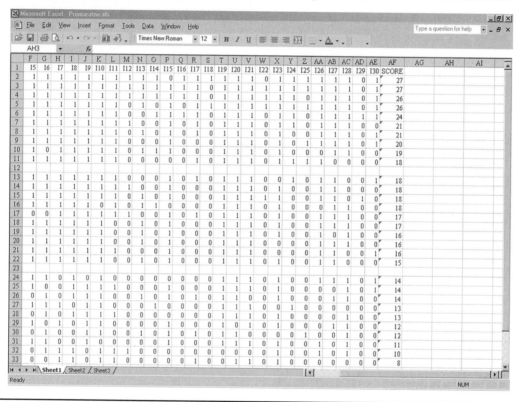

B. Examine the computer output shown in Table 4.3 for an NRT in terms of *IF* and *ID*. These results are real data from a pilot version of the Reading Comprehension subtest of the English Language Institute Placement Test at UHM. [Hint: Item-total correlations can be interpreted much like item discrimination (see Chapter 7).] If you were responsible for choosing five of the fifteen items for a revised version of the test, which five would you choose? Why? [See APPLICATION EXERCISES ANSWER KEY for my choices.]

Table 4.3 Computer analysis of 15 items

ITEM	GROUP	(Difficulty)	A	B	C	D	E	(Correlation)
1	HIGH	(93.0)	284*	1	2	5	0	(0.153)
	LOW		260	1	18	13	0	
2	HIGH	(65.6)	11	11	229*	43	0	(0.295)
	LOW		39	39	154	81	0	
3	HIGH	(88.2)	18	5	5	263*	0	(0.122)
	LOW		13	13	12	252	0	
4	HIGH	(73.8)	237*	12	40	3	0	(0.189)
	LOW		195	13	76	5	0	
5	HIGH	(45.5)	19	4	98	169*	0	(0.310)
	LOW		39	14	143	96	0	
6	HIGH	(83.8)	5	10	273*	3	0	(0.394)
	LOW		23	42	216	11	0	
7	HIGH	(68.4)	10	251*	11	20	0	(0.469)
	LOW		14	148	29	100	0	
8	HIGH	(55.2)	84	6	13	189*	0	(0.231)
	LOW		102	19	37	134	0	
9	HIGH	(58.1)	15	5	52	220*	0	(0.375)
	LOW		29	7	136	120	0	
10	HIGH	(39.8)	25	166*	46	55	0	(0.399)
	LOW		51	67	91	83	0	
11	HIGH	(92.6)	4	0	286*	2	0	(0.468)
	LOW		10	15	255	12	0	
12	HIGH	(77.4)	268*	6	10	9	0	(0.468)
	LOW		184	13	57	37	0	
13	HIGH	(66.3)	1	9	246*	36	0	(0.414)
	LOW		9	48	141	92	0	
14	HIGH	(86.2)	271*	0	2	19	0	(0.276)
	LOW		233	17	18	24	0	
15	HIGH	(62.4)	39	5	46	202*	0	(0.205)
	LOW		75	15	40	162	0	

* Note that the correct option is indicated by an asterisk.

C. Now look back at Screen 4.6 (p. 81). If your task was to select the best 15 CRT items out of the twenty shown in the table on the basis of the *DI*, which would you choose and why? [See APPLICATION EXERCISES ANSWER KEY for my choices.]

D. Next, examine Screen 4.9. Calculate the *B*-index for each item for a 70 percent cut-point. How do you interpret the indexes that result? [See APPLICATION EXERCISES ANSWER KEY.]

Screen 4.9 Example item data for *B*-index calculations

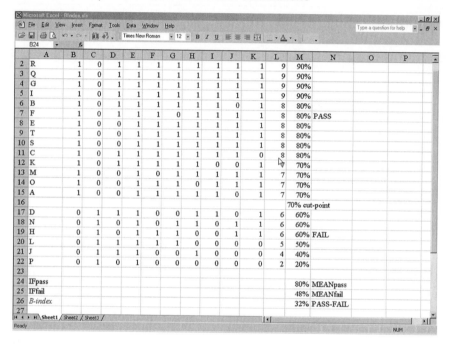

	A	B	C	D	E	F	G	H	I	J	K	L	M	N
2	R	1	0	1	1	1	1	1	1	1	1	9	90%	
3	Q	1	0	1	1	1	1	1	1	1	1	9	90%	
4	G	1	0	1	1	1	1	1	1	1	1	9	90%	
5	I	1	0	1	1	1	1	1	1	1	1	9	90%	
6	B	1	0	1	1	1	1	1	1	0	1	8	80%	
7	F	1	0	1	1	1	0	1	1	1	1	8	80%	PASS
8	E	1	0	0	1	1	1	1	1	1	1	8	80%	
9	T	1	0	0	1	1	1	1	1	1	1	8	80%	
10	S	1	0	0	1	1	1	1	1	1	1	8	80%	
11	C	1	0	1	1	1	1	1	1	1	0	8	80%	
12	K	1	0	1	1	1	1	1	0	0	1	7	70%	
13	M	1	0	0	1	0	1	1	1	1	1	7	70%	
14	O	1	0	0	1	1	1	0	1	1	1	7	70%	
15	A	1	0	0	1	1	1	1	1	0	1	7	70%	
16													70% cut-point	
17	D	0	1	1	1	0	0	1	1	0	1	6	60%	
18	N	0	1	0	1	0	1	1	0	1	1	6	60%	
19	H	0	1	0	1	1	1	0	0	1	1	6	60%	FAIL
20	L	0	1	1	1	1	1	0	0	0	0	5	50%	
21	J	0	1	1	1	0	0	1	0	0	0	4	40%	
22	P	0	1	0	1	0	0	0	0	0	0	2	20%	
23														
24	IFpass												80%	MEANpass
25	IFfail												48%	MEANfail
26	*B*-index												32%	PASS-FAIL
27														

5

DESCRIBING LANGUAGE TEST RESULTS

INTRODUCTION

The purpose of describing the results on a test is to provide test developers and test users with a picture of how the students performed on it. In order to show how testers graphically and statistically describe test results, I will first illustrate several useful ways of visually displaying sets of numbers (also known as **data**) with reference to the frequency of occurrence of each score. Such graphs help testers, teachers, and students to understand the results on the test more easily. Then, I will briefly discuss the differences between three scales of measurement that are essential for understanding many of the statistics that will follow in this book. Next, I will introduce descriptive statistics, which provide a useful set of tools for describing sets of data. In this section on descriptive statistics, I will cover one type that is used for describing the central tendency of a set of numbers and another set that is used for characterizing the dispersion of numbers away from the central tendency. After looking at how to calculate statistics of central tendency and dispersion using your spreadsheet, I will end the chapter with a discussion of how best to go about describing test results, whether the results are for NRT or CRT purposes. Along the way, I will intersperse explanations of how to do the above statistics in your spreadsheet program.

DISPLAYING DATA

If I were to ask my neighbor how frequently people in our neighborhood read their mail, she would probably answer something like once per day. If I were to ask how frequent a score of 69 is in Table 5.1 the answer would clearly be "four people received 69."

Frequency is the term that is used to describe this very common-sense sort of tallying procedure. Frequency can be used to indicate how many people did the same thing on a certain task, or how many people have a certain characteristic, or how many people fall into a certain set of categories. Thus, frequency is particularly useful when dealing with data that are in categories. However, it is not restricted to looking at categories because other types of data can easily be converted to categories. For instance, to figure out the frequency of students receiving a score of 69 in Table 5.1, just count up the number of 69s in the score column. To calculate the frequency at each score level on the test, just tally the number of students who got each score, and record the results as shown in the last two columns of Table 5.1. Thus, frequency is one numerical tool for reorganizing test score data into categories. But why bother going to all this trouble?

Table 5.1 Score frequencies

Students	Score	Tally	Frequency
Shenan	77	/	1
Robert	75	/	1
Randy	72	//	2
Mitsuko	72		
Millie	70	//	2
Kimi	70		
Kazumoto	69	////	4
Kako	69		
Joji	69		
Jeanne	69		
Issaku	68	//	2
Iliana	68		
Dean	67	/	1
Corky	64	//	2
Bill	64		
Archie	61	/	1

Frequencies are useful because they provide one way to summarize data, and thereby reveal patterns that might not otherwise be noticed. For instance, in Table 5.2, the frequencies of the score values are arranged from high to low scores in what is called a **frequency distribution**. Table 5.2 shows the score values from 60 to 77, the frequency at each score level (that is, the number of students), the cumulative frequency, and the cumulative percentage. Each **cumulative frequency** can be viewed as the number of students who scored at or below the score in question. The **cumulative percentage** is the same thing but expressed as a percentage of the total number of students. Thus in the example, four people scored 69 (frequency), which made a cumulative total of 10 students at or below 69 on the test (cumulative frequency). These 10 students amounted to 63% of the group (cumulative percentage). Or put another way, 63 percent of the students scored at or below a score of 69 on the test. The concept of cumulative percentage is particularly important for interpreting NRT results, as I will describe in Chapter 6, because knowing the percent of other examinees falling below or above each student is an integral part of interpreting NRT scores.

Table 5.2 Frequency distribution

Score Value	Cumulative Frequency	Cumulative Frequency	Percentage
77	1	16	100%
76	0	15	94%
75	1	15	94%
74	0	14	88%
73	0	14	88%
72	2	14	88%
71	0	12	75%
70	2	12	75%
69	4	10	63%
68	2	6	40%
67	1	4	25%
66	0	3	19%
65	0	3	19%
64	2	3	19%
63	0	1	6%
62	0	1	6%
61	1	1	6%
60	0	0	0%

GRAPHIC DISPLAY OF FREQUENCIES

However, frequency data can be displayed in far more graphic and appealing ways than the plain, ordinary frequency distribution shown in Table 5.2 above. Such graphic displays of scores generally come in one of three forms: a histogram, a bar graph, or a frequency polygon. All three are drawn on two axes: a horizontal line (also called the **abscissa**, or *X* **axis**) and a vertical line (also called the **ordinate**, or *Y* **axis**). These are shown in Figure 5.1.

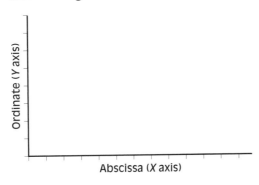

Figure 5.1 Abscissa and ordinate

A **histogram** of the frequencies of a set of scores is normally displayed by assigning score values to the horizontal line (abscissa) and putting the possible frequency values on the vertical line. An "X," asterisk, dot, or other symbol is then marked to represent each student who received each score as shown in Figure 5.2a. If bars are drawn side-by-side instead of Xs to represent the score frequencies, the result is a **bar graph**, as shown in Figure 5.2b (created using a spreadsheet's graphing function). Likewise, when dots are placed where the top X would be at each score value, then connected by lines, the result is a **frequency polygon** as shown in Figure 5.2c (a spreadsheet graph). All three of these graphs used for displaying test results are important because they can help teachers understand what happened when their students took a test. Another excellent reason for teachers to understand how such graphs work is that such techniques are sometimes used to misrepresent or distort information graphically (see Huff & Geis 1993). For example, take a look at Figure 6.7 (p. 128) in the next chapter. You will find that the standardized scores on the vertical or ordinate line are truncated (i.e., ranging only from 48 to 54, whereas the whole range of possible scores is from 20 to 70) and stretched out in such a way that the differences between the graduate and undergraduate students look big. Such strategies can make results look more dramatic than they would otherwise look if the entire range of scores is shown without magnification. Thus, understanding how graphs work can help teachers to successfully defend their program against harmful external misrepresentations about enrollments, budgets, teaching loads, and so forth.

a. Histogram

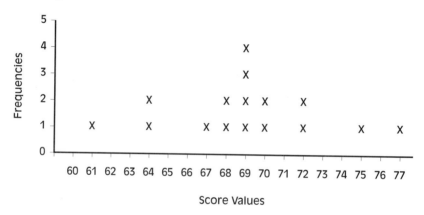

b. Bar graph

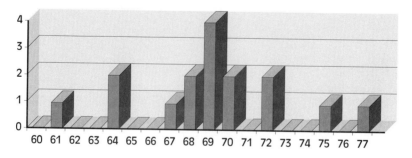

c. Frequency polygon

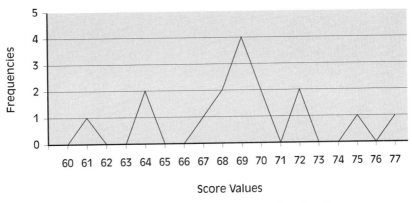

Figure 5.2 Graphic representation of frequency distributions

CREATING GRAPHS IN EXCEL™

Now, let's consider how such graphs can be created using a spreadsheet program. Screen 5.1 displays the test score data graphically, and can allow teachers to quickly summarize the patterns of the test results by viewing the charts. In the following sections, you will enter test score and frequency data from Screen 5.1 in *Excel*. Then you will create a bar and line chart to analyze the data visually.

Enter the data and initiate the Chart Wizard in *Excel*.

1. Open the *Excel* program on your computer.
2. Using Screen 5.1 as a guide, type the headings **Scores** in Cell A1, **Frequencies** in Cell B1, and then type the score and frequency data below the headings.
3. Highlight the data in the range B2:B19, and then click **Insert**, **Chart**. The *Excel* **Chart Wizard** will start on your screen.

Screen 5.1 Creating bar and line graphs in *Excel*

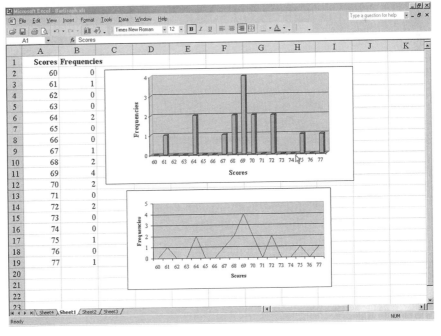

Create a bar chart and adjust *X* axis numbers.

1. In the *Chart Wizard* window, on the *Standard Types* tab, under *Chart type*, click **Column**. Select the first column chart example in the second row, and then click **Next**.
2. In the *Chart Wizard* window, on the *Data range* tab, confirm that the data are outlined by a moving box in the spreadsheet. The chart wizard will create the bar chart using the data in the range =Sheet1!$B$2:$B$19, as shown in the *Data range* box.
3. Click on the *Series* tab, and then in the *Category (X) axis labels* box, click on the icon to the right of the white area. A *Chart Source Data* window will display. You will define the source data so the chart uses the correct number series for the scores: highlight Cells A2 through A19, and then press ENTER. *Excel* will display a preview of the graph with the correct score numbers on the *X* axis.
4. Click **Next**.

Create bar graph titles and adjust the orientation.

1. In the *Chart Wizard* window, on the *Titles* tab, in the *Category (X) axis* box, type **Scores,** and then type **Frequencies** in the *Value (Z) axis* box. *Excel* will display a preview of the graph with the titles.
2. Click **Finish**. The bar graph will display on the spreadsheet.
3. To adjust the title Frequencies so that it is oriented at a 90 degree angle, right-click on the *Frequencies* label, and select *Format Axis Title*.
4. In the *Format Axis Title* window, on the *Alignment* tab, type **90** in the *Degrees* box and click the **OK** button. The chart will display the Frequencies title with the correct orientation. If the chart format looks different from the graph in Screen 5.1, then you may change fonts, number scaling, alignment, etc. by right-clicking on specific areas of the graph that you wish to adjust.

Create a line chart using *Excel*.

The preceding paragraphs explained how to create a bar graph in your spreadsheet. The creation of a frequency polygon (line chart) is a similar process except that you select a different type of chart when using the *Chart Wizard*, while using the same data used for the bar charts. By using a line chart, the data is displayed in a different format, which is useful for summarizing the test scores at a glance.

1. Highlight the data, and then click **Insert**, **Chart**. The *Excel Chart Wizard* will start on your screen.
2. In the *Chart Wizard* window, on the *Standard Types* tab, under *Chart type*, click **Line**. Select the first chart example, located in the first row, and then click **Next**.
3. In the *Chart Wizard* window, on the *Data Range* tab, confirm that the data are outlined by a moving box in the spreadsheet. The *Chart Wizard* will create the bar chart using the data in the range =Sheet1!$A$1:$B$19, as shown in the *Data range* box.
4. Click on the *Series* tab, and then in the *Category (X) axis labels* box, click on the icon to the right of the white area. A *Chart Source Data* window will display. You will define the source data so the chart uses the correct number series for the scores: highlight Cells A2 through A19, and then press ENTER. *Excel* will display a preview of the graph with the correct score numbers on the *X* axis.
5. Click **Next**.
6. Create graph titles and adjust the orientation, as performed in the previous section, to change the format of your line chart to reflect the chart in Screen 5.1.

Unfortunately, descriptions of language tests most often omit these very useful forms of graphs. Hence, test developers and test score users are missing out on one kind of test description that could help them to understand what the scores on the test mean. I strongly advise teachers to graph their test results in one way or another and consider what the graphs may be showing them. Fortunately, graphing numbers has become relatively easy in today's personal-computer-oriented world.

SCALES OF MEASUREMENT

All quantifiable data are by definition countable or measurable in some way. However, various types of data must be handled in different ways. Typically, three types of **scales** appear in the language teaching literature. The three scales represent three different ways of observing, organizing, and quantifying language data. The three scales are the nominal, ordinal, and continuous scales. In addition to organizing data in different ways, the three scales can also be thought of as supplying varying amounts of information. In fact, the amounts of information can be arranged hierarchically from least to most information as shown in Table 5.3. This is why they are sometimes referred to as "levels of measurement" (Bachman 1990). I will start by discussing the scale that provides the least information, the nominal scale, and then gradually move down the table toward the scale that provides the most information, the continuous or ratio scale.

Table 5.3 Three scales of measurement

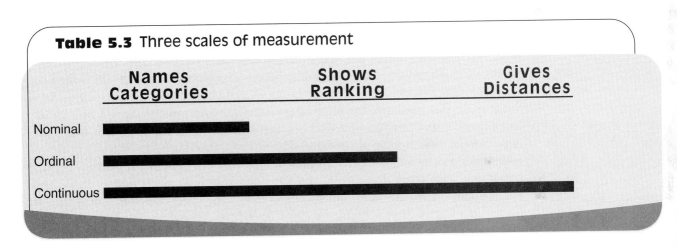

	Names Categories	Shows Ranking	Gives Distances
Nominal	▬▬▬		
Ordinal	▬▬▬▬		
Continuous	▬▬▬▬▬▬		

NOMINAL SCALES

Nominal scales are used for categorizing and naming groups. Most language teaching professionals will sometimes need to categorize language students into groups. Some of the most common categories or groupings for people would be gender, nationality, native language, educational background, socio-economic status, level of language study, membership in a particular language class, or even whether or not the students say that they enjoy language study. However, nominal scales are by no means restricted to people. Almost anything that the human mind can conceptualize can be categorized, grouped, and counted on nominal scales. The list of possible nominal scales is unlimited. However, in order to be a nominal scale, one condition must always be met: each observation on the scale must be independent, that is, each observation must fall into one, and only one, category. The essence of the nominal scale is that it names independent categories into which people or objects can be classified.

ORDINAL SCALES

Like the nominal scale, an **ordinal scale** names a group of observations, but, as its label implies, an ordinal scale also orders, or ranks, the data. For instance, I might want to rank my students from best to worst in some ability based on a test that I have administered to them. To do this, I would need to arrange the students' scores from high to low and then simply rank the students, using ordinal numbers. The highest student would be first, the next student second, then third, fourth, and so on. This would be an ordinal scale for my group of students. Other ordinal scales may also be of interest to language teachers. For instance, ordinal scales might be used to quantify the salary or seniority rankings of teachers within a language program, or to quantify the rankings for the relative difficulty of morphemes or structures like those measured on structure tests. If the data are arranged in order and labeled with ordinal numbers (first, second, third, and so forth), those data are on an ordinal scale. More exactly, an ordinal scale orders, or ranks, people or objects, with each point on the scale being ranked in a position that is *more than* and *less than* the other points on the scale.

CONTINUOUS SCALES

Continuous scales represent the ordering of a named group of data, but they provide additional information. A continuous scale also shows the distances between the points in the rankings. For instance, language test scores are usually on continuous scales. Consider the test scores shown in the second column in Table 5.4. Notice, in the last column, that the students can be categorized into four groups (top, upper middle, lower middle, and lower groups) on a nominal scale and that the students can be also ranked on an ordinal scale as shown in the third column. However, the test scores themselves provide much more information than either of the other two scales because continuous scale scores indicate the distances between the students' scores on the test. For example, Shenan scored 12 points higher than Robert, but Robert was only 3 points higher than Randy. Note also that the distances between some of the middle scores are only one point each. In short, continuous scales contain information about the distances between students' scores that is missing on ordinal and nominal scales. Hence, continuous scales provide more information than either ordinal or nominal scales. Examples of continuous scales include virtually all language tests, whether for placement, proficiency, achievement, or diagnosis, as well as other scales used to measure attitudes, learning styles, and so forth.

Table 5.4 Three example scales

Students	Test Scores (Continuous)	Rankings (Ordinal)	Frequencies (Nominal)		
Shenan	97	1	/	1	"Top
Robert	85	2	/	1	Group"
Randy	82	3	/	1	
Mitsuko	71	4	/	1	
Millie	70	5.5	//	2	"Upper
Kimi	70	5.5			Middle
Kazumoto	69	7	/	1	Group"
Kako	68	8	/	1	
Joji	67	10	///	3	"Lower
Jeanne	67	10			Middle
Issaku	67	10			Group"
Iliana	66	12	/	1	
Dean	62	13	/	1	"Lower
Corky	59	14	/	1	Group"
Bill	40	15	/	1	
Archie	31	16	/	1	

One problem arises among statisticians due to the fact that the distances between points on the scale are assumed to be equal. On the test shown in the second column of Table 5.4, the distance between scores of 25 and 27, which is 2 points, is assumed to be the same as the distance between 96 and 98, which is also 2 points. The problem is that some items on a language test may be much more difficult than others so the distances between scores may not, in fact, be equal. Items that make a difference between high scores like 96 and 98 might be considerably more difficult than items, at the other end of the scale, that make the difference between scores of 25 and 27. The assumption of equal distances is one that language testers worry about but also learn to live with.

In virtually all cases, the tests that teachers design for their language programs produce scores that can be treated as continuous scales, and so it should be. Nevertheless, knowing about the different types of scales is important because some of the analyses presented later in this book assume an understanding of the differences between continuous, ordinal, and nominal data.

DESCRIPTIVE STATISTICS

At a minimum, teachers should examine the descriptive statistics whenever they administer a test. **Descriptive statistics** are numerical representations of how a group of students performed on a test. Generally, test developers are responsible for providing descriptive statistics (see APA 1999) so that all test result users can create a mental picture of how the students performed on the test. Two aspects of group behavior are crucial in descriptive statistics: the middle of the group and the individuals. Both are important because the user of the test results must be able to visualize the middle (or typical) behavior of the group as well as the performances of those students who varied from the typical behavior. In statistical terms, these two aspects of group behavior are called central tendency and dispersion. I will cover each in turn conceptually in some detail before showing how to do these statistics in your spreadsheet program.

CENTRAL TENDENCY

Central tendency is the first aspect of a test to consider. **Central tendency** describes the most typical behavior of a group. Four statistics are used for estimating central tendency: the mean, the mode, the median, and the midpoint. Note that, in the examples used below, the mean, mode, median, and midpoint all turn out to be the same (with a value of 69 in these cases). Please, don't assume that they would always turn out the same in real testing results.

Mean

The **mean** is probably the single most often reported indicator of central tendency. The mean is virtually the same as the arithmetic average that most teachers calculate in grading classroom tests. The mean is cleverly symbolized by the letter M. Another way to define a statistical concept is to give its formula, so mean is defined as the following:

$$M = \frac{\Sigma X}{N}$$

M = mean N = number of scores
X = scores Σ = sum (or add)

In order to help clarify the reading of such formulas, I will briefly explain this one in a step-by-step manner. The formula simply says: to get the mean (M), add up (Σ) the scores (X), and divide by the number of scores (N). These steps are shown in Table 5.5. To find the mean in the example: (a) sum, or add up the scores, (b) find the number of scores, and (c) divide the sum of the scores by the number of scores. So the mean in the example in Table 5.5 would be 69. As mentioned above, this set of calculations probably looks very familiar since most teachers use the arithmetic average in looking at the results of a classroom test. What they are checking in the process is almost exactly the same as the mean and therefore is an indicator of the central tendency, or typical performance, of their class on the test.

Table 5.5 Calculating the mean

Students (X)	Scores	Calculations
Shenan	77	*a.* ΣX = Sum of scores = 77 + 75 + 72 + 72 + 70 + 70 + 69
Robert	75	+ 69 + 69 + 69 + 68 + 68 + 67 + 64 + 64 + 61 = 1104
Mitsuko	72	
Iliana	72	*b.* N = *Number of scores* = 16
Millie	70	
Kimi	70	*c.* $M = \dfrac{\Sigma X}{N} = \dfrac{1104}{16} = 69$
Kazumoto	69	
Kako	69	
Joji	69	
Jeanne	69	
Issaku	68	
Corky	68	
Dean	67	
Randy	64	
Bill	64	
Archie	61	

Like the formula for the mean, all other equations in this book will always be explained in a recipe-book style with examples. In the case of this formula, the steps were very easy because the formula and the concept of the mean are just another way of expressing something that teachers already know how to do. However, in general, formulas provide more precision for defining and discussing statistical concepts. So language testers use such formulas much like linguists and language teachers use terms like "syntax" and "phonology" when everyone else calls these concepts grammar and pronunciation. Such formulas are just part of learning to speak language testing.

Mode

Another indicator of central tendency is the mode. The **mode** is that score which occurs most frequently. In Table 5.5 above, what would the mode be? It would be 69, the only score received by four students. A memory device that I use to keep the mode straight in my mind is that the word *mode* can mean fashionable (as in *à la mode*)[3]. Thus, the mode would be that score which is most fashionable, or the one received by the most students. No statistical formula is necessary for this straightforward idea. You can identify it by lining up the scores in order and figuring out which one is the most common. While you are looking, be sure to check for more than one mode because it is possible for a set of scores to have two or more modes. Such distributions of scores are referred to as being **bimodal** (if there are two peaks), **trimodal** (if there are three peaks), and so on.

---

[3] Contrary to popular belief in the United States, the French phrase *à la mode* does not mean "with ice cream."

Median

The **median** is that point below which 50 percent of the scores fall and above which 50 percent fall. Thus, in the set of scores 100, 95, 83, 71, 61, 57, 30, the median is 71 because 71 has three scores above it (100, 95, and 83) and three scores below it (61, 57, and 30). What is the median for the following set of scores: 11, 23, 40, 50, 57, 63, 86? Fifty, right?

In real data, cases arise that are not so clear. For example, what is the median for these scores: 9, 12, 15, 16, 17, 27? In such a situation, when there is an even number of scores, the median is taken to be midway between the two middle scores. In this example, the two middle scores are 15 and 16 so the median is 15.5. Does that make sense? If so, what is the median for these scores: 11, 28, 33, 50, 60, 62, 70, 98? Your answer should have been 55 because that is the point halfway between the two middle scores, 50 and 60, which leaves four scores above the median and four below it as shown on the following continuum:

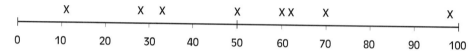

There are other cases where there might be more than one numerically equal score at the median, for instance, 40, 45, 49, 50, 50, 50, 57, 64, 77. Here, the midpoint is clearly 50 because there is an odd number of like scores at the median separating equal numbers of scores on either side.

There are still other situations that may arise in determining the median but the important thing to remember is that the median is the point that divides the scores 50/50, much like the median in a highway divides the road into two equal parts. However, in sets of test scores, the median may have a fraction because students rarely cooperate to the degree that highways do.

Midpoint

The **midpoint** in a set of scores is that point halfway between the highest score and the lowest score on the test. The formula for calculating the midpoint is:

$$\text{Midpoint} = \frac{\text{High} + \text{Low}}{2}$$

For example, if the lowest scorer on a test was 30 and the highest was 100, the midpoint would be halfway between these two scores. To use the formula: (a) identify the high and low scores (100 and 30 in this example), (b) add the low score to the high one (100 + 30 = 130), and (c) divide the result by 2 (130/2 = 65 = midpoint). Or, formulaically:

$$\text{Midpoint} = \frac{100 + 30}{2} = \frac{130}{2} = 65$$

To briefly review central tendency, four such measures of central tendency exist: the mean, the mode, the median, and the midpoint. Each of these measures has its strengths and weaknesses. None is necessarily better than the others, though the mean is most commonly reported. They simply serve different purposes and are appropriate in different situations, as you will see at the end of the chapter.

To further review central tendency, look at Table 5.5 (p. 99). I have explained that the mean, or arithmetic average, in Table 5.5 was 69. The mode, or most frequent score, also turned out to be 69. The median, that score which divided the scores 50/50, was also 69. The midpoint, halfway between the high score of 77 and the low score of 61, was also 69. In this contrived example, all four measures of central tendency turned out to be the same, that is, 69. However, as you will see in Table 5.8 (p. 109) these four indices for actual test data are seldom so similarly well-centered and in agreement. For that reason alone, all four should be used. Furthermore, as I will explain further in Chapter 6, the degree to which these four indices of central tendency are similar is one indication of the degree to which a set of scores is normally (as in norm-referenced) distributed.

DISPERSION

With a clear understanding how to examine the central tendency of a set of scores, the next step is to consider **dispersion**, or how the individual performances vary from the central tendency. Four indicators of the dispersion are commonly used for describing distributions of test scores: the range, the high and low, the standard deviation, and the variance.

Range

Most teachers are already familiar with the concept of **range** from tests that they have taken or given in class. Simply put, the range is the number of points between the highest score on a measure and the lowest score plus one (one is added because the range should include the scores at both ends). Thus, in Table 5.5 (p. 99), where the highest score is 77 and the lowest is 61, the range is 17 points ($77 - 61 + 1 = 17$). To see why I argued that 1 should be added in calculating the range, count up the number of numbers in the range from 61 to 77:

| | | | | | | | | | | | | | | | | |
|61|62|63|64|65|66|67|68|69|70|71|72|73|74|75|76|77|

You should get a total of 17 numbers. If 1 is not added, the range would be 16 instead of 17 with the result that one of the numbers (either the 61 or the 77 in this case) would be left out. However, I also need to tell you that some statistics books advocate calculating the range without adding 1. Regardless of how it is calculated, the range provides some idea of how individuals vary from the central tendency.

However, the range only reflects the magnitude of the outer edges (high and low) of all the variation in scores and, therefore, can be strongly affected by a test performance that is not really representative of the group of students as a whole. For instance, if I add another student named Emma, who scored 26, to the bottom of Table 5.5 (p. 99), the range will be much larger than 17. With Emma included, the range is 52 ($77 - 26 + 1 = 52$). However, her performance on the test is so different from the performances of the other students that she does not appear to belong in this group. Such a person may be an **outlier**, a person who, for some reason, does not belong to the group. To check this, I would talk to Emma in an attempt to discover what was going on during the test. Perhaps she will reveal that she had already decided to drop the course at the time of the test so she did not study and had to guess on most of the test. If she is included in calculating the range, a value of 52 is obtained. If she is excluded, a value of 17 is the result. These ranges are quite different. In a sense, the range of 52 (obtained with the outlier included) is wrong in that it does not really represent the performances of the group. So I might be tempted to exclude her and report the range as 17. However, I can never be 100 percent sure that an outlier is not a natural part of the group so I am more likely to be open and honest about the situation and report the range with and without the outlier. I would also want to explain why I think that the outlier is not part of the group.

In short, the range is a weak measure of dispersion because factors like Emma's personal decision can strongly affect it, even though they are extraneous to students' performances on the test. Regardless of this problem, the range is usually reported as one indicator of dispersion and should be interpreted by test score users as just what it is: the number of points between the highest and lowest scores on a test, including both of them.

High and low

The range gives some idea of how far the scores on a test spread along the continuum of possible scores, but it does not show where on the continuum the whole set of scores lies. For example, the range for the scores in Table 5.5 is 17 points ($77 - 61 + 1 = 17$), but a range of 17 points can be found at many places along the continuum of possible scores. For instance, a group of students with very weak ability levels might have scores from 21 to 37 and still have a range of 17 points ($37 - 21 + 1 = 17$), while another group with very high abilities might have scores from 81 to 97 and still have a range of 17 points ($97 - 81 + 1 = 17$). Thus, in addition to showing the range, it is often necessary and desirable to show what the actual lowest score and highest score were. So, when reporting that the range was 17 points, it would be helpful for readers if you were to add that the **low score** was 61 and the **high score** was 77, thus showing not only how wide the spread of scores was, but also where along the scale they were located.

Standard deviation

The standard deviation is an averaging process, and as such, it is not affected as much by outliers as the range. Consequently, the standard deviation is generally considered a stronger estimate of the dispersion of scores. I define the **standard deviation** as a sort of average of the differences of all scores from the mean. This is not a rigorous statistical definition but rather one that will serve well for conveying the meaning of this statistic. The formula that will be used here to calculate the statistic says very much the same thing but in mathematical shorthand. Remember that M is the symbol for the mean, that X represents the scores, that Σ indicates that something must be added up, and that N stands for the number of scores. The formula for the standard deviation (S, s, or SD) is:

$$S = \sqrt{\frac{\Sigma(X - M)^2}{N}}$$

M = mean N = number of scores
X = scores Σ = sum (or add)

Starting from the inside and working outward, subtract the mean from each score ($X - M$), then square each of these values ($X - M)^2$, and add them up $\Sigma(X - M)^2$. This sum is then divided by the number of scores $\frac{\Sigma(X - M)^2}{N}$, and the square root of the result of

Table 5.6 Standard deviation

Students	Score a. (X)	−	Mean (M)	=	Difference b. (X − M)	Difference Squared c. (X − M)²
Shenan	77	−	69	=	8	64
Robert	75	−	69	=	6	36
Mitsuko	72	−	69	=	3	9
Iliana	72	−	69	=	3	9
Millie	70	−	69	=	1	1
Kimi	70	−	69	=	1	1
Kazumoto	69	−	69	=	0	0
Kako	69	−	69	=	0	0
Joji	69	−	69	=	0	0
Jeanne	69	−	69	=	0	0
Issaku	68	−	69	=	−1	1
Corky	68	−	69	=	−1	1
Dean	67	−	69	=	−2	4
Randy	64	−	69	=	−5	25
Bill	64	−	69	=	−5	25
Archie	61	−	69	=	−8	64

d. $\Sigma(X-M)^2 = 240$

e. $S = \sqrt{\dfrac{\Sigma(X-M)^2}{N}} = \sqrt{\dfrac{240}{16}} = \sqrt{15} = 3.87$

that operation $S = \sqrt{\dfrac{\Sigma(X-M)^2}{N}}$ is the standard deviation. Let's take a look at Table 5.6 to make this clear.

Remember that the mean in Table 5.5 (p. 99) was 69. Using the same scores and mean, Table 5.6 illustrates the steps required to calculate the standard deviation: (a) line up each score with the mean, (b) subtract the mean from each score, (c) square each of the "differences" from the mean, (d) add up all the squared values, (e) insert the results into the formula and calculate the result. In the example, the result after taking the square root is 3.87. I will now go back to the original definition to make sure all this is crystal clear.

In my definition, the standard deviation is "a sort of average (ignoring the squaring and square root, notice that something is added up and divided by *N*—similar to what happens in calculating an average) of the differences of all scores from the mean" (so it turns out that the difference of each student's score from the mean is what is being averaged). Thus, the standard deviation is a sort of average of the differences of all scores from the mean. These differences from the mean are often called **deviations** from the mean—hence the label *standard deviation*.

I call the standard deviation a "sort of" average because it involves squaring certain values and taking a square root at the end. In the example in Table 5.6 the deviations are reported in Column b. under (X − M). Notice that adding up the deviations including both the positive and negative values will yield zero. Such a result will usually be obtained because typically about half the deviations will be positive (above the mean) and half will be negative (below the mean). Thus, they will usually add to zero or a value very close to zero. To get around this problem, each value is squared as shown in column c. under $(X - M)^2$. Then the resulting numbers can be added with a result other than zero. After the sum of these numbers is divided by N in the averaging process, the result is brought back down to a score value by taking its square root. In other words, the square root is taken to counteract the squaring process that went on earlier.

The standard deviation is a very versatile and useful statistic as I will explain in much more detail in the next chapter, but for now, keep in mind that the standard deviation is a good indicator of the dispersion of a set of test scores around the mean. The standard deviation is usually better than the range because it is the result of an averaging process. By averaging, the effects are lessened of any extreme scores not attributable to performance on the test (that is, outliers like Emma with her personal problem).

Sometimes, another slightly different formula is used for the standard deviation:

$$S = \sqrt{\frac{\Sigma(X - M)^2}{N - 1}}$$

To explain this version (called the "$N - 1$" formula), I must first clarify the difference between a sample and a population. A **sample** is a subset selected, randomly or otherwise, to represent a population. From another angle, a **population** is the whole group from which the sample is selected. Thus, if a sample of 16 students is taken from the whole population of 2000 students in a particular school, the sample is the group of 16 students and the population is the group of 2000 students that the population represents. The reason I needed to explain all this is that the $N - 1$ formula given above is appropriate for samples (particularly if they are small, numbering less than 30 students), while the N formula is generally used in this book for populations. As long as you are testing all the students appropriate for the particular testing situation, which is the case most of the time, you are justified in using the simpler N formula. Note that the sample size in Table 5.6 is only 16, which is less than 30, but since it is the entire population of students to be tested, I can justify using the N formula.

Variance

The variance is another descriptive statistic for dispersion. As indicated by its symbol, S^2, the test **variance** is equal to the squared value of the standard deviation. Thus, the formula for the test variance looks very much like the one for the standard deviation except that both sides of the equation are squared. Squaring the left side of the standard deviation equation is easy. To square the right side of the standard deviation equation, all that is necessary is to remove the square root sign. What is left is the formula for the test variance.

$$S^2 = \sqrt{\frac{\Sigma(X - M)^2}{N}}$$

Hence, **test variance** can easily be defined, with reference to this formula, as the average of the squared differences of students' scores from the mean. Test variance can also be defined as the square of the standard deviation, or as an intermediary step in the calculation of the standard deviation. Note that, just like the standard deviation, the variance can also be calculated using an N formula or an $N - 1$ formula for exactly the same reasons as those stated for the standard deviation. For much more discussion of the concept of variance, see Chapter 10.

THE SPREADSHEET APPROACH TO DESCRIPTIVE STATISTICS

You will be happy to learn that all of the above central tendency and dispersion statistics can be calculated using functions in your spreadsheet. The functions in *Excel* for these statistics are as follows:

Number of students (*N*)	= COUNT(range)
Mean	= AVERAGE(range)
Mode	= MODE(range)
Median	= MEDIAN(range)
Midpoint	= (MAX(range)+MIN(range))/2
High	= MAX(range)
Low	= MIN(range)
Range	= MAX(range)−MIN(range)+1
Standard deviation (the *N* formula)	= STDEVP(range)
Standard deviation (the *N* - 1 formula)	= STDEV(range)
Variance (the *N* formula)	= VARP(range)
Variance (the *N* - 1 formula)	= VAR(range)

Screen 5.2 (p. 106) shows all of these formulas applied to the data from Table 5.1 (p. 90), and Screen 5.3 (p. 106) shows the results of those calculations. (Note that I have used the **Format Cells** menus discussed earlier in the book to format eight of the numbers to show two places to the right of the decimal.)

Entering all the formulas shown in Screen 5.2 for Test A was not an easy task, as you know if you followed along in your spreadsheet. The payoff comes when you are able to copy those formulas into other columns. With the example data, simply block out the results for Test A and copy them to the same position below Test B. In other words, block out the range from B19 to B30 and copy that block to the range from C19 to C30. The results should look like Screen 5.4.

Screen 5.2 Formulas for calculating example descriptive statistics in a spreadsheet

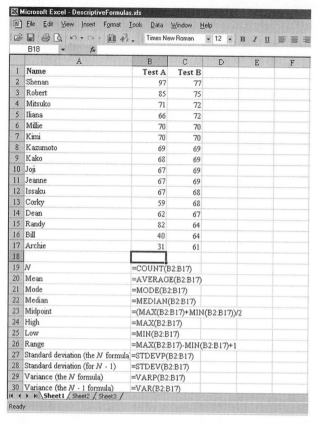

Screen 5.3 Results of example descriptive statistics in a spreadsheet

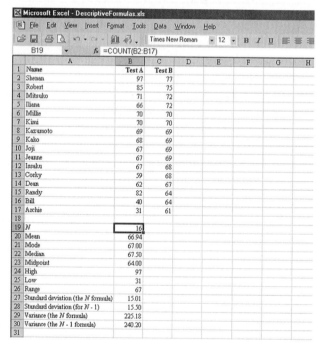

Screen 5.4 Results of copying example descriptive statistics

	A	B	C	D	E	F
1	Name	Test A	Test B			
2	Shenan	97	77			
3	Robert	85	75			
4	Mitsuko	71	72			
5	Iliana	66	72			
6	Millie	70	70			
7	Kimi	70	70			
8	Kazumoto	69	69			
9	Kako	68	69			
10	Joji	67	69			
11	Jeanne	67	69			
12	Issaku	67	68			
13	Corky	59	68			
14	Dean	62	67			
15	Randy	82	64			
16	Bill	40	64			
17	Archie	31	61			
18						
19	N	16	16			
20	Mean	66.94	69.00			
21	Mode	67.00	69.00			
22	Median	67.50	69.00			
23	Midpoint	64.00	69.00			
24	High	97	77			
25	Low	31	61			
26	Range	67	17			
27	Standard deviation (the N formula)	15.01	3.87			
28	Standard deviation (for N - 1)	15.50	4.00			
29	Variance (the N formula)	225.18	15.00			
30	Variance (the N - 1 formula)	240.20	16.00			
31						

REPORTING DESCRIPTIVE STATISTICS

WHAT SHOULD BE INCLUDED?

To review, let's consider the report that test developers often write up to explain the results of administering their test. In such reports, they typically describe at least two aspects of the results on the test: central tendency and dispersion. Central tendency indicates the middle, or typical, score for the students who took the test. Central tendency indicators come in four forms: the mean (arithmetic average), mode (most often received score), the median (score that splits the group 50/50), and the midpoint (the score halfway between the highest and lowest scores).

In addition, test developers usually provide some indicators of the dispersion of scores, or the way individuals varied around the typical behavior of the group. Dispersion indicators come in three forms: the range (the difference between the highest and lowest scores, including both), the standard deviation (a sort of average of how far individuals varied from the mean), and the test variance (a sort of average of the squared differences of students' scores from the mean).

Two other descriptive statistics are commonly reported. Mercifully, these statistics do not require any calculations. The number of students who took the test (N) is one such statistic. For instance, if 130 students took the test, the test developer should report that $N = 130$. They should also report the number of items (k) that were on the test. Thus on a test with 50 items, the test developer should report that $k = 50$.

Under circumstances where one focus of the report is on the individual test items or on selecting items for revising and improving the test, the means for the following item statistics might also be reported: the item facility index, the item discrimination index, the difference index, and the B-index. These mean item statistics are calculated just like the mean for a set of scores, but the individual item statistics are used instead of students' scores.

So far in this chapter, I have covered numerous statistics that can help in analyzing and reporting test results. Deciding which indicators to calculate and report in a particular testing situation will depend on whether the test is an NRT or CRT, on the statistical sophistication of the audience (the test users), and on how clear the results need to be. But in most cases, test developers should consider all available graphic and statistical ways of describing test data so they can provide the clearest possible description of how the students performed on the test. The best rule of thumb to follow would be, when in doubt, report too much information rather than too little.

How Should Descriptive Test Statistics Be Displayed?

The next step is to consider how to present the statistics once they are calculated. Test developers may find themselves presenting test results to colleagues, to funding agencies, or to a journal in the form of research. Most often, the purpose is to summarize the information so that everyone involved can better understand how well the tests worked or how well the students performed on them. In most cases, descriptive test statistics are displayed in the form of a table.

Table 5.7 shows one way to display such statistics. The table shows very real listening, reading, vocabulary, and writing subtest results from a now retired version of the English Language Institute Placement Test (ELIPT) at the University of Hawaii at Manoa (UHM).

Table 5.7 ELI placement test results

| STATISTICS | SUBTEST | | | |
	LISTENING	READING	VOCABULARY	WRITING
N	153.00	153.00	154.00	153.00
total possible (k)	55.00	60.00	100.00	100.00
mean (M)	34.76	40.64	69.34	75.08
mode	32.00	43.00	86.00	77.00
median	34.45	41.00	71.67	75.50
midpoint	34.50	39.00	59.50	69.00
low-high	17-52	21-57	20-99	4494
range	36.00	37.00	80.00	51.00
S	7.29	7.48	16.08	8.94

The results shown in Table 5.7 are one fall semester's administration of the ELIPT. Notice that the table has row labels and column labels, and that there are four columns and nine rows of results. The first column label indicates that the first column is for the row labels (STATISTICS). The other four columns are for the four subtests. Notice that the labeling for subtests is in two levels. The first level shows that those four columns are subtests by having the label SUBTEST with a line over each of the individual subtest labels (LISTENING, READING, VOCABULARY, and WRITING) in the second level. In addition, the rows inside the table have labels in the first column for the various statistics that are reported.

Notice how very neatly and clearly this table presents a great deal of information that can easily be examined and interpreted by the test user. This clarity results partly from the fact that the table is not cluttered with vertical lines. The columns of numbers are enough to orient the reader's eye both horizontally and vertically. The horizontal lines that do appear serve only to define the boundaries of the table itself and separate the column labels from the statistical results. Notice also how each number (except those for the low-high) has been rounded off to two decimal places, even when not necessary (for instance, those for *N* and total possible), for the sake of presenting a neat and symmetrical table.

Table 5.8 ELI placement test results

Subtest	N	k	M	mode	median	midpoint	low-high ranges		
				Central Tendency			**Dispersion**		
Listening	153	55	34.76	32	34.45	34.50	17-52	36	7.29
Reading	153	60	40.64	43	41.00	39.00	21-57	37	7.48
Vocabulary	154	100	69.34	86	71.67	59.50	20-99	80	16.08
Writing	153	100	75.08	77	75.50	69.00	44-94	51	8.94

Table 5.8 displays exactly the same information with the column labels changed to row labels and vice versa. Many other possible variations exist, and the form that test developers choose to use will depend on their purposes in displaying the statistics. In some cases, they may wish to present data in a histogram, bar graph, or frequency polygon. For instance, histograms for each of the ELIPT subtests helped us to examine the degree to which each subtest was producing a normal distribution. The histogram for the ELIPT listening subtest is shown in Figure 5.3, just as it came off of the computer. Notice that the orientation of the graph is different from the histograms elsewhere in this chapter. The sideways orientation resulted from the fact that the scores were plotted on the ordinate (or, vertical *Y* axis) and the frequencies along the abscissa (or, horizontal *X* axis). This orientation is a product of the way the computer program was "thinking" and printing rather than a question of convenience for the humans who must interpret the graph. Nevertheless, nobody should have any problem visualizing the distribution of scores the way they are presented, though some may have to turn the book sideways to do so.

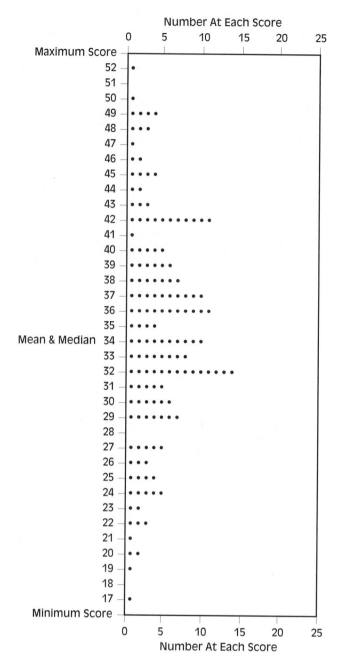

Figure 5.3 Histogram ELIPT listening subtest

REVIEW QUESTIONS

1. What is a frequency distribution? Why might you want to use a frequency distribution to describe the behavior of your students on a test if you already have the descriptive statistics?

2. What are the three scales of measurement discussed in this chapter? How are they different?

3. How would you define central tendency? What are four ways to estimate it? Which is most often reported?

4. What is dispersion? Which of the four indices for dispersion are most often reported?

5. Why should you describe your students' behavior on a measure in terms of both central tendency and dispersion?

6. Which of these axes in Figure 5.3 (p. 110) is the ordinate and which the abscissa? Go ahead and label them.

APPLICATION EXERCISES

A) Examine the descriptive statistics shown in Table 5.9 and answer the questions that follow.

Table 5.9 Summary test statistics for three TOEFL subtests (and total) with separate cloze and writing sample scores for the same students

Measure	Possible score	M	S	N
Cloze	50	15.3	7.31	207
TOEFL Listening	68	50.4	10.50	207
TOEFL Structure	68	50.4	8.80	207
TOEFL Reading	68	51.3	9.01	207
Total TOEFL	677	507.0	57.17	207
Writing Sample	100	61.0	12.43	118

A1) How many subtests are there on the TOEFL?

A2) a. What is the mean for the TOEFL Reading subtest?
   b. What is the standard deviation?
   c. And how many students took it?

A3) a. Which test has the smallest possible score?
   b. Which appears to have the largest?

A4) a. Which test had the smallest number of students taking it?
   b. And why do you suppose this is the case?

A5) a. Which test appears to have the widest dispersion of scores?
   b. How do you know that?

A6) What additional information would you have liked to see in this table to help you interpret the results of these tests?

B) The scores shown in Screen 5.5 (p. 112) are based on a subsample of 30 Sri Lankan high school students who took four different 30-item variations of the cloze type of test. (The data are taken from Premaratne 1987.) Look at the data labeled tests A–D and answer the questions.

Screen 5.5 Sri Lankan High School cloze test data

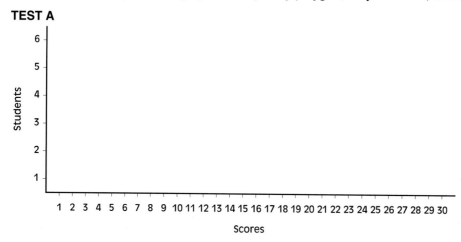

Student ID#	TEST A	TEST B	TEST C	TEST D
1	27	19	28	28
2	27	20	27	29
3	20	16	18	23
4	21	17	24	25
5	21	15	26	19
6	18	13	25	26
7	11	6	24	23
8	16	11	24	21
9	17	12	24	23
10	14	8	22	17
11	12	8	19	18
12	24	18	28	29
13	10	8	10	23
14	14	8	26	21
15	13	7	26	22
16	19	13	24	19
17	18	15	25	18
18	18	14	23	24
19	17	14	20	25
20	26	20	24	28
21	15	11	17	24
22	16	11	22	21
23	12	9	20	18
24	16	11	21	21
25	14	12	22	22
26	13	11	17	21
27	18	13	20	24
28	8	8	14	19
29	26	21	25	27
30	18	13	21	23

B1) Begin by graphing the results of each test. Please do so by hand in the spaces provided below. Use a histogram, bar graph, or frequency polygon, as you see fit, or mix and match.

TEST A

(Blank graph: y-axis "Students" 1–6, x-axis "Scores" 1–30)

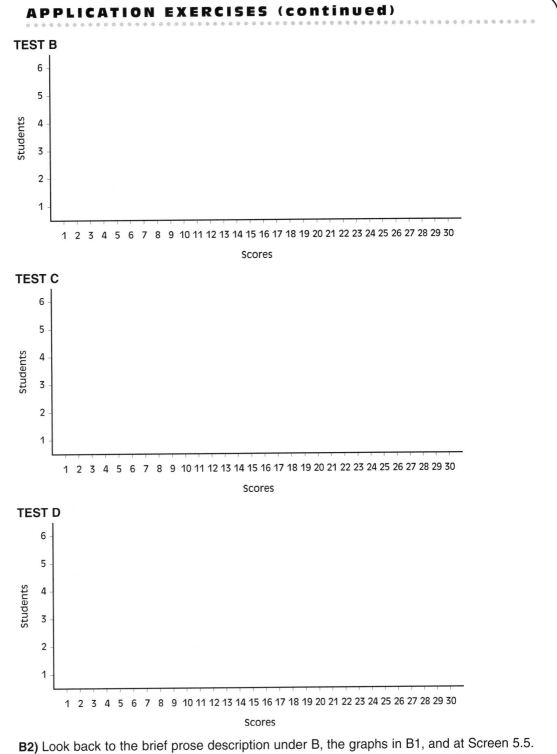

TEST B

TEST C

TEST D

B2) Look back to the brief prose description under B, the graphs in B1, and at Screen 5.5. How many students took each test? How many items were there on each test? In terms of central tendency, what was the mean, mode, median, and midpoint for each of the tests? In terms of dispersion, what was the standard deviation, variance, low-high, and range for each of the tests? Use your spreadsheet program to organize and analyze these descriptive statistics if at all possible.

6

INTERPRETING LANGUAGE TEST SCORES

INTRODUCTION

The purpose of developing language tests, administering them, and sorting through the resulting scores is to make decisions about your students. The sorting process is sometimes called test score interpretation. This chapter is about interpreting the performances of students on both norm-referenced and criterion-referenced tests. The descriptive statistics discussed in the previous chapter help to visualize the students' performances in terms of central tendency and dispersion. As explained in this chapter, descriptive statistics can also help language teachers to understand more complex patterns in the test behavior of their students. As a foundation, the discussion will begin with three concepts: probability distributions, the normal distribution, and standardized scores. Knowing about these three concepts will help teachers to understand what has happened on a test administration and will enable them to report students' scores in the context of the entire score distribution. As a result, each score will have more meaning to the students, as well as to the administrators and teachers involved. Naturally, it will be useful if we can save some time and energy in making these decisions by using a spreadsheet program.

PROBABILITY DISTRIBUTIONS

Early in life, most people discover that the **probability** of getting heads on any given flip of a coin is 50/50. This probability can also be expressed as a 1 in 2 chance or 50 percent. Regardless of how it is phrased, the concept is a familiar one. In more formal terms, such a probability is determined by dividing the number of expected outcomes (one—heads in this case) by the number of possible outcomes (two—both heads and tails are possibilities). In the case of the coin flip, one expected outcome is divided by the number of possible outcomes, which yields 1/2, or .50, which indicates a 50 percent probability of getting heads on any particular flip of a coin.

Expected outcomes represent those events for which a person is trying to determine the probability (heads in the example above). The **possible outcomes** represent the number of potentially different events that might occur as the events unfold (two in the example). The probability of a given event, or set of events, is the ratio of the expected outcomes to the possible outcomes. This ratio ranges from 0 to 1.0, and is commonly discussed in percentage terms. Thus, a ratio of .50, as discussed above, is also referred to as a 50 percent chance of getting heads.

Another way of keeping track of probabilities is to plot them out as they occur, perhaps in the form of a histogram like the ones in the previous chapter. Typically, a histogram is designed so that the number of actual outcomes is on the ordinate and the number of possible outcomes is on the abscissa. Figure 6.1a shows how the histogram would look for coin flips if they were to occur as follows: tails, heads, heads, tails, tails, heads, tails, tails.

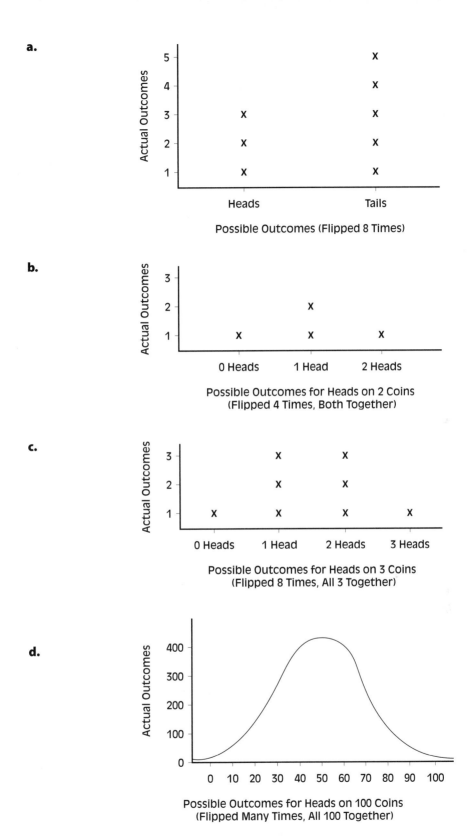

Figure 6.1 Histograms of coin flips

The result of plotting the coin flips as they occurred is a graph of the **distribution**, or arrangement, of the outcomes. This distribution helps picture the events that occurred in a more vivid manner than simply knowing the numbers (three heads and five tails). Another way to plot the events involved in coin flipping is to plot the probable, or likely, distributions for many more than the two possible events described above. Consider, for instance, the possibilities for outcomes of heads only, but for two coins flipped at the same time, instead of just one coin. A typical distribution for heads on two coins (flipped together) given four sets of flips is shown in Figure 6.1b. Notice that the distribution in Figure 6.1b shows heads only ("heads only" were used to get randomly distributed numbers ranging from 0 to 100), and that the histogram indicates all possible outcomes for heads given that two coins are being flipped at the same time (that is, 0, 1, or 2 heads). Notice also that the following events are plotted: zero heads one time, one head two times, and two heads one time. Figure 6.1c shows the distribution for heads on three coins being flipped together given eight sets of flips. Notice that, as the number of coins is increased, the distribution of events grows more complex. Consider what would probably happen if I were to plot the occurrences of heads for 100 coins flipped together, given thousands of sets of flips. If I were to do so and connect the tops of each column, the resulting frequency polygon would look something like the one shown in Figure 6.1d. This figure should look familiar to anyone who has ever worked with the concept of normal distribution, or the bell curve. Such normal distributions will occur in distributions like those just discussed, as long as enough coin flips are involved. Notice that these distributions occur because of the probabilities of those coins landing on the various possible numbers of heads.

NORMAL DISTRIBUTION

Normal distribution does occur. The graphs of the coin flip distributions demonstrate that. Moreover, as the number of possible events gets larger, plots of those events increasingly take the shape of the bell curve. Additional evidence comes from the biological sciences, where repeated observations generally show that living organisms grow, multiply, and behave in relatively predictable patterns. Many of these patterns take the shape of the **normal distribution**, which is a pattern for a set of data that takes the shape of a bell-shaped curve. In a normal distribution, the data will tend to be concentrated near the center and decrease symmetrically on both sides.

For example, consider the 28 trees that grow in Mauka Park near where I live. If I were to measure them, I could plot their heights roughly as shown in Figure 6.2a. Each tree is represented by an "x" on the five-foot height closest to the actual height of the tree. Notice that the result is a histogram of the distribution of heights among the trees in Mauka Park. Such visual representation could equally well be accomplished by using a frequency polygon (as shown in Figure 6.2b). Notice how the shape of the curve in the polygon looks suspiciously, but not exactly, like the normal curve.

a. Histogram

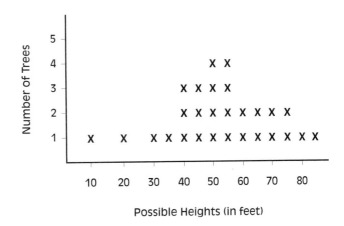

b. Frequency polygon

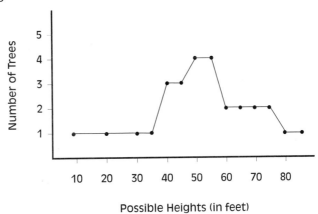

Figure 6.2 Distribution of the heights of trees

a. Histogram

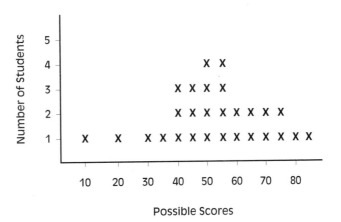

b. Frequency polygon

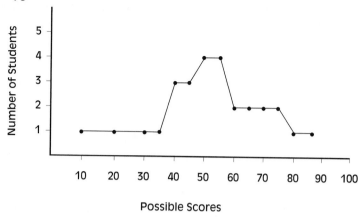

Figure 6.3 Students' scores on hypothetical language test

The numbers along the abscissa could just as easily have been the measurements of another type of organism, that is, scores measuring the language performance of language students, perhaps on a 100-point test as shown in Figure 6.3. Notice that their scores look reasonably normal, a distribution that is quite common among language students. Similar distributions would likely occur in graphs of their ages, their heights, or their IQ scores as well.

So the normal distribution is often observed in the behavior of language students. In fact, I have done so repeatedly over the years. However, like in the coin-flip examples, as the number of outcomes increases, the distributions will tend to look more and more normal. Hence, teachers should remember that in a small number of outcomes, the distribution may be somewhat lopsided as in Figures 6.2 and 6.3. As the number of outcomes increases, teachers can reasonably expect the distribution to become increasingly normal. However, they should never take this for granted.

Visual inspection of a distribution will provide valuable information about the normality of the distribution of events involved, that is, inspection can reveal just how wide, lopsided, or normal the distribution is. Remember also that a class of say 15 students is typically too small of a group to expect a perfectly normal distribution of scores on even the best norm-referenced test. But what is a large enough group? Well, 1,000,000 students would certainly be enough. But in more realistic terms, a good rule of thumb to remember is that events tend to approach normal distribution (if indeed it exists in the distribution) when the number of observations is about 30. This rule of thumb seems to work out fairly well in reality. However, in most norm-referenced test development situations, the developers should try to get the largest sample of students possible in order to maximize the chances of getting a normal distribution. After all, creating a normal distribution of scores is a major goal of norm-referenced tests.

In the previous chapters, I explained that criterion-referenced decision making may be almost completely independent of the normal distribution. Nonetheless, plotting the CRT scores of a group of students can never hurt. While CRT distributions are often quite different from NRT distributions, inspecting them can provide as much information about the CRT involved as the normal distribution does about NRTs.

Therefore, to the surprise of many teachers, the normal distribution of scores, or something close to it, really does occur if the purpose of the test is norm-referenced and the number of students is sufficiently large. Hence, teachers should never dismiss the idea of the normal distribution out of hand. With a group of say 160 students taking the Hypothetical Language Test, I could reasonably expect a normal distribution that would look something like the frequency polygon shown in Figure 6.4. This normal distribution illustrates a pattern that occurs and recurs in nature as well as in human behavior. More importantly, this pattern can help in sorting out the test performance of language students.

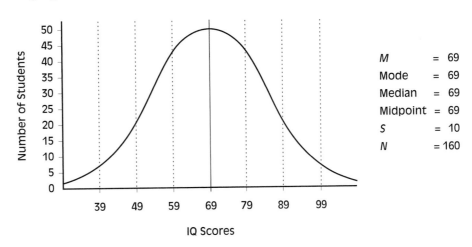

Figure 6.4 Mean and standard deviation in a normal distribution

CHARACTERISTICS OF NORMAL DISTRIBUTIONS

The two most important characteristics of a normal distribution were covered in the previous chapter: central tendency and dispersion. A third useful characteristic is the notion of percents in the distribution. One way this concept can be useful is in exploring the percents of students who fall within different score ranges on a test. Mostly, I will explore the notion of percents in terms of the normal distribution, but I will also discuss potential exceptions to the theoretical model of normal distribution later in the chapter.

Central tendency

Recall that **central tendency** indicates the typical behavior of a group and that four different estimates can be used: the mean, mode, median, and midpoint. All four of these estimates should be somewhere near the center or middle if a distribution is approximately normal. In fact, in a perfectly normal distribution, all four indicators of central tendency would fall on exactly the same score value as shown in Figure 6.4, right in the middle of the distribution. Note in Figure 6.4 that the mean, mode, median, and midpoint all equal the same value, 69. Also note that a perfect normal distribution is an ideal that we compare our real data to, knowing that there will always be some departures from such perfection.

Dispersion

Like central tendency, **dispersion** is predictable in a normal distribution. Remember that dispersion describes how the individual scores disperse, or vary, around the central tendency. This concept is commonly estimated statistically by using the range and standard deviation. In a theoretical normal distribution, testers expect the lowest score on the test (39 in Figure 6.4) and the highest score (99 in the example) to be exactly the same distance from the center, or mean. This is apparently true in the example. Both are 30 points above or below the mean. Thus, in this case, the **range** is symmetrical.

The other indicator of dispersion is, of course, the standard deviation. Conveniently, the standard deviation in Figure 6.4 is a nice round number, 10. Typically, the standard deviation in a normal distribution will fall in the pattern shown in Figure 6.4. One standard deviation above the mean ($+1S$) will fall on the score which is equal to the $M + 1S$, or in this case $69 + 10 = 79$. Similarly, two standard deviations below the mean will fall on the score, which is equal to $M - 2S$, or $69 - 20 = 49$. In short, the **standard deviation** is a regular distance measured in score points, which marks off certain portions of the distribution, each of which is equal in length along the abscissa.

Consider a hypothetical situation in which teachers administered an IQ (Intelligence Quotient) test to 947 elementary school students. The mean, mode, median, and midpoint all turned out to be 100, and the standard deviation was 15 with a range of 91 points (low score = 55 and high = 145). Can you imagine what such a distribution of scores might look like under these conditions? Try to make a rough sketch of the distribution. Start with a vertical line for the mean and assume that mean = mode = median = midpoint. Now put in a line for each of three standard deviations above the mean and three below, as well. Then draw a rough normal curve to fit the standard deviation markers. Finally, compare the drawing to the distribution shown in part A of the Application Exercises section at the end of the chapter. Both distributions should look about the same.

Percents/Percentages

Once central tendency and dispersion are understood as they apply to the normal distribution, some inferences can be made about the **percents**, or **percentages** (I use these terms interchangeably in this book to refer to the result of 100 times the proportion that results from dividing a subgroup of data points by the total number of data points) of students who are likely to fall within certain score ranges in the distribution. First, recall that the mean, mode, median, and midpoint should all be the same in a normal distribution. Also recall that the median is the score below which 50 percent of the cases should fall, and above which 50 percent should be. Given these facts, teachers can predict with fair assurance that 50 percent of their students' scores will be above the median (or mean, or mode, or midpoint) in a normal distribution. In like manner, researchers have repeatedly shown that 34.13 percent of the scores will fall within one standard deviation above the mean as shown in Figure 6.5. That means that about 34.13 percent of the students scored between 41 and 51 points on this particular test. Since the distribution under discussion is normal and therefore bell-shaped, the curve is symmetrical. Thus 34.13 percent of the students are also likely to score between 31 and 41 points on the test, or within one standard deviation below the mean.

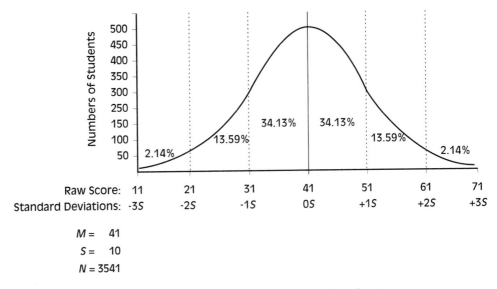

Figure 6.5 Approximate percentages under the normal distribution

Thus, in a normal distribution, about 68 percent of the students (34.13% + 34.13% = 68.26%) are likely to fall within one standard deviation on either side of the mean (plus or minus). But that leaves 31.74 percent of the students (100% − 68.26% = 31.74%) not yet explained in the distribution. Notice in Figure 6.5 that 13.59 percent of the students scored between the first and second standard deviations (+1S to +2S) above the mean (or between 51 and 61 score points in this particular distribution). Likewise, 13.59 percent will usually score between one standard deviation below the mean (−1S) and two standard deviations below the mean (−2S) (or between 21 and 31 score points in this case).

At this point, about 95.44 percent of the students in the distribution are accounted for (34.13% + 34.13% + 13.59% + 13.59% = 95.44%). The remaining 4.56 percent of the students are evenly divided above and below the mean: 2.14 percent in the area between the second and third standard deviations above the mean (+2S to +3S) and 2.14 percent in the area between the second and third standard deviations below the mean (−2S to −3S). This leaves .28 percent unexplained, .14 percent of whom would theoretically fall above +3S in the distribution, and .14 percent of whom would theoretically fall below −3S. This pattern of percents for students' scores within the various areas under the curve of the normal distribution is fairly regular and predictable, and some interesting things can be learned from such patterns, as I will explain in the next section.

LEARNING FROM DISTRIBUTIONS

I should stress that so far I have been discussing the theoretical normal distribution, that is, the normal distribution in its purest idealized form, or the distribution that testers would like to find in their NRT results. I am not implying that the same patterns do not occur in reality or that they do not exist. Nor am I skeptical about the existence of such distributions or about their characteristics. I know they exist in mathematical probability distributions (as shown in the distributions for coin flips), and I have often seen very close approximations occur in the test scores of my own students.

These distributions have also been observed by countless other testers and researchers in our discipline and in other disciplines. Such distributions do occur with the same regularity as the distribution of 50 percent heads and 50 percent tails for coin flips *if the number of scores is large enough and the test is at the appropriate level of difficulty.*

Once teachers have accepted the notion of normal distribution, they can benefit from a number of inferences that can be made from this predictable pattern of scores. In addition to knowing the percents of students who will score within certain score ranges on a measure, they can learn what percentiles mean in terms of exactly where an individual's score falls in the normal distribution. Perhaps more importantly, they can learn what happens when departures from the normal distribution occur (that is, when distributions are *not* normal) and what language testers do when things go wrong and deviate from normality.

Using percents/percentages

To review briefly the concept of percents, or percentages, if I ask teachers what percentage of their paychecks goes to buying food each week, they can figure it out easily. They would simply divide the amount of money they spend on food each week by the total amount they earn per week and multiply the result times 100. Similarly, referring back to Figure 6.5 (p. 121), the following questions should be easy to answer:

1. What percentage of students has scores above the mean?
2. What percentage has scores falling between 31 and 41 points on this test? Or scores between the mean and one standard deviation below the mean?
3. About what percentage fall within one standard deviation of the mean, plus and minus, that is, between 31 and 51 on this test?
4. Approximately, what percentage has scores below 31?

To answer Question 1, remember that 50 percent of the students should fall below the mean and 50 percent above it. For Question 2, examine the percentage shown in the space between the scores of 31 and 41. This should be 34.13 percent, right? For Question 3, add the two percentages given in the spaces between 31 and 51 (that is, 34.13% + 34.13% = 68.26%). To answer Question 4, find the percentage of the students who scored 31 or below (that is, 2.14% + 13.59% = 15.73%).

Percentiles, another category of inferences, stems from the foregoing notion of percents under the normal distribution. However, as I will explain, percentiles relate more directly to the performance of each individual student.

Percentiles

Percentiles are not any trickier than percentages. In effect, Question 4 in the previous section was about percentiles because it could be rephrased as follows: what percentile score would a score of 41 (the mean) represent? Such a score would represent about the 50th percentile. Thus a **percentile** can be defined as the total percentage of students who scored equal to or below a given point in the normal distribution.

Given this definition, what percentile would a score of 21 represent in Figure 6.5? Or 31? Or 51? Or 61? They would be about the 2nd (2.14% to be more precise), 16th (2.14% + 13.59% = 15.73 16%), 84th (50% + 34.13% = 84.13% ≈ 84%), and 98th (50% + 34.13% + 13.59% = 97.72% ≈ 98%) percentile, respectively, right? To make this idea somewhat more personal, any teacher should be able to think back to the percentile score he or she received on any standardized test (for instance, ACT, SAT, or GRE). Consider someone who scored in the 84th percentile on the GRE quantitative subtest. This means that her score was equal to or higher than 84 percent of the other students who took the test (but also lower than 16 percent).

The concepts of percent (or percentage), on the one hand, and percentile, on the other, are being used fairly carefully in this book. Since they were used in Chapter 1 to delineate very real differences between NRTs and CRTs, they will continue to enter the discussion. For the moment, remember that percents or percentages are associated with CRTs and that the percentiles just discussed are very much a part of NRT decisions as are the standardized scores that come next.

STANDARDIZED SCORES

One result of the different ideas discussed above has been the evolution of different scoring systems. The best place to begin discussing these different scoring systems is with the notions of raw scores and weighted scores. **Raw scores** are the actual numbers of items answered correctly on a test (assuming that each item gets one point). Most teachers are familiar with this type of score. **Weighted scores**, on the other hand, are those scores that are based on different weights for different questions on a test. For instance, a teacher might give 1 point for each of the first 20 questions on a test, then 3 points each for the next 10 questions, and 5 points each for the last 5 questions. This type of scoring is fairly common in language courses. Standardized scores are yet a third way to record, interpret, and report test results. Unfortunately, standardized scores are often somewhat mysterious to language teachers, so I will attempt now to make this concept more concrete.

Remember that percentiles, or **percentile scores**, indicate how a given student's score relates to the test scores of the entire group of students. Thus a student with a percentile score of 84 had a score equal to or higher than 84 percent of the other students in the distribution and a score equal to or lower than 16 percent. **Standard scores** represent a student's score in relation to how far the score varies from the test mean in terms of standard deviation units. The three most commonly reported types of standard scores are z, T, and CEEB scores.

z SCORES

The **z score** is a direct indication of the distance that a given raw score is from the mean in standard deviation units. The z score for each student can be calculated on any test by using the following formula:

$$z = \frac{X - M}{S}$$

X = student's score
M = mean
S = standard deviation

In other words, to calculate a student's z score, first subtract the mean from the student's score; then divide the result by the standard deviation for the test. If a student scored 51 in the distribution shown in Figure 6.5 (p. 121), where $M = 41$ and $S = 10$, the z score for that student would be as follows:

$$z = \frac{51 - 41}{10} = \frac{10}{10} = 1 = +1.0$$

This student's z score would be $+1.0$, or one standard deviation unit above the mean. If another student scored 21 raw score points on the same test, that student's z score would be:

$$z = \frac{21 - 41}{10} = \frac{-20}{10} = -2 = -2.0$$

The student with a z score of -2.0 is two standard deviations below the mean.

A quick look at Figure 6.6 (p. 125), will reveal that z scores, which are labeled three rows below the bottom of the distribution, are in exactly the same positions as those points marked off for the standard deviations just above them. Observe that the mean for the z scores is zero and that logically, the standard deviation for any set of z scores will be 1.0. Again, with reference to Figure 6.6, notice that the raw scores have a mean of 41 and a standard deviation of 10. In view of that information, answer the following questions:

1. How many standard deviations above the mean would a raw score of 51 be?
2. What would the z score be for a student whose raw score was 11?
3. What would the z score be for a raw score of 71?
4. Now the tricky one. How many standard deviations above or below the mean would a raw score of 41 be?

To answer Question 1, just remember that a raw score of 51 is one standard deviation above the mean (equivalent to a z score of $+1.0$). For Question 2, subtract the mean of 41 from the score of 11 ($11 - 41 = -30$) and divide the result by the standard deviation ($-30 \div 10 = -3.0$). Thus, $z = -3.0$. To answer Question 3, look at Figure 6.6 and decide how many standard deviations a score of 71 is above the mean. Three, right? If it is three standard deviations above the mean, the equivalent z score must be $+3.0$. To answer Question 4, just remember that in this example the mean is 41, so a raw score of 41 is neither above nor below the mean of 41 (it *is* the mean) and the mean for a set of z scores is always 0.0.

In short, a z score indicates the number of standard deviations that a student's score falls away from the mean. This value will always be plus ($+$) if the student scored above the mean, minus ($-$) if the score was below the mean, and zero if the student scored right on the mean. Note that z scores seldom turn out to be perfectly round numbers like those found in the examples above. These were used so that the demonstration would be clear. In fact, uneven z scores, like $+1.67$, 0.71, or -3.13, are much more likely to occur in real test data. Nevertheless, the steps involved in calculating z will be exactly the same.

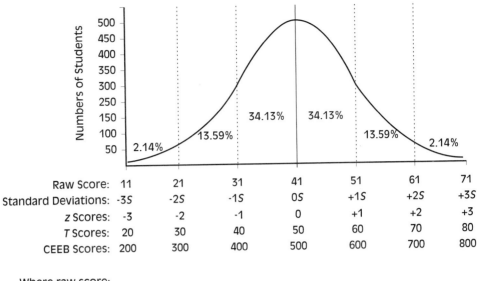

Raw Score:	11	21	31	41	51	61	71
Standard Deviations:	-3S	-2S	-1S	0S	+1S	+2S	+3S
z Scores:	-3	-2	-1	0	+1	+2	+3
T Scores:	20	30	40	50	60	70	80
CEEB Scores:	200	300	400	500	600	700	800

Where raw score:

$$M = 41$$
$$S = 10$$
$$N = 3541$$

Figure 6.6 Comparison of standard score distributions

T SCORES

When reporting z scores to students, several problems may arise. The first is that z scores can turn out to be both positive and negative. The second is that z scores are relatively small, usually ranging from about -3.00 through 0.00 to $+3.00$. Thirdly, z scores usually turn out to include several decimal places. Most students (and their parents) just will not understand if they get a score of -1 on a test. Or, 0.00. Or, even $+3.43$. Such scores are difficult to understand without a long and involved explanation like the one I have presented. One technique that testers have used to circumvent these problems is to transform the z scores into **T scores**. The T score transformation is done by rather arbitrarily multiplying the z score by 10 and adding 50. The formula for this simple transformation is:

$$T = 10z + 50$$

The following are some examples of applying this T score transformation:

For $z = -2$ $T = 10(-2) + 50$
$$= -20 + 50$$
$$= 30$$

For $z = 0$ $T = 10(0) + 50$
$$= 0 + 50$$
$$= 50$$

For $z = +1$ $T = 10(+1) + 50$
$$= 10 + 50$$
$$= 60$$

T scores at least give the illusion of looking more like "real" scores than z scores and will probably be more readily accepted by students and their parents. Note that row four of Figure 6.6 above shows a mean for T scores of 50 and a standard deviation of 10 for the distribution of T scores. In the same sense that the mean and standard deviation for a set of z scores should always be 0 and 1, respectively, the mean and standard deviation for a set of T scores will always be 50 and 10.

CEEB SCORES

College Entrance Examination Board (CEEB) scores (used for the SAT, GRE, TOEFL paper-and-pencil, and other tests) are another variation of the z score that is often reported in the U.S. To convert z scores to **CEEB scores**, multiply the z score by 100 and add 500, as follows:

$$CEEB = 100z + 500$$

The results for transforming the same z scores as those shown above for T scores would be as follows:

For $z = -2$ 　$\begin{aligned} CEEB &= 100(-2) + 500 \\ &= -200 + 500 \\ &= 300 \end{aligned}$

For $z = 0$ 　$\begin{aligned} CEEB &= 100(0) + 500 \\ &= 0 + 500 \\ &= 500 \end{aligned}$

For $z = +1$ 　$\begin{aligned} CEEB &= 100(+1) + 500 \\ &= 100 + 500 \\ &= 600 \end{aligned}$

Clearly, CEEB scores are very similar to T scores. In fact, they are exactly the same except that CEEB scores always have one extra zero. So to convert from a T score to CEEB, just add a zero. In other words, if a student's T score is 30, his or her CEEB score will be 300. The mean for a distribution of CEEB scores will always be 500 with standard deviation of 100. The fifth row of Figure 6.6 confirms these facts.

COMPUTER-BASED TOEFL SCORES

Educational Testing Service has recently created a new type of standardized scores for computer-based TOEFL scores, the subtest scores reportedly range from 0 to 30, while the total scores range from 0 to 300. To understand these scores and relate them to paper-and-pencil TOEFL scores, see ETS (2004).

STANDARDIZED AND PERCENTILE SCORES

Even though standardized scores are generally clear to test developers, percentile scores are more widely and easily understood by students, teachers, and the general public. Thus, percentile score reports will be clearer to many more people than standardized scores. Table 6.1 (p. 127), is a conversion table for z, T, and CEEB scores to percentiles, or vice versa. Note that these conversions assume that the raw scores are normally distributed and that the conversions are only accurate to the degree this assumption of normality is met.

Table 6.1 Converting standardized scores to percentiles

z	T	CEEB	Percentile	z	T	CEEB	Percentile
3.0	80	800	99.9	−0.1	49	490	46.0
2.9	79	790	99.8	−0.2	48	480	42.1
2.8	78	780	99.7	−0.3	47	470	38.2
2.7	77	770	99.6	−0.4	46	460	34.5
2.6	76	760	99.5	−0.5	45	450	30.9
2.5	75	750	99.4	−0.6	44	440	27.4
2.4	74	740	99.2	−0.7	43	430	24.2
2.3	73	730	98.9	−0.8	42	420	21.2
2.2	72	720	98.6	−0.9	41	410	18.4
2.1	71	710	98.2	−1.0	40	400	15.9
2.0	70	700	97.7	−1.1	39	390	13.6
1.9	69	690	97.1	−1.2	38	380	11.5
1.8	68	680	96.4	−1.3	37	370	9.7
1.7	67	670	95.5	−1.4	36	360	8.2
1.6	66	660	94.5	−1.5	35	350	6.7
1.5	65	650	93.3	−1.6	34	340	5.5
1.4	64	640	91.9	−1.7	33	330	4.5
1.3	63	630	90.3	−1.8	32	320	3.6
1.2	62	620	88.5	−1.9	31	310	2.9
1.1	61	610	86.4	−2.0	30	300	2.3
1.0	60	600	84.1	−2.1	29	290	1.8
0.9	59	590	81.6	−2.2	28	280	1.4
0.8	58	580	78.8	−2.3	27	270	1.1
0.7	57	570	75.8	−2.4	26	260	0.8
0.6	56	560	72.6	−2.5	25	250	0.6
0.5	55	550	69.1	−2.6	24	240	0.5
0.4	54	540	65.5	−2.7	23	230	0.4
0.3	53	530	61.8	−2.8	22	220	0.3
0.2	52	520	57.9	−2.9	21	210	0.2
0.1	51	510	54.0	−3.0	20	200	0.1
0.0	50	500	50.0				

To use Table 6.1, begin by finding the correct standard score column, then, find the actual standard score that is to be converted into a percentile, and look across the row for the percentile equivalent. For example, to convert a z score of 1.7 to a percentile score, look down the left column (labeled z) until you get to the z score of 1.7, then search three columns to the right (in the column for percentiles) and find the percentile equivalent, which turns out to be 95.5. All other conversions will work about the same way.

THE IMPORTANCE OF STANDARDIZED SCORES

All language teachers should understand standardized scores for a number of reasons. First, knowing about standardized scores can help teachers to understand standardized test score reports, which are often reported as *T*, or CEEB scores, and sometimes as percentiles. Many tests report their scores as standardized scores. For example, in language testing, ETS reports the paper-and-pencil TOEFL scores as T scores for the subtest scores (for listening comprehension, writing and analysis, and reading comprehension) and as CEEB scores for the total scores. Hence an *average* student in the normative population would have an overall score of 500 on this test. Computer-based TOEFL scores are on an entirely different scale ranging from 0 to 300. Convenient conversion tables are provided by Educational Testing Service at their website (ETS 2004).

Second, knowing about standardized scores can help language teachers examine the relationships between performances of different groups on two or more tests of different lengths. Such comparisons are difficult to make unless the scores are converted to a common scale. If the scores of interest are first converted to standardized scores and then compared, the problem of different lengths is effectively circumvented as shown in Figure 6.7 below. Notice in Figure 6.7 (Farhady 1982, p. 49) that a comparison is being made between the relative performances of graduate and undergraduate international students on six different ESL tests (which were all of different lengths). To make these comparisons, the researcher (Farhady 1982) first converted the raw scores into standardized T scores. He could equally well have used CEEB or even z scores.

Third, knowing about standardized scores can help teachers examine the relative position of any individual student on different tests or on different administrations of the same test. Thus students can be monitored over time, using different forms of the same overall proficiency test to see if their positions have changed in the distributions relative to other students.

In short, percentiles, and standardized scores, including z scores, T scores, and CEEB scores, are becoming increasingly common throughout the world. As such, knowing about standardized scores is essential to making responsible norm-referenced decisions and to reporting the results of norm-referenced tests.

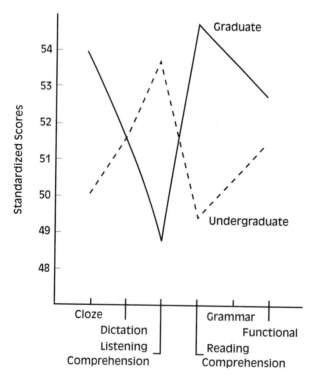

Figure 6.7 Difference due to university status in student performance on study measures

Skewed distributions

At this point, the primary characteristics of normal distributions and the types of inferences that can be drawn from them should be clear. However, for a variety of reasons, the distributions of language students' scores may not always be normal. Several things can go wrong, but the most common problem is that a distribution will be skewed. Skewing usually occurs because the test was either too easy or too difficult for the group of students who took it. However, as I will explain later, a skewed distribution is not always bad.

Skewedness

A **skewed** distribution is easy to spot by visual inspection of a histogram, bar graph, or frequency polygon of scores. A skewed distribution is one that does not have the prototypical symmetrical "bell" shape. For example, a distribution of family incomes in the United States would be skewed with most of us "scrunched up" near the bottom of the distribution and a few thousand very rich people spread way out toward the high end of the scale.

The scores may be scrunched up toward the higher end of the scale as shown in Figure 6.8a, in which case the distribution is negatively skewed. Or, the scores may be scrunched up toward the lower end of the scale as in Figure 6.8b. In this latter case, the distribution would be considered positively skewed. I have always found the assignment of the negative and positive distinctions in discussions of skewedness to be counter-intuitive. To keep them straight, I always try to remember that skewed distributions characteristically have a "tail" pointing in one of the two possible directions. When the tail is pointing in the direction of the lower scores (−), the distribution is said to be **negatively skewed**. When the tail points toward the higher scores (+), the distribution is **positively skewed**.

a. Negatively-skewed distribution

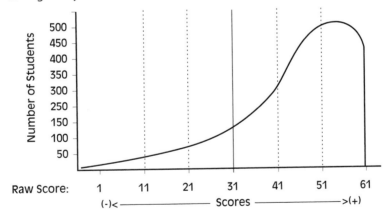

b. Positively skewed distribution

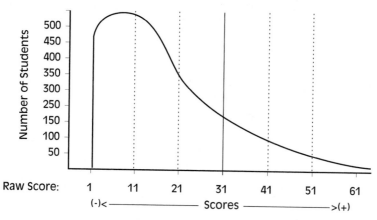

Figure 6.8 Skewed distributions

A number of implications may arise from such non-normal distributions. First, many of the statistics used to analyze tests assume a normal distribution. In most cases, such statistics are based on comparisons of the central tendency and dispersion of scores. When a distribution of test scores is non-normal, perhaps negatively skewed, most of the students have scored well. Thus they are "scrunched up" toward the top of the scale and the usual indicators of dispersion (range, standard deviation, and variance) will be depressed by what is sometimes called a **ceiling effect**. If all the students have scored so high on a measure that the dispersion is depressed, the related statistics may be impossible to interpret. Under such conditions, particularly in examining NRT results, the assumption of normality that underlies most of the common testing statistics is not met. Thus applying such statistics may become an exercise in futility. The results of such analyses will be difficult, if not impossible, to interpret responsibly. As a result, all language testers must learn to spot skewed distributions in their norm-referenced test results so that they can make proper interpretations based on the statistics being used.

In other words, when language testers look at the descriptive statistics for a test, a picture of the distribution should come to mind. Consider a test administered to 112 students, which has a range of 56 raw score points (45 to 100), a mean of 71, and a standard deviation of 9. What would the distribution look like? Can you draw it? Consider another administration of the same test where the range is 70 points (31 to 100), but the mean is 92, and the standard deviation is 8.25. What would this distribution look like? The distribution would be skewed, right? Notice that the top score is 100 and the mean is 92, so only one standard deviation of 8.25 can fit between the mean of 92 and the top score of 100. So the distribution is skewed, but which way (positive or negative) is it skewed? Remember, when in doubt, just sketch out the distribution and examine the *tail*. Which way is the tail pointing—toward the low scores (negative skew) or toward the high scores (positive skew)?

Another relatively easy way to detect a skewed distribution is to examine the indicators of central tendency. As pointed out in the previous chapter, the four indicators of central tendency (mean, mode, median, and midpoint) should be the same, or very similar, if the distribution is normal. Conversely, if they are very different, the distribution is probably skewed. In fact, the more skewed a distribution is, the more these indicators are likely to diverge. Note also that they will diverge in different directions for positive and negative skewing. As pointed out in Figure 6.9, a negatively-skewed distribution will likely have indicators that vary from low to high as follows: midpoint, mean, median, and mode. A positively-skewed distribution will usually have indicators that vary in the opposite order from low to high: mode, median, mean, and midpoint. Thus when differences in central tendency estimates occur, especially large differences, remember to inspect a histogram of the scores to check for skewing.

a. Negatively-skewed distribution

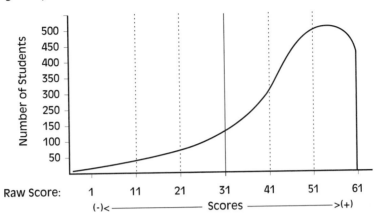

b. Positively-skewed distribution

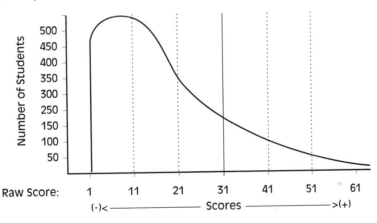

Figure 6.9 Skewed distributions

As I will explain below, a skewed distribution on an NRT usually means that the test is not functioning well with the particular group of students. However, on a CRT, a skewed distribution may be the very pattern that teachers would most like to find in the scores of their students. For instance, on a pre-test, before the students have studied the material in a course, the teacher would want most of the students to score rather poorly on the course CRT with perhaps a few students doing better than the rest. Such a positively-skewed distribution at the beginning of a course would indicate that most of the students do not know the material and therefore need to take the course. At the end of the term, the teacher would hope that most of the students had learned the material and therefore would score very well on the CRT. In this case, a negatively-skewed distribution would indicate that most of the students had learned the material well and that the teaching and learning had gone well. As with many other aspects of language testing, interpretation of the distributions of scores is related to the purpose of administering the test.

Peaked distributions

Even if a distribution is not skewed, the height of the distribution relative to its width is important. **Kurtosis** is one way of looking at the degree to which the curve in the middle of a distribution is steep, or the degree to which the distribution is peaked. If the height of the peak, relative to the width, is too different from what would be expected in a normal distribution, that is, either too peaked (referred to as **leptokurtic**) or too flat (referred to as **platykurtic**), problems may arise in applying testing statistics. Hence testers should always check for this condition. Simple inspection of a histogram will reveal the degree to which the distribution appears to have a normal shape, or depart from that shape.

Abnormally skewed or peaked distributions may both be signs of trouble in a norm-referenced test, so language testers should always verify, at least by visual inspection of a graph of the scores, that the distribution is normal.

NRT AND CRT DISTRIBUTIONS

All the foregoing discussion of the normal distribution and standardized scores applies to interpreting the results of norm-referenced proficiency or placement tests. Recall from Chapter 1 that the decisions based on NRTs are called relative decisions and that the interpretation of the scores focuses on the relative position of each student vis-à-vis the rest of the students with regard to some general ability. Thus, the normal distribution and each student's position in that distribution, as reflected by their percentile or standardized score, make sense as viable tools for score interpretation.

Recall also that interpreting the results of criterion-referenced diagnostic and achievement tests is entirely different. CRT decisions are labeled absolute because they focus, not on the student's position relative to other students, but rather on the percent of material that each student knows, largely without reference to the other students. Thus, at the beginning of a course, the distribution of scores on a CRT is likely to be positively skewed if the students actually need to learn the material covered in the course. However, at the end of the course, if the test reflects the course objectives, the teacher hopes the students will all score fairly high. In other words, the distribution of scores at the end of instruction will be negatively skewed on a good CRT if reasonably efficient language teaching and learning are taking place.

Item selection for CRTs involves retaining those items which students answer poorly at the beginning of the course (that is, they need to learn the material) and answer well at the end of instruction (that is, they learned it). This pattern will show up in the *IF*s (recall that item facility is the proportion of students who answered a particular item correctly) on the pre-test and post-test as well as in the *DI* (recall that the difference index is calculated by subtracting the pre-test *IF* from the post-test *IF*). The result of revising the CRTs on the basis of these item statistics will usually be that any existing differences between the pre-test and post-test distributions will be magnified. Thus, ideal distributions for a CRT would be like those shown in Figure 6.10. So certain conditions exist under which a skewed distribution is not only desirable but also something that testers may aim for in revising their CRTs.

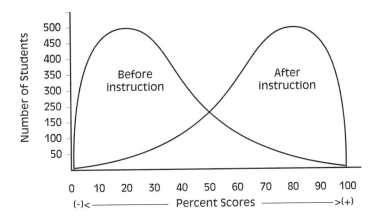

Figure 6.10 Ideal CRT distributions

The trick is not just to create the negatively-skewed distribution at the end of instruction. After all, such a distribution can be created by simply making the test much too easy for the students. The trick is to create, *through instruction*, a negatively-skewed distribution on a well-designed test that previously indicated a positively-skewed distribution before the instruction took place. In other words, students who needed the instruction (as shown by the positively-skewed pre-test distribution) learned from that instruction (as shown by the negatively-skewed post-test results).

One problem that arises in trying to set up this type of test analysis is the potential problem of practice effect. The practice effect occurs when the scores on a second administration are higher, not because of instruction, but rather because the students have already experienced, or "practiced," the same test on a previous occasion. One way around this is called counterbalancing. To do counterbalancing, testers need to develop two parallel forms (for instance, forms A and B) of the CRT so that they are very similar, objective-by-objective. During the pre-test, half of the students (randomly selected) take Form A and half take Form B. After instruction, the first half then takes Form B and the second half takes Form A. Note that putting the students' names on the tests ahead of time for the second administration will help insure that the right students take the right form. Counterbalancing insures that no student takes exactly the same test twice. Hence, the practice effect is minimized.

At the same time, the appropriate CRT statistics can still be applied. Recall that the difference index is usually based on an intervention strategy in which the teacher administers a pre-test before instruction, intervenes by teaching whatever is relevant, and then administers a post-test. Even though no student took the same test twice, the difference index can be calculated for each item on each form by subtracting the *IF* for the pre-test results from the *IF* for the post-test. Even though the students are not the same on the pre-test and post-test results for each item, they do represent non-masters at the beginning and masters at the end of the course, so *DI*s based on these results are legitimate. Selecting "good" items and revising on the basis of these statistics remains logical, as do any other comparisons of the distributions of scores that the teacher may wish to make. In other words, the teacher can make inferences from the performances on these two forms in a pre-test and post-test, but without worrying too much about a potential practice effect.

You should be pleased to learn that all the standardized scores discussed in this chapter can be calculated using formulas in your spreadsheet. The first exercise calculates a set of z scores in the *Excel*™ program. You will type the student names and test scores in the spreadsheet, and then enter formulas to calculate z, T, and CEEB scores. Finally, you will copy the standardized test score formulas to the other cells in the spreadsheet to perform calculations for all the students.

Enter Headings, Data, Mean, and Standard Deviation

1. Open the *Excel* program on your computer.
2. Using Screen 6.1 as a guide, type the following headings:
   In Cell A1, type **Name**.
   In Cell B1, type **Raw Score**.
   In Cell C1, type z.
   In Cell D1, type T.
   In Cell E1, type **CEEB**.
   In Cell A19, type **Mean**.
   In Cell A20, type **SD**.

Screen 6.1 Calculating z, T and CEEB scores using *Excel*

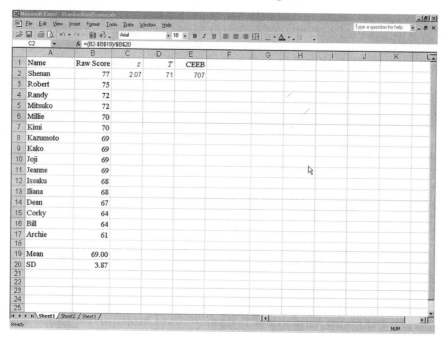

3. Type the student names in Cells A2 to A17, and then type the raw scores in Cells B2 to B17, as seen in Screen 6.1.
4. In Cell B19, enter **69.00**, which is the figure for the mean calculated for the class.
5. In Cell B20, enter **3.87**, which is the figure for the standard deviation.

Enter z, T, and CEEB test score formulas.

1. In Cell C2, type the formula **=(B2−$B$19)/$B$20** to calculate the z score for Shenan. The dollar sign is inserted in front of B and 19, and B and 20, so that the column and row will not change when the formula is copied to the other cells. The mean is subtracted from the score of 77, and then divided by the standard deviation, which calculates the z score of 2.07 in this case.
2. If the figure in C2 has multiple decimal places (i.e., 2.067183), round the number to two decimal places. Click **Format**, **Cells**, and then click the *Number* tab. Under *Category*, select **Number**, and then type **2** in the *Decimal places* box.
3. To calculate the T score, click Cell D2, and then type **=(10*C2)+50**. The resulting T calculation will be 71.
4. To calculate the CEEB score, click Cell E2, and then type **=(100*C2)+500**. The resulting CEEB calculation will be 707.

Copy the formulas and verify the results.

Entering all the formulas shown in Screen 6.1 for Shenan's z, T, and CEEB scores was not an easy task. However, as you will remember from earlier exercises, the payoff comes when you are able to copy those formulas into other rows. Follow the steps below to calculate the scores for the other students, and then verify the figures using the mean and standard deviation formulas.

1. Highlight Cells C2 to E2, and then click **Edit**, **Copy**. A moving box will display around the cells.
2. Click Cells C3 to E17, and then click **Edit**, **Paste**. The results of the calculations will display in the cells for the other students, as seen in Screen 6.2.

Screen 6.2 Copying the standardized score calculations

	A	B	C	D	E	F
1	Name	Raw Score	z	T	CEEB	
2	Shenan	77	2.07	71	707	
3	Robert	75	1.55	65	655	
4	Randy	72	0.77	58	577	
5	Mitsuko	72	0.77	58	577	
6	Millie	70	0.26	53	526	
7	Kimi	70	0.26	53	526	
8	Kazumoto	69	0.00	50	500	
9	Kako	69	0.00	50	500	
10	Joji	69	0.00	50	500	
11	Jeanne	69	0.00	50	500	
12	Issaku	68	-0.26	47	474	
13	Iliana	68	-0.26	47	474	
14	Dean	67	-0.52	45	448	
15	Corky	64	-1.29	37	371	
16	Bill	64	-1.29	37	371	
17	Archie	61	-2.07	29	293	
18						
19	Mean	69.00	0.00	50.00	500.00	
20	SD	3.87	1.00	10.00	100.00	

3. Click Cells B19 and B20, and then click **Edit, Copy**. Paste the results in Cells C19 to E20. The calculations for the mean and standard deviation for the z, T, and CEEB scores are used as a crosscheck to verify that the student formulas are correct.

4. Save the spreadsheet (perhaps as Screen 6.2), as the student names can also be used in Chapter 7.

REVIEW QUESTIONS

1. What is the probability of drawing a queen of spades from a deck of 52 cards? How many expected outcomes are involved? How many possible outcomes? What is the ratio of expected to possible outcomes? What is the probability of drawing the queen of hearts? Of drawing any queen?

2. Draw an ideal normal distribution. Start by drawing two lines—an ordinate and an abscissa. Then mark off a reasonable set of scores along the abscissa and some sort of frequency scale along the ordinate. Make sure that you represent the mean, mode, median, and midpoint with a vertical line down the middle of the distribution. Also include six lines to represent each of three standard deviations above and below the mean. Remember to include the following standard deviation labels: $-3S$, $-2S$, $-1S$, 0, $+1S$, $+2S$, $+3S$. Then actually draw a normal curve to fit the data.

3. Now go back and put in the approximate percents of students that you would expect to find within each score range on the distribution (between the lines that mark off the standard deviations).

4. Also label the main z scores that would correspond to the standard deviation lines. And the equivalent T scores. And CEEB scores, too.

5. About what percent of students would you expect to score within plus and minus one standard deviation of the mean?

6. About what percentage of students would you expect to score below a z score of -1? Below a T score of 60? Below a CEEB score of 500?

7. In Table 1, what would the percentile score be for a *z* score of +1? A *T* score of 40? A CEEB score of 650?

8. What would a positively skewed distribution look like? What about a negatively-skewed distribution? For what category of tests would skewed distributions be a sign that there is something wrong? For what category of tests would a skewed distribution be a good sign? How is this possible and how does it work?

9. Why is counterbalancing a good idea in a CRT development project? How does it work? And what is the practice effect?

10. Do you now believe that normal distribution occurs? Under what conditions? Do you now know what the normal distribution indicates and what you should do for various kinds of tests if the normal distribution does not occur for some reason?

APPLICATION EXERCISES

A. Look at the frequency polygon and answer the questions that follow:

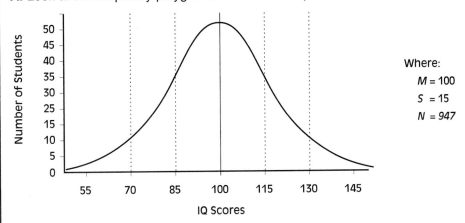

Where:
M = 100
S = 15
N = 947

A1. What percentile score would an IQ score of 85 represent?

A2. About what percentage of students scored between 70 and 115?

A3. If Iliana had a score of 177 on this test, about how many standard deviations would she be above the mean? Does this mean that she is really intelligent?

A4. What would Iliana's *z* score be? *T* score? CEEB score?

B. In the table below, the raw score mean is 50, and the raw score standard deviation is 7. Fill in all the missing spaces by using the available information and what you now know about distributions and standardized scores.

Student	Raw score	z score	T score	CEEB score
A	64		70	
	___	___	___	___
B	50			
	___	___	___	___
C		−1.0		
	___	___	___	___
D		−1.5		350
	___	___	___	___
ETC.				

C. Study the table below and answer the questions that follow:

Test	Raw scores			Standardized scores	
	k*	**M**	**S**	**M**	**S**
A	110	60	25	500	100
B	75	60	15	50	10
C	50	11	4	0	1
* Remember, k = number of items on the test					

C1. Which test (A, B, or C) shows standardized scores that are probably:

  a. z scores? _____

  b. T scores? _____

  c. CEEB scores? _____

C2. In raw scores, which test has:

  a. the largest standard deviation? _____

  b. the lowest mean? _____

  c. the largest number of items? _____

  d. a negatively-skewed distribution? _____

C3. In test C, a raw score of:

  a. 11 would equal what z score? _____

  b. 7 would equal what T score? _____

  c. 19 would equal what CEEB score? _____

D. In Table 5.1 of the previous chapter, there were some scores given for Robert, Millie, and others. Now calculate standardized scores from these raw scores. To make your task a little easier, assume that the mean was 69.00 and the standard deviation is a nice even 4.00. Lay out a new table that gives not only their raw scores, but also the z, T, and CEEB score for each student.

E. Collect some data from your students, plot them out, and decide for yourself whether they are normally distributed. Try doing all of this in your spreadsheet program. Remember to collect a fairly large number of scores, or ages, or heights, or whatever you decide to measure.

CHAPTER 7

CORRELATION IN LANGUAGE TESTING

INTRODUCTION

In the last two chapters, I discussed the importance of descriptive statistics and various interpretations of those statistics—whether for adopting, developing, or adapting norm-referenced or criterion-referenced tests. However, a test can have wonderful descriptive statistics, produce scores that are beautifully distributed and still have problems. Before examining these potential problems, which have to do with the reliability, dependability, and validity of tests, I must cover a set of useful test analysis tools called correlational analyses. This family of statistical analyses can help teachers understand the degree of relationship between two sets of numbers. For example, a teacher might want to know if there is a real relationship between attendance (number of days in class) and classroom achievement (grades in the same class expressed on a 1.00 to 4.00 scale), or if it is just in her imagination. Correlational analyses can not only help determine the degree of relationship between two sets of numbers like these, but also whether that relationship is significant (in a statistical sense), as well as meaningful (in a logical sense). With these concepts in hand, teachers will then be in a position to effectively consider test reliability, dependability, and validity, which are presented in Chapters 8 to 10.

PRELIMINARY DEFINITIONS

One of the most valuable sets of analytical techniques covered in this book is the correlational family of statistics. The purpose of **correlational analyses** in language testing is to examine how the scores on two tests compare with regard to dispersing, or spreading out, the students. Essentially, correlation is the "go-togetherness" of two sets of scores. Figure 7.1a shows two sets of scores lined up in columns. Notice that the two sets are in exactly the same order, that is, the student who scored highest on Test X also scored highest on Test Y; the same is true for the second highest, third highest, fourth highest, and so forth.

The degree to which two sets of scores **covary**, or vary together, is estimated statistically by calculating a **correlation coefficient**. Such a coefficient is a numerical value that can reach a magnitude as high as +1.0 if the relationship between the scores on two tests is perfect and positive, that is, in the same direction (see Figure 7.1a). Alternatively, a correlation coefficient can be negative with a value as strong as −1.0 if the relationship is perfectly negative, that is, in the opposite direction (see Figure 7.1b). A zero can also result if no relationship can be shown between the two sets of numbers.

To begin doing correlational analysis, testers line up the scores side-by-side as shown in Figures 7.1a and 7.1b. Setting up a table of scores is easy. Consider the scores tabled in 7.1a. All that is necessary is that three columns be labeled, in this case one for the students' names, a second for their scores on Test X, and a third for their scores on Test Y. This table also organizes the data such that each row in the table represents one student's record for these tests.

A scatterplot of the information will also prove useful in examining correlations. A **scatterplot** is a form of visual representation (similar to the histogram, bar graph, and frequency polygon described in Chapter 5) that allows for representing two sets of scores at the same time and examining their relationship. Usually, the increments in the range of possible scores for one test will be marked off along the X axis (or abscissa) and those for the other test along the Y axis (or ordinate). A mark is then plotted for each student at the point where the coordinates for that student's two scores meet. For instance in the scatterplot shown in Figure 7.1a, Dean scored 21 on Test Y and 20 on Test X. If you were to draw a line straight up from 20 on the horizontal axis and another line straight across from a score of 21 on Test Y, they would intersect at the point represented by a diamond (♦) in the figure. If you repeat the process for each of the other students, the results will look like the diamonds plotted in the same figure. Notice that the scatterplot presents exactly the same information as the corresponding table, but that the scatterplot displays the data in an entirely different way.

a. A perfect positive correlation

Students	Text X	Test Y
Dean	21	20
Randy	31	30
Iliana	41	40
Jeanne	51	50
Kimi	61	60
Shenan	71	70
Kako	81	80

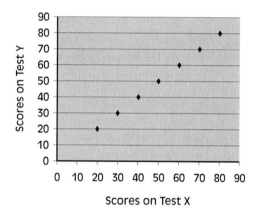

b. A perfect negative correlation

Students	Text W	Test Z
Dean	12	61
Randy	22	51
Iliana	32	41
Jeanne	42	31
Kimi	52	21
Shenan	62	11
Kako	72	1

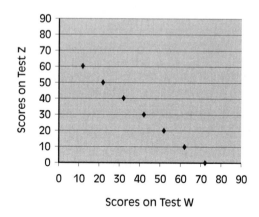

Figure 7.1 Examples of correlation

A correlation coefficient that represents a perfect relationship like that shown in Figure 7.1a will be positive and take on the maximum value of +1.0. Such a correlation will occur only if the two sets of scores line up the students in exactly the same order, that is, only if the ranking of the scores is 100 percent similar. Such a correlation coefficient indicates a very strong positive correlation and the plot for a perfect correlation, positive or negative, will always form a straight line like that shown in Figure 7.1a. This line is the reason such relationships are called linear (more about this below).

A correlation coefficient can also be negative in value and as high in magnitude as −1.0. For such a high negative correlation to occur, the relationship between the two sets of scores must be exactly the opposite, or negative, as shown in Figure 7.1b. In other words, as the scores on one test go up, the scores on the other go down, or put another way, students who scored high on one test scored low on the other and vice versa. The negative sign in front of the coefficient shows that the relationship between the two tests is in the opposite direction. Though negative, the relationship shown in Figure 7.1b is nevertheless very strong because students who have high scores on Test W scored low on Test Z, and vice versa.

When no relationship at all is found between two sets of numbers, the coefficient will be 0 or something very close to 0. Coefficients either positive or negative up to about +.40, or −.40 indicate fairly weak relationships. Relatively strong correlations would be those that range from +.80 to +1.0, or −.80 to −1.00. Just remember that the further a coefficient is from 0 toward +1.0 or −1.0 the stronger the relationship is between whatever sets of numbers are involved.

Table 7.1 Correlation of two sets of test scores

Students	Test X	Test Y
Shenan	97	77
Robert	85	75
Randy	82	64
Mitsuko	71	72
Millie	70	70
Kimi	70	70
Kazumoto	69	69
Kako	68	69
Joji	67	69
Jeanne	67	69
Issaku	67	68
Iliana	66	72
Dean	62	67
Corky	59	68
Bill	40	64
Archie	31	61

Summary of descriptive statistics:

		Test X	Test Y
N	=	16	16
M	=	66.94	69.00
S	=	15.01	3.87
Range	=	67	17

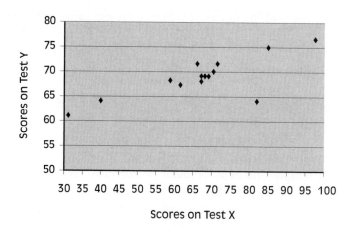

Table 7.1 and the associated scatterplot present a slightly more realistic situation because real scores seldom line up perfectly. This correlation coefficient is called the **Pearson product-moment correlation coefficient**, which is the statistic of choice for comparing two sets of continuous scale data like the scores shown in the table. In this case, the correlation coefficient turns out to be .78 (the calculations for this statistic will be explained below). A coefficient of this magnitude indicates that there is a fairly strong positive correlation between these two groups of data. In other words, the two tests are spreading the students out in very much the same way. Note also, though, that the students are not in exactly the same order on the two tests and that the distances between students are not exactly the same on each scale. In fact, the descriptive statistics given at the bottom of Table 7.1 indicate that the two tests are different in central tendency (as indicated by the means) and even more so in dispersion (as indicated by the standard deviations and ranges). Nevertheless, the correlation coefficient shows that the two sets of scores "go together" to a fairly high degree.

CALCULATING THE PEARSON PRODUCT-MOMENT CORRELATION COEFFICIENT

Calculating the Pearson product-moment correlation coefficient, if taken step-by-step, is not any more demanding than calculating the standard deviation was in Chapter 5. It looks very daunting, but by taking it in steps, you will find it's actually quite easy (or perhaps: boring, but easy). The Pearson product-moment correlation coefficient is usually symbolized by r, or r_{xy} (because it is also known as the regression coefficient).

As mentioned above, the process of looking at the degree of relationship between two sets of numbers begins with lining up the scores for two tests administered to the same group of students, or collecting any two sets of continuous scale information (like age, years of language study, and so forth). Ultimately, pairs of continuous scale numbers for each student should be lined up in two columns like those shown in Table 7.1. In cases where there are **missing data**, that is, when there is only one score for a given student, leave that student out of the analysis. Once the data are lined up properly in two columns with no missing data, everything is ready for calculating a Pearson product-moment correlation coefficient.

The formula for the Pearson product-moment correlation coefficient will be explained in terms of two sets of test scores because this is a language testing book, but remember the numbers could equally well be any other continuous scale data. The best formula for understanding what you are doing while calculating the Pearson product-moment correlation coefficient is the following:

$$r_{xy} = \frac{\Sigma(X - M_x)(Y - M_y)}{N S_x S_y}$$

r_{xy} = Pearson product-moment correlation coefficient
X = each student's score on Test X
M_x = mean on Test X
S_x = standard deviation on Test X
Y = each student's score on Test Y
M_y = mean on Test Y
S_y = standard deviation on Test Y
N = the number of students who took the two tests

Notice that the formula has many elements, but that they are all familiar. For example, N, M, S, and even $(X - M)$ should all be familiar to you from previous formulas. Here, however, you will notice that some of the symbols have a subscript x as is the case for M_x and S_x. These subscripts simply mean that these particular symbols are the mean and standard deviation for Test X. Similarly, M_y and S_y are the mean and standard deviation for Test Y. Thus $(X - M_x)$ would be the deviation of each student's score from the mean on Test X, and $(Y - M_y)$ would be the same for Test Y. Given this information, calculating a correlation coefficient is not difficult at all. [Note that, doing these calculations by hand, you may find small differences between your calculations and what you see in the table. These differences are probably due to differences in rounding. This data was calculated in a spreadsheet program, which carries all of the numbers in memory to 14 places to the right of the decimal at all times, regardless of what is showing. If you did the same calculations by hand, you were probably rounding as you went along, and the cumulative differences show up increasingly as you move from left to right. The differences are minor, and are not very important.]

Table 7.2 Calculating a correlation coefficient (for Table 7.1 data)

Column 1 Students	2 X	−	3 M_x	=	4 $(X-M_x)$	5 y	−	6 M_y	=	7 $(y-M_y)$	8 $(y-M_y)(y-M_y)$
Shenan	97	−	66.94	=	30.06	77	−	69.00	=	8.00	240.50
Robert	85	−	66.94	=	18.06	75	−	69.00	=	6.00	108.38
Randy	82	−	66.94	=	15.06	64	−	69.00	=	−5.00	−75.31
Mitsuko	71	−	66.94	=	4.06	72	−	69.00	=	3.00	12.19
Millie	70	−	66.94	=	3.06	70	−	69.00	=	1.00	3.06
Kimi	70	−	66.94	=	3.06	70	−	69.00	=	1.00	3.06
Kazumoto	69	−	66.94	=	2.06	69	−	69.00	=	0.00	0.00
Kako	68	−	66.94	=	1.06	69	−	69.00	=	0.00	0.00
Joji	67	−	66.94	=	0.06	69	−	69.00	=	0.00	0.00
Jeanne	67	−	66.94	=	0.06	69	−	69.00	=	0.00	0.00
Issaku	67	−	66.94	=	0.06	68	−	69.00	=	−1.00	−0.06
Iliana	66	−	66.94	=	−0.94	72	−	69.00	=	3.00	−2.81
Dean	62	−	66.94	=	−4.94	67	−	69.00	=	−2.00	9.88
Corky	59	−	66.94	=	−7.94	68	−	69.00	=	−1.00	7.94
Bill	40	−	66.94	=	−26.94	64	−	69.00	=	−5.00	134.69
Archie	31	−	66.94	=	−35.94	61	−	69.00	=	−8.00	287.50

$$\Sigma(X-M_x)(Y-M_y) = 729.00$$

N	= 16	16
M	= 66.94	69.00
S	= 15.01	3.87
Range	= 67	17

$$r_{xy} = \frac{\Sigma(X - M_x)(Y - M_y)}{NS_xS_y} = \frac{729.00}{16(15.01)(3.87)} = \frac{729.00}{929.90} = .7838552 \approx .78$$

Table 7.2 shows the calculations for the data set shown in Table 7.1:

1. The data were copied and the mean and standard deviation were calculated for each set. These descriptive statistics are shown at the bottom of columns 2 and 5 of Table 7.2 for tests X and Y, respectively.

2. The means for Test X and for Test Y were placed repeatedly in columns 3 and 6 so that the mean could easily be subtracted from each score on tests X and Y. The results of these repeated subtractions were placed in columns 4 and 7 for tests X and Y, respectively. For example, Shenan's score of 97 on Test X (column 2) minus the mean of 66.94 on Test X (column 3) is 30.06 (column 4), or *his deviation from the mean on Test X*; his score of 77 on Test Y (column 5) minus the mean of 69.00 on Test Y (column 6) is 8.00 (column 7), or *his deviation from the mean on Test Y*. This process was repeated for each student.

3. The results of the subtractions for both tests X and Y (see columns 4 and 7) were then multiplied times each other for each student and the results were placed in column 8. For instance, Shenan's deviation from the mean of 30.06 on Test X (column 4) was multiplied by his deviation from the mean of 8.00 on Test Y (column 7). The result, or the **cross-product**, of Shenan's deviations, was 240.50 (column 8). This process was repeated for each student.

4. The cross-products for all the students (column 8) were then summed (added up) as shown at the bottom of column 8. This resulted in a value of 729.00.

5. Returning to the formula for the correlation coefficient (below the table), the sum of the cross-products, 729.00, was substituted into the formula as the numerator. The values 16, 15.01, and 3.87 were then appropriately substituted (from the

information given below the table to the left) for N, S_x, and S_y, respectively, in the denominator of the formula. When the three numbers in the denominator were multiplied, the result was $16 \times 15.01 \times 3.87 = 929.90$. Dividing the numerator by the denominator, the result was $729.00 \div 929.90 = .7838552$, or approximately .78.

Clearly then, calculating the Pearson product-moment correlation coefficient really is not difficult, though it may be a bit tedious sometimes. Hence such calculations are usually done on a computer or advanced hand calculator if at all possible. However, with this formula in hand, teachers are in a position to calculate this correlation coefficient by hand. More importantly, working through the formula should have removed some of the mystery that surrounds this statistic.

However, calculating the correlation coefficient is far from the final step. The tester must also check the assumptions that underlie this statistic to make sure that they have been met and must interpret the results in terms of statistical significance and meaningfulness.

ASSUMPTIONS OF THE PEARSON PRODUCT-MOMENT CORRELATION COEFFICIENT

One requirement of the Pearson r, which is really a design requirement, is that the two sets of numbers must both be continuous scales, rather than ordinal or nominal scales (see the discussion in Chapter 5 (pp. 95–96) for definitions of these terms). It is not that correlational analysis cannot be applied to nominal and ordinal scales, but statistics other than the Pearson product-moment correlation coefficient must be used to do so.

In addition to the continuous-scale design requirement, there are three assumptions that underlie the Pearson product-moment correlation coefficient:

1. Independence–each pair of scores is independent from all other pairs.
2. Normally distributed–each of the two sets of numbers is normally distributed.
3. Linear–the relationship between the two sets of scores is linear.

These assumptions must be met for the statistic to be properly applied and interpreted.

The assumption of **independence** requires that each pair of scores be unrelated to all other pairs of scores. In other words, when the pairs of test scores are in two columns, no student should appear twice in either column (because, for example, he or she took the two tests twice) and thus created two pairs of scores related to each other, and no student should have copied the answers from another student (also creating related pairs). In short, to properly apply the Pearson r, there must be no systematic association between pairs of scores. Hence, language teachers who wish to use correlational analysis should insure that this assumption is met during the test administration and analysis stages.

The second assumption is that each of the sets of scores must be **normally distributed**. Another way to state this would be that neither of the two distributions can be skewed (for more on skewed distributions, see Chapter 6, p. 129). If one or the other is not normal, the magnitude of any resulting correlation coefficients will be affected. Typically, if either distribution is skewed the value of the correlation coefficient will be depressed to an unpredictable degree. The normality assumption can usually be checked by examining the descriptive statistics for each test or by visually inspecting histograms, bar graphs, or frequency polygons of the distributions of scores for skewedness. The importance of checking for skewedness cannot be over-emphasized. While perfect normality is not assumed here, you should look to make sure that neither of the distributions is markedly skewed, that is, markedly non-normal.

The most important of the three assumptions is that the relationship between the two sets of scores should be **linear**. In other words, fitting a straight line through the points on the scatterplot must make sense. Figures 7.1a and b show ideal situations where a perfect correlation is represented by a perfectly straight line. A glance at the scatterplot in Figure 7.1a will give you an idea of what the ideal straight line relationship for a perfect positive correlation (+1.00) looks like. And, scatterplot 7.1b illustrates the same thing, but for a perfect negative correlation (−1.00). In reality, such perfect linear relationships are seldom obtained.

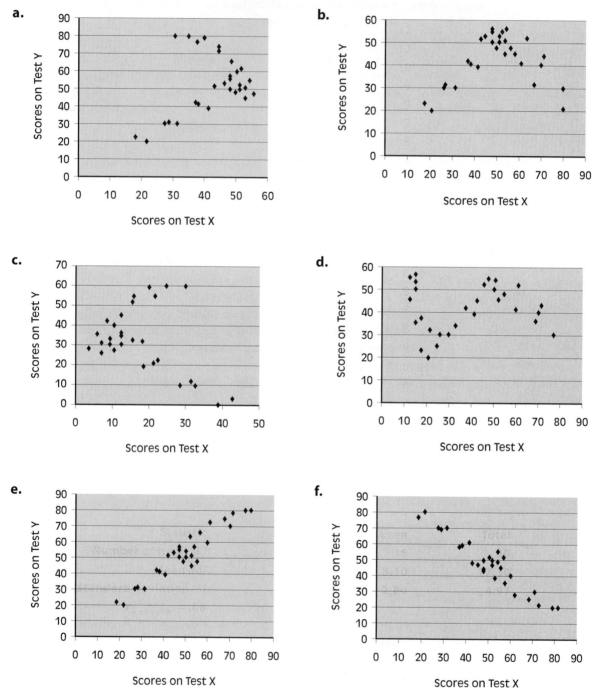

Figure 7.2: Curvilinear (a. - d.) & linear (e. and f.) scatterplots

Figures 7.2a-d offer alternative situations that may arise in real data. Figures 7.2a-d are all examples of **curvilinear** relationships because they form a curve when plotted out. Curvilinear relationships should not be analyzed using a Pearson *r*. Such relationships often occur when one of the sets of numbers is a function of time. Consider, for instance, a situation in which a teacher is interested in the degree of relationship between the number of division problems a student can correctly answer per minute and the number of minutes elapsed. If the number of division problems correctly solved per minute was plotted on a *Y* axis and the number of minutes plotted on the *X* axis, a positive relationship might show up for the first ten or twenty minutes while the student improved in ability to answer division problems, but the number of problems per minute would probably drop off as the student became tired and bored with division. The scatterplot might consist of a positive correlation line during the first few minutes and a negative line once fatigue set in. The positive and negative relationships combined into the same scatterplot would produce a curvilinear relationship that would look something like the one shown in Figure 7.2b.

The scatterplots shown in Figures 7.2a, 7.2b, 7.2c, and 7.2d are all curvelinear in one way or another, with 7.2d being the most complex (could we call it "S" linear?). The scatterplots shown in Figures 7.2e and 7.2f are more typical of the form of a linear relationship of a strong positive correlation (Figure 7.2e) or a strong negative correlation (Figure 7.2f). The best way to check the assumption of linearity is to visually examine a scatterplot of the data. While perfect linearity is not assumed here, you should look for some indication that fitting a straight line through the data would make sense.

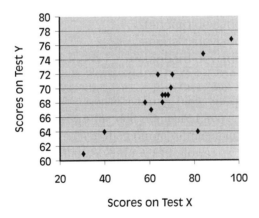

Figure 7.3 Scatterplot for data in Table 7.2

Now, once again, consider the data in Table 7.2. A scatterplot of these data is shown in Figure 7.3. Notice that the data appear to be fairly linear in this scatterplot with one exception: one diamond is alone below and to the right of the rest of the plotted points. This data point may be what is referred to as an **outlier** because it is far away from the general clustering of all the other data points. An outlier, if that is what this case is, must be handled with special care. The first trick is to figure out who is involved. Looking carefully at the diamond, I could tell that the student had a score of 82 on Test X and 64 on Test Y. Looking back at Table 7.1 or 7.2 I noticed that Randy had these scores. Since he was so different from the pattern found for all the other students, I wanted to further investigate why he did so well on one test, but so poorly on the other. Interviewing him, I found out that, for personal reasons, he was furious with his brother when he arrived at Test Y and remained angry throughout the examination. Based on this information, I had to decide if I was logically justified in leaving him out of the analysis. Sometimes doing so is a good idea because, in a sense, an outlier is creating a small curvilinear twist in the data.

Table 7.3 Calculating Pearson r (for Table 7.1 data—without outlier)

Column 1 Students	2 X	−	3 M_x	=	4 $(X−M_x)$	5 y	−	6 M_y	=	7 $(y−M_y)$	8 $(y−M_y)(y−M_y)$
Shenan	97	−	65.93	=	31.07	77	−	69.33	=	7.67	238.31
Robert	85	−	65.93	=	19.07	75	−	69.33	=	5.67	108.13
Mitsuko	71	−	65.93	=	5.07	72	−	69.33	=	2.67	13.54
Millie	70	−	65.93	=	4.07	70	−	69.33	=	0.67	2.73
Kimi	70	−	65.93	=	4.07	70	−	69.33	=	0.67	2.73
Kazumoto	69		65.93	=	3.07	69	−	69.33	=	−0.33	-1.01
Kako	68	−	65.93	=	2.07	69	−	69.33	=	−0.33	-0.68
Joji	67	−	65.93	=	1.07	69	−	69.33	=	−0.33	-0.35
Jeanne	67	−	65.93	=	1.07	69	−	69.33	=	−0.33	-0.35
Issaku	67	−	65.93	=	1.07	68	−	69.33	=	−1.33	-1.42
Iliana	66	−	65.93	=	0.07	72	−	69.33	=	2.67	0.19
Dean	62	−	65.93	=	−3.93	67	−	69.33	=	−2.33	9.16
Corky	59	−	65.93	=	−6.93	68	−	69.33	=	−1.33	9.22
Bill	40	−	65.93	=	−25.93	64	−	69.33	=	−5.33	138.21
Archie	31	−	65.93	=	−34.93	61	−	69.33	=	−8.33	290.97

$\Sigma(X-M_x)(Y-M_y) = 809.33$

N	= 15	15
M	= 65.93	69.33
S	= 14.97	3.77
Range	= 67	17

$$r_{xy} = \frac{\Sigma(X - M_x)(Y - M_y)}{NS_xS_y} = \frac{809.33}{15(14.97)(3.77)} = \frac{809.33}{846.55} = .9560333 \approx .96$$

In this case, because of his extraordinary anger, I felt justified in eliminating this outlier from the analysis, and doing so made a very dramatic difference in the results as shown in Table 7.3. Notice that leaving the outlier out of the analysis changed many of the descriptive statistics slightly and sharply affected the magnitude of the correlation coefficient. Instead of .78, the correlation is now .96. This reanalysis illustrates the degree to which an outlier can affect the results of correlational analysis. Notice in Figure 7.4 (for the results given in Table 7.3), that the outlier is no longer there and that the relationship now appears marvelously linear. Thus the assumption of linearity has been met. In situations where outliers are an issue, the tester should report both sets of results, with and without the outlier, and explain why the outlier was removed.

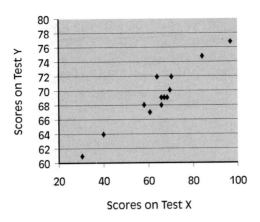

Figure 7.4 Scatterplot for data in Table 7.3

CALCULATING THE PEARSON CORRELATION COEFFICIENT WITH A SPREADSHEET

Naturally, you could calculate the Pearson product-moment correlation coefficient in your *Excel*™ spreadsheet. In the following exercise, you will enter data into the spreadsheet, enter a formula to calculate the correlation coefficient of the test scores, and compare the results with the calculations in Table 7.2. Then, you will create a scatterplot graph using the *Excel **Chart Wizard*** to visually analyze the two sets of test results. After finishing the exercise, you will see that using a spreadsheet may save you considerable time and effort in calculating the correlation coefficient of test scores.

Copy or Enter Headings and Data in an Excel Spreadsheet.

1. Open the *Excel* program on your computer.
2. Using the spreadsheet that you created near the end of Chapter 6, you can copy the heading and the student names from column A, and paste the data to a new *Excel* spreadsheet. Copy only the student names without the test scores or calculations created in the exercise.
3. If you didn't create a spreadsheet in Chapter 6, then using Screen 7.1 as a guide, type the following headings:

   In Cell A1, type **Students**.
   In Cell B1, type **Test X**.
   In Cell C1, type **Test Y**.

Screen 7.1 Calculating a correlation coefficient

	A	B	C	D	E	F	G
					E1	=CORREL(B2:B16,C2:C16)	
1	Students	Test X	Test Y		0.9558	= correlation	
2	Shenan	97	77				
3	Robert	85	75				
4	Mitsuko	71	72				
5	Millie	70	70				
6	Kimi	70	70				
7	Kazumoto	69	69				
8	Kako	68	69				
9	Joji	67	69				
10	Jeanne	67	69				
11	Issaku	67	68				
12	Iliana	66	72				
13	Dean	62	67				
14	Corky	59	68				
15	Bill	40	64				
16	Archie	31	61				

4. In Cells B2 to B17, and C2 to C17, type the test score data, as shown in Screen 7.1.

Calculate the Pearson correlation coefficient and compare method calculations.

1. In Cell E1, type the formula **=CORREL(B2:B17,C2:C17)**. This will calculate a correlation coeffieicent for the two ranges using the function =CORREL(RANGE,RANGE2).

2. The results of the calculation, .9558, will display in Cell E1. The figure .9558 differs slightly from .9560333, which was obtained in Table 7.3. When you round both figures to two places, the result is .96, which is exactly the same for manual and Excel spreadsheet calculation methods.

Use a chart to create a scatterplot graph for the data sets.

1. In *Excel,* click **I**nsert, **C**hart. The *Excel Chart Wizard* will start on your screen.

2. In the *Chart Wizard* window, on the *Standard Types* tab, under *Chart Type*, click *XY Scatter*. Select the first chart example in the top row, and then click **Next**.

Screen 7.2 Creating a scatterplot graph in *Excel's* Chart Wizard, and selecting a chart type

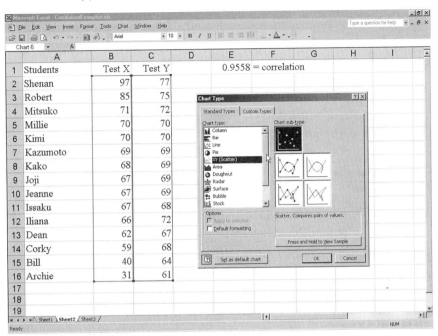

3. In the chart **Source Data** window, on the **Data Range** window, highlight Cells B2 to C17, and then verify that **Columns** is selected. A preview of the scatterplot chart will display in the window, as shown in Screen 7.3. Click **Next**.

Screen 7.3 Entering data ranges and previewing the graph

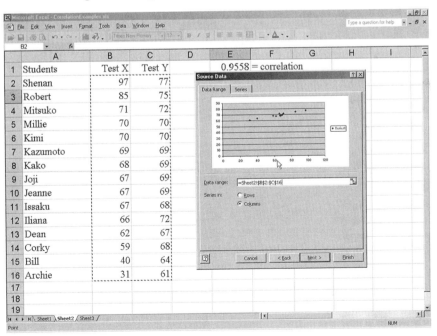

4. In the ***Chart Options*** window, on the ***Titles*** tab, in the ***Chart Title*** box, type **Plot for Correlation Coefficient**.

5. In the ***Value (X) axis*** box, type **Test X**, and then in the ***Value (Y) axis*** box, type **Test Y**. The title and labels will display in the preview of the chart, as shown in Screen 7.4.

Screen 7.4   Adding a graph title and labels

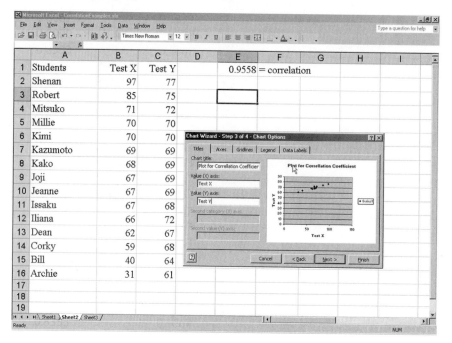

6. Click **Finish**. The scatterplot chart will display in the spreadsheet, as shown in Screen 7.5.

Screen 7.5   Finished scatterplot graph

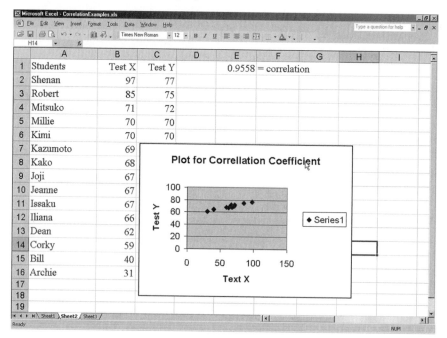

7. If the chart format looks different from the graph above, then you may change fonts, number scaling, alignment, etc., by right-clicking on specific areas of the graph that you wish to adjust.

8. Save your spreadsheet, as the student names and raw test scores can be used in the exercise at the end of the chapter.

INTERPRETING CORRELATION COEFFICIENTS

Once the correlation coefficient is in hand with the assumptions clearly met, testers must interpret the coefficient from two different perspectives. First, they must check to see if the coefficient is statistically significant; then and only then, they should decide if the coefficient is also meaningful.

STATISTICAL SIGNIFICANCE

If I were to line up 100 completely random numbers in one column and 100 other random numbers in a second column, I could calculate a correlation coefficient and plot the relationship. What would it look like? Figure 7.5 shows a scatterplot of the relationship between two sets of random numbers. Clearly, Figure 7.5 shows no linear relationship between the two sets of numbers because fitting a straight line to the data would be impossible. Thus by visual inspection alone, I can fairly safely say that there is no relationship between these two sets of numbers. Yet, a correlation coefficient of $r_{xy} = -.0442$ was calculated for these data, so some degree of correlation, or relationship, seems to exist. How is this possible?

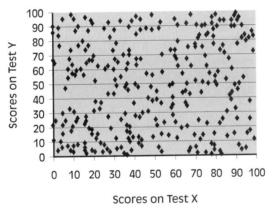

Figure 7.5 Scatterplot for two sets of random data

It turns out that calculating correlation coefficients between sets of random numbers will most often result in non-zero values. This happens because of chance factors. In other words, even random numbers may haphazardly produce correlation coefficients of some magnitude. In fact, they will seldom turn out to be exactly zero, even when random numbers are used. Examples of such spurious coefficients are shown in Table 7.4, where I show correlation coefficients that I calculated on the basis of repeated sets of random numbers. Notice that the first column of the table gives the Trial (the first

Table 7.4 Correlation coefficients from random numbers

Trial	N = 100	N = 50	N = 10	N = 5
1	−.0517	+.0755	−.3319	+.9281
2	+.1150	+.0185	+.4787	+.5879
3	+.1762	+.2191	−.1488	+.8543
4	+.0384	+.0273	−.2828	+.9032
5	−.1448	+.2192	−.2969	+.3692
6	+.1259	−.0637	+.6394	+.6441
7	−.0216	−.0306	−.0757	+.2468
8	+.0373	−.1658	+.3567	−.8413
9	+.0133	+.0817	−.3801	−.5772
10	−.0442	+.1232	+.4890	−.6933

correlation calculated, the second, the third, and so on) while the other four columns give the correlations for differing sizes of random number sets, that is, for sets of 100 pairs of random numbers, 50 pairs, 10 pairs, and 5 pairs of random numbers.

Notice also that none of the correlation coefficients is exactly zero, and that as the size of the number sets decreases the distances that the coefficients vary from zero seem to increase. In the column with samples of 100, the highest chance correlation is +.1762; in the 50s column, it is +.2192; in the 10s column, it is +.6394; and in the 5s column, it is +.9281. This may be fairly astounding to most readers, but these results really happened, and similar results will happen again if I replicate these trials using different sets of random numbers.[4] Notice also in Table 7.4 that the results for 100 pairs and 50 pairs are not too different, but the very small sample sizes of 10 and five seem to produce, respectively, high and very high correlation coefficients by chance alone. The message that should come through loud and clear is that testers should avoid using small numbers of students when doing correlational analysis because such groups can produce very large correlation coefficients by chance alone.

In interpreting any correlation coefficient, then, one important issue is whether the results could have occurred by chance alone. Fortunately, statisticians have worked out a strategy to help testers determine the probability that a correlation coefficient occurred by chance. The strategy compares any calculated correlation coefficient, called an **observed correlation**, with the appropriate **critical correlation** shown in Table 7.5. If the observed coefficient is larger than the critical value, a high and specific probability exists that the observed correlation coefficient did not occur by chance alone. The trick is to decide which critical correlation value in the table is the correct one to refer to.

---

[4] To do this for yourself, you will need to know that you can generate a random number by using the =RAND() function in your *Excel* spreadsheet. I usually multiply the resulting random number by 100 so the result will be somewhere between 0 and 100 like a test score. To do all this, I put the cursor in the cell where I want my first random number and type =**RAND()*100** and hit the ENTER key. Then, I copy that cell and paste it to the other cells where I want random numbers. The result is a set of randomly generated numbers.

Table 7.5 Critical values of the Pearson product-moment correlation coefficient*

| | Directional Decision: Sound reasons to expect either a positive or a negative correlation | | Non-directional Decision: Do not know direction of correlation | |
	95% Certainty $p < .05$	99% Certainty $p < .01$	95% Certainty $p < .05$	99% Certainty $p < .01$
N-2				
1	.9877	.9995	.9969	1.0000
2	.9000	.9800	.9500	.9900
3	.8054	.9343	.8783	.9587
4	.7293	.8822	.8114	.9172
5	.6694	.8329	.7545	.8745
6	.6215	.7887	.7067	.8343
7	.5822	.7498	.6664	.7977
8	.5494	.7155	.6319	.7646
9	.5214	.6851	.6021	.7348
10	.4973	.6581	.5760	.7079
11	.4762	.6339	.5529	.6835
12	.4575	.6120	.5324	.6614
13	.4409	.5923	.5139	.6411
14	.4259	.5742	.4973	.6226
15	.4124	.5577	.4821	.6055
20	.3598	.4921	.4227	.5368
25	.3233	.4451	.3809	.4869
30	.2960	.4093	.3494	.4487
35	.2746	.3810	.3246	.4182
40	.2573	.3578	.3044	.3932
45	.2428	.3384	.2875	.3721
50	.2306	.3218	.2732	.3541
60	.2108	.2948	.2500	.3248
70	.1954	.2737	.2319	.3017
80	.1829	.2565	.2172	.2830
90	.1726	.2422	.2050	.2673
100	.1638	.2301	.1946	.2540

* Adapted from Fisher and Yates 1963.

To decide which critical value is appropriate in Table 7.5, I first decide whether any sound logical or theoretical reasons exist for expecting the correlation to be either positive or negative. Such reasons are usually based on an existing theory, or previous research findings, or both. If such reasons exist, I will use a **directional decision** as shown in the second and third columns of the table. In contrast, if I have no way of knowing which way the relationship might go, I would be making a **non-directional decision** and need to examine the fourth and fifth columns in the table. In other words, my expectations before calculating the coefficient are related to the probabilities of a coefficient occurring by chance alone. So I should begin by using the sets of columns, directional or non-directional, that best describe those expectations.

Next, I must decide the degree to which I want to be sure of my results. Since I can never be 100 percent sure, I will probably want to settle for one of the traditional levels. In language testing, such decisions are traditionally set at 95 percent or 99 percent. If I decide that I want the 95 percent level, only a five percent chance exists, or less than .05 probability ($p < .05$), that I will be wrong in deciding that my correlation coefficient occurred for other than chance reasons. In other words, with this certainty level, I can be 95 percent sure that I am right in rejecting the notion that my observed correlation coefficient is really due to chance alone. I would be safer yet if I set that level at $p < .01$, thereby insuring that, if my observed correlation coefficient exceeds the critical value, only a 1 percent chance exists, or less than .01 probability, that I will be wrong in deciding that my observed correlation coefficient occurred for other than chance reasons. In other words, I can also set my certainty level so that I can be 99 percent sure that I am right in rejecting the idea that my observed correlation coefficient is really due to chance alone. Therefore, after deciding whether the directional or non-directional columns apply to my decision, I will also need to decide on whether I want to use the 95 or 99 percent certainty column to find my critical value.

As shown in Table 7.4, the number of random numbers used in the calculation of correlation coefficients can affect the fluctuations in chance correlations. Hence, the number of students involved also has a bearing on the critical value as shown in the left-most column of Table 7.5. To find the correct number that applies to my correlation coefficient, I must subtract two from the number of students who took the two tests (that is, the number of pairs of scores involved in my calculations, minus 2) and move down the left-hand column to the correct number ($N - 2$). Moving across that row, I must then find the correct column for my chosen probability level (.01 or .05) within the directional or non-directional columns. The value that is in the place where that row and column intersect is the critical value that my observed correlation must exceed (regardless of its sign, + or −) to be considered **statistically significant**, or due to factors other than chance with the appropriate degree of certainty (that is, 95 percent or 99 percent).

For example, the correlation obtained in Table 7.2 of .78 would be worth checking for statistical significance. Say I have sound reasons for expecting any correlation calculated between these two tests will be positive. Perhaps they are both very similar multiple-choice tests of French grammar and therefore, if there is any relationship at all, I would expect it to be positive. This would mean that I will use a directional decision and must only choose between columns 2 and 3 in Table 7.5. Because of my cautious nature and the importance of being correct in this case, I decide that I want to be correct with 99 percent certainty. Hence, my decision is further narrowed in that my critical value must be somewhere in the third column. Next, I must go back to the data and check the number of students, in this case $N = 16$. Therefore, $N - 2 = 16 - 2 = 14$. Moving down the left column until I reach the number 14, I find the correct row. Moving to the right in that row until I reach the correct column (column 3: directional at 99 percent certainty), I then find the critical value, .5742. Since the magnitude (regardless of sign) of the observed correlation coefficient, .78, is larger than the critical value, .5742 (that is .7800 > .5742), I know that the correlation coefficient is statistically significant at $p < .01$. In other words, there is only a 1 percent probability that this correlation coefficient occurred by chance alone. Put another way, I can be 99 percent sure that the correlation coefficient occurred for reasons other than chance.

Let's also consider an example that will logically turn out to be due to chance. Most (95 percent) of the correlations shown in Table 7.4 should reasonably turn out to be due to chance alone. Let's take the coefficient furthest to the right in the last row of Table 7.4.

At $-.6933$, this coefficient is fairly high in magnitude but is negative and is based only on five pairs of scores. In checking this coefficient for statistical significance, I must first decide whether there is any logical reason to expect either a positive or negative correlation in this situation. Since the data are random numbers, I have no reason to expect a positive correlation or a negative correlation. Thus, I am looking at a non-directional decision. I will also use the relatively liberal .05 probability level because nobody will be hurt if this decision turns out wrong. I look down the left column until I reach 3 ($N - 2 = 5 - 2 = 3$) for the correct row; then, I move to the right in that row until I reach the correct column, non-directional at 95 percent certainty (fourth column), and find that the critical value is .8783. Since the magnitude (regardless of sign) of the observed correlation coefficient, $-.6933$, is not larger than the critical value, .8783, I can make no claims about the correlation coefficient being statistically significant at $p < .05$. Hence, I must accept that this correlation coefficient could have occurred by chance alone, and it would be safest if I accepted that it probably does not differ from 0.00.

MEANINGFULNESS

The statistical significance of a correlation coefficient is useful to know because the tester can then argue that an observed coefficient probably did not occur by chance alone, but statistical significance does not imply that the coefficient is *significant* in the sense of meaningful. Instead, statistical significance is a necessary precondition for a meaningful correlation, but it is not sufficient in itself. A quick look at Table 7.5 (p. 155) will reveal that correlations as low as .1638 would be significant for directional decisions at $p < .05$ if 102 students were taking the tests. But the question would remain as to whether such a low coefficient would be meaningful. **Meaningfulness** is not probabilistic and absolute; rather, meaningfulness requires a judgment about the degree to which a coefficient (already shown to be significant) is also interesting.

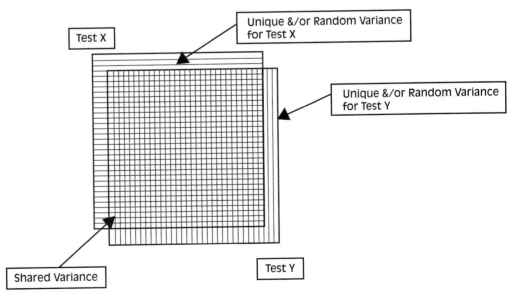

Figure 7.6 Overlapping variance to illustrate coefficient of determination

One statistical tool that will help in making such judgments is called the **coefficient of determination**, which is simply the correlation coefficient, r_{xy}, squared. Thus, to get the coefficient of determination, you just need to square the value of the correlation coefficient. That is why the symbol for this statistic is r_{xy}^2. The result is a coefficient that directly represents the proportion of overlapping variance between two sets of scores. In other words, this coefficient tells you what proportion of the variance in the two sets of scores is common to both, or the degree to which the two tests are lining up the students in about the same way. Figure 7.6 illustrates what the coefficient of determination means. Consider a correlation coefficient of .80 between tests X and Y. If I marked that .80 point off on the bottom horizontal edge and right vertical edge of a square representing Test X (the square with horizontal stripes in Figure 7.6), I would be in a position to overlay another square representing Test Y (the square with vertical stripes) at those two points such that the overlapping variance would be represented by a third smaller square shared by both measures (the smaller, checkered square). To find the area of this smaller square, I would logically multiply the distance along the bottom, .80, times the distance up the right, also .80, and get .64. A quicker way to accomplish the same thing would be to square the value of the correlation coefficient .80 and obtain the area of the overlapping, or shared, variance.

The area of overlap can be interpreted as the proportion of variance on one measure that is common to the other measure, and vice versa. Or, by moving the decimal point to the right two places, the coefficient of .64 can be interpreted as a percentage. In other words, 64 percent of the variance in Test X is shared with Test Y. Likewise, 64 percent of the variance on Test Y is shared with Test X. By extension, the remaining 36 percent ($100\% - 64\% = 36\%$) of variance on each test can be said to be unique to that measure and/or totally random in nature.

Table 7.6 Correlation coefficients and corresponding coefficients of determination

Correlation Coefficient (r_{xy})	Coefficient of Determination (r_{xy}^2)	Error Variation ($1 - r_{xy}^2$)
1.00	1.00	.00
.90	.81	.19
.80	.64	.36
.70	.49	.51
.60	.36	.64
.50	.25	.75
.40	.16	.84
.30	.09	.91
.20	.04	.96
.10	.01	.99

Table 7.6 illustrates how precipitously the coefficients of determination drop in magnitude when compared with their respective correlation coefficients. For instance, consider a correlation of .90, which has a corresponding squared value of .81 as shown in the second row of Table 7.6. That means that about 81 percent, or approximately four-fifths of variance is shared between whatever two measures are involved. By extension, 19 percent of the variance is unaccounted for, that is, it is unique or random. A correlation of .80 has a squared value of .64, or about two-thirds overlap. A correlation of .70, when squared, yields .49, which indicates that there is less than half the variance shared between the two sets of scores. A correlation of .60 squared gives .36, which shows that only about one-third of the variance is common to the two sets of scores; .50 squared is .25, which indicates about one-quarter is shared; .30 squared is .09, or less than one-tenth overlapping variance; .20 squared is .04, or less than one-twentieth overlapping variance; and .10 squared is .01, or less than one-hundredth overlapping variance.

Thus, correlation coefficients of .00 to .59 might be considered to be low correlations because they represent less than one-third overlap, while correlations of .60 to say .79 might be viewed as moderate correlations that represent one-third to two-thirds overlapping variance, and correlations of .80 to 1.00 might be viewed as high correlations that represent two-thirds to complete overlapping variance. Note that the same relationships hold whether the correlation is positive or negative. Also note that all such interpretations will depend on the importance of the decision, the types of information the correlation coefficient is based on, typical correlations found in previous related research, and so forth.

Thus, after all the work of calculating a correlation coefficient and deciding whether it is statistically significant, as well as calculating a coefficient of determination, someone must ultimately examine the magnitude of the correlation coefficient to determine if it is meaningful in a particular situation for a particular purpose. In some situations, only a very high correlation coefficient makes sense. Other times, a relatively low coefficient will provide useful information. In the next two chapters on reliability and the one on validity, I will demonstrate some of the applications that can be made of such correlational analyses.

CORRELATION MATRIXES

One useful way to efficiently present a large number of correlation coefficients is to use a **correlation matrix** like the one shown in Table 7.7a (p. 160). The correlation coefficients displayed in Table 7.7a are those among the independent scores of seven tasks (E20, A21, B20, F05, F09, E21, and C14) and the total of those scores. These correlation coefficients are based on data taken from Form Q of a task-based performance test reported in Brown, Hudson, Norris, and Bonk (2002). The authors lined up all the individual task scores and the total score for a group of 30 students and calculated correlation coefficients for all possible pairings of these scores. The correlation matrix shown in Table 7.7a is an economical way of displaying this information. To read the table, start with the correlation coefficient between the Task E20 and A21, which turns out to be .67 and is found straight across from E20 at the point just below A21. By using the labels in the left column and those across the top as coordinates, teachers can isolate the correlation coefficient for any combination of the scales.

Table 7.7b presents an elaboration of same basic matrix. This second table is provided simply to illustrate some of the other features that might occur in such a correlation matrix. Notice that the second table contains the same correlation coefficients. The asterisks for these correlation coefficients refer to the $p < .01$ below the table, which means that all these coefficients were statistically significant at the .01 level. Thus those with asterisks are relationships that are probably due to other than chance factors, while those without asterisks are probably due to chance alone and cannot be interpreted as being different from zero.

Table 7.7a Matrix of correlation coeffcients

Tasks	E20	A21	B20	F05	F09	E21	C14	Total
E20		.67	.55	.31	.49	.67	.40	.78
A21			.48	.27	.46	.60	.46	.76
B20				.07	.41	.30	.38	.61
F05					.29	.38	.17	.54
F09						.66	.48	.76
E21							.54	.84
C14								.70
Total								

Table 7.7b Matrix of correlation coeffcients and coefficients of determination

Tasks	E20	A21	B20	F05	F09	E21	C14	Total
E20	1.00	.67*	.55*	.31	.49*	.67*	.40	.78*
A21	.45	1.00	.48*	.27	.46*	.60*	.46*	.76*
B20	.30	.23	1.00	.07	.41	.30	.38	.61*
F05	.10	.07	.00	1.00	.29	.38	.17	.54*
F09	.24	.21	.17	.08	1.00	.66*	.48*	.76*
E21	.45	.36	.09	.14	.44	1.00	.54*	.84*
C14	.16	.21	.14	.03	.23	.29	1.00	.70*
Total	.61	.58	.37	.29	.58	.71	.49	1.00

$*p < .01$

Notice also that a series of 1.00s runs diagonally across the second table. These 1.00s represent the correlation between the scores on each of the tasks (and total) and themselves. Of course, any set of numbers should correlate perfectly with itself, so this makes sense. The main function of these 1.00s (collectively called **the diagonal** because of the way they descend diagonally across the table) is to divide the correlations above and to the right of the diagonal from the numbers below and to the left of the diagonal. In this case, the new numbers below the diagonal are the coefficients of determination for the same correlations found above the diagonal. In other words, they are the squared values of the corresponding correlation coefficients above the diagonal. For instance, the correlation coefficient of .78 in the upper right corner (between E20 and Total), when it is squared, equals .61, which is found in the lower left corner (between Total and E20). Remember, the coefficient of determination can usefully be interpreted as the percent of shared, or overlapping, variance between the two sets of scores. A correlation matrix, then, is one way to present a great deal of information in a small amount of space.

POTENTIAL PROBLEMS WITH CORRELATIONAL ANALYSIS

There are a number of ways in which interpretations of results can go awry in applying correlational analysis to the problems of test development. Three potential pitfalls may occur: restriction of range, skewedness, and causality.

RESTRICTION OF RANGE

If a tester chooses to base a correlational analysis on a sample that is made up of fairly homogeneous language proficiency levels (perhaps students from one semester level out of the six available in a high school German program), the sample itself can have dramatic effects on the analysis. Without realizing it, the range of talent may have been restricted, and such a restriction will tend to make any resulting correlation coefficients much lower. I will discuss this issue more in Chapter 10, where I will also demonstrate the effects of restrictions in range on correlation coefficients when they are used to analyze the reliability and validity of tests. For the moment, I will only stress that restrictions in the range of students taking the tests involved in a correlation coefficient may be one reason for mediocre or low correlation coefficients. Put another way, if a tester wants to maximize the possibilities of finding a strong correlation, if indeed a strong relationship exists, then the full range of possible abilities should be included so the samples are representative of the students for whom the two measures were designed.

SKEWEDNESS

Skewed distributions can likewise depress the values of correlation coefficients. This effect occurs if either (or both) of the tests is skewed. Hence, it is important to check the assumption of normality when doing correlational analysis. Remember, anyone can detect such skewing by examining graphs (histograms, bar graphs, or frequency polygons) of the distribution of scores, or the descriptive statistics for each of the tests as was discussed earlier. Most importantly, remember that skewedness will tend to depress correlation coefficients and should therefore be avoided so that the results do not end up being lower than the actual degree of relationship that could exist between the two sets of scores.

Another major error that novices make in interpreting even a high correlation between the scores on one test with those on another is in thinking that it indicates a causal relationship. One test, though highly related to another, cannot be said to be "causing" the differences in scores on the other test. This is easily illustrated by considering that there is probably a strong relationship, or correlation, between the number of fires per year in each city in the U.S. and the number of firemen working in those cities. Yet fairness would never allow anyone to say either that the firemen cause fires or that fires cause the firemen. Yes, a relationship exists, but not a causal one. So it is wisest to entirely avoid making causal statements based on correlational evidence alone.

ANOTHER USEFUL TYPE OF CORRELATION ANALYSIS

The Pearson r is a very useful statistic for investigating the degree of relationship between two sets of continuous scale numbers. Since most sets of test scores are considered continuous scales, the Pearson r is most often appropriate. However, occasions may arise when testers may want to explore the degree of relationship between two sets of numbers that are not continuous scales. Statisticians have developed a number of alternative procedures for analyzing different types of scales. The one that most commonly appears in test analyses is the point-biserial correlation coefficient (r_{pbi}), which is often used to estimate the degree of relationship between a nominal scale (right or wrong on a particular item) and a continuous one (the total scores on the test). The point-biserial correlation coefficient is derived from and is designed to estimate the Pearson r. Therefore, in most ways, the interpretation of this statistic is the same as the interpretation of Pearson r.

POINT-BISERIAL CORRELATION COEFFICIENT

Under what conditions would one need to compare a nominal scale with a continuous scale in terms of the degree of relationship? One way to use r_{pbi} would be to estimate the degree of relationship between being male or female and language aptitude test scores. Do you think that there would be any relationship between students' gender and their performance on such an aptitude test? If so, the point-biserial correlation coefficient could help investigate the degree of gender bias in a test.

More likely, I would be interested in the degree to which individual items on one of my tests are related to total test scores. Such item-to-whole-test correlations are often used to estimate the item discrimination. In fact, it was just such correlation coefficients that I reported in Table 4.3 (p. 87) in place of item discrimination indexes. In such a situation, I am comparing a dichotomous nominal scale (the correct or incorrect answer on each item usually coded as 1 or 0) with a continuous scale (total scores on the test). The appropriate statistic to apply (when examining the relationship between a nominal scale, like right or wrong, and a continuous scale) is the **point-biserial correlation coefficient**.

Screen 7.6 Calculating r_{pbi} using the spreadsheet program

Names	I1	I2	I3	I4	I5	I6	I7	I8	I9	I10	etc.....	Total
Shenan	1	1	1	1	1	1	0	1	1	0	etc.....	77
Robert	1	0	1	1	1	1	0	1	0	0	etc.....	75
Mitsuko	1	0	0	1	1	1	0	1	0	0	etc.....	72
Iliana	1	1	0	1	1	1	0	0	0	0	etc.....	72
Millie	1	1	1	1	1	0	0	1	0	0	etc.....	70
Kimi	1	1	0	1	1	0	1	1	1	0	etc.....	70
Kazumoto	1	0	1	1	1	1	0	1	0	0	etc.....	69
Kako	1	1	0	1	1	0	0	1	0	0	etc.....	69
Joji	1	0	1	0	1	0	1	1	0	0	etc.....	69
Jeanne	1	1	0	0	1	1	0	0	1	0	etc.....	69
Issaku	1	0	1	0	1	0	1	0	0	0	etc.....	68
Corky	1	1	0	0	1	1	1	1	1	0	etc.....	68
Dean	1	1	0	0	1	0	1	0	1	0	etc.....	67
Randy	1	1	1	0	1	0	1	0	0	0	etc.....	64
Bill	1	0	0	0	1	0	1	0	1	0	etc.....	64
Archie	0	0	0	0	1	0	1	1	0	0	etc.....	61
r_{pbi}	0.53	0.16	0.29	0.71	0.00	0.62	-0.68	0.33	0.03	0.00		
ID	0.20	0.00	0.40	1.00	0.00	0.60	-1.00	0.40	-0.40	0.00		

The data in Screen 7.6 are set up to illustrate calculating r_{pbi} between items and total scores. Notice that the items have been coded 1 for correct and 0 for incorrect just as they have been elsewhere in this book. To calculate the r_{pbi} for each item, you could use the following formula:

$$r_{pbi} = \frac{M_p - M_q}{S_t}\sqrt{pq}$$

r_{pbi} = point-biserial correlation coefficient
$\quad M_p$ = mean on the whole test for those students who answered correctly (i.e., coded as 1s)
$\quad M_q$ = mean on the whole test for those students who answered incorrectly (i.e., coded as 0s)
$\quad S_t$ = standard deviation for whole test
$\quad p$ = proportion of students who answered correctly on the whole test (i.e., coded as 1s)
$\quad q$ = proportion of students who answered incorrectly on the whole test (i.e., coded as 0s)

Notice that the formula has no elements that are completely new. Hence, the reader should be able to calculate a point-biserial correlation coefficient on the basis of this formula alone. But again, an example might help. Consider Item 1 from Screen 7.6 and look at its correlation with the total scores:

Item One

$$r_{pbi} = \frac{M_p - M_q}{S_t} \sqrt{pq} = \frac{69.5333 - 61.0000}{3.8730} \sqrt{.9375 \times .0625}$$

$$= \frac{8.5333}{3.8730} \sqrt{.0586} = 2.2033 \times .2421 = .5334 \approx .53$$

Using four places to the right of the decimal for accuracy, the mean of the total scores for those students who answered Item 1 correctly (M_p of those coded as 1) was 69.5333 as shown in the first row below the item response table, while the mean for those students who answered incorrectly (M_q of those coded as 0) was 61.0000. In addition, the standard deviation for the total scores was 3.8730. The proportion of students in the p group is 15 out of 16 (as shown in the third row below the main table) or .9375 so the proportion in the q group is .0625 (as shown in the fourth row below the table). Substituting all these values into the formula for Item 1 and solving it as shown, the correlation turns out to be .5334, or about .53, which is the same value as that shown in Screen 7.6 (p. 163) for I1. The same processes would lead to the r_{pbi} values for items 2–10 in Screen 7.6.

The strategy for interpreting r_{pbi} is very similar to the one described above for the Pearson product-moment correlation coefficient. Table 7.5 (p. 155) is even appropriate for determining if the observed correlation is statistically significant. Again, the comparison will be between the observed correlation coefficient and the critical value. If the observed coefficient is larger than the critical value, a high and specific probability exists that the coefficient did not occur by chance alone. Again, the trick is to decide which coefficient in the table is the correct one to use.

CALCULATING THE POINT-BISERIAL CORRELATION COEFFICIENT WITH A SPREADSHEET

Naturally, you could calculate the point-biserial correlation coefficient in your *Excel* spreadsheet using the formula as I did in the example above. However, in the following exercise, I want to show you a shortcut that would save you considerable time and effort. Below, you will enter data.

Copy or enter headings and data in an Excel spreadsheet.

1. Open the *Excel* program on your computer.
2. Using the spreadsheet that you created from the last exercise, you can copy the headings and the student names from Column A, and paste the data to a new *Excel* spreadsheet. Copy only the student names without the correlation coefficient formulas created in the exercise.
3. If you didn't create a spreadsheet in the previous exercise, then, using Screen 7.6 as a guide, type the following headings:
   In Cell A1, type **Names**.
   In Cells B1 to K1, type **I1** to **I10** (test score items 1 to 10).
   In Cell M1, type **Total**.
   In Cell A19, type r_{pbi}.
   In Cell A20, type **ID**.
4. In Cells B2 to K17, type the test score data, as shown in Screen 7.6.

Screen 7.7: Calculating r_{pbi} using *Excel*

	A	B	C	D	E	F	G	H	I	J	K	L	M	N
	Names	I1	I2	I3	I4	I5	I6	I7	I8	I9	I10	etc.....	Total	
1														
2	Shenan	1	1	1	1	1	1	0	1	1	0	etc.....	77	
3	Robert	1	0	1	1	1	1	0	1	0	0	etc.....	75	
4	Mitsuko	1	0	0	1	1	1	0	1	0	0	etc.....	72	
5	Iliana	1	1	0	1	1	1	0	0	0	0	etc.....	72	
6	Millie	1	1	1	1	1	0	0	1	0	0	etc.....	70	
7	Kimi	1	1	0	1	1	0	1	1	1	0	etc.....	70	
8	Kazumoto	1	0	1	1	1	1	0	1	0	0	etc.....	69	
9	Kako	1	1	0	1	1	0	0	1	0	0	etc.....	69	
10	Joji	1	0	1	0	1	0	1	1	0	0	etc.....	69	
11	Jeanne	1	1	0	0	1	1	0	0	1	0	etc.....	69	
12	Issaku	1	0	1	0	1	0	1	0	0	0	etc.....	68	
13	Corky	1	1	0	0	1	1	1	1	1	0	etc.....	68	
14	Dean	1	1	0	0	1	0	1	0	1	0	etc.....	67	
15	Randy	1	1	1	0	1	0	1	0	0	0	etc.....	64	
16	Bill	1	0	0	0	1	0	1	0	1	0	etc.....	64	
17	Archie	0	0	0	0	1	0	1	1	0	0	etc.....	61	
18														
19	r_{pbi}	0.53	0.16	0.29	0.71	0.00	0.62	-0.68	0.33	0.03	0.00			
20	ID	0.20	0.00	0.40	1.00	0.00	0.60	-1.00	0.40	-0.40	0.00			
21	Prop Correct	0.9375	0.5625	0.4375	0.5000	1.0000	0.4375	0.5000	0.6250	0.3750	0.0000			
22	Prop Wrong	0.0625	0.4375	0.5625	0.5000	0.0000	0.5625	0.5000	0.3750	0.6250	1.0000			

Calculate the point-biserial correlation coefficient and copy the formula.

As long as the item data are a nominal scale coded 1 or 0 and the total scores are a continuous scale, as shown Screen 7.7, you can simply use the same =CORREL function you used for calculating the Pearson correlation, and you will get a value that is mathematically equivalent to the point-biserial correlation coefficient. For each test score item, you will use the following function: =CORREL(RANGE1,RANGE2). In the example shown in Screen 7.7, I calculated the correlation between the nominal scale 1s and 0s in the range B2:B17, and the interval scale scores in the range M2:M17.

1. Click Cell B19, and then enter the formula **=CORREL(B2:B17,$M2:$M17)**. The dollar signs are inserted in front of the Ms so that the column will not change when the formula is copied to the other cells.
2. Press ENTER. The correlation coefficient of .153 will display for Item 1.
3. Highlight Cell B19, and then click **Edit**, **Copy**. A moving box will display around the cell.
4. Click Cells C19 to K19, and then click **Edit**, **Paste**. The results of the calculations will be displayed in the cells for the other items, as shown in Screen 7.6.
5. In columns I5 and I10, #DIV/0 will be displayed because the formula cannot manipulate the items with a standard deviation of zero (the answers for I5 and I10 were the same for all students). In cells F19 and K19, enter **0** to correct the calculation (zero standard deviation leads to zero correlation).

Compare point-biserial correlation coefficient to item discrimination values.

In Screen 7.7, you will notice that the item discrimination values in Cells B20 to K20 (item discrimination values from the Screen 4.5 in Chapter 4) are added so that readers can compare the results obtained by using *ID* with the results calculated by using r_{pbi}.

1. To calculate these values, open the spreadsheet that you created in Chapter 4.
2. Click Cells B24 to K24, and then click **Edit**, **Copy**. A moving box will display around the cells.
3. In the current spreadsheet that you are comparing values, click in Cells B20 to K20, and then click **Edit**, **Paste**. The results of the calculations for *ID* will display in the cells for the other students, as shown in Screen 7.7.
4. If you did not create the spreadsheet in Chapter 4, then enter the formula to calculate item discrimination manually, and copy and paste the formula to the other cells.

In both cases, the goal is to estimate how well each item is separating the better students on the whole test from the weaker students. Clearly the two different methods do not produce exactly the same results. Items 4 and 6 appear to be effective as "discriminators" using either method, and items 2, 5, 7, 9, and 10 appear to be ineffective "discriminators" using either method. However, the r_{pbi} seems to indicate that Item 1 is a good discriminator when *ID* does not and the reverse appears to be true for Items 3 and 8. Part of the discrepancy between *ID* and r_{pbi} results is probably due to the small numbers of students involved in this example.

In any case, item analysis statistics are only tools to help in selecting the best items. If a tester has both *ID* and r_{pbi} available, both statistics can help in making decisions about which items to keep in a revised version of a norm-referenced test. More importantly, the statistics should never take the tester far from the common sense notions involved in developing sound test items.

REVIEW QUESTIONS

1. What is correlational analysis? What is a correlation coefficient? If I say that two sets of scores covary, what do I mean?

2. How high and how low can a correlation coefficient go? Near what value would you expect a correlation coefficient to be if absolutely no relationship exists between two sets of numbers?

3. What are the one design requirement and three assumptions underlying the Pearson product-moment correlation coefficient? What does each assumption require and how would you check to see if each has been met?

4. What is a linear relationship between two sets of numbers? What would a scatterplot of such a relationship look like? What would some of the possible scatterplots for curvilinear relationships look like?

5. How do you know whether a correlation coefficient that you have calculated is statistically significant? What are the steps involved in finding this out? Once you know that a correlation coefficient is significant at $p < .05$, what does that mean?

6. Can sets of random numbers produce correlation coefficients that turn out to be statistically significant in a small percent of the trials? Why, or why not?

7. Does the fact that a correlation coefficient is statistically significant mean that it is necessarily meaningful?

8. How do you calculate the coefficient of determination, and what does it mean in terms of percents and interpreting the degree of overlap between two sets of test scores?

9. What is the point-biserial correlation coefficient used for and how is it commonly used in item analysis?

APPLICATION EXERCISES

A. Screen 7.8 shows the raw scores for Tests Z and Y in the second and third columns. The descriptive statistics for each are just below the table. Based on these scores and statistics, calculate a Pearson r correlation coefficient (either by hand or in your spreadsheet program).

Screen 7.8 Data for applications exercises on Pearson r

	A	B	C
1	Students	Test Z	Test Y
2	Shenan	87	77
3	Robert	75	75
4	Randy	72	64
5	Mitsuko	61	72
6	Millie	60	70
7	Kimi	60	70
8	Kazumoto	59	69
9	Kako	58	69
10	Joji	57	69
11	Jeanne	57	69
12	Issaku	57	68
13	Iliana	56	72
14	Dean	52	67
15	Corky	49	68
16	Bill	30	64
17	Archie	21	61
18			
19	N	16	16
20	M	56.94	69.00
21	S	15.01	3.87
22	Range	67	17

B. Is the correlation coefficient you calculated in A above statistically significant? Meaningful?

C. The table below contains data from six students on a dichotomous scale (0 or 1) for Items and a continuous scale (0 – 100) for Total Scores. Calculate the r_{pbi} for each of the four items (either by hand or in your spreadsheet program). Notice that the mean and standard deviation for the Total Scores is given below the table. You will need some of this information to calculate r_{pbi}.

		Items			
Student	1	2	3	4 ... ETC.	Total Scores
Robert	1	0	1	0 ...	100
Mitsuko	1	0	1	0 ...	90
Randy	1	0	1	0 ...	80
Bill	0	1	1	0 ...	60
Kazumoto	0	1	1	0 ...	50
Archie	0	1	1	0 ...	40

$M = 70$; $SD = 10$;

LANGUAGE TEST RELIABILITY

INTRODUCTION

A test, like any other type of instrument used to measure, should give the same results every time it measures (if it is used under the same conditions), should measure exactly what it is supposed to measure (not something else), and should be practical to use. If my son uses a tape measure to measure my height and finds that I am 71 inches tall one time, I would expect to be about the same height if he measures me again 30 minutes later. In addition, I would reasonably assume that the scale that he is using to measure me was designed to measure height and does not turn out to be measuring weight. Finally, the instrument that he is using must be practical so that it is not too inconvenient or difficult for him to use. In language testing terms, these considerations are called reliability, validity, and usability. I discussed the usability, or practicality, issues in some depth in Chapter 2. I will cover test reliability for norm-referenced tests in this chapter, then, test dependability (the analogy to reliability for CRTs) in Chapter 9, and test validity in Chapter 10.

The fundamental problem in this chapter and the next is that a certain amount of error exists whenever measurements take place. Even in measuring on relatively stable scales like meters, liters, and kilograms, nobody can count on the results being exactly the same every time because the measurement instruments inevitably have small flaws that cause inaccuracies or because the person using the instruments makes small almost imperceptible errors. Because measurements are error prone and because measurements are often very important, many countries have established some equivalent to the U.S. Bureau of Weights and Standards to watch over the consistency and accuracy of measuring devices.

In testing language, the problem is that measuring for language proficiency, placement, achievement, diagnosis, or other mental traits of human beings is much harder to do consistently than measuring the heights or weights of those same people. The very difficulty of measuring mental traits explains why consistency is of particular concern to language testers. In this chapter, I will explain the numerous strategies that language testers use in developing NRTs, that is, the calculation and interpretation of reliability coefficients and the standard error of measurement to examine the consistency of measurement. To construct any tests that measure consistently, language testers must first understand the potential sources of consistent and inconsistent test score variance.

SOURCES OF VARIANCE

The performances of students on any test will tend to vary from each other, but their performances can vary for a variety of reasons. In the best of all possible worlds, all the variance in test scores would be directly related to the purposes of the test. For example, consider a relatively straightforward test of the spelling rules of English. At first glance, teachers might think that the variance in students' performances on such a test could be attributed entirely to their knowledge of the spelling rules of English. Unfortunately, reality is not quite that simple and clear. Many other factors may be potential sources of score variance on this spelling test. These variables fall into two general sources of variance: (a) those creating variance related to the purposes of the test (called meaningful variance here), and (b) those generating variance due to other extraneous sources (called **measurement error**, or **error variance**).

In order for the meaningful variance to be most informative, the concept being tested must be very carefully defined and thought through so that the items are a straightforward reflection of the purpose for which the test was designed. For instance, on the example spelling test, the test could be carefully designed to assess specific spelling rules. However, if exactly the same spelling words are used on the test that were used in classroom exercises, the variance in scores may be due partly to knowledge of the spelling rules, but also partly to remembering the spelling words. Some students may be answering items correctly because they know the spelling rules and can apply them, while others are getting them right because they memorized the isolated spelling words. This type of ambiguity can cause serious problems because, in most cases, a test should have a clearly-defined purpose that is not confounded with other sources of variance.

Thus, the **meaningful variance** on a test will be defined here as that variance which is directly attributable to the testing purposes. (This is essentially a test validity issue, which I will therefore discuss at more length in Chapter 10.) A number of issues were covered in Chapters 1 and 2—issues that can help teachers to think through the purposes of various types of tests. Once those purposes are clear, thinking about the meaningful variance on any test should be relatively easy.

Table 8.1 Potential sources of meaningful test variance for communicative competence

COMPONENTS OF LANGUAGE COMPETENCE:
Organizational Competence
Grammatical Competence
Vocabulary
Morphology
Syntax
Phonology/graphemes
Textual Competence
Cohesion
Rhetorical organization
Pragmatic Competence
Illocutionary Competence
Ideational functions
Manipulative functions
Heuristic functions
Imaginative functions
Sociolinguistic Competence
Sensitivity to differences in dialect or variety
Sensitivity to differences in register
Sensitivity to naturalness
Ability to interpret cultural references and figures of speech

Bachman (1990, as well as Bachman and Palmer 1996) provided an outline of the components of language competence (shown in Table 8.1, p. 170)—an outline that may prove helpful in thinking about these issues. This outline provides some of the many factors that language teachers might want to consider including in defining the purpose of a given test. For instance, in designing part of the listening comprehension section of the ELI Placement Test at the University of Hawaii, we referred to Bachman's organizational framework, and we decided to include a component to assess the students' comprehension of cohesion in academic lectures (see Table 8.1, under **Textual Competence** within *Organizational Competence*). Thus, the Bachman and Palmer framework helped us to define and include a purpose that we might not otherwise have thought of.

Naturally, other models of language learning exist that may prove useful in defining meaningful variance on a test, especially as the field of language learning and teaching continues to develop new ways of looking at these issues. Consider for instance how the types of syllabuses, or organizational frameworks, used in a curriculum could affect the purposes of the tests that would result (see Brown 1995a for more on syllabuses). A group of elementary school ESL teachers might prefer to organize their curriculum and testing purposes around a structural syllabus going from the simplest structures of English to more difficult structures. Another group of high school Spanish teachers might prefer to organize their curriculum and testing purposes around various language functions as in a functional syllabus. Yet another group of adult education EFL teachers in Amsterdam might want to develop curriculum and testing purposes centered on tasks that the students must perform in the language. The point is that, regardless of how teachers decide on the purpose of a given test, they must clearly define that purpose so that they know what sources of meaningful variance they should be focusing on.

Unfortunately, other factors, unrelated to the purpose of the test, almost inevitably enter into the performances of the students. For instance, in a set of scores from the example spelling test, other potential sources of score variance might include: variables in the environment like noise, heat, etc.; the adequacy of administration procedures; factors like health and motivation in the examinees themselves; the nature and correctness of scoring procedures; or even the characteristics of the set of items selected for this particular test. All these factors might be contributing to the success or failure of individual students on the test—factors that are not directly related to the students' knowledge of spelling rules.

MEASUREMENT ERROR

Measurement error (also sometimes called **error variance**) is a term that describes the variance in scores on a test that is not directly related to the purpose of the test (see the examples in the previous paragraph). The summary provided in Table 8.2 clarifies the types of issues that are generally associated in the testing literature with measurement error.

Table 8.2 Checklist for potential sources of error variance

- ☐ Variance due to environment
  - ☐ location
  - ☐ space
  - ☐ ventilation
  - ☐ noise
  - ☐ lighting
  - ☐ weather
- ☐ Variance due to administration procedures
  - ☐ directions
  - ☐ equipment
  - ☐ timing
  - ☐ mechanics of testing
- ☐ Variance due to scoring procedures
  - ☐ errors in scoring
  - ☐ subjectivity
  - ☐ evaluator biases
  - ☐ evaluator idiosyncrasies
- ☐ Variance attributable to the test and test items
  - ☐ test booklet clarity
  - ☐ answer sheet format
  - ☐ particular sample of items
  - ☐ item types
  - ☐ number of items
  - ☐ item quality
  - ☐ test security

- ☐ Variance attributable to examinees
  - ☐ health
  - ☐ fatigue
  - ☐ physical characteristics
  - ☐ motivation
  - ☐ emotion
  - ☐ memory
  - ☐ concentration
  - ☐ forgetfulness
  - ☐ impulsiveness
  - ☐ carelessness
  - ☐ testwiseness
  - ☐ comprehension of directions
  - ☐ guessing
  - ☐ task performance speed
  - ☐ chance knowledge of item content

VARIANCE DUE TO ENVIRONMENT

The first potential source of measurement error shown in Table 8.2 is the environment in which the test is administered. The very location of the test administration can be one source of measurement error if it affects the performance of the students. Consider for instance the possible effects of administering a test to a group of students in a library with people quietly talking nearby, as opposed to administering it in a quiet auditorium that contains only examinees and proctors. Clearly, the difference in the noise levels of the surroundings could cause some variance in test scores that is not related to the purpose of the test. Similarly, the amount of space available to each student can become a factor. Moreover, noise can be a factor that will affect the performance of students, particularly on a listening comprehension test, but also on other types of tests if the noise distracts the students from the items at hand. Indeed, lighting, ventilation, weather, or any other environmental factors can serve as potential sources of measurement error if they affect the students' performances on a test. Hence, the checklist in Table 2.5 (p. 35) should be used when setting up a test administration so the effects of environment as a source of measurement error can be minimized.

Variance Due to Administration Procedures

Another potential source of measurement error involves the procedures that are used to administer the test. For instance, if the directions for filling out the answer sheets or for doing the actual test are not clear, score variance may be created that has nothing to do with the purpose of the test. If the results from several administrations are to be combined and the directions are inconsistent from administration to administration, another source of measurement error will exist. Likewise, if the quality of the equipment and the timing are not the same each time a test is administered, sources of measurement error are being created. Consider, for instance, a situation in which the students take a six-minute taped dictation test (three readings, the second with pauses so that students have time to write) played to them on a small cassette recorder, as compared to another group that takes the same dictation, but a teacher reads it aloud from a script—reading a bit louder, clearer, and more slowly than the cassette tape. If all other factors are held constant, which group do you think will do best? The second group will do better with the teacher reading louder, slower, and more clearly, right? Thus, equipment and timing can create error variance that is not related to the central purpose of the test. Indeed, any issues related to the mechanics of testing may inadvertently become sources of measurement error. Hence, error variance may be caused by factors such as differences in: the helpfulness of the proctors, the speed with which the directions are delivered, the attitudes of the proctors toward the students, the anxiety level of the proctors, and so forth. Again, careful attention to the checklist shown in Table 2.5 (p. 35) should help to minimize the effects of administration procedures as a source of error variance.

Variance Attributable to Examinees

A large number of potential sources of error variance are directly related to the condition of the students when they take the test. The sources include physical characteristics like differences among students in their fatigue, health, hearing, or vision. For example, if five students in a class are coming down with the flu at the time that they are taking a test, their poor physical health may be a variable that should be considered as a potential source of measurement error. Depending on the tasks involved on a test, color blindness or other more serious physical differences could also become important sources of measurement error.

Other factors that would more appropriately be termed psychological factors include differences among students (or in individual students over time) in motivation, emotional state, memory, concentration, forgetfulness, impulsiveness, carelessness, and so forth.

The experience of students with regard to test taking can also affect their performances. This experience, sometimes termed **testwiseness**, includes the ability to easily comprehend almost any test directions, or knowledge of guessing strategies (developed by some students to an art form), or strategies for maximizing the speed of task performance.

In addition, just by chance, through classes or life experience, some of the students may have topic knowledge that will help them with certain of the questions on a test in a way that is not related to the purpose of the test. By and large, the issues related to the condition of the students are their responsibility; however, testers must be aware that they are potential sources of measurement error, and attempt to minimize their effects.

VARIANCE DUE TO SCORING PROCEDURES

Factors over which testers have considerably more control are related to the scoring procedures used. Human errors in doing the scoring are one common source of measurement error. Another source is variance in judgments that may occur in any of the more subjective types of tests (for example, in composition and interview ratings). The problem is that the subjective nature of the scoring procedures can lead to evaluator inconsistencies or biases having an effect on the students' scores. For instance, if a rater is affected positively or negatively by the sex, race, age, or personality of the interviewee, these biases can contribute to the measurement error. An evaluator may also simply have certain idiosyncrasies that contribute to measurement error. Perhaps one composition rater is simply tougher than the others. Then a student's score is affected by whether or not the rating is done by this particular rater. Careful adherence to the checklists provided in Tables 2.4 (p. 32) and 2.5 (p. 35) should help to minimize scoring procedures as a source of measurement error. Careful rater selection and training can also help.

VARIANCE ATTRIBUTABLE TO THE TEST AND TEST ITEMS

The last general source of measurement error is the test itself and its items. For instance, the clarity of the test booklet may become a factor if some of the booklets were smudged in the printing process, or the format of the answer sheets may be an issue if some of the students are familiar with the format while others are not. Item selection may also become an issue if the particular sample of items chosen is for some reason odd or unrepresentative of the purpose of the test. The type of items chosen can also be an issue if that type is new to some of the students or is a mismatch with the purpose of the test. The number of items used on a test is also a potential source of measurement error. If only a small number of items is used, we know that the measurement will not be as accurate as a larger number of items. For instance, a thirty-item multiple-choice test will clearly measure more accurately than a one-item test. Once that premise is accepted, differences in the accuracy of measurement for other numbers of items simply become a matter of degrees. The quality of the items can also become a source of measurement error if that quality is poor or uneven. Lastly, test security can become an issue, particularly if some of the students have managed to get a copy of the test beforehand and prepared for that particular set of questions. To minimize the effects of the test itself and the test items on measurement error, testers should use Tables 2.4 (p. 32), 2.5 (p. 35), and 3.1 (p. 43) to 3.3 (p. 51) as carefully as possible.

All the foregoing sources of measurement error may be affecting students' scores on any given test. Such effects are undesirable because they are creating variance in the students' scores that is unrelated to the purpose(s) of the test. Therefore, every effort must be made to minimize these effects. Many of the procedures and checklists previously described in this book were designed to do just that: minimize the sources of error variance in a test and its administration.

In the remainder of this chapter, I will cover ways of estimating the effects of error variance on the overall variance in a set of test scores. This is an important issue because, if I know the degree to which error variance is affecting test scores (that is, the unreliability of a test), I can also determine the degree to which error variance is NOT affecting test scores (that is, the reliability of a test). Knowing about the relative reliability of a test can help me decide the degree to which I should be concerned about all the potential sources of measurement error presented in Table 8.2 (p. 172).

RELIABILITY OF NRTS

In general, **test reliability** is defined as the extent to which the results can be considered consistent or stable. For example, if language teachers administer a placement test to their students on one occasion, they would like the scores to be very much the same if they were to administer the same test again one week later. Such consistency is desirable because they do not want to base their placement decisions on an unreliable (inconsistent) test, which might produce wildly different scores if students were to take it again and again. Placement decisions are important decisions that can make big differences in the lives of the students involved in terms of the amounts of time, money, and effort they will have to invest in learning the language. Since most language teachers are responsible language professionals, they want the placement of their students to be as accurate and consistent as possible so they can responsibly serve their students' language learning needs.

The degree to which a test is consistent, or reliable, can be estimated by calculating a **reliability coefficient** ($r_{xx'}$). A reliability coefficient is like a correlation coefficient in that it can go as high as $+1.00$ for a perfectly reliable test. But the reliability coefficient is also different from a correlation coefficient in that it can only go as low as 0.00 because a test cannot logically have less than zero reliability. In those rare cases where testers find negative values for the reliability of a test, they should first go back and check for errors in their calculations; then, if their mathematics is 100 percent correct, they should round their negative result upward to 0.00 and accept that the results on the test have zero reliability (that is, they are totally unreliable, or random).

Reliability coefficients, or reliability estimates as they are also called, can be interpreted as the percent of systematic, or consistent, or reliable variance in the scores on a test. For instance, if the scores on a test have a reliability coefficient of $r_{xx'} = .91$, by moving the decimal two places to the right, the tester can say that the scores are 91% consistent, or reliable, with 9% measurement error ($100\% - 91\% = 9\%$), or random variance. If $r_{xx'} = .40$, the variance on the test is only 40 percent systematic and 60 percent of the variances due to measurement error.

As I explain next, language testers use three basic strategies to estimate the reliability of most tests: test-retest, equivalent forms, and internal-consistency strategies. I will also show how certain types of productive language tests (like compositions and oral interviews) necessitate estimating the reliability of ratings or judgments.

TEST-RETEST RELIABILITY

Of the three basic reliability strategies, **test-retest reliability** is the one most appropriate for estimating the stability of a test over time. The first step in this strategy is to administer whatever test is involved two times to a group of students. The testing sessions should be far enough apart time-wise so that students are not likely to remember the items on the test, yet close enough together so that the students have not changed in any fundamental way (like learning more language). Once the tests are administered twice and the pair of scores for each student are lined up in two columns, simply calculate a Pearson product-moment correlation coefficient between the two sets of scores (as shown in Chapter 7). The correlation coefficient will provide a test-retest reliability estimate that is a **conservative estimate** (that is, erring on the low side rather than the high side if it is not 100% accurate) of the reliability of the test over time. This reliability estimate can then be interpreted as the percent of reliable variance on the test. Admittedly, administering a test two times to the same group of students is not a very attractive proposition for the teachers or the students—clearly a major drawback for this reliability strategy. However, situations do arise in which the test-retest strategy is the most logical and practical alternative for estimating reliability.

EQUIVALENT-FORMS RELIABILITY

Equivalent-forms reliability (sometimes called **parallel-forms reliability**) is similar to test-retest reliability. However, instead of administering the same test twice, the tester administers two different but equivalent tests (for example, Forms A and B) to a single group of students. Then, the tester calculates a correlation coefficient between the two sets of scores, and that indicates the degree of relationship between the scores on the two forms. The resulting equivalent-forms reliability coefficient can be directly interpreted as the percent of reliable, or consistent, variance on either form of the test. However, note that this strategy provides an estimate of the consistency of scores across forms rather than over time, as was the case with test-retest reliability.

One question that always arises in discussing equivalent-forms reliability is the issue of what constitutes equivalence between two forms. Of course, writing parallel items for each form will help create equivalent or parallel forms. At least, the items on the two forms should be similar because the goal is to make the two forms as similar as possible. The number of items on each test should be the same as well. From a strict statistical point of view, equivalent (or parallel) forms produce scores that have equal means, equal standard deviations, and equal correlations with some third measure of the same knowledge or skills. Therefore, to establish the equivalence of two forms, you simply need to show that: (a) the means and standard deviations are quite similar and (b) the two forms correlate about equally with some third measure.

Clearly, however, developing two forms, establishing their equivalence, administering the two forms to a hapless group of students, and calculating the correlation coefficient between the scores is a fairly cumbersome way to go about estimating the reliability of each form. However, conceptually it is correct, and sometimes this strategy is useful.

INTERNAL-CONSISTENCY RELIABILITY

To avoid the work and complexity involved in the test-retest and equivalent-forms strategies, testers most often use internal-consistency strategies to estimate the **internal-consistency reliability**. As the name implies, internal-consistency reliability strategies estimate the consistency of a test using only information internal to a test, that is, available in one administration of a single test.

The easiest internal-consistency strategy to understand conceptually is called the **split-half method**. This approach is very similar to the equivalent-forms technique except that, in this case, the equivalent forms are created from the single test being analyzed by dividing it into two equal parts. The test is usually split on the basis of odd- and even-numbered items. The odd-numbered and even-numbered items are scored separately as though they were two different forms. A correlation coefficient is then calculated for the two sets of scores. This coefficient gives the reliability for either the odd-numbered items or the even-numbered items—either half, but just half of the test. If all other things are held constant, a longer test will usually be more reliable than a short one, and the correlation calculated between the odd-numbered and even-numbered items must therefore be adjusted to provide a coefficient that represents the full-test reliability. This adjustment of the half-test correlation to estimate the full-test reliability is accomplished by using the **Spearman-Brown prophecy formula**. The applicable formula is:

$$r_{xx'} = \frac{(n)r}{(n-1)r+1}$$

$r_{xx'}$ = full-test reliability

r = correlation between the two test halves

n = number of times the test length is to be increased

For example, let's say the half-test correlation coefficient is calculated between the even-numbered and odd-numbered items, and it turns out to be .60. In this case, the formula would be applied as follows:

$$r_{xx'} = \frac{(n)r}{(n-1)r+1} = \frac{(2).60}{(2-1).60+1} = \frac{1.20}{1.60} = .75$$

So the adjusted full-test reliability is .75, and that is the value that the tester should report as the split-half reliability (adjusted).

Let's consider a fuller set of data as shown in Table 8.3. Let's say these are the scores on the odd-numbered and even-numbered items on a cloze test for 30 students. Note that the odd-numbered items have been scored separately from the even-numbered ones in Table 8.3 and that they have been lined up into two columns representing the two scores for each student. The Pearson r calculated for these two sets of scores turns out to be .66. Since this is the half-test correlation between the odd-numbered and even-numbered items, it is labeled $r_{odd-even}$.

Table 8.3 Split-half reliability

	ODD	EVEN	
	13	14	
	13	14	
	12	14	
	14	12	
	12	12	
	11	10	
	12	9	
	11	9	
	12	7	
	10	8	
	9	9	
	10	8	
	11	7	
	11	7	
	9	8	
	9	8	
	8	8	
	8	8	
	9	7	
	9	6	
	5	9	
	8	6	
	8	6	
	6	7	
	6	7	
	9	3	
	7	5	
	6	5	
	3	7	
	5	3	
Statistic	**Odd**	**Even**	**Total**
Number of items *(k)*	15	15	30
Mean *(M)*	9.20	8.10	17.30
Standard deviation *(S)*	2.66	2.80	4.97

$$r_{odd\text{-}even} = .66$$

The Spearman-Brown formula should then be used to provide an estimate of what the full-test reliability is. Inserting the .66 half-test correlation value (shown at the bottom of the table) into the formula where r appears, and 2 where n appears, the necessary calculations are simple:

$$r_{xx'} = \frac{(n)r}{(n-1)r+1} = \frac{(2).66}{(2-1).66+1} = \frac{1.32}{1.66} = .77952 \approx .80$$

The result, $r_{xx'}$, is an internal-consistency reliability estimate calculated using the split-half method on the data from a single administration of a single test. This result was made possible by separately scoring the odd-numbered and even-numbered items on the test and treating them as if they were two forms.

CRONBACH ALPHA

Conceptually, the split-half method is the easiest of the internal-consistency procedures to understand. However, others are easier to calculate. For instance, one way of calculating the **Cronbach alpha coefficient** (α) offers an alternative procedure for calculating the split-half reliability, one which will give very similar results. The formula is as follows:

$$\alpha = 2\left(1 - \frac{S^2_{odd} + S^2_{even}}{S^2_{total}}\right)$$

α = split-half reliability for the full test
S_{odd} = standard deviation for the odd-numbered items
S_{even} = standard deviation for the even-numbered items
S_{total} = standard deviation for the total test scores

Referring once again to Table 8.3 (p. 178), find the values for the standard deviations for the odd-numbered items, the even-numbered items, and the total test scores (given at the bottom of the table). Substitute those values into Cronbach's formula and solve for α as follows:

$$\alpha = 2\left(1 - \frac{S^2_{odd} + S^2_{even}}{S^2_{total}}\right) = 2\left(1 - \frac{2.66^2 + 2.80^2}{4.97^2}\right) = 2\left(1 - \frac{7.0756 + 7.8400}{24.7009}\right)$$

$$= 2\left(1 - \frac{14.9156}{24.7009}\right) = 2(1 - .6038484) = 2(.3961516) = .7923931 \approx .79$$

Notice that the .79 Cronbach α value obtained here is very similar to the .80 value calculated using the split-half (adjusted) method, but also note that the Cronbach α is much easier to calculate.

KUDER-RICHARDSON FORMULAS

Among the many other variations of internal-consistency reliability, the most commonly reported are the Kuder-Richardson formula 20 (K-R20) and formula 21

(K-R21) (Kuder & Richardson 1937). I would like to discuss these formulas in reverse order by beginning with **Kuder-Richardson formula 21**. The easiest internal consistency estimate to calculate is that produced by the K-R21 formula:

$$\text{K-R21} = \frac{k}{k-1}\left(1 - \frac{M(k-M)}{kS^2}\right)$$

K-R21 = *Kuder-Richardson formula 21*
k = number of items
M = mean of the test scores
S = standard deviation of the test scores

To calculate K-R21, a tester only needs to know the number of items, the mean, and the standard deviation on the test. The tester does not have to administer the test twice, or develop two forms; the tester does not have to score the odd-numbered and even-numbered items separately; and the tester does not have to calculate a correlation coefficient. Hence, the K-R21 formula is relatively easy to use in those situations where it can be applied.

For instance, applying the K-R21 formula to the data used in Table 8.3, I begin by marshalling my information, which means I have to look below the table for the mean (17.30), standard deviation (4.97), and number of items (30). Substituting those values into the formula and solving for the K-R21 reliability estimate are accomplished as follows:

$$\text{K-R21} = \frac{k}{k-1}\left(1 - \frac{M(k-M)}{kS^2}\right) = \frac{30}{29}\left(1 - \frac{17.30(30-17.30)}{30 \times 4.97^2}\right)$$

$$= 1.0345\left(1 - \frac{219.71}{741.03}\right) = 1.0345(1 - .2965) = 1.0345 \times .7035 = .7278 \approx .73$$

While this method of calculating reliability is relatively simple, new language testers must understand one thing about calculating K-R21 for real language tests. Notice that the .73 result of the K-R21 formula is considerably lower (even though it is based on the same data) than the .79 and .80 results obtained using the Cronbach α and split-half (adjusted) methods. This difference is due to the fact that the K-R21 is a conservative estimate of the reliability of a test, that is, if it is in error, the error should always be one of underestimation for the reliability of the test. However in language testing, it can provide a serious underestimate. In my experience, the K-R21 usually does not give a very serious underestimate for multiple-choice language tests. However, for some types of tests, like the cloze procedure, the K-R21 may produce a very serious underestimate, as compared to other approaches for estimating internal-consistency reliability.

Since the data in Table 8.3 (p. 178) are from a cloze test, I am not surprised that a fairly large difference occurs in the reliability estimates produced for this test by the split-half (adjusted) and Cronbach α strategies on the one hand and the K-R21 formula on the other. While the difference between .79 and .73 may not seem too large, I have found far more substantial K-R21 underestimates of cloze reliability in previous studies (Brown 2002). Results adapted from these studies are shown in Table 8.4. Notice how very much lower the K-R21 estimates are in comparison to the other types of estimates.

Table 8.4 K-R21 estimates for cloze procedure

Reliability Estimate	GP 1	GP 2	GP 3	GP 4
Cronbach alpha	.66	.61	.67	.67
K-R20	.64	.60	.67	.67
Split-half adjusted by Spearman-Brown prophecy formula	.67	.63	.61	.67
Flanagan's coefficient	.66	.63	.61	.67
Rulon's coefficient	.66	.63	.61	.67
K-R21	.48	.36	.56	.55

The **Kuder-Richardson formula 20** (K-R20) avoids the problem of underestimating the reliability of certain language tests. Although it is marginally more difficult to calculate, K-R20 is considered a much more accurate estimate of reliability than K-R21. K-R20 is estimated using the following formula:

$$\text{K-R20} = \frac{k}{k-1}\left(1 - \frac{\Sigma S_i^2}{S_t^2}\right)$$

K-R20 = Kuder-Richardson formula 20
k = number of items
S_i^2 = item variance
S_t^2 = test score variance

This formula contains some elements that may not be familiar to the reader. The first of these is the sum of the item variances, symbolized by ΣS_i^2. These **item variance** values are derived from the concept of item facility (recall that item facility is the proportion of students who answered each item correctly; examples are shown at the bottom of Table 8.5). As shown in Table 8.6, the calculations begin by lining up the *IF* values for each item. Recall that these represent the proportion of students who answered each item correctly. Next, calculate $1 - IF$ for each item. Subtracting the *IF* from 1.00 yields the proportion of students who answered each item incorrectly. These results must then be lined up with their corresponding *IF* values as shown in Table 8.6. The next step is to multiply the *IF* times $(1 - IF)$, which yields the item variance, or $S_i^2 = IF(1 - IF)$. In other words, the item variance for each item is equal to the proportion of students who answered correctly by the proportion who answered incorrectly. As shown in Table 8.6, these item variance values for each item are then lined up in their own column, which in turn is summed for all the items. This sum is substituted into the numerator of the second fraction in the K-R20 formula.

Table 8.5 Item variance data (adapted from Screen 3.12) for calculating K-R20

ID	I1	I2	I3	I4	I5	I6	I7	I8	I9	I10	I11	I12	I13	I14	I15	I16	I17	I18
1	1	1	1	1	1	1	1	1	1	1	1	1	0	1	0	1	1	1
2	0	1	1	1	1	1	1	1	1	1	1	1	1	1	0	1	1	0
20	0	1	1	1	1	1	1	1	1	1	1	1	1	1	1	0	1	0
29	1	1	1	1	1	1	1	1	1	1	1	0	1	0	1	1	1	1
12	1	1	0	1	1	1	1	1	1	1	1	0	1	1	1	1	1	0
5	1	1	0	1	1	1	1	1	1	1	1	0	0	0	1	0	0	0
4	1	1	0	1	1	1	1	1	1	1	1	0	1	0	1	1	0	0
3	1	1	1	1	1	1	1	1	1	1	1	0	0	1	1	0	1	0
16	1	1	0	1	1	0	1	1	1	1	1	0	0	0	1	0	0	0
30	1	1	0	1	1	1	1	1	1	1	1	0	0	0	1	0	0	0
17	0	1	1	1	1	1	1	1	1	1	1	1	1	1	1	0	0	0
6	1	1	0	1	1	1	1	1	1	1	0	0	0	0	1	0	1	0
27	0	0	0	1	1	1	1	1	1	1	0	0	1	0	0	0	0	0
18	0	1	1	1	1	1	1	1	1	1	0	0	0	1	1	0	0	0
19	0	1	0	1	1	1	1	1	1	0	0	0	1	0	1	0	0	0
9	0	1	0	1	1	1	1	1	0	1	0	0	0	0	0	0	0	0
22	0	1	1	1	1	1	1	1	1	1	1	0	1	1	1	0	1	0
8	0	1	0	1	1	1	1	1	1	1	0	0	0	0	0	0	0	0
24	1	0	0	1	1	1	1	1	1	1	1	0	1	1	0	0	0	0
21	0	0	0	1	1	1	1	1	1	1	0	0	0	0	1	0	1	0
14	1	1	0	1	1	1	1	1	1	1	1	1	1	1	1	0	0	0
10	1	0	0	1	0	1	1	1	1	1	0	0	0	1	1	0	1	0
25	1	1	0	0	1	1	1	1	1	1	1	0	0	0	0	0	0	0
15	1	1	0	0	1	1	1	0	1	1	1	0	1	1	1	0	0	0
26	1	1	0	1	0	1	0	0	1	1	1	0	0	0	0	0	1	0
23	1	0	0	1	0	1	0	0	1	1	0	0	0	0	1	0	0	0
11	1	1	0	1	1	1	1	1	1	1	1	1	1	0	0	0	0	0
7	0	0	0	0	0	1	1	0	1	1	0	1	0	0	1	0	1	0
13	0	1	0	0	0	1	1	0	0	1	1	0	0	0	0	0	0	0
28	0	0	0	0	0	0	1	1	0	1	1	0	0	0	0	0	1	0
IF	0.5667	0.7667	0.2000	0.8667	0.8000	0.8333	0.8000	0.8667	0.9000	0.9333	0.6667	0.2333	0.4667	0.2333	0.7333	0.1333	0.4333	0.0667
ID	0.2000	0.4000	0.5000	0.4000	0.5000	0.2000	0.6000	0.4000	0.3000	0.1000	0.6000	0.3000	0.4000	0.4000	0.3000	0.4000	0.5000	0.2000

Table 8.5 Item variance data (adapted from Screen 3.12) for calculating K-R20 (continued)

I19	I20	I21	I22	I23	I24	I25	I26	I27	I28	I29	I30	Scores	Proportion
1	1	1	0	1	1	1	1	1	1	0	1	27	0.9000
1	1	1	1	1	1	1	1	1	1	0	1	27	0.9000
1	1	1	1	1	1	0	1	1	1	0	1	26	0.8667
1	1	1	1	1	1	1	1	1	1	0	1	26	0.8667
1	1	1	0	1	1	0	1	1	1	1	1	24	0.8000
1	1	1	0	1	0	0	1	1	1	0	0	21	0.7000
1	1	1	0	0	0	0	1	1	1	0	1	21	0.7000
1	1	1	0	1	0	0	0	1	1	0	1	20	0.6667
1	1	1	0	1	1	1	1	1	1	1	0	19	0.6333
1	1	1	0	0	0	0	0	1	0	0	0	18	0.6000
1	1	1	1	1	1	0	1	1	0	0	1	18	0.6000
1	1	1	0	0	0	0	0	1	0	1	0	18	0.6000
1	1	1	0	1	0	0	1	1	1	0	0	18	0.6000
1	1	1	0	0	0	0	1	0	1	0	0	17	0.5667
1	1	1	0	1	1	0	1	1	1	0	0	17	0.5667
1	1	1	0	0	0	0	1	0	0	0	0	16	0.5333
1	1	1	0	0	0	0	1	1	0	0	0	16	0.5333
1	1	1	0	0	1	1	1	1	0	1	1	16	0.5333
1	1	1	0	0	0	0	1	1	0	0	0	15	0.5000
1	1	1	0	1	0	0	0	0	1	0	1	14	0.4667
1	1	0	0	0	1	1	0	1	1	0	1	14	0.4667
1	1	1	0	0	1	0	1	0	0	0	1	14	0.4667
1	1	1	0	0	0	0	0	0	0	0	0	13	0.4333
1	1	1	0	0	0	0	0	0	0	0	0	13	0.4333
1	1	1	0	1	0	1	0	1	1	0	0	12	0.4000
1	1	0	0	0	0	0	0	0	1	0	0	12	0.4000
1	1	1	0	1	0	0	1	0	1	0	0	11	0.3667
0	0	0	0	1	0	0	0	0	1	0	0	10	0.3333
0	1	1	0	1	0	0	0	0	0	0	0	8	0.2667
0.9333	0.9333	0.9000	0.1333	0.8333	0.3000	0.2000	0.7000	0.7000	0.7333	0.0667	0.3667	17.3000	0.5766667 M_p
0.2000	0.2000	0.3000	0.3000	0.2000	0.6000	0.4000	0.6000	0.6000	0.1000	0.1000	0.5000	4.9700	0.1656667 S_p

Table 8.6 Calculating item variances

ITEM #	IF	1 - IF	IF (1 - IF)
1	0.5667	0.4333	0.2456
2	0.7667	0.2333	0.1789
3	0.2000	0.8000	0.1600
4	0.8667	0.1333	0.1156
5	0.8000	0.2000	0.1600
6	0.8333	0.1667	0.1389
7	0.8000	0.2000	0.1600
8	0.8667	0.1333	0.1156
9	0.9000	0.1000	0.0900
10	0.9333	0.0667	0.0622
11	0.6667	0.3333	0.2222
12	0.2333	0.7667	0.1789
13	0.4667	0.5333	0.2489
14	0.2333	0.7667	0.1789
15	0.7333	0.2667	0.1956
16	0.1333	0.8667	0.1156
17	0.4333	0.5667	0.2456
18	0.0667	0.9333	0.0622
19	0.9333	0.0667	0.0622
20	0.9333	0.0667	0.0622
21	0.9000	0.1000	0.0900
22	0.1333	0.8667	0.1156
23	0.8333	0.1667	0.1389
24	0.3000	0.7000	0.2100
25	0.2000	0.8000	0.1600
26	0.7000	0.3000	0.2100
27	0.7000	0.3000	0.2100
28	0.7333	0.2667	0.1956
29	0.0667	0.9333	0.0622
30	0.3667	0.6333	0.2322

$4.6200 =$ SUM OF ITEM VARIANCES (ΣS_i^2)

The other element of the K-R20 formula that is probably unfamiliar is the one symbolized by S_i^2. This is just a new label for an old concept. S_i^2 represents the variance for the whole test—that is, the standard deviation of the test scores squared.

Consider the example data once again. Based on the information provided in Table 8.6, the test variance (4.97^2, as shown at the bottom right corner of Table 8.3, or bottom of the second column from the right in Table 8.5), sum of the item variances (4.62), and number of items (30) can be substituted into the formula to calculate K-R20 as follows:

$$\text{K-R20} = \frac{k}{k-1}\left(1 - \frac{\Sigma S_i^2}{S_t^2}\right) = \frac{30}{29}\left(1 - \frac{4.62}{4.97^2}\right) = 1.0345\left(1 - \frac{4.62}{24.70}\right)$$

$$= 1.0345(1 - .1870) = 1.0345 \times .8130 = .8410485 \approx .84$$

Notice that the result of these calculations, though based on the same data as those above for the split-half (adjusted), Cronbach α, and K-R21 reliabilities, is a considerably higher estimate (at .84) than any of the others, which were .80, .79, and .73, respectively.

Which estimate is the correct one? Because all these estimates are underestimates of the true reliability of the test, they are all correct but lower than the true state of affairs. In other words, none will overestimate the actual state of reliability in the test being analyzed, so they can all be safely interpreted. However, the single most accurate and flexible of these estimates (as they are calculated here) is the K-R20. Nevertheless, the other three approaches have advantages that sometimes outweigh the need for accuracy. For instance, the split-half (adjusted) version makes more sense conceptually than any other estimate for explaining how internal-consistency reliability works. In addition to the fact that it gives a fairly accurate estimate of the reliability of a test, it is useful for teaching about reliability, as I am doing in this book (and as you may end up doing with your colleagues). Therefore, there may be reasons why you would want to use the split-half variety on some occasions. The K-R21 formula has the advantage of being quick and easy to calculate. So, for situations where a quick, rough estimate of reliability is sufficient, this may be the formula of choice. If the items on a test are weighted in some sense, like two points for each item in one section and only one point each in another, then Cronbach α might be the statistic of choice because it can be applied to tests with weighted items, it is easy to calculate, and it is reasonably accurate. In contrast, K-R20 can only be applied when the items are scored correct/incorrect with no weighting scheme of any kind. If accuracy is the main concern, then the K-R20 formula clearly should be used if at all possible.

However, in all cases, remember that the error will be in the direction of an underestimate of the actual reliability of the test. Testers simply have to decide how much of an underestimate they are willing to accept in terms of the amount of work involved, the accuracy of the estimate, and whether a weighting scheme needs to be applied in scoring the items.

This coverage of internal-consistency reliability has necessarily been brief. Numerous other strategies exist for estimating internal consistency, some of which appear in Table 8.4 (p. 181) (e.g., Flanagan's coefficient, Rulon's coefficient, Guttman coefficient, etc.). The strategies chosen for presentation in this book were selected on the basis of their conceptual clarity, ease of calculation, accuracy of results, and frequency of appearance in the language testing literature. In most cases, these strategies should provide all the necessary tools for calculating internal-consistency reliability in most language programs. Remember, internal-consistency estimates are the ones most often reported by language testers because they have the distinct advantages of being estimable from a single form of a test administered only once.

RELIABILITY OF RATER JUDGMENTS

Two other types of reliability may be necessary in language testing situations where raters make judgments and give scores for the language produced by students. Raters usually are necessary when testing students' productive skills (speaking and writing) as in composition, oral interviews, role plays, etc. As I will explain next, testers most often rely on interrater and intrarater reliabilities in such situations.

Interrater reliability is usually estimated by looking at the scores produced by two raters, lining those scores up in columns, and calculating a correlation coefficient between the two sets of scores. The resulting coefficient provides an estimate of the interrater reliability of the judgments being made in either set of ratings. A real-world example of this application is shown in Table 8.7, in which three scores (in columns) are shown for each of 55 students (in rows). These are the three ratings assigned by three different teachers to each student's composition on the ELIPT from one small spring semester administration.

Table 8.7 Three ratings for each of 55 compositions (writing sample subtest of the ELIPT)

Student ID	Rater1	Rater2	Rater3	Student ID	Rater1	Rater2	Rater3
A 1	66	66	72	A51	80	67	74
A 2	84	72	67	A52	82	78	74
A 3	62	66	56	B 2	63	65	67
A 5	79	90	68	B 3	60	57	69
A 6	73	67	67	B 5	60	73	65
A 8	76	78	71	B 6	73	71	69
A 9	72	82	64	B 9	64	77	82
A11	63	54	57	B10	68	74	61
A13	57	62	71	B11	65	62	66
A16	58	76	81	B13	84	78	82
A19	72	71	70	B14	41	46	37
A20	61	63	71	B17	87	91	81
A25	68	79	62	B18	71	68	77
A30	62	87	87	B20	69	63	54
A31	61	67	72	B21	61	59	58
A32	73	87	78	B23	66	74	67
A36	70	76	63	B24	65	70	64
A37	70	71	68	C 2	67	77	70
A38	95	80	89	C 3	67	67	57
A40	67	81	71	C 4	53	66	65
A41	76	75	77	C 5	88	87	90
A43	68	53	55	C 6	83	90	67
A44	75	64	69	C 9	59	69	62
A46	87	85	75	C11	68	72	66
A47	64	69	61	C12	59	75	71
A48	73	60	65	C13	68	72	75
A49	63	60	69	C14	87	93	90
				C15	64	64	65

Table 8.8 gives the correlation coefficients between each of the three possible pairings of ratings assigned by the raters in this test administration. They are not as high as I would like. However, recall that the number of items (or number of ratings in this case) can have a dramatic effect on the magnitude of the reliability coefficient. Since we are likely to average or add up all the available ratings in scoring each student, it may be useful to calculate the reliability of the ratings taken together. Remember the interrater correlations provide estimates of the reliability of each single

set of ratings. Two or three sets of ratings are likely to be higher in reliability when taken together than a single rating, so adjusting the reliability to account for such larger numbers of raters is generally advisable.

> **Table 8.8** Interrater correlations for writing sample ($N = 55$)
>
> | | | | |
> |---|---|---|---|
> | R1 | 1.000 | | |
> | R2 | 0.632 | 1.000 | |
> | R3 | 0.571 | 0.662 | 1.000 |
> | | R1 | R2 | R3 |

The Spearman-Brown prophecy formula (explained in the discussion of split-half reliability) can be used for this purpose. Remember, the formula for this adjustment was:

$$r_{xx'} = \frac{n \times r}{(n - 1)r + 1}$$

$r_{xx'}$ = full-test reliability
r = correlation between the two test halves
n = number of times the test length is to be increased

I could apply the adjustment to any one of the coefficients reported in Table 8.8, but my naturally careful approach to all statistics leads me to use the lowest estimate, .571 in this case. Adjusted for two ratings ($n = 2$) from this single set estimate, the Spearman-Brown prophecy formula is applied as follows:

$$r_{xx'} = \frac{n \times r}{(n - 1)r + 1} = \frac{(2).571}{(2 - 1).571 + 1} = \frac{1.142}{1.571} = .7269255 \approx .73$$

However, since the actual decisions in this case are based on three sets of ratings, a more appropriate adjustment would be for three ratings ($n = 3$) in order to estimate approximately what the reliability is for all three raters combined, as follows:

$$r_{xx'} = \frac{n \times r}{(n - 1)r + 1} = \frac{(3).571}{(3 - 1).571 + 1} = \frac{1.713}{2.142} = .799198 \approx .80$$

Intrarater reliability is typically estimated by getting two sets of scores produced by the same rater for the same group of students (say a rater scores one group's set of compositions on two successive occasions about two weeks apart), and calculating a correlation coefficient between those two sets of scores. The resulting coefficient provides an estimate of the intrarater reliability of the judgments being made by that rater on either of the two occasions (as with the interrater reliability), if the two sets of ratings are to be averaged or added up in the decision-making process, the Spearman-Brown prophecy formula can be used to estimate the reliability of the two ratings taken together. Intrarater reliability coefficients provide estimates of the consistency of judgments over time.

Interpreting Reliability Estimates

Reporting the degree to which a test is reliable is often necessary in the process of developing and defending a new language test. I have shown a number of alternatives from which teachers can choose to estimate the reliability of their norm-referenced tests. However, regardless of the type of reliability involved, the interpretation of the coefficients is about the same. The central concern is with how consistent the test is in terms of the percent of variance in the scores that is reliable and the percent that is attributable to error. If $r_{xx'} = .33$, then 33 percent of the variance in the test scores is reliable, and the remaining 67 percent is measurement error. Hence, a reliability estimate of .33 indicates that the test scores are not very reliable for the particular group of students involved and that the test should either be seriously revised or replaced altogether.

Remember that reliability estimates are derived from the performances of a particular group of people. Hence, the estimate is linked to that group. In other words, the tester can only make claims about the reliability of a test with reference to that particular group of students; or perhaps very cautiously, claims can be made about the probable level of reliability when the test is administered to a *very similar* group of students with about the same range of abilities.

Standard Error of Measurement

Reliability coefficients are just one useful way of looking at the issue of norm-referenced test consistency. Such coefficients can, indeed, be used to estimate how reliable the test is in percentage terms. Another, perhaps more concrete, way of looking at the consistency of a set of test scores is called the **standard error of measurement** (SEM). Conceptually, this statistic is used to determine a band around a student's score within which that student's score would probably fall if the test were administered repeatedly to the same person. Based on the percentages in the normal distribution (discussed in Chapters 5 and 6), the SEM can also be used to estimate the probability with which the tester expects those scores to fall within one SEM of where it is, or two SEMs, or even three SEMs. Consider Test A, a 100-item test administered in the Haleakala Immigrant Services Center ESL program, for which the standard error of measurement is 5 (that is, SEM = 5). I can conclude from this SEM that a particular student, Xiao Lao, who scored 80, will score within a band of one SEM plus (80 + 5 = 85) or minus (80 − 5 = 75) 68% of the time if she takes the test over and over again (without learning in the process). I base this interpretation on the notion that a standard deviation would exist for the hypothetical normal distribution of the chance fluctuations (error) in Xioa Lao's scores, and that the percentages under the normal distribution discussed in Chapter 6 would apply. The deviation of these errors across all students is the SEM, and errors within one SEM plus or minus would occur about 68% of the time (34.13% + 34.13% = 68.26% ≈ 68%).

The purpose of the SEM, then, is to estimate a sort of average of the distribution of error deviations across all the students who took the test. On the basis of this statistic, a tester can estimate with certain probabilities how far students' scores will vary by chance alone if the students were to take the test repeatedly. Using this information, the tester can be fairly sure that, for any student, error alone can cause the scores to vary within a band of plus or minus one SEM (±1 SEM, or ± 5 points in this example) 68% of the time. For Xiao Lao, whose score was 80, this SEM indicates that, by chance alone, her scores could vary between 75 and 85 points 68% of the time if she were to take the test repeatedly. If testers want to be even more sure of this band, they can extend it out further to two SEMs (5 + 5 = 10) plus (80 + 10 = 90) or minus (80 − 10 = 70) on either side of the observed raw score. The tester would then be relatively sure that Xiao Lao's score would consistently fall between 70 and 90 (95% of the time, based on the percentages under the normal distribution).

To calculate the SEM, I will need the standard deviation of the test and any of the reliability coefficients discussed previously. The formula for calculating SEM is relatively simple:

$$SEM = S\sqrt{1 - r_{xx'}}$$

SEM = standard error of measurement
S = standard deviation of the test
$r_{xx'}$ = reliability estimate for the test

I apply this formula to the data shown in Tables 8.3, 8.5, and 8.6, for which $S = 4.97$ and $r_{xx'} = .84$ (using K-R20). The resulting SEM based on the formula is:

$$SEM = S\sqrt{1 - r_{xx'}} = 4.97\sqrt{1 - .84} = 4.97\sqrt{.16} = 4.97 \times .40 = 1.988 \approx 2.0$$

This is a much lower figure than the SEM calculated for Xiao Lao's test; therefore, the band of chance fluctuations in students' scores is narrower. However, as with all statistics, this one is relative to other factors that must be considered at the same time. In comparing the SEM found here with the one produced by the test that Xiao Lao took, note that this test only had 30 items while Xioa Lao's test had 100 items. Nevertheless, in this case, the SEM of 2.0 indicates that there would only be relatively small fluctuations in the students' scores if they were to take the test repeatedly.

A corollary to all this is that the narrower the SEM is, the narrower the band of possible fluctuations will be, or the more consistently the raw scores represent the students' actual abilities. Thus, with all other factors held constant, a test that has a small SEM is more consistent than one with a large SEM. In a sense, the SEM is easier to interpret than a reliability coefficient because it is expressed in terms of raw score bands rather than the more abstract percentage interpretations typically used to interpret reliability estimates.

This difference extends to the use of these statistics for real-life decision-making purposes, where the SEM is often far more important than any reliability coefficient. The SEM is especially useful in deciding the "fate" of students who are on the borderline for some decision that can affect their lives in important ways. For example, perhaps the test that Xiao Lao took was for purposes of placement into adult-education English courses. This decision is a fairly important one for Xiao Lao. After all, if the test inaccurately places her into a level below her true ability, it would unjustly cost her extra time, energy, and money if she had to take courses she did not need. In such a situation, most language professionals would like placement to be as accurate and fair as possible.

Unfortunately, our unlucky Xiao Lao scored 80, and the cut-point between the second and third levels of ESL study was 82 points. Into which course should she be placed? She is clearly within one SEM (5 points) of the cut-point, so she might score into the third level if she were to take the test again, yet her actual score indicates that she should be placed into the second level. A responsible decision about Xiao Lao, or any student in a similar situation, would probably involve getting more information about her proficiency (for example, an additional composition, or oral interview) before making the decision about which way she should be placed. Clearly then, the SEM can be a very important way to apply the concept of reliability in a very practical sense to the actual decision making in a language program. The SEM should be considered, therefore, and reported right along with reliability coefficients for any norm-referenced test.

USING A SPREADSHEET TO CALCULATE NRT RELIABILITY

In this section, I will explain step-by-step how to use your *Excel*™ spreadsheet to calculate NRT reliability estimates for split-half (adjusted), Cronbach alpha, K-R20, K-R21, and the standard error of measurement. To calculate interrater or intrarater reliability estimates, you will simply need to combine what you learned in the previous chapter about calculating correlation coefficients in your spreadsheet with the explanation below in Screen 8.2 and the associated discussion for applying the Spearman-Brown prophecy formula.

SPLIT-HALF (ADJUSTED) AND CRONBACH ALPHA

To calculate split-half (adjusted) reliability and the Cronbach alpha coefficient explained in this chapter, I begin by creating a score for the odd-numbered items for the first student. In Screen 8.1, you will see the item level data that we have worked with before. I began by labeling two columns at the top (AG and AH) as **Odd** and **Even**. Then, in Cell AG2, I added up the ones and zeros in the cells that represented the odd-numbered items for the first student. I did so by typing the following: **=B2+D2+F2+H2+J2+L2+N2+P2+R2+T2+V2+X2+Z2+AB2+AD2**.

Once I hit ENTER for Cell AG2, I had the score for the first student's odd-numbered items. I then copied Cell AG2 and pasted it to Cell AH2. Since all the cells that were being added up in Cell AG2 moved over one column when copied to Cell AH2, that operation provided the total for all the even-numbered items, as well. With the odd and even scores for the first student in Cells AG2 and AH2, respectively, I then copied those two cells and pasted them down the entire column from AG3 to AH31 for all the students as shown in Screen 8.1.

I also labeled and calculated the mean, standard deviation, and variance for the total scores in Cells AF33 to AF35 using the functions shown in Screen 8.1. Once I had entered each of those functions, I copied them into the corresponding spaces below the Odd and Even scores in Cells AG33 to AG35 and AH33 to AH35. The resulting statistics are shown in Screen 8.2.

Screen 8.1 Data set-up and first steps in calculating split-half (adjusted) and Cronbach alpha reliability estimates

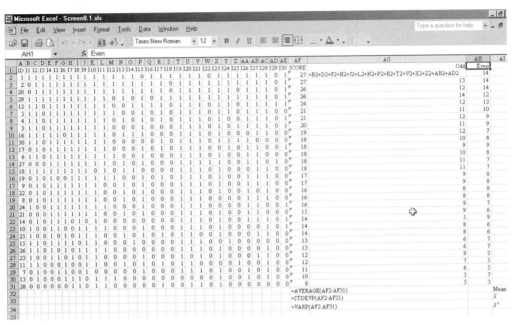

Screen 8.2: Remaining steps in calculating split-half (adjusted) and Cronbach alpha reliability estimates

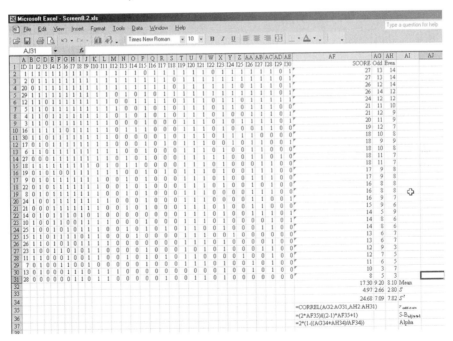

The next step in estimating the split-half (adjusted) reliability is to label and calculate the Pearson product-moment correlation coefficient. I labeled it $r_{odd\text{-}even}$ in Cell AI35 of Screen 8.2 and calculated it by using **=CORREL(AG2:AG31,AH2:AH31)** as shown in Cell AF35. That correlation coefficient yields the half-test reliability, but of course I want the full-test reliability so I need to apply the Spearman-Brown prophecy formula. The spreadsheet cannot read the formula as it was presented earlier in the chapter. Instead, I must label the Spearman-Brown adjustment (abbreviated "S-B adjust" in Cell AI36) and apply the formula in its linear algebra equivalent as shown in Cell AF36 of Screen 8.2, which shows $=(2*AF35)/((2-1)*AF35+1)$.

Step-by-step, that formula is saying:

1. Multiply two times the half-test correlation (in Cell AF35) and isolate the result in parentheses.
2. Subtract 1 from 2 and isolate that result in parentheses.
3. Multiply the result of Step 2 times the half-test correlation (in AF35) and add 1, then isolate the result in parentheses.
4. Divide the result of Step 1 by the result of Step 3, and hit ENTER.
5. The final result of .79 is shown in Cell AF36 in Screen 8.3.

To calculate the Cronbach alpha described earlier in the chapter, I label it **Alpha** in cell AI37 and apply the Cronbach alpha formula in its linear algebra equivalent as shown in Cell AF37 of Screen 8.2, which shows $=2*(1-((AG34+AH34)/AF34))$.

Step-by-step, that formula is saying:

1. Add the variance for the odd items (AG34) to the variance for the even items (AH34) and isolate the result in parentheses.
2. Divide the result of Step 1 by the variance for the whole test (AF34) and isolate the result in parentheses.
3. Subtract the result of Step 2 from 1 and isolate the result in parentheses.
4. Multiply the result of Step 3 times 2, and hit ENTER.
5. The final result of .79 is shown in Cell AF37 of Screen 8.3.

Naturally, you will want to save these results, probably under a new file name so you don't lose this work if something goes wrong with your computer.

Screen 8.3 Results of calculating split-half (adjusted) and Cronbach alpha reliability estimates

SCORE	Odd	Even	
27	13	14	
27	13	14	
26	12	14	
26	14	12	
24	12	12	
21	11	10	
21	12	9	
20	11	9	
19	12	7	
18	10	8	
18	9	9	
18	10	8	
18	11	7	
18	11	7	
17	9	8	
17	9	8	
16	8	8	
16	8	8	
16	9	7	
15	9	6	
14	5	9	
14	8	6	
14	8	6	
13	6	7	
13	6	7	
13	6	7	
12	9	3	
12	7	5	
11	6	5	
10	3	7	
8	5	3	
17.30	9.20	8.10	Mean
4.97	2.66	2.80	S
24.68	7.09	7.82	S^2
0.66			$r_{odd-even}$
0.79			S-B$_{adjusted}$
0.79			Alpha

Starting over with the same data set, but without the split-half (adjusted) or Cronbach alpha calculations to clutter things up, I begin setting up the data for calculating K-R20 and K-R21 (as shown in Table 8.4) by labeling the IF, $1-F$, and S_i^2 (in Cells A33 to A35) then calculating those values for I1 as shown in Cells B33 to B35. I do so in the following steps.

1. Calculate the IF for I1 by averaging the ones and zeros for that item (by typing **=AVERAGE(B2:B31)** in Cell B33 and hitting ENTER).
2. Calculate one minus the IF for I1 by subtracting the value in B33 from one (by typing **=1−B33** in Cell B34 and hitting ENTER).
3. Calculate the item variance for I1 by multiplying IF found in B33 times the $1-IF$ found in B34 (by typing **=B33*B34** in Cell B35 and hitting ENTER).
4. Copy Cells B33 to B35 and paste them across the bottom of the other items in the range C33 to AE35 as shown in Table 8.4.

Screen 8.4 First steps in calculating K-R20 & K-R21 formulas

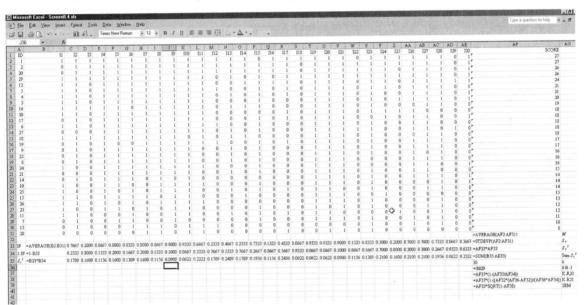

Once I have the item variances in hand for all the items, I continue setting up the data for calculating K-R20 and K-R21 (as shown in Screen 8.5) by labeling the M, S_T, S_T^2, Sum S_i^2, k, and $k/k-1$ (in cells AG32 to AG37), then calculating those values for the total scores in Cells AF32 to AF37. I do so in the following steps.

1. Calculate the mean by typing **=AVERAGE(AF2:AF31)** in Cell AF32 and hitting ENTER.
2. Calculate the standard deviation (using the n formula) by typing **=STDEVP(AF2:AF31)** in Cell AF33 and hitting ENTER.
3. Calculate the total test variance, or standard deviation squared, by typing **=AF33*AF33** in Cell AF34 and hitting ENTER.
4. Add up the item variances for all the items found in Row B35 to AE35 by typing **=SUM(B35:AE35)** in Cell AF35 and hitting ENTER.

5. There are 30 items, so type **30** in Cell AF36 and hit **ENTER**.
6. The result of $k/k-1$ will be 30 divided by 29, so I type **=30/29** in Cell AF37 and hit **ENTER**.

The results of steps 1–6 are shown in Cells AF32 to AF37 of Screen 8.6.

Screen 8.5 Second set of steps in calculating K-R20 & K-R21 formulas

Microsoft Excel - Screen8.5.xls

File Edit View Insert Format Tools Data Window Help

AF19   fx =SUM(B19:AE19)

	X	Y	Z	AA	AB	AC	AD	AE	AF	AG	AH
1	123	124	125	126	127	128	129	130		SCORE	
2	1	1	1	1	1	1	0	1		27	
3	1	1	1	1	1	1	0	1		27	
4	1	1	0	1	1	1	0	1		26	
5	1	1	1	1	1	1	0	1		26	
6	1	1	0	1	1	1	1	1		24	
7	1	1	0	1	1	1	0	0		21	
8	1	0	0	1	1	1	0	1		21	
9	1	0	1	1	1	1	0	1		20	
10	1	0	0	0	1	1	0	0		19	
11	1	1	1	1	0	0	0	0		18	
12	0	1	0	1	1	0	0	1		18	
13	1	0	0	1	0	0	0	0		18	
14	1	0	0	1	1	0	1	0		18	
15	1	0	0	0	1	1	0	0		18	
16	1	0	0	1	1	1	0	0		17	
17	1	0	0	1	1	1	0	0		17	
18	1	0	0	1	0	1	0	0		16	
19	0	0	0	1	1	1	0	0		16	
20	0	0	0	1	1	0	0	1		16	
21	1	0	0	1	1	0	0	0		15	
22	1	0	0	1	1	1	0	1		14	
23	1	0	0	0	0	1	0	1		14	
24	1	0	0	0	1	1	0	0		14	
25	0	1	0	0	0	0	0	0		13	
26	1	0	0	0	0	1	0	0		13	
27	1	0	0	0	1	1	0	0		12	
28	0	0	1	0	0	1	0	0		12	
29	1	0	0	1	0	1	0	0		11	
30	1	0	0	1	0	1	0	0		10	
31	1	0	0	0	0	0	0	0		8	
32									=AVERAGE(AF2:AF31)	M	
33	0.8333	0.3000	0.2000	0.7000	0.7000	0.7333	0.0667	0.3667	=STDEVP(AF2:AF31)	S_T	
34	0.1667	0.7000	0.8000	0.3000	0.3000	0.2667	0.9333	0.6333	=AF33*AF33	S_T^2	
35	0.1389	0.2100	0.1600	0.2100	0.2100	0.1956	0.0622	0.2322	=SUM(B35:AE35)	Sum S_i^2	
36									30	k	
37									=30/29	k/k-1	
38									=AF37*(1-(AF35/AF34))	K-R20	
39									=AF37*(1-((AF32*(AF36-AF32))/(AF36*AF34)))	K-R21	
40									=AF33*SQRT(1-AF38)	SEM	

Sheet1 Sheet2 Sheet3

Ready

Now that I have all the bits and pieces I need to calculate K-R20 or K-R21, the final step for each is to actually calculate it.

To calculate K-R20, I label it in Cell AG38 and apply the K-R20 formula in its linear algebra equivalent as shown in Cell AF38 of Screen 8.5, which shows **=AF37*(1−(AF35/AF34))**.

Step-by-step, that formula is saying:
1. Inside the parentheses to the right of the asterisk, divide the sum of the item variances (AF35) by the total test variance (AF34) and isolate the result in parentheses.
2. Subtract the result of Step 1 from 1 and isolate that result in parentheses.
3. Multiply the result of Step 2 by the result of dividing k by $k-1$ (already calculated in AF37) and hit **ENTER**.
4. The resulting value should be .84, as shown in Cell AF38 of Screen 8.6

Screen 8.6 Results of calculating K-R20 & K-R21 formulas

Microsoft Excel - Screen8.6.xls
File Edit View Insert Format Tools Data Window Help

ID	I1	I2	I3	I4	I5	I6	I7	I8	I9	I10	I11	I12	I13	I14	I15	I16	I17	I18	I19	I20	I21	I22	I23	I24	I25	I26	I27	I28	I29	I30	SCORE
1	1	1	1	1	1	1	1	1	1	1	1	1	1	1	1	0	1	1	1	1	1	1	1	1	1	1	1	1	0	1	27
2	0	1	1	1	1	1	1	1	1	1	1	1	1	1	1	1	0	1	1	1	1	1	1	1	0	1	1	1	0	1	27
20	0	1	1	1	1	1	1	1	1	1	1	1	0	1	1	0	1	1	1	1	1	1	1	1	1	1	1	1	0	1	26
29	1	1	1	0	1	1	1	1	1	1	1	0	0	1	1	1	1	0	1	1	1	1	1	0	1	1	1	1	1	1	24
12	1	1	0	1	1	1	1	1	1	1	1	0	0	0	1	0	1	0	1	1	1	0	1	0	1	1	1	1	0	1	21
5	1	1	0	1	1	1	1	1	1	1	1	0	1	0	1	0	1	0	1	1	1	0	1	0	0	0	1	1	0	1	21
4	1	1	1	1	1	1	1	1	1	1	0	0	0	0	1	0	1	0	1	1	1	0	1	0	1	0	1	1	0	1	20
3	1	1	1	1	0	1	1	1	1	1	1	0	1	1	1	0	0	0	1	1	0	1	0	0	0	1	1	1	0	0	19
16	1	1	0	1	1	1	1	1	1	1	0	0	0	0	1	1	1	1	1	1	1	0	1	0	0	0	1	1	0	1	18
30	0	1	0	1	1	1	1	1	1	1	0	0	0	0	1	0	1	0	1	1	1	0	1	1	0	0	1	1	1	0	18
17	1	1	0	1	1	1	1	1	1	1	0	0	0	0	1	0	1	0	1	1	1	0	0	0	1	0	1	1	0	0	18
6	1	1	1	1	1	1	1	1	1	0	1	0	0	0	0	0	1	0	1	1	1	0	0	1	1	0	1	0	0	0	18
27	0	0	0	1	1	1	1	1	1	1	1	0	0	1	0	0	0	0	1	1	1	1	1	1	0	0	1	1	0	1	18
18	1	1	1	1	1	1	1	1	0	1	1	0	1	1	0	0	0	0	1	1	1	0	0	0	1	1	1	1	0	0	18
19	0	1	0	1	0	0	1	1	1	1	1	1	0	0	1	0	1	0	1	1	1	0	0	1	1	1	1	0	0	0	17
9	0	1	0	1	1	1	1	1	1	1	0	0	1	0	1	0	1	0	1	0	1	0	0	0	1	1	1	0	0	0	16
22	0	1	0	1	1	1	1	1	1	1	0	0	0	0	1	0	1	0	1	0	0	0	1	0	1	1	1	0	0	0	16
8	0	0	0	1	1	1	1	1	1	1	0	0	0	0	1	0	1	0	1	0	1	0	0	0	1	1	1	0	0	1	16
24	1	0	0	1	1	1	1	1	1	1	0	0	0	0	1	0	1	0	1	0	0	0	1	0	0	1	1	0	0	1	15
21	0	0	0	1	1	1	1	1	1	1	0	0	0	0	1	0	1	0	1	0	1	0	0	0	1	1	1	0	0	1	14
14	0	1	0	1	1	1	0	1	0	1	0	0	0	0	1	0	1	0	1	1	1	0	0	0	0	0	1	0	0	1	14
10	1	0	0	1	0	1	1	1	1	0	0	0	0	0	1	0	1	0	1	1	0	0	0	1	1	0	1	0	0	0	14
25	1	0	0	1	0	1	0	1	0	0	1	0	0	0	1	0	1	1	1	0	0	0	1	0	0	0	1	0	0	0	13
15	1	0	0	1	1	1	1	0	1	0	0	0	0	1	0	0	1	0	1	0	0	0	0	0	1	0	1	0	0	0	13
26	1	0	1	0	1	0	1	0	0	0	1	0	0	0	1	0	1	0	1	0	1	0	0	0	1	1	1	0	0	0	12
23	1	0	0	0	1	0	0	1	0	0	0	0	0	0	1	0	1	0	1	1	0	0	0	0	1	0	1	0	0	0	12
11	1	1	0	0	0	1	0	0	1	0	0	0	0	0	1	0	0	1	0	1	1	0	0	0	0	1	0	1	0	0	11
7	0	1	0	0	1	0	1	0	0	0	1	0	0	0	1	0	0	1	0	1	0	0	0	1	0	1	0	1	0	0	10
13	0	1	0	0	0	0	1	1	0	1	1	0	0	0	0	0	1	0	1	0	1	0	1	0	0	0	0	0	0	0	10
28	0	0	0	0	0	0	1	1	0	1	0	0	0	0	0	0	1	0	1	0	1	0	1	0	0	0	0	0	0	0	8

Summary statistics:

- 17.30 M
- 4.97 S_I
- 24.68 S_T^2
- 4.62 Sum S_I^2
- 30 k
- 1.03 $k/k-1$
- 0.84 K-R20
- 0.73 K-R21
- 1.98 SEM

	I1	I2	I3	I4	I5	I6	I7	I8	I9	I10	I11	I12	I13	I14	I15	I16	I17	I18	I19	I20	I21	I22	I23	I24	I25	I26	I27	I28	I29	I30
IF	0.5667	0.7667	0.2000	0.8667	0.8000	0.8333	0.8000	0.8667	0.9000	0.9333	0.6667	0.2333	0.4667	0.2333	0.7333	0.1333	0.4333	0.0667	0.9333	0.9333	0.9000	0.1333	0.8333	0.3000	0.2000	0.7000	0.7000	0.7333	0.0667	0.3667
1-IF	0.4333	0.2333	0.8000	0.1333	0.2000	0.1667	0.2000	0.1333	0.1000	0.0667	0.3333	0.7667	0.5333	0.7667	0.2667	0.8667	0.5667	0.9333	0.0667	0.0667	0.1000	0.8667	0.1667	0.7000	0.8000	0.3000	0.3000	0.2667	0.9333	0.6333
S_I^2	0.2456	0.1789	0.1680	0.1156	0.1600	0.1389	0.1600	0.1156	0.0900	0.0622	0.2222	0.1789	0.2489	0.1789	0.1956	0.1156	0.2456	0.0622	0.0622	0.0622	0.0900	0.1156	0.1389	0.2100	0.1600	0.2100	0.2100	0.1956	0.0622	0.2322

To calculate K-R21, I label it in Cell AG39 and apply the K-R21 formula in its linear algebra equivalent as shown in Cell AF39, which shows
$$=AF37*(1-((AF32*(AF36-AF32))/(AF36*AF34))).$$
Step-by-step, that formula is saying:
1. At the far right, multiply the number of items (AF36) times the total test variance (AF34) and isolate that result in parentheses.
2. Then, looking to the left of the / sign, subtract the mean (AF32) from the number of items (AF36) and isolate the result in parentheses.
3. Multiply the result of Step 2 times the mean (AF32) and isolate the result in parentheses.
4. Divide the result of Step 3 by the result of Step 2 and isolate the result in parentheses.
5. Subtract the result of the previous step from 1 and isolate the result in parentheses.
6. Multiply the result of Step 5 by the result of dividing k by $k-1$ (already calculated in AF37) and hit ENTER.
7. The resulting value should be .73, as shown in Cell AF39 of Screen 8.6.

Naturally, you will want to save these results, again probably under a new file name.

To calculate the standard error of measurement (SEM) using the K-R20 reliability, I label it in Cell AG40 and apply the SEM formula in its linear algebra equivalent as shown in Cell AF40, which shows **=AF33*SQRT(1−AF38),** as shown in Screen 8.5. In words, I multiply the standard deviation (in Cell AF33) times the square root of 1 minus K-R20 isolated in parentheses. The result, SEM = 1.98, is shown in Screen 8.6.

To sum up briefly, a number of factors affect the reliability of any norm-referenced test (see Tables 8.1 & 8.2). Some of these factors are more directly within the control of testers than are other factors. However, language test developers and users must realize that, if all other factors are held constant, the following statements are usually true:

1. A longer test tends to be more reliable than a short one;
2. A well-designed and carefully-written test tends to be more reliable than a shoddy one;
3. A test made up of items that assess similar language material tends to be more reliable than a test that assesses a wide variety of material;
4. A test with items that discriminate well tends to be more reliable than a test with items that do not discriminate well;
5. A test that is well-centered and disperses the scores efficiently (that is, a test that produces normally-distributed scores) tends to be more reliable than a test that has a skewed distribution;
6. A test that is administered to a group of students with a wide range of abilities tends to be more reliable than a test administered to a group with a narrow range of abilities;

In other words, if testers want to maximize the possibility that a test designed for NRT purposes will be reliable, they should make sure that the test is as long as is reasonable, is well designed and carefully written, assesses relatively homogeneous material, has items that discriminate well, is normally distributed, and is administered to a group of students whose abilities are as widely dispersed as logically possible within the context.

REVIEW QUESTIONS

1. What are some of the sources of measurement error? And how is measurement error related to the meaningful variance on a test?

2. Why are the procedures for NRT reliability estimation different from those for CRT reliability?

3. What are the three basic types of NRT reliability discussed in the chapter? What are the conceptual differences among the three types?

4. What are interrater and intrarater reliability? And for what types of tests would they be most appropriate?

5. Which of the three types of NRT reliability is the intrarater reliability most similar to? Why? And the interrater approach?

6. What is the standard error of measurement? For decision-making purposes, is it better to have a large or small SEM?

7. What are the factors that affect the reliability of an NRT, and what steps can you take to maximize such reliability?

A. Screen 8.7 shows the item responses for 30 students who took a 20-item NRT. Like Screen 4.8, these data are for the Sri Lankan high school students in Premaratne 1987. Notice that the *IF* values, 1-*IF*, and *IV* are given at the bottom of the table and that the total scores as well as the odd-numbered and even-numbered scores are given in the columns to the right. In the bottom right corner, you will also find the mean and standard deviation for the total scores, the odd-numbered scores, and the even-numbered scores. Given the information in Screen 8.7, calculate each of the following reliability estimates (either by hand or in your spreadsheet program):

Screen 8.7 Reliability application for NRTs

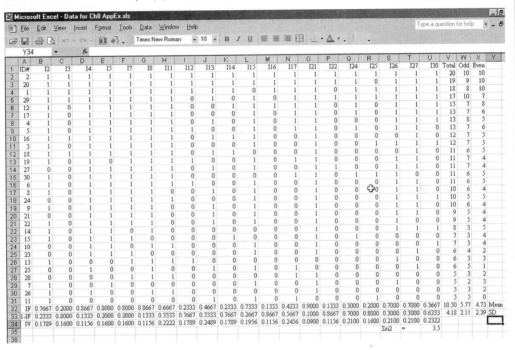

A1. Cronbach α =

A2. K-R21 =

A3. K-R20 =

A4. Split-half reliability (remember to use the half-test correlation and Spearman-Brown prophecy formula) =

B. What do the reliability estimates that you calculated in A1-A4 mean to you in terms of consistency of this test as an NRT?

C. What would the SEM be (based on the K-R20 estimate that you found)?

D. If you had a set of scores assigned by two raters to 30 compositions, you would have two scores for each student. How would you determine the degree to which the scores given by the raters were consistent? What is this type of reliability called? What application of the Spearman-Brown formula should you make in calculating interrater reliability?

CHAPTER 9

LANGUAGE TEST DEPENDABILITY

INTRODUCTION

As noted previously (particularly in Chapters 1 and 5), CRTs will not necessarily produce normal distributions, especially if they are functioning correctly. On some occasions, such as at the beginning of instruction, CRTs may produce normal distributions, but the tester cannot count on the normal distribution as part of the strategy for demonstrating the reliability of a CRT. If all the students have learned the material, the tester would like them all to score near 100 percent on the end-of-course achievement CRT. Hence, a CRT that produces little variance in scores is an ideal that testers seek in developing CRTs. In other words, a low standard deviation on the course post-test may actually be a positive byproduct of developing a sound CRT. This is quite the opposite of the goals and results when developing a good NRT, which ideally should approximate a normal distribution of scores to the greatest extent possible.

As far back as Popham and Husek (1969) the appropriateness of using correlational strategies for estimating the reliability of CRTs was questioned, because such analyses all depend in one way or another on normal distribution and a large standard deviation. Consider the test-retest and equivalent-forms strategies. In both cases, a correlation coefficient is calculated. Since correlation coefficients are designed to estimate the degree to which two sets of numbers go together, scores that are very tightly grouped, because of skewing or homogeneity of ability levels, will probably *not* line the students up in similar ways. As that standard deviation approaches zero, so do any associated correlation coefficients. Correlation coefficients used for estimating interrater and intrarater reliability will be similarly affected by such circumstances. A quick glance back at the K-R20 and K-R21 formulas will also indicate that, as the standard deviation goes down relative to all other factors, so do these internal-consistency estimates. In short, all the strategies for reliability discussed in Chapter 8 are fine for NRTs because they are very sensitive to the magnitude of the standard deviation, and a relatively high standard deviation is one result of developing a norm-referenced test that effectively spreads students out into a normal distribution.

However, those same reliability strategies may be quite inappropriate for CRTs because CRTs are not developed for the purpose of producing variance in scores. Fortunately, many other strategies have been worked out for investigating their consistency—strategies that do not depend on a high standard deviation; in general, they fall into three categories (Berk 1984, p. 235): threshold loss agreement, squared-error loss agreement, and domain score dependability. These three strategies have been developed specifically for CRT consistency estimation. Note that these strategies provide tools for analyzing CRTs that have only recently become available to language testers. Like all statistics, they should be used with caution and interpreted carefully as just what they are: estimates of test consistency.

Notice in the previous paragraph that the terms *agreement* and *dependability* are used with reference to CRTs in lieu of the term *reliability*. In this book, the terms **agreement** and **dependability** are used exclusively for estimates of the consistency of CRTs, while the term reliability is reserved for NRT consistency estimates. This distinction helps teachers and testers keep the notions of NRT reliability separate from the ideas of CRT agreement and dependability.

THRESHOLD LOSS AGREEMENT APPROACHES

As shown in Brown (1990a) and Brown and Hudson (2002), two of the **threshold loss agreement** statistics that are prominent in the literature are also straightforward enough mathematically to be calculated in most language teaching situations. These two statistics are the agreement coefficient and the kappa coefficient. Both of these coefficients measure the consistency of master/non-master classifications as they were defined in Chapter 4. Recall that a master is a student who knows the material or has the skill being tested, while a non-master is a student who does not. These two threshold loss agreement approaches are sometimes called **decision consistency** estimates because they gauge the degree to which decisions that classify students as masters or non-masters are consistent. In principle, these estimates require the administration of a test on two occasions. I will base my conceptual explanations on this relatively impractical strategy. Then I will cover some time-saving strategies that Subkoviak (1988) reported for estimating the agreement and kappa coefficients from the data of a single test administration.

AGREEMENT COEFFICIENT

The **agreement coefficient** (p_o) provides an estimate of the proportion of students who have been consistently classified as masters and non-masters on two administrations of a CRT. To apply this approach, the test should be administered twice, such that enough time has been allowed between the administrations for students to forget the test, but not so much time that they have learned any substantial amount. Using a predetermined cut-point, the students are classified on the basis of their scores into the master and non-master groups on each test administration. The cut-points are usually determined by the purpose of the test. On an achievement test, for instance, a passing score might be considered 60 percent or higher. If this achievement test were administered twice near the end of a term of instruction, the tester would need to tally the number of students who passed (masters) and those who failed (non-masters) on the two administrations.

		ADMINISTRATION 2		
		Masters	Non-masters	
ADMINISTRATION 1	Masters	**A**	**B**	A + B
	Non-masters	**C**	**D**	C + D
		A + C	B + D	A+B+C+D

Figure 9.1 Master/Non-master classifications for two test administrations

Figure 9.1 shows the way to categorize the results on the two tests in order to calculate p_o. In some cases, classifications agree between the two tests. Thus, when students turn out to be masters on both administrations of the test, the tester should count up the number who were masters on both and record the resulting number in cell A in Figure 9.1. Similarly, the number of students classified as non-masters by both tests should go in cell D. In other cases, the classifications disagree between the two administrations. Some students may be classified as masters on the first administration and non-masters on the second. This number should appear in cell B, while those students classified as non-masters on the first administration and masters on the second should go in cell C. Notice that A + B and C + D are totaled to the right of Figure 9.1, and A + C and B + D are also totaled below that figure. Note also that A + B + C + D is shown in the bottom right corner for the total of all four. These additions to the right and below are called **marginals** (probably because they appear in the margins of such figures).

Consider a contrived example for the sake of understanding how the agreement coefficient works: A group of 110 students takes two administrations of a post-test, the master/non-master classifications are shown in Figure 9.2. Notice that 77 out of the 110 students are classified as masters by both administrations, while 21 others are classified as non-masters by both administrations. In addition, 12 students (12 = 6 + 6 students in cells C and B) are classified differently by the two administrations.

ADMINISTRATION 2

	Masters	Non-masters	
Masters	77	6	83
Non-masters	6	21	27
	83	27	110

ADMINISTRATION 1

Figure 9.2 Example master/non-master classifications for two test administrations

With this information in hand, the calculation of the agreement coefficient merely requires application of the following formula:

$$p_o = \frac{A + D}{N}$$

p_o = agreement coefficient
A = number of students in cell A
D = number of students in cell D
N = total number of students

Substituting the values found in Figure 9.2, the calculations turn out as follows:

$$p_o = \frac{A + D}{N} = \frac{77 + 21}{110} = \frac{98}{110} = .8909 \approx .89$$

This result indicates that the test classified the students in the same manner with about 89 percent agreement. Thus, the decision consistency is about 89% and this CRT appears to be very consistent.

Notice that, if all the students were classified in exactly the same way in both administrations, the coefficient would be 1.00 [for example, $(A + D) / N = (80 + 30) / 110 = 1.00$]. Thus, 1.00 is the maximum value that this coefficient can have. However, unlike the reliability coefficients discussed previously for NRTs, the agreement coefficient can logically be no lower than the value that would result from a chance distribution across the four cells. For 120 students, you might reasonably find 30 students per cell by chance alone. This would result in a coefficient of .50 [$(A + D) / N = (30 + 30) /120 = 60 / 120 = .50$]. Thus, for all two-way classifications like that shown in Figure 9.2, the agreement coefficient can logically be no lower than what would occur by chance alone. That is to say, no lower than .50. This is very different from NRT reliability estimates, which can have a logical lower limit of .00.

KAPPA COEFFICIENT

The **kappa coefficient** (κ) was developed to adjust for this problem of a chance lower limit by adjusting to the proportion of consistency in classifications beyond that which would occur by chance alone. The adjustment is given in the following formula:

$$\kappa = \frac{(p_o - p_{chance})}{(1 - p_{chance})}$$

p_o = agreement coefficient
p_{chance} = proportion classification agreement that could occur by chance alone
= $[(A + B)(A + C)+(C + D)(B + D)] / N^2$

As mentioned above, two-way classifications, like those shown in Figure 9.2, will always have a certain P_{chance} level. Hence, before calculating the κ value, a tester must calculate P_{chance} for the particular classification table involved. These levels will differ, of course, depending on the score used as a cut-point in making the absolute decision. For the example data, the calculations would be as follows:

$$P_{chance} = \frac{[(A + B)(A + C)+(C + D)(B + D)]}{N^2} = \frac{[(83)(83) + (27)(27)]}{110^2} = \frac{[6889 + 729]}{12100} = \frac{7618}{12100} = .6296$$

$$\kappa = \frac{(p_o - p_{chance})}{(1 - p_{chance})} = \frac{(.89 - .63)}{(1 - .63)} = \frac{.26}{.37} = .7027 \approx .70$$

The kappa coefficient is an estimate of the classification agreement that occurred beyond what would be expected by chance alone and can be interpreted as a percentage of agreement by moving the decimal two places to the right. Since kappa represents the percentage of classification agreement beyond chance, it is usually lower than the agreement coefficient. Like the agreement coefficient, it has an upper limit of 1.00, but unlike the agreement coefficient with its chance lower limit, the kappa coefficient has the more familiar lower limit of .00.

Estimating threshold loss agreement from a single test administration

Because administering a test twice is cumbersome and hard on everyone involved, several approaches have been worked out to estimate threshold agreement from one administration (see Brown & Hudson 2002). Historically, these approaches have been far too complex for practical application by anyone but a statistician. However, Subkoviak (1988) presented practical approaches for approximating both the agreement and kappa coefficients. In order to approximate either of these coefficients from a single test administration, a tester needs two values. The first is a value for the cut-point score converted to a standard score (as discussed in Chapter 6). This is calculated using the following formula:

$$z = \frac{c - .5 - M}{S}$$

z = standardized cut-point score
c = raw cut-point score
M = mean
S = standard deviation

The second value is one of the NRT internal-consistency reliability estimates (split-half adjusted, Cronbach α, or K-R20). Once the tester has the standardized cut-point score and an internal-consistency reliability estimate in hand, it is just a matter of checking the appropriate table (Table 9.1 for the agreement coefficient, or Table 9.2 for the kappa coefficient). In either table, you can find the value of the respective coefficient by looking in the first column for the z value (regardless of sign, + or −) closest to the obtained value, and scanning across that row until reaching the column headed by the reliability coefficient closest to the observed reliability value. Where the row for the z value meets the column for the reliability coefficient, an approximate value is given for the threshold agreement of the CRT in question. Table 9.1 gives the approximations for the agreement coefficients, and Table 9.2 gives the same information for kappa coefficients (both are adapted from Subkoviak 1988).

Table 9.1 Approximate values of the agreement coefficient

z	Reliability								
	0.10	**0.20**	**0.30**	**0.40**	**0.50**	**0.60**	**0.70**	**0.80**	**0.90**
0.00	0.53	0.56	0.60	0.63	0.67	0.70	0.75	0.80	0.86
0.10	0.53	0.57	0.60	0.63	0.67	0.71	0.75	0.80	0.86
0.20	0.54	0.57	0.61	0.64	0.67	0.71	0.75	0.80	0.86
0.30	0.56	0.59	0.62	0.65	0.68	0.72	0.76	0.80	0.86
0.40	0.58	0.60	0.63	0.66	0.69	0.73	0.77	0.81	0.87
0.50	0.60	0.62	0.65	0.68	0.71	0.74	0.78	0.82	0.87
0.60	0.62	0.65	0.67	0.70	0.73	0.76	0.79	0.83	0.88
0.70	0.65	0.67	0.70	0.72	0.75	0.77	0.80	0.84	0.89
0.80	0.68	0.70	0.72	0.74	0.77	0.79	0.82	0.85	0.90
0.90	0.71	0.73	0.75	0.77	0.79	0.81	0.84	0.87	0.90
1.00	0.75	0.76	0.77	0.77	0.81	0.83	0.85	0.88	0.91
1.10	0.78	0.79	0.80	0.81	0.83	0.85	0.87	0.89	0.92
1.20	0.80	0.81	0.82	0.84	0.85	0.86	0.88	0.90	0.93
1.30	0.83	0.84	0.85	0.86	0.87	0.88	0.90	0.91	0.94
1.40	0.86	0.86	0.87	0.88	0.89	0.90	0.91	0.93	0.95
1.50	0.88	0.88	0.89	0.90	0.90	0.91	0.92	0.94	0.95
1.60	0.90	0.90	0.91	0.91	0.92	0.93	0.93	0.95	0.96
1.70	0.92	0.92	0.92	0.93	0.93	0.94	0.95	0.95	0.97
1.80	0.93	0.93	0.94	0.94	0.94	0.95	0.95	0.96	0.97
1.90	0.95	0.95	0.95	0.95	0.95	0.96	0.96	0.97	0.98
2.00	0.96	0.96	0.96	0.96	0.96	0.97	0.97	0.97	0.98

For instance, perhaps a CRT achievement test had a mean of 58.47, a cut-point of 60 out of 100, a standard deviation of 6.10, and a K-R20 reliability estimate of .86. To obtain the standardized cut-point score (z), the tester would first need the following formula:

$$z = \frac{c - .5 - M}{S} = \frac{60 - .5 - 58.47}{6.10} = \frac{1.03}{6.10} = .1689 \approx .17$$

To approximate the agreement coefficient by following Subkoviak's instructions, the tester would next check Table 9.1 at the row for z that is the closest to .17 (.20 in this case) and then look across the top for the reliability closest to .86 (.90 in this case). Where the identified row and column intersect, the tester finds a value of .86 for the approximate agreement coefficient. Following the same steps in Table 9.2 yields an estimate for the kappa coefficient, $\kappa = .71$ in this case.

Table 9.2 Approximate values of the kappa coefficient

	Reliability								
z	0.10	0.20	0.30	0.40	0.50	0.60	0.70	0.80	0.90
0.00	0.06	0.13	0.19	0.26	0.33	0.41	0.49	0.59	0.71
0.10	0.06	0.13	0.19	0.26	0.33	0.41	0.49	0.59	0.71
0.20	0.06	0.13	0.19	0.26	0.33	0.41	0.49	0.59	0.71
0.30	0.06	0.12	0.19	0.26	0.33	0.40	0.49	0.59	0.71
0.40	0.06	0.12	0.19	0.25	0.32	0.40	0.48	0.58	0.71
0.50	0.06	0.12	0.18	0.25	0.32	0.40	0.48	0.58	0.70
0.60	0.06	0.12	0.18	0.24	0.31	0.39	0.47	0.57	0.70
0.70	0.05	0.11	0.17	0.24	0.31	0.38	0.47	0.57	0.70
0.80	0.05	0.11	0.17	0.23	0.30	0.37	0.46	0.56	0.69
0.90	0.05	0.10	0.16	0.22	0.29	0.36	0.45	0.55	0.68
1.00	0.05	0.10	0.15	0.21	0.28	0.35	0.44	0.54	0.68
1.10	0.04	0.09	0.14	0.20	0.27	0.34	0.43	0.53	0.67
1.20	0.04	0.08	0.14	0.19	0.26	0.33	0.42	0.52	0.66
1.30	0.04	0.08	0.13	0.18	0.25	0.32	0.41	0.51	0.65
1.40	0.03	0.07	0.12	0.17	0.23	0.31	0.39	0.50	0.64
1.50	0.03	0.07	0.11	0.16	0.22	0.29	0.38	0.49	0.63
1.60	0.03	0.06	0.10	0.15	0.21	0.28	0.37	0.47	0.62
1.70	0.02	0.05	0.09	0.14	0.20	0.27	0.35	0.46	0.61
1.80	0.02	0.05	0.08	0.13	0.18	0.25	0.34	0.45	0.60
1.90	0.02	0.04	0.08	0.12	0.17	0.24	0.32	0.43	0.59
2.00	0.02	0.04	0.07	0.11	0.16	0.22	0.31	0.42	0.58

These approximations of the agreement and kappa coefficients are underestimates of the values that would be obtained using two test administrations. Thus, they are safe estimates but will always be on the low side of what the tester would obtain in a two-administration situation. Hence, if they are low, the tester might want to double-check the consistency of the test by using other approaches. Using a variety of approaches is a good idea in any case.

Threshold loss agreement coefficients focus on the degree to which classifications in clear-cut categories (master or non-master) are consistent. **Squared-error loss agreement** strategies also do this, but they do so with "sensitivity to the degrees of mastery and nonmastery along the score continuum" (Berk, 1984, p. 246). Thus, squared-error loss agreement approaches attempt to account for the distances that students are from the cut-point—that is, the degree of mastery and non-mastery rather than just the dichotomous categorization, that is, whether a person qualifies as a master or non-master. Thus, in most cases where a cut-point is being used, the squared-error loss agreement will provide more information than either the agreement or kappa coefficients.

I present only the **phi(lambda) dependability index** (Brennan, 1980, 1984, 2001) here because it is the only squared-error loss agreement index that can be estimated using a single test administration, and because Brennan has provided a short-cut formula for calculating this index that can be based on raw score test statistics. Adapted to the symbols of this book, the formula is as follows:

$$\Phi(\lambda) = 1 - \left[\frac{1}{k-1} \left(\frac{M_p(1 - M_p) - S_p^2}{(M_p - \lambda)^2 + S_p^2} \right) \right]$$

$\Phi(\lambda)$ = phi(lambda) dependability index
λ = cut-point expressed as a proportion
k = number of items
M_p = mean of proportion scores (or the mean divided by the number of items)
S_p = standard deviation of proportion scores (or the standard deviation
      divided by the number of items)

Consider once again the example shown in Table 8.5 (pp. 182–183) as though it were a CRT. Notice that the proportion scores, given in the column furthest to the right in the table, are the raw scores divided by the number of items. The mean (.57666667) and standard deviation (.1656667) of these proportion scores are the M_p and S_p in the formula for the $\Phi(\lambda)$ coefficient. The k indicates the total number of items, or 30 in this case, and the λ is the cut-point expressed as a proportion. For the example, the cut-point for mastery has been set at 70 percent (or $\lambda = .70$ if expressed as a proportion). Substituting all these values into the $\Phi(\lambda)$ formula:

$$\Phi(\lambda) = \Phi(.70) = 1 - \left[\frac{1}{k-1} \left(\frac{M_p(1 - M_p) - S^2_p}{(M_p - \lambda)^2 + S^2_p} \right) \right]$$

$$= 1 - \left[\frac{1}{30 - 1} \left(\frac{.5766667(1 - .5766667) - .1656667^2}{(.5766667 - .70)^2 + .1656667^2} \right) \right]$$

$$= 1 - \left[\frac{1}{29} \left(\frac{.2441222 - .0274454}{.0152111 + .0274454} \right) \right] = 1 - \left[.0344828 \left(\frac{.2166768}{.0426565} \right) \right]$$

$$= 1 - (.0344828 \times 5.0795728) = 1 - .1751578 = .8248422 \approx .82$$

The result of .82 means that the scores on this test are about 82 percent dependable for making decisions at the .70 cut-point. Remember, this is a short-cut index of dependability that takes into account the distances of students from the cut-point for the master/non-master classification. The full-blown version of this analysis is better overall, but such analyses are beyond the scope of this volume (see Brennan 1984, 2001 for more on this topic).

Domain Score Dependability

All the threshold loss and squared-error loss agreement coefficients described previously have been criticized because they are dependent in one way or another on the cut-score. Alternative approaches, called *domain score estimates of dependability,* have the advantage of being independent of the cut-score. However, in principle, they apply to domain-referenced interpretations rather than to all criterion-referenced interpretations. **Domain-referenced tests** (DRTs) are defined here as a type of CRT that is distinguished primarily by the ways in which items are sampled. For DRTs, the items are sampled from a general, but well-defined, domain of behaviors (e.g., overall business English ability), rather than from individual course objectives (e.g., the course objectives of a specific intermediate level business English class), as is often the case in what might be called **objectives-referenced tests** (ORTs). The results on a DRT can therefore be used to describe a student's status with regard to the domain in a manner similar to the way in which ORT results are used to describe the student's status on small subtests for each course objective. Thus, the terms *domain-referenced* and *objectives-referenced* describe variant sampling techniques within the overall concept of criterion-referenced testing. If objectives-referenced tests are viewed as defining a domain of their own within the scope of the course objectives, any analyses appropriate for DRTs can be taken to also be appropriate for ORTs. One way of analyzing the consistency of domain-referenced tests (and by extension, objectives-referenced tests) is the *phi coefficient.*

The **phi dependability index** (Φ) is also known as the *generalizability coefficient for absolute error* (for more on generalizability theory, see Brennan 2001; Shavelson & Webb 1991; for more on its applications in second language settings, see Kunnan 1992; Stansfield & Kenyon 1992; Bachman, Lynch, & Mason 1995; Brown & Ross 1996; Brown 1999b; Brown & Hudson 2002). Phi is a general-purpose estimate of the domain-referenced dependability of a test. This interpretation assumes that the items are sampled from a well-defined domain and gives no information about the reliability of the individual objectives-based subtests. Nevertheless, phi does provide a handy way to estimate the overall dependability of the scores without reference to a cut-score. The formula that is presented here is derived from information presented by Brennan (1984, 2001). The resulting formula for the phi coefficient is:

$$\Phi = \frac{\dfrac{nS_p^2}{n-1}[\text{K–R20}]}{\dfrac{nS_p^2}{n-1}[\text{K–R20}] + \dfrac{M_p(1-M_p)-S_p^2}{k-1}}$$

n = number of persons who took the test
k = number of items
M_p = mean of proportion scores
S_p = standard deviation of proportion scores (using the N formula rather than $N-1$)
$K\text{-}R20$ = Kuder-Richardson formula 20 reliability estimate

What is necessary for calculating this coefficient of dependability is the number of students, number of items, mean of the proportion scores, standard deviation of the proportion scores, and the K-R20 reliability estimate. Once again using the data in Table 8.5 (pp. 182–183) as though it is a CRT, k is the number of items (30 in this case); n is the number of students (30); M_p is the mean (.5766667) of the proportion scores; S_p is the standard deviation (.1656667) of the same proportion scores; and K-R20 is the traditional reliability estimate (.8410485) demonstrated earlier in the chapter. Substituting all these values into the formula gives the following result:

$$\Phi = \frac{\dfrac{nS_p^2}{n-1}[\text{K–R20}]}{\dfrac{nS_p^2}{n-1}[\text{K–R20}] + \dfrac{M_p(1-M_p)-S_p^2}{k-1}}$$

$$= \frac{\dfrac{30 \times (.1656667)^2}{30-1}[.8410485]}{\dfrac{30 \times (.1656667)^2}{30-1}[.8410485] + \dfrac{.5766667(1-.5766667)-.1656667^2}{30-1}}$$

$$= \frac{\dfrac{.8233620}{29}[.8410485]}{\dfrac{.8233620}{29}[.8410485] + \dfrac{.2166768}{29}} = \frac{.0238787}{.0238787 + .0074716}$$

$$= \frac{.0238787}{.0313503} = .7616737 \approx .76$$

The result of .76 means that the scores on this test are about 76 percent dependable for testing this particular domain. It is important to note that this result for phi exactly matches the result obtained in a full set of generalizability study procedures (including analysis of variance, estimation of G-study variance components, estimation of D-study elements, and finally calculation of the phi, or G coefficient for absolute error)—all of which are well beyond the scope of this book, but are explained in the citations at the top of this section. In other words, although the full generalizability study would be clearer conceptually, precisely the same result has been obtained here using only n, k, M_p, S_p, and K-R20 reliability.

There are several additional points related to these CRT consistency estimates that I must stress. First, some of the coefficients presented in this chapter are related in rather predictable ways. Second, certain cautions are important when doing these calculations—especially those for the phi coefficient.

Relationships

Certain predictable relationships exist among some of the NRT reliability coefficients and the phi dependability index. One interesting relationship that Brennan (1984, pp. 315-316; 2001, pp. 48-49) demonstrates is that, for a given test, K-R21 will always be less than (or equal to) Φ, which will in turn be less than (or equal to) K-R20, as follows:

$$\text{K-R21} \leq \Phi \leq \text{K-R20}$$

Using the example data in Table 8.5 (where K-R21 = .73; Φ = .76; and K-R20 = .84), it is clear that indeed:

$$.73 \leq .76 \leq .84$$

This fact has one important implication: If K-R21 is indeed always lower than (or equal to) Φ, then K-R21 can serve as a conservative "rough and ready" underestimate of the domain-referenced dependability (Φ) of a test.

Cautions

In doing calculations for the phi or phi(lambda) estimates that I demonstrated in this chapter, three cautions must be observed. First, these formulas are only applicable when the items on the test are dichotomously scored (i.e., right or wrong). Second, the n formula (rather than the $n - 1$ formula) should be used in calculating the means and standard deviations of the proportion scores that are used in the phi and phi(lambda) formulas. Third, when doing all the calculations, as much accuracy as possible should be maintained. In other words, throughout the calculations, as many places should be carried to the right of the decimal point as possible. Rounding, then, should be avoided until the final coefficient is estimated.

In addition, the full-blown versions of phi and phi(lambda) coefficients are related to the variance components involved in the test and, as Brennan states, "it is strongly recommended that, whenever possible, one report variance components, and estimate indices of dependability in terms of variance components" (1984, p. 332). Thus, if the resources are available for doing a full-fledged generalizability study, a G-study is the best way to proceed.

CONFIDENCE INTERVALS

I must cover one last statistic in this section on CRT dependability, the **confidence interval** (CI). The CI functions for CRTs in a manner analogous to the standard error of measurement (SEM) that I described in Chapter 8 for NRTs. More explicitly, the CI can be used to estimate a band around each student's score (plus or minus one CI), within which they would probably score with 68 percent probability if they were to take the test again. This thinking can also extend out two bands plus or minus to obtain a 95 percent probability, or three bands for 98 percent probability (recall that these are based on percents in the normal distribution as discussed in Chapter 6). Formulaically, the confidence interval is as follows:

$$CI = \sqrt{\frac{M_p(1 - M_p) - S_p^2}{k - 1}}$$

k = number of items
M_p = mean of proportion scores
S_p = standard deviation of proportion scores (using the N formula rather than $N - 1$)

For the example data shown in Table 8.5 (pp. 182-183), the CI would be calculated as follows:

$$CI = \sqrt{\frac{M_p(1 - M_p) - S_p^2}{k - 1}} = \frac{.5766667(1 - .5766667) - .1656667^2}{30 - 1} = \sqrt{\frac{.2166768}{29}}$$

$$= \sqrt{.0074716} = .0864384 \approx .086$$

In interpreting such CIs, remember that it is a confidence interval for the proportion scores. Thus, the CI of .086 indicates that a student with a proportion score of .70 would score between .614 and .786 (or within a band of one CI plus or minus) 68 percent of the time if the test was repeatedly administered. In other words, the interpretation of the CI for CRT dependability is very much analogous to the interpretation for the SEM when it is applied to the interpretation of NRT reliability (for more on CI, see Brennan, 1984, 2001).

USING A SPREADSHEET TO CALCULATE CRT DEPENDABILITY

In this section, I will explain step-by-step how to use your *Excel*™ spreadsheet to calculate CRT dependability estimates including the agreement, kappa, phi(lambda), and phi estimates, as well as the confidence interval.

Agreement and Kappa Estimates (Using the Subkoviak Method)

I find it easiest to use a calculator and pencil to calculate the standardized z score necessary for finding the agreement and kappa estimates (using the Subkoviak method). I then use my spreadsheet program and methods like those explained in Screens 8.1 to 8.6 and the associated text to calculate either K-R20 or Cronbach alpha. With the standardized z score and one of the reliability estimates in hand, I then refer to Table 9.1 to get the agreement coefficient and to Table 9.2 to get the kappa coefficient (as explained on the previous page).

The Phi(lambda) Coefficient

Screen 9.1 Setting up for calculating CRT dependability estimates

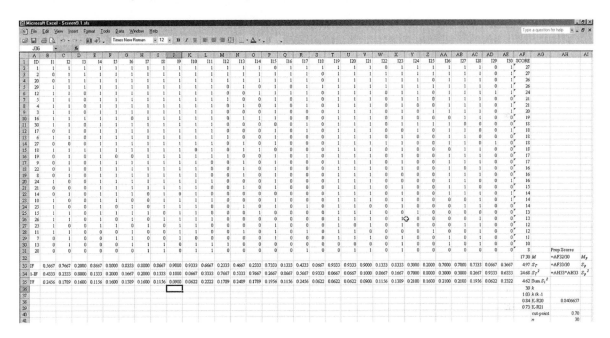

To calculate the phi(lambda) coefficient, I begin by assembling all the statistics I need to calculate this coefficient. In Screen 9.1, you will see the item level data that we have worked with before including the raw score mean, standard deviation, and variance for the total scores in Cells AF32 to AF34. To calculate phi(lambda) and phi, I will need to convert these three raw score statistics to their proportion score equivalents. I have labeled these three proportion score statistics as M_p, S_p, and S_p^2 in Cells AI32 to AI24. I calculate M_p in Cell AH32 by using the formula **=AF32/30,** which tells the computer to use the value in Cell AF32 (i.e., the value of M) and divide it by **30** (i.e., the number of items). I then copy that formula into the cell below it (AH33), which becomes **=AF33/30** and calculates S_p (naturally, you can type out the formula if you like, instead of copying it as I did). The final step is to calculate S_p^2 in Cell AH34, which I do by squaring the result in Cell AH33 (i.e., by multiplying it times itself) as follows: **=AH33*AH33**. [Note that S_p^2 should be calculated by squaring the value of S_p rather than on the basis of dividing the raw score variance (S_T^2) by 30, because that latter strategy will yield an incorrect value.] To calculate phi(lambda) and phi, I will also need to express the K-R20 statistic that I previously calculated to at least seven decimal places. I have done that in Cell AH38 by typing **=AF38** to copy the K-R20 value to that cell and by adjusting the number of decimal places as explained earlier in the book. Finally, I have labeled the cut-point and number of examinees in Cells AG40 and AG41, and typed in those two values in Cells AH40 and AH41; in this case, **0.70** (or 70%) is the cut point and **30** is the number of examinees. The results of all these operations are shown in the same cells in Screen 9.2.

Screen 9.2 Results of Screen 9.1 and formulas for calculating phi(lambda), phi, and *CI*

	AF	AG	AH	AI	AJ	AK	AL	AM	AN	AO
20	16									
21	15									
22	14									
23	14									
24	14									
25	13									
26	13									
27	12									
28	12									
29	11									
30	10									
31	8		Prop Scores							
32	17.30	M	0.5766667	M_p						
33	4.97	S_T	0.1655854	S_p						
34	24.68	S_T^2	0.0274185	S_p^2						
35	4.62	Sum S_i^2								
36	30	k								
37	1.03	k/k -1								
38	0.84	K-R20	0.8406657							
39	0.73	K-R21								
40		cut-point	0.70							
41		n	30							
42		Phi(lambda)	=1-((1/(AF36-1))*(((AH32*(1-AH32))-AH34)/(((AH32-AH40)*(AH32-AH40))+AH34)))							
43		Phi(top)	=((30*AH34)/(30-1))*AH38							
44		Phi(error)	=((AH32*(1-AH32))-AH34)/(AF36-1)							
45		Phi	=AH43/(AH43+AH44)							
46		CI	=SQRT(AH44)							

To calculate the phi(lambda), I label it in Cell AG42 and apply the phi(lambda) formula in its linear algebra equivalent as shown in Cell AH42 of Screen 9.2, which shows **=1−((1/(AF36−1))*(((AH32*(1−AH32))−AH34)/ (((AH32−AH40)*(AH32−AH40))+AH34))).**

Step-by-step, that formula is saying:

1. Begin those calculations working to the right of the first parenthesis by dividing 1 by the isolated result of the number of items (AF36) minus one, and isolate that result in parentheses.
2. Then multiply the mean of the proportion scores (AH32) times the isolated result of 1 minus the mean of the proportion score (AH32) and isolate the result in parentheses.
3. Subtract the result of Step 2 minus the variance of the proportion scores (AH34) and isolate that result in parentheses.
4. Then subtract the mean of the proportion scores (AH32) minus the cut-point (AH40) and isolate the result in parentheses.
5. Multiply the result of Step 4 times itself and isolate the result in parentheses.
6. Add the result of Step 5 to the variance of the proportion scores (AH34) and isolate the result in parentheses.
7. Divide Step 3 by Step 6 and isolate the result in parentheses.
8. Multiply the result of Step 1 times the result of Step 7, and isolate the result in parentheses.
9. Subtract 1 minus the result of Step 8 and hit ENTER.
10. The final result of .8247101 shown in Cell AH42 of Screen 9.3 can now be rounded to .82.

Naturally, you will want to save these results, probably under a new file name, so you don't lose them if something goes wrong with your computer.

Screen 9.3 Results of formulas in Screen 9.2 for phi(lambda), phi, and CI

	AF	AG	AH	AI	AJ	AK	AL	AM	AN	AO	AP
1	SCORE										
2	27										
3	27										
4	26										
5	26										
6	24										
7	21										
8	21										
9	20										
10	19										
11	18										
12	18										
13	18										
14	18										
15	18										
16	17										
17	17										
18	16										
19	16										
20	16										
21	15										
22	14										
23	14										
24	14										
25	13										
26	13										
27	12										
28	12										
29	11										
30	10										
31	8	Prop Scores									
32	17.30 M	0.5766667 M_p									
33	4.97 S_T	0.1655854 S_p									
34	24.68 S_T^2	0.0274185 S_p^2									
35	4.62 Sum S_i^2										
36	30 k										
37	1.03 k/k -1										
38	0.84 K -R20	0.8406657									
39	0.73 K -R21										
40		cut-point	0.70								
41		n	30								
42		Phi(lambda)	0.8247101								
43		Phi(top)	0.0238446								
44		Phi(error)	0.0074725								
45		Phi	0.7613916								
46		CI	0.0864439								
47											
48											

THE PHI COEFFICIENT AND CONFIDENCE INTERVAL

Look back at the formula for the phi coefficient and you will see that all of the calculations above the line in the numerator are repeated below the line in the denominator. At the same time, there are additional calculations over to the right in the denominator, which turn out to be the error term we need in calculating both the phi coefficient and the confidence interval (*CI*). Because of this, I will calculate the top part and the error parts of the phi coefficient separately in the spreadsheet and then quite easily calculate phi and *CI*.

In Screen 9.2, I begin by labeling the two parts of the phi formula as Phi(top) and Phi(error) in Cells AG43 and AG44, respectively, and calculating the top part in its linear algebra equivalent as shown in Cell AH43 of Screen 9.2, which shows **=((30*AH34)/(30−1))*AF38.**

Step-by-step, the calculations for the Phi(top) value are:
1. Begin by multiplying the number of examinees, 30 in this case, times the variance of the proportion scores (AH34), and isolate the result in parentheses.
2. Then subtract 1 from the number of examinees and isolate the result in parentheses.
3. Divide the result of Step 1 by the result of Step 2 and isolate the result in parentheses.
4. Multiply the result of Step 3 times the K-R20 (with seven places to the right of the decimal in AH38) and hit the ENTER key to get the Phi(top) result in Cell AH43.

Next, I calculate the Phi(error) in its linear algebra equivalent as shown in Cell AH44 of Screen 9.2, which shows $=((AH32*(1-AH32))-AH34/(AF36-1)$.
Step-by-step, the calculations for the Phi(error) value are:
1. Multiply the mean of the proportion scores (AH32) times the isolated result of 1 minus the mean of the proportion score (AH32).
2. Subtract the result of Step 1 minus the variance of the proportion scores (AH34) and isolate that result in parentheses.
3. Then divide the result of Step 2 by the isolated result of the number of items (AF36) minus one and hit the ENTER key to get the value of the Phi(error).

To calculate the phi coefficient and *CI*, I begin by labeling the two in Cells AG45 and AG46, respectively. I calculate the phi coefficient in Cell AH45 by dividing the Phi(top) (AH43) by the isolated result of the Phi(top) (AH43) plus the Phi(error) (AH44) and hitting the ENTER key using the following: $=AH43/(AH43+AH44)$.

As shown in Screen 9.2, to calculate the *CI* in Cell AH46, I simply take the square root of the Phi(error) and hit the ENTER key using the following: $=SQRT(AH44)$.

The results of all these calculations for Phi(top), Phi(error), phi, and *CI* are shown in Cells AH43 to AH46 in Screen 9.3, which are very similar to the results obtained in the formulas in the text above. The slight differences are very minor and are due to rounding.

● FACTORS AFFECTING THE CONSISTENCY OF CRTS

As with norm-referenced tests, a number of factors may affect the consistency of a criterion-referenced test. Many of these factors are exactly the same as those listed in Table 8.1. However, some factors are more directly under the control of the test developers than others. If all other factors are held constant, the following will usually be true for CRT development:
1. A longer test will tend to be more consistent than a short one;
2. A well-designed and carefully-written test will tend to be more consistent than a shoddy one;
3. A test made up of items that test similar language material will tend to be more consistent than a test assessing a wide variety of material;
4. A test with items that have relatively high difference indexes, or *B*-indexes, will tend to be more consistent than a test with items that have low ones;
5. A test that is clearly related to the objectives of instruction will tend to be more consistent than a test that is not obviously related to what the students have learned.

In other words, to maximize the possibility that a test designed for CRT purposes will be dependable, make sure that it is as long as is reasonable, is well designed and carefully written, assesses relatively homogeneous material, has items that produce high difference indexes, and is clearly related to the instructional objectives of the course or program in which it is used.

REVIEW QUESTIONS

1. What are the three basic types of CRT dependability discussed in the chapter?
2. What two different statistics are used to estimate threshold loss agreement dependability?
3. What statistic is presented in this book to estimate squared-error loss agreement dependability? Why is this approach sometimes preferable to the threshold loss agreement approach?
4. What statistic is presented in this book to estimate domain score dependability?
5. What is the confidence interval (CI) in the context of CRT dependability?
6. What are the factors that affect the dependability of a CRT?
7. What steps can you take to maximize the dependability of a CRT?

A. Figure 9.3 shows a hypothetical set of master/non-master classifications for a CRT administered on two occasions ten days apart.

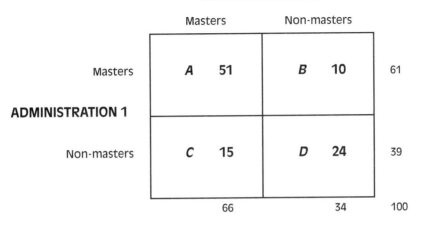

Figure 9.3 Application for hypothetical master/non-master classifications on two administrations of a test

Given the information in Figure 9.3, calculate each of the following CRT reliability estimates:

A1. agreement coefficient =

A2. kappa =

B. Table 9.3 (pp. 218-219) shows the item responses for 30 students who took a 30-item CRT. Assume that the cut-point is a raw score of 24 (80 percent), or a proportion of .80 on this CRT. Notice that the *IF* values, 1-*IF*, and *IV* are given at the bottom of the table and that the proportion scores are given in the columns to the right. In the bottom right corner, you will also find the mean and standard deviation for the total scores and the proportion scores.

Table 9.3 Dependability application for CRTs

ID#	I1	I2	I3	I4	I5	I6	I7	I8	I9	I10	I11	I12	I13	I14	I15	I16	I17
12	1	1	1	1	1	1	1	1	1	1	1	1	1	1	1	1	1
2	1	1	1	1	1	1	1	1	1	1	1	1	1	1	1	1	1
1	1	1	1	1	1	1	1	1	1	1	1	1	1	1	1	1	1
20	1	1	1	1	1	1	1	1	1	1	1	1	1	1	1	1	0
29	1	1	1	1	0	1	1	1	1	1	1	1	1	1	1	0	1
6	1	1	1	0	1	1	1	1	1	1	1	1	1	1	1	0	1
19	1	1	1	1	1	1	1	1	0	1	1	1	1	1	1	0	1
4	1	1	1	1	1	0	1	1	1	1	1	1	1	0	1	1	1
21	1	1	1	1	1	0	0	1	1	1	0	1	1	1	1	0	1
18	1	1	1	0	1	1	1	1	0	1	1	1	1	1	1	0	1
27	1	1	1	1	1	1	0	1	0	1	1	1	1	1	1	1	1
13	1	1	1	1	0	1	1	1	1	1	1	1	1	0	1	0	1
7	1	1	0	1	1	1	1	0	0	1	1	1	1	0	0	0	1
30	1	1	1	1	1	0	0	1	0	1	1	1	1	1	1	0	0
3	1	1	1	1	1	1	1	1	1	1	1	1	1	1	0	0	1
9	1	1	0	1	1	1	1	1	1	0	0	1	1	1	1	0	1
25	1	1	1	1	1	0	0	1	0	1	0	1	1	1	1	0	1
15	1	1	0	1	1	1	0	0	1	0	1	1	1	1	1	0	1
24	1	1	0	1	1	0	1	1	1	1	1	1	0	1	0	1	0
22	1	1	1	0	0	1	0	1	0	0	1	1	1	1	0	0	1
8	1	1	0	1	1	1	1	1	1	0	0	1	1	1	1	0	0
14	1	1	1	0	1	0	0	0	0	1	0	1	1	0	1	1	1
26	1	1	1	0	1	0	1	1	1	1	1	0	1	1	0	0	0
16	1	0	0	1	1	1	1	0	0	1	1	0	1	1	0	0	0
28	1	1	1	1	1	1	0	0	0	0	0	1	1	1	1	1	1
5	1	1	1	0	1	0	1	1	0	1	0	1	1	1	0	0	1
23	1	1	1	1	0	0	0	0	0	1	0	1	0	0	1	0	1
17	1	1	1	1	1	0	1	0	0	0	0	0	1	1	1	0	1
11	1	1	1	0	1	0	0	1	0	0	0	1	1	1	0	0	1
10	0	1	0	0	1	0	0	1	0	1	0	1	1	1	1	1	0
IF	0.9667	0.9667	0.7667	0.7333	0.8667	0.6000	0.6333	0.7667	0.5000	0.7667	0.6333	0.9000	0.9333	0.8667	0.7333	0.3333	0.7667
1-IF	0.0333	0.0333	0.2333	0.2667	0.1333	0.4000	0.3667	0.2333	0.5000	0.2333	0.3667	0.1000	0.0667	0.1333	0.2667	0.6667	0.2333
S_i^2	0.0322	0.0322	0.1789	0.1956	0.1156	0.2400	0.2322	0.1789	0.2500	0.1789	0.2322	0.0900	0.0622	0.1156	0.1956	0.2222	0.1789

Table 9.3 Dependability application for CRTs (continued)

I18	I19	I20	I21	I22	I23	I24	I25	I26	I27	I28	I29	I30	Total	Proportion	
1	1	1	1	1	1	1	1	1	1	1	1	0	29	0.9667	
1	1	1	1	1	1	1	1	1	1	1	1	0	29	0.9667	
0	1	1	1	1	1	1	1	1	1	1	0	1	28	0.9333	
1	1	1	1	1	1	1	1	1	1	1	1	0	28	0.9333	
1	1	1	1	1	1	1	1	1	1	1	1	0	27	0.9000	
1	1	1	1	1	1	0	1	1	1	1	1	0	26	0.8667	
1	1	0	1	1	1	1	1	1	1	0	1	0	25	0.8333	
1	1	0	1	1	1	0	1	1	1	1	1	0	25	0.8333	
1	1	0	1	1	1	1	1	1	0	1	1	1	24	0.8000	
1	1	0	1	1	1	1	1	0	1	1	1	0	24	0.8000	
1	0	0	1	1	1	1	1	1	1	1	0	0	24	0.8000	
1	0	0	1	1	0	1	1	1	1	1	1	0	23	0.7667	
1	1	0	1	1	1	1	1	1	1	1	1	0	23	0.7667	
1	1	1	1	1	1	1	1	1	1	0	1	0	23	0.7667	
1	0	0	1	1	1	1	1	0	0	1	0	0	23	0.7667	
1	1	0	1	1	1	1	1	1	1	1	0	0	23	0.7667	
1	1	0	1	1	1	1	1	1	1	1	0	0	22	0.7333	
1	0	1	1	1	1	1	1	1	1	1	0	0	22	0.7333	
1	1	0	1	1	1	1	0	1	1	1	0	0	21	0.7000	
1	1	1	1	1	1	1	1	1	1	1	0	0	21	0.7000	
1	0	0	1	1	0	1	1	1	1	1	1	0	21	0.7000	
1	1	0	1	1	1	1	1	1	1	1	1	0	21	0.7000	
1	1	1	1	1	0	1	1	1	1	0	1	0	21	0.7000	
1	1	0	1	1	1	1	0	1	1	1	0	0	19	0.6333	
1	0	0	1	1	1	0	0	1	1	0	0	0	19	0.6333	
1	1	0	1	1	1	0	0	1	0	1	1	0	18	0.6000	
0	1	0	1	1	1	1	1	1	1	0	1	0	18	0.6000	
1	1	0	1	0	1	1	0	1	0	1	0	0	18	0.6000	
1	0	0	1	1	1	1	0	1	1	1	1	0	18	0.6000	
1	0	0	1	1	1	1	0	1	0	1	1	0	17	0.5667	
0.9333	0.7333	0.3333	1.0000	1.0000	0.9000	0.9000	0.8333	0.8333	0.9000	0.8000	0.7333	0.0667	22.70	0.7566667	M_p
0.0667	0.2667	0.6667	0.0000	0.0000	0.1000	0.1000	0.1667	0.1667	0.1000	0.2000	0.2667	0.9333	3.35	0.1116667	S_p
0.0622	0.1956	0.2222	0.0000	0.0000	0.0900	0.0900	0.1389	0.1389	0.0900	0.1600	0.1956	0.0622	$\Sigma S_i^2 = 4.18$	.6471832	K-R20

Given the information in Table 9.3, calculate (either by hand or in your spreadsheet program) each of the following dependability estimates:

B1. agreement coefficient (you will also need to use Table 9.1 to do this) =

B2. kappa coefficient (you will also need to use Table 9.2 to do this) =

B3. phi(lambda) dependability index =

B4. phi dependability index =

B5. confidence interval (CI) for phi =

CHAPTER 10
LANGUAGE TEST VALIDITY

INTRODUCTION

In the previous two chapters, I argued that consistency is a necessary and important quality that should be monitored in tests. However, demonstrating reliability or dependability is not sufficient in itself for claiming that a test is doing a good job. For example, the *Test of English as a Foreign Language (TOEFL)* (ETS 2003) is considered a reliable test of overall ESL proficiency. The reliability coefficients reported for the paper-and-pencil TOEFL in the *TOEFL Test and Score Manual* (ETS 1997) were as follows: Listening Comprehension = .90, Structure and Written Expression = .86, Vocabulary and Reading Comprehension = .89, and Total Scores = .95. The corresponding SEM values were reported to be fairly low at 2.0, 2.7, 2.4, and 13.9. Thus, focusing solely on reliability, this test must inevitably be described as a very good measure.

However, validity is a separate but equally important issue. For instance, if the TOEFL were administered to a group of international students as a test of their abilities in mathematics, the reliability would be high because the test would spread the students out rather consistently along a continuum of scores. However, the TOEFL is clearly not valid for the purpose of testing mathematical ability. This is not to say that anyone ever claimed that TOEFL should be used to test mathematics or that TOEFL is not valid for measuring overall ESL proficiency. The point is that, a test can be reliable without being valid. In other words, a test can consistently measure something other than that for which it was designed. Hence test reliability and validity, though related, are different test characteristics. In fact, reliability can be viewed as a precondition for validity, that is, a test cannot be valid unless it is first reliable. A test cannot be said to be systematically testing what it claims to measure unless it is first shown to be systematic (i.e., consistent).

Test validity will be defined here as the degree to which a test measures what it claims, or purports, to be measuring. Validity is especially important when it is involved in the decisions that teachers regularly make about their students. Teachers certainly want to base their admissions, placement, achievement, and diagnostic decisions on tests that are actually testing what they claim to measure. Adopting, developing, and adapting tests for such decisions is difficult enough without having to also worry about whether the tests are measuring the wrong student characteristics, abilities, proficiencies, etc. Hence, in all cases, after insuring that a test is practical and reliable, teachers should consider its validity.

Three main strategies have traditionally been used to investigate validity: content validity, construct validity, and criterion-related validity. Once again, it is necessary to distinguish between norm-referenced tests (NRTs) and criterion-referenced tests (CRTs) in terms of how the results are analyzed. Recall that NRTs are designed to produce a normal distribution with relatively high variance among the scores. In contrast, CRTs are designed to measure what has been learned and, therefore, cannot be expected to necessarily produce variance among scores (for instance, when all the students know all the material at the end of a course).

Only the content and construct validity strategies are applicable for analyzing the validity of CRTs, because these two strategies do not depend on the magnitude of the variance in the test scores. The third strategy, criterion-related validity, does not lend itself to investigating the validity of CRTs because it is based on correlational analysis. Since the distributions of scores on CRTs may be skewed, especially when they are working well, the assumption of normal distribution, which underlies correlational analysis, is not met. Hence, the results of a criterion-related validity study for a CRT would be difficult, if not impossible, to interpret. NRTs, on the other hand, can be analyzed from all three strategies: content, construct, and criterion-related.

Regardless of which strategy is used to demonstrate and defend validity, the strongest arguments will be built around at least two, or in the case of NRTs all three, of these strategies. Notice that I am advocating that test developers "defend" and build "arguments" for the validity of their tests. I strongly feel that test developers are responsible for convincing people who are considering adopting their tests that their product is testing what it claims to measure. Also remember, investigation of validity would only be necessary after the consistency of the scores produced by the test has been established. In addition, remember that a test should only be used for the particular purposes and for the specific types of students for which that test was designed. Thus, validity is not about the test itself so much as it is about the test when the scores are interpreted for some specific purpose. In fact, it is much more accurate to refer to the validity of the scores and interpretations that result from a test than to think of the test itself as being valid.

As mentioned earlier, content and construct validity strategies are both appropriate for investigating the validity of NRTs and CRTs. Therefore in this chapter, content and construct validity will be covered under one major heading. The third strategy, criterion-related validity, which is dependent on test score variance, is suitable primarily for NRTs. Hence, criterion-related validity will be covered in a section of its own, followed by a discussion of several other issues: the matter of setting standards, also know as cut-points on a test, issues of testing bias and washback. The chapter will end with a discussion on the place of testing in language curriculum.

TRADITIONAL VALIDITY STRATEGIES FOR BOTH NRTs AND CRTs

As mentioned above, only two of the traditional approaches (content validity and construct validity) used for demonstrating **validity** apply to both NRTs and CRTs. These two will be covered here.

CONTENT VALIDITY

In order to investigate **content validity,** testers must decide whether the test is a representative sample of the content the test was designed to measure. To address this issue, testers will usually end up making some sorts of judgments, usually in the form of ratings given to students' language oral or written output. To maximize the efficiency of these judgments, the testers may need to focus particularly on the organization of the different types of items that they have included on the test and on the specifications for each of those item types. This content validation process may take many forms, depending on the particular language teaching situation and staff, but the goal will always be to establish an argument that the test is a representative sample of the content the test claims to measure.

Overall strategy for establishing content validity

Consider the problems involved in adopting, developing, or adapting a Tagalog listening comprehension proficiency test. The first step might be to decide what the test should be designed to measure. The simple answer would be Tagalog listening comprehension. But, what is Tagalog listening proficiency? To figure out the nature of Tagalog listening proficiency, it may help to analyze it into component parts. Perhaps, such analysis will lead those designing the test to decide that Tagalog listening proficiency is made up of distinguishing minimal pairs, understanding vocabulary in context, listening for facts, listening for inference, listening for gist, listening for main ideas, etc. The testers might then want to talk to some Tagalog listening teachers and get their ideas on the components of Tagalog listening proficiency. Thus, thinking about validity may initially involve defining what it is that the testers wanted to measure in the first place. If they cannot define who they want to test and what content they want to assess, how can they possibly determine the degree to which the test is measuring what it is designed to measure?

Assuming that the testers and teachers reach a consensus on what they want to test, they might find that no such measure exists. Being uncompromisingly professional, they would then probably decide to develop a new test that is valid for the purpose of testing Tagalog listening proficiency—as defined by them. They would then want to outline and organize the different types of items that they have identified as important and decide how many of each they want to end up with on the final version of the test.

The test developers should also write out item specifications if at all possible for each of the testing objectives that they have collectively identified as components of Tagalog listening proficiency. As explained in Chapter 3, item specifications include a general description, a sample item, stimulus attributes, response attributes, and supplemental lists. Recall also that the purpose of each item specification is to make it possible for any item writer to produce items that test about the same thing. Thus, clear item specifications can help to make items much more consistent and also more valid in the sense that, when specifications are used, the items are more likely to match those specifications, which in turn match the objectives of the test. This match between the items and the specifications can be verified as part of the argument for content validity.

Whether or not testers use formal item specifications, they will probably want to get together with the relevant teachers and write items for each of the testing objectives that they feel are important to Tagalog listening proficiency. They will need to write enough items (about 50 percent to 100 percent more than they will need for the final version of the test) so they can throw some of the non-reliable items out in the revision process. In the end, they must have enough items left so that each testing objective can be adequately represented on the test.

Once they have done field testing by administering and revising the test using the appropriate item analysis strategies, they will want to do all the things discussed in Chapters 5, 8, and 9, such as examine the descriptive statistics, calculate a reliability coefficient (or dependability estimate) or two, and look at the SEM (or CI). At that point, they will be in a position to explore the content validity of their new test. One way to do this would be to convene a panel of Tagalog listening comprehension experts to judge the degree to which the items on their new test actually represent the testing objectives of Tagalog listening proficiency (i.e., the objectives the testers and teachers had already agreed on).

If those experts disagree as to whether the items represent the proficiency in question and its underlying elements, the testers may have to return to the drawing board for at least some portions of the test. If, on the other hand, the experts agree that the test is representative of Tagalog listening proficiency, the testers would have built at least one argument for the content validity of their test for purposes of measuring Tagalog listening proficiency as defined by them and their colleagues and confirmed by experts. Unfortunately, this procedure is only accurate to the extent that the biases of the experts do not interfere with their judgment of the test. Hence test developers may wish to take certain steps to insure that the experts' judgments are as unclouded as possible.

In order to do this, the testers should first insure that the experts really are experts and that, at least to a degree, the experts share the kinds of professional viewpoints the testers and their colleagues have. In other words, if the group developing the test favors the *ACTFL Proficiency Guidelines* (ACTFL 1986, 2004) as *the* way of defining language proficiency, they probably should not bring in experts who have written articles criticizing those guidelines (for example, Savignon 1985; or Bachman & Savignon 1986). Similarly, if the testers favor a communicative approach to language teaching, they would be foolish to invite experts who believe firmly in a structural approach. On the other hand, testers will probably never find experts who agree 100 percent with their definition and categories of items for Tagalog listening proficiency. This is fine. After all, the testers and their colleagues may be able to learn something from an outsider's fresh perspective.

Second, the test developers must recognize that judgments of the quality of individual items may not be absolutely black-and-white. An item may be a 70 percent match or 80 percent match with what the test developers want to test. Therefore, instead of having the experts rate the questions either acceptable or not acceptable, the test developers may want to provide the experts with a more subtle rating scale. Such a scale should be designed to help the experts focus in on each item and make as objective a judgment as possible. At the same time the particular scale used will depend on the type of information and the amount of detail needed. For instance, testers in one situation might need for each item to be judged on a scale from 1 to 5. In another situation, testers might benefit more from a rating sheet that simply asks the expert to estimate the percent of match to the testing goals. Or perhaps, a group of testers needs even more information and therefore decides to have three 1 to 5 scales for each item: one for the form of the item, a second for the content, and a third for match to the overall goals of the course.

Table 10.1 Content validity judgment scale

SEASSI PROFICIENCY EXAMINATION

Name_____

LISTENING COMPREHENSION SUBTEST

| | MATCH TO ACTFL GUIDELINES | | | | |
	No Match				Perfect Match

INTERMEDIATE-LOW

13) MAGKANO MO IPINAGBIBILI ANG TELEBISYONG ITO?	1	2	3	4	5
A. Opo, ang mahal.					
B. Isa po.					
K. P6,000.00 po.*					
D. Cash lang po.					
14) NASAAN KA NITONG NAKARAANG SABADO AT LINGGO?	1	2	3	4	5
A. Noong Linggo.					
B. Nasa Baguio po.*					
K. Dalawang araw po sa isang linggo.					
D. Tanghali na po akong gumising noong Linggo.					
15) PAPASOK KA BA SA ESKUWELAHAN BUKAS?	1	2	3	4	5
A. Opo, dahil kailangang pumasok.*					
B. Opo, pumasok po ako.					
K. Bukas po ang pasok sa eskuwela.					
D. May pasok po.					
16) ANO ANG GINAGAWA NIYA SA KANYANG LIBRENG ORAS?	1	2	3	4	5
A. Wala rin po siyang gaanong pera.					
B. Nagtratrabaho po siya mula 8:00 hanggang 5:00.					
K. Nagbibihis na po siya ngayon.					
D. Lumalangoy po siya.*					

* Correct answer

Table 10.1 shows a small part of one such scale that was developed for judging the validity of a Tagalog listening proficiency test developed at UHM (Brown, Cook, Lockhart, & Ramos 1991). Notice that the overall layout of the rating sheet focuses the expert's attention on the individual test items. The stems are given in capital letters because they were actually heard on audiotape by the test takers (rather than written above the options). However, the test takers are asked to read the four options as shown and select the one that makes the most sense as a response to the taped utterance. Notice that the rating scale asks for the expert to rate the degree to which the item matches the ACTFL Guidelines. Since the items had originally been developed to match the nine different levels described for listening comprehension proficiency in the *ACTFL Proficiency Guidelines,* that scale was considered appropriate for experts to use in rating each item on a scale of 1 to 5 for the degree of match to those descriptions. Whether or not the items (and indirectly the ACTFL descriptions) were an adequate reflection of what they expected of their students at each level was handled as a separate but related issue.

The reader may have noticed that Table 10.1 is very similar to Table 4.2 (p. 78) in the chapter on item analysis. That is correct. All of what was presented on item quality (including Tables 3.1–3.3., pp. 43, 47, and 51) and content analysis (including Table 4.2 on page 78) has direct bearing on content validity. The discussions in Chapters 3 and 4 were simply focused on the single item level, whereas this discussion is covering the validity of the resulting test scores and their interpretations. Overall validity is nevertheless highly related to the individual item validities.

An example of the importance of item planning in regards to content validity

In the process of developing a test like the one described above, sound planning can help in creating a sound test as well as in building a strong argument for content validity. Sound planning involves working out a rational blueprint for what to include in the test and in approximately what proportions. Thus, test developers should be very careful about planning the test objectives and specifying the types and proportions of items that will appear. After all, they may be asked to justify their rationale at a later date.

Consider the following plan, which was used to develop items for tests designed to measure non-native English speakers in their engineering-English reading and listening abilities (described in more detail in Brown 1984b, 1988b; or Erickson & Molloy 1983). A group of seven graduate students at UCLA (including myself) set out to develop tests for purposes of testing graduate-level engineering students (non-native speakers of English) at UCLA. We were breaking new ground with this test development project, and we soon discovered that nobody had any idea what the components of engineering-English reading ability might be. After consulting with engineering professors and examining the literature on English for specific purposes (ESP), we decided to test as broad a spectrum of item types as we could and, in the process, discovered that our perceptions as linguists were quite different from those of the engineering professors. As a result, we found that two distinct categories of item types emerged in our plan: one that we labeled linguistic factors and another that we called engineering factors. The individual item types for each category were as follows:

Item Plan

I. Linguistic factors
    A. Cohesion
        1. Reference items
        2. Substitution items
        3. Lexical cohesion items
        4. Conjunction items
    B. Non-technical vocabulary items
II. Engineering factors
    A. Fact items
    B. Inference items
    C. Lexis
        1. Subtechnical vocabulary items
        2. Technical vocabulary items
    D. Scientific rhetorical function items

Figure 10.1 Two categories of test items for engineering students

Two sets of three tests (one set of three to test reading comprehension and one set of three to test lecture listening comprehension) were developed in this project. The three reading comprehension tests were developed from three reading passages taken from sophomore-level engineering textbooks. (We chose sophomore-level texts because we had been advised by the engineering professors that this was the last year we would find common core texts that all engineers would understand, given that the students specialize into different types of engineering after this point.) For each of the three reading passages, we wrote three to five questions for each of the item types in the plan outlined above. The lecture listening tests were similarly developed from three videotapes of engineering lectures with the same overall item organization plan. Because we were trying to produce a new type of test, we had necessarily planned very carefully, basing our selection of item types on the best available information in ESP and on the insights of engineering professors who knew the content area. (For an excellent overview of much more recent developments in ESP testing, see Douglas 2000.) Since we were also trying to create three reading and three lecture listening tests that were more or less parallel, we felt the need to lay out our item plan very clearly before charging ahead. The net result was that, after we developed the tests, the item plan became part of the content validity argument.

Content validity and other types of validity

One problem that may arise in looking exclusively at content validity is that the performance of the particular group of students who took the test can be overlooked. In the same sense that a test can only be said to be consistent for a particular group of students (or very similar students), a test can only be said to be valid for testing specific types of students for particular purposes. Put another way, the students who are tested in the development process on a test become part of the definition of that purpose, because language tests must be designed with particular students in mind. As a result, a test can only be considered reliable and valid for a particular context (or for contexts that are very similar) and purpose. In a sense, the context is defined by the type of decision involved, the type of students involved, as well as the testing objectives. For example, the test designed to test the engineering-English reading and listening abilities for UCLA students would not be a valid test to give to test the English abilities of hotel workers.

Once test developers have established content validity, which is based on characteristics of the test itself, they must immediately explore other validity arguments, ones that are related to the performances of real live students on the test (i.e., construct or criterion-related).

CONSTRUCT VALIDITY

An understanding of the concept of a psychological construct is prerequisite to understanding construct validity. A **psychological construct** is an attribute, proficiency, ability, or skill defined in psychological theories. Consider, for example, "love." Love is a name for a very complex set of mental processes that go on in the human mind. Everyone knows about love and accepts that it exists. Yet, love goes on largely inside the individuals involved and is therefore, very difficult to observe. Nevertheless, love is an example of a psychological construct. It goes on; it is accepted; yet it is hard to observe because it goes on inside the head. Some other psychological constructs that are perhaps more pertinent to the topic at hand are language aptitude, intelligence, overall language proficiency, etc.

Since these constructs occur inside the brain, they must be observed indirectly if they are to be observed at all. This job often falls to the language tester, because only tests (broadly defined) can efficiently measure such constructs. In terms of test validity, the major problem with psychological constructs is that testers cannot take a construct out of a student's brain and show that a test is in fact measuring it. The only recourse is to demonstrate indirectly through some kind of experiment that a given test is measuring a particular construct. Since such demonstrations are always indirect, the results must be interpreted very carefully. Nonetheless, such experiments are the most straightforward strategy available to testers for establishing construct validity. The experiment may take numerous forms, but the easiest to understand initially are the differential-groups and intervention types of studies.

Differential-groups studies

Sometimes, studies are designed to compare the performances of two groups on a test. Such studies are called **differential-groups studies** because, in conducting such studies, the tester is trying to show that the test scores differentiate between groups: one group which obviously has the construct that is being measured and another that clearly does not have it (similar to the difference index described in Chapter 4, page 80). For instance, consider the Tagalog listening proficiency construct discussed on pages 221–224. If I wanted to demonstrate the construct validity of that test, I might locate two groups of students who are similar in all ways except that one group is made up of non-native speakers of Tagalog with very little Tagalog listening comprehension ability, while the other group has high ability. For example, I might identify a group of third-year Tagalog students, a group of second-year Tagalog students, and group of first-year students. I could then administer the Tagalog proficiency test to all these students and analyze the results. If the third-year students scored high on the test, while the second-year students scored relatively low and the first-year students scored lowest of all, I would have a fairly strong argument for the construct validity of the test scores. In other words, I would have shown that the test differentiates between students who have a great deal of the Tagalog listening proficiency construct (third-year Tagalog students) and those who have less of the construct (second-year students). I would have further demonstrated that the test differentiates between those who have only a little of the construct (second-year students) and those who have very little of it (first-year students). Especially when coupled with evidence of content and/or criterion-related validity, this line of reasoning forms a convincing argument that the test scores reflect the construct that the test was designed to measure.

A more concrete example of a construct validity study is provided by the engineering-English testing project described on pages 225–226. The three engineering-English reading tests were analyzed by experts and revised to form a single three-passage test with 20 items each, resulting in a test with 60 items. The next step was to establish the validity of the new 60-item reading test. We had already contributed to the necessary arguments for validity by carefully planning with engineering professors and defining various theoretical categories of item types that we wanted to pilot. The next step was to administer the test and find out how well the scores reflected what we thought we were assessing.

To this end, a differential-groups experiment was set up to address the validity question both at the total test score level and at the individual item type level. The validity question we wanted answered was whether or not our test was valid for purposes of measuring overall engineering-English reading ability for norm-referenced decisions about international engineering students who wanted to study engineering in English-speaking countries. All the students in this differential-groups study were graduate students and were studying either at UCLA or at Zhongshan University in the People's Republic of China (PRC). Two nationalities were tested: native speakers of English who were Americans, and non-native speakers of English who were Chinese from the PRC. (We chose Chinese because we were setting up an English for Science and Technology program in the PRC that would include many engineers and graduate students in engineering.) Two academic majors were also involved: engineers and non-engineers (all humanities students in the sense that they had varied backgrounds at the undergraduate level but were currently doing graduate work in TESL/TEFL). Four groups were formed in this differential-groups study based on their majors and nationalities (see Figure 10.2): (a) American engineers, (b) American TESL/TEFL, (c) Chinese engineers, and (d) Chinese TESL/TEFL. As shown in Figure 10.2, the number of students (n) in each of these groups was 29.

Major

	Engineer	TESL/TEFL	
American	$M = 50.52$ $n = 29$	$M = 44.79$ $n = 29$	$M = 47.66$ $n = 58$
Nationality Chinese	$M = 36.97$ $n = 29$	$M = 27.38$ $n = 29$	$M = 32.17$ $n = 58$
	$M = 43.74$ $n = 58$	$M = 36.09$ $n = 58$	

Figure 10.2 Means and marginals for differential groups

After the test was administered to these four groups of students and the reliability was investigated (K-R20 was .85 for the targeted international students), descriptive statistics were calculated as shown in Figure 10.2 (Brown 1984b). Not surprisingly, the American engineers scored highest with a mean (M) of 50.52 out of 60, and the Chinese non-engineers (TESL/TEFL) scored lowest with a mean of 27.38. In addition, all engineers together had a mean of 43.74, thereby outscoring the TESL/TEFL students who had a combined mean of 36.09. This alone would lend credence to our validity argument in the sense that the test scores were clearly reflecting something related to engineering reading ability. Since our focus was on the international students, the construct validity of the test was further supported by the fact that the Chinese engineers also outscored their non-engineer countrymen with means of 36.97 and 27.38, respectively.

The next step in the analysis involved using analysis of variance (**ANOVA**) procedures. Unfortunately, you cannot do this sort of ANOVA in *Excel*™. In any case, a full explanation of ANOVA is well beyond the scope of this book (for introductions to the use of more advanced statistics in language studies, see Brown 1988a, 2001; Hatch & Lazaraton 1991; Rietveld & van Hout 1993; Brown & Rodgers, 2002). One strategy you might consider using is to simply calculate and look at the means in any group comparisons you wish to make. If the differences between means are large, that fact will provide some support for any validity arguments that may be associated with the group comparisons you are making.

Back to the example study at hand, using ANOVA, the mean differences between nationalities and between majors were found to be statistically significant at $p < .01$, as shown in Table 10.2. However, notice that Source in an ANOVA table (like that shown in Table 10.2 from Brown 1984b) refers to the source of variance measured. In this case, both academic major (engineers versus TESL/TEFL students) and nationality (Americans versus Chinese) are contributing to significant differences among the means of the four groups. In other words, ANOVA is used to investigate whether differences among group means are significantly different from each other, in the same sense that correlation coefficients can be shown to be significantly different from zero (see Chapter 7, p. 139 and following). The particular ANOVA used here indicates that the testers could be 99 percent sure ($p < .01$) that the mean differences observed between engineers and TESL/TEFL students (Major), as well as between Americans and Chinese (Nationality) are due to factors other than chance. In short, the test appears to differentiate between engineers and non-engineers, as well as between natives and non-natives, for other than chance reasons. Hence, this differential-groups study could be used to argue for the construct valid of our test scores for purposes of measuring engineering-English reading proficiency.

Table 10.2 Results of two-way ANOVA

Source	SS	df	MS	F
Major	1699.45	1	1699.45	35.88*
Nationality	6951.76	1	6951.76	146.75*
Major x Nationality	108.14	1	108.14	2.28
Residual (error)	5305.65	112	47.37	
Total	14064.99	115	122.30	

* $p < .01$

An intriguing question that remained was why the native TESL/TEFL (non-engineers), who had a mean of 44.79, outscored (by nearly eight points) the Chinese engineers, who had a mean of 36.97. Was it possible that engineering-English reading ability as measured in this test was more reliant on language ability than on engineering factors?

To investigate this question, omega squared analysis was performed. Again, a full explanation of this form of statistical analysis is beyond the scope of this book (see Keppel 2002 for a clear description of this procedure). In a nutshell, this type of analysis is derived from the results of an ANOVA—in this case, the ANOVA shown in Table 10.2. Omega squared analysis is a way of estimating the percent of variance among scores in the ANOVA design that is attributable to each of the factors involved.

As shown in Table 10.3, the Nationality factor in this study apparently accounted for about 49 percent of the variance in scores while the Major factor explained about 12 percent of that variance. In other words, knowledge of the language, at least in terms of native/non-native differences, appears to be a much more important factor in explaining score variation than is Major in terms of engineering/non-engineering differences. From a validity point of view, the interaction between the Major and Nationality factors (Major x Nationality) in this study did not contribute significantly to the score variance so it was ignored. However, the residual, or error (i.e., variance not explained by the factors included in this study) is more worrisome. The results in Table 10.3 (Brown 1984b) indicate that 39 percent of the variance among scores was not accounted for by Major or Nationality. Hence 39 percent of the variance can only be considered random until further study can identify more systematic sources. Nevertheless, for a new test designed to measure an entirely new area of language proficiency, these results were encouraging from a construct validity viewpoint insofar as they indicated that roughly 61 percent (Major + Nationality = 11.71 + 48.93 = $60.64 \approx 61$) of the variance in the scores on the test was attributable to something related to engineering knowledge or English language reading ability.

Table 10.3 Results of omega squared analysis

Source	Omega squared	Percent of variance
Major	.1171	11.71
Nationality	.4893	48.93
Major x Nationality	.0041	.41
Residual (error)	.3894	38.94
Total	.9999	99.99

One other benefit can be derived from having both a clear item plan to defend content validity and a differential-groups study to defend construct validity. Both strategies can be combined to provide useful insights and information about different item types. Consider the analysis of the engineering-English reading test that is shown in Table 10.4 (Brown 1988b). Observe that percent scores are provided in the body of the table for each of the groups (labeled across the top) and for each of the item types (labeled in the left column). Notice that the same pattern of performances exists in this table that appeared in Figure 10.2, that is, the American engineers performed best on each item type just as they did on the overall test mean. Their performance is followed in order by the American TESL students, Chinese engineers, and Chinese TEFL students. This pattern holds true for each item type, as the reader can see by reading each line from left to right across Table 10.4. Notice also that some item types appear to have been easier than others and that in general the linguistic items appear to be easier than the engineering items for all the groups involved in this validity study.

Table 10.4 Performance of differential groups on each content type

Factors	Americans		Chinese	
Item Type	Engineers %	TESL %	Engineers %	TESL %
Linguistic factors				
Reference	82	67	60	52
Substitution	100	79	77	41
Lexical cohesion	94	64	63	55
Conjunction	85	80	66	65
Non-technical vocabulary	97	95	78	72
Engineering factors				
Fact	89	81	62	48
Inference	90	69	59	36
Subtechnical vocabulary	71	65	59	28
Technical vocabulary	80	52	42	21
Rhetorical functions	92	91	81	50

This more detailed look at the content and construct validity of the test led to the conclusion that the table indicates:

> ... that the engineering items are more efficient than the linguistic ones. There are only 34 percentage points between high and low group scores (American engineers and Chinese TEFL) for the linguistic items, while the same figure for the engineering items is 49 points. Using only the engineering items might also be more justified, from a theoretical standpoint, as more "authentic" engineering tasks after Widdowson's (1978, p. 80) distinction between "genuine" and "authentic." (Brown 1988b, p. 198)

Such additional information proved useful in further exploring the degree to which the test was measuring the construct in question, what that construct might be, and what content might most efficiently assess the construct. In other words, the study of validity can cause the test developer to take a long, hard look at what is being measured and how that construct should be defined—both theoretically and practically.

The results of this study are typical in that validity is never absolute. Rather validity is a relative quality that can be demonstrated experimentally to exist, but only in probabilistic terms. Interestingly, in the process of investigating the degree to which this engineering reading test assessed the construct involved, something about the construct was also learned. Engineering-English reading ability, *as measured by this test,* relies more on language ability than on factors related to engineering itself. Thus, this validation study helped us to understand the degree to which the test was assessing the engineering-English reading ability construct (see Brown 1984b), but also helped us to discern which of the components of the engineering-English reading ability construct might be most important (see Brown 1988b).

The general strategy for establishing test validity involves using a variety of strategies to marshal evidence, and then arranging that evidence into logical arguments. Thus, in the case of the engineering-English reading test, the argument is based both on showing the content validity through description of careful item planning and on demonstrating the degree of construct validity through a differential-groups experiment. The combined evidence supports the claim that the test measures overall engineering-English reading ability for NRT proficiency decisions about international students—at least for the groups involved in this validation study. The evidence and arguments may or may not be convincing to potential test *users,* but that is not their problem. Test *developers* are responsible for convincing test users of validity. From a common sense point of view, if a potential test user is not convinced of the practicality, consistency, and validity of our engineering-English reading test, they should avoid using it.

Intervention studies

Another way to address the same set of validity problems is to set up **intervention studies.** Intervention studies are similar to differential-groups studies but are conducted with only one group of students. In order to do an intervention study for the engineering-English reading test, we could administer the test at the beginning of a course for students studying English for engineering reading. We could then re-administer the test at the end of their course. If they perform much better on the second administration than on the first, we have built an argument for the construct validity of the test scores.

This intervention strategy is often the one that makes the most sense in classroom teaching situations and is particularly well suited to criterion-referenced testing where the purpose is to assess learning. Since CRT item analysis also works best in this pre-test/post-test design, testers can accumulate the validity information they need in the process of gathering item analysis data. In fact, using an intervention study in support of the construct validity of the scores on a CRT turns out to be quite a natural process.

Of course the logic of the decision to run an intervention study is based on the assumption that students actually do learn something, engineering-English reading in the example above. A problem could arise, however, if the students all skipped classes constantly or if the teacher taught general grammar instead of engineering reading. In such a case, differences in pre-test/post-test scores on the engineering-English reading test might be small or non-existent. Obviously, such results would not necessarily indicate a problem with the validity of the test; however, it may be very difficult for a test developer to know what has caused the test scores. Fortunately, students usually attend classes regularly and teachers typically address the general goals of the course. So intervention studies often make a good deal of sense, especially when investigating CRT construct validity.

Numerous other approaches exist for investigating construct validity. Occasionally in our field, multitrait-multimethod studies have been done (as explained in Brown 2001), factor analytic techniques (e.g., Kunnan 1992; Sasaki 1996; Brown, Cunha, & Frota 2001; Kondo-Brown & Brown 2004), and structural equation modeling (e.g., Kunnan 1995; Sasaki 1996) have been used to study validity. Neither of these is particularly practical in most classroom testing situations so they are not explained here.

Regardless of the techniques used, the basic strategy in studying construct validity is always the same. The tester conducts an experiment to investigate the degree to which the test scores reflect the construct that the test was designed to measure. Naturally, such construct validation will be strongest and most convincing if it is a cumulative process of gathering evidence based on a variety of experiments.

CRITERION-RELATED VALIDITY: A TRADITIONAL STRATEGY FOR NRTs

The concept of **criterion-related validity** (not to be confused with criterion-referenced tests) involves demonstrating validity by showing that the scores on the test being validated correlate highly with some other, well-respected measure of the same construct. For instance, to demonstrate the criterion-related validity of a new test, let's call it the Test of Overall ESL Proficiency (TOESLP), the test developers might administer it to a group of international students wishing to study in the United States. As a **criterion measure** (i.e., the other, well-respected measure of the same construct), the test developers might also administer the *TOEFL*. The TOEFL is a good test to administer because it is a well-established test of overall academic English proficiency (the construct under investigation). Once the two tests are administered to a group (preferably a large group representative of the new test's target population), the test developers can calculate a correlation coefficient for the relationship between the two sets of scores and determine the degree to which the scores on the two tests go together, or overlap. For example, let's say the correlation coefficient (also called a **validity coefficient** in this context) turns out to be $r_{xy} = .95$. Such a validity coefficient would indicate a very strong relationship between the two sets of scores. In fact, the scores on the two tests would appear to be spreading the students out in almost exactly the same way.

Based on this correlation, the test developers could argue that, since the TOESLP scores appear to produce a distribution of scores very similar to the TOEFL scores, the TOESLP provides results that are virtually the same as TOEFL results. If this is true, and if the TOEFL is indeed a well-established measure of overall ESL proficiency, it follows that the TOESLP is a valid test of overall ESL proficiency (as that construct is measured by TOEFL). In short, the testers would have demonstrated the criterion-related validity of the TOESLP scores. If test users believe that the criterion measure, in this case TOEFL, is a valid measure of overall ESL proficiency, then they really must believe that the TOESLP is also valid for that purpose.

To make this even clearer, recall that the squared value of a correlation coefficient can be directly interpreted as the percentage of overlap between the two measures. Since the criterion-related validity estimate is a correlation coefficient, the squared value of a validity coefficient can also be directly interpreted as the percentage of overlap between the two measures. For example, if the scores on the TOESLP were correlated at $r_{xy} = .95$ with the scores on TOEFL, one could simply square the .95 value ($r_{xy}^2 = .95^2 = .9025 \approx .90$) and then make the claim that the variance in the TOESLP scores overlaps about 90 percent with the variance of the TOEFL scores. This squared value, as you may recall, is called the **coefficient of determination** (see p. 158).

One source of confusion that arises from reports about criterion-related validity studies is that it is sometimes called concurrent or predictive validity. These two labels are just variations on the same theme. **Concurrent validity** is criterion-related validity but indicates that both measures were administered at about the same time, as in the TOESLP example. **Predictive validity** is also a variant of criterion-related validity, but this time the two sets of numbers are collected at different times. In fact, for predictive validity, the purpose of the test should logically be "predictive." Imagine that a French aptitude test has been administered and the testers want to interpret the scores in terms of how well they predict students' achievement in French courses as measured by their grades after one semester. A correlation coefficient between scores on the test and course grades would indicate how well the test predicts grades, that is, an indication of its predictive validity for purposes of testing French achievement.

Basically, criterion-related validity is a subset of the ideas discussed under construct validity. Demonstration of criterion-related validity usually also entails designing an experiment, but in this case, one group of students takes two tests: the new test that testers are developing and another test that is already a well-established measure of the construct involved.

Restrictions of Range and NRT Validity

Remember, as discussed in Chapter 7, testers generally should avoid restricting the range of abilities in any groups being tested unless they have a very good reason for doing so. If a tester chooses to base a correlational analysis on a sample with fairly homogeneous language proficiency, the sample itself can have dramatic effects on the analysis. For example, if only students at the lowest level of study in a particular language program were chosen to be tested, this choice could unwittingly be restricting the range of abilities, which would, in turn, tend to result in lower correlation coefficients. An example of the degree to which this can affect results is shown in Table 10.5 (Brown 1984b). This table presents a number of sets of testing statistics. The results are systematically arranged from the group with the widest range of abilities at the top to narrower and narrower ranges of ability moving down the table.

Table 10.5 Ranges of abilities in relationship to reliability and validity of a cloze test

Sample	S	range	$r_{xx'}$	r_{xy}
1978A	12.45	46	.95	.90
1978B	8.56	33	.90	.88
1981A	6.71	29	.83	.79
1981B	5.59	22	.73	.74
1982A	4.84	22	.68	.59
1982B	4.48	20	.66	.51
1982C	4.07	21	.53	.40
1982D	3.38	14	.31	.43

Notice that the ranges of abilities are generally reflected in both the standard deviation and the range. Both statistics get much smaller further down the columns. Notice also the rather dramatic relationship between this systematic restriction of range and both the reliability ($r_{xx'}$) and validity (r_{xy}) coefficients. The startling thing about this table is that these results are based on exactly the same cloze test administered to different samples of students with different ranges of overall language abilities. In this example, the effect of restriction of range is so great that the particular cloze test involved here may appear to be the most highly reliable and valid cloze test ever created or a hands-down loser as the worst. And this difference depends almost entirely on differences in the ranges of ability among the samples. The message here is that descriptive statistics should always be examined whenever such analyses are conducted. And testers should look not only at the reliability and validity coefficients, but also at the amount of dispersion in the scores as indicated by the range and standard deviation. By doing so, testers may notice things that they would otherwise have missed—things that can change how they interpret their results and how they view the validity of their scores.

STANDARD SETTING

Since the purpose of most language tests is to make decisions about students, validity is often linked to the degree to which the test is accurate for decision making. As discussed in Chapters 8 and 9, the accuracy of a decision is a test consistency issue and can be enhanced by using the SEM (or CI) as part of the decision-making process—especially for students who fall near cut-points. On the other hand, the appropriateness of a cut-point (and the decisions that result) is a test validity issue.

This whole area of concern is called standard setting. **Standard setting**[5] is defined here as the process of deciding where and how to make cut-points. In all language programs, decisions must be made at least partially on the basis of test scores. In order to make such decisions, standards must be set. Basically, five types of decisions require setting standards of performance; teachers and administrators must often decide whether a student should be: (a) admitted into an institution, (b) placed in the elementary, intermediate, or advanced level of a program, (c) diagnosed as knowing certain objectives and not knowing others, (d) passed to the next level of study, or (e) certified as having successfully achieved the objectives of a course or program. Thus **standards** might be defined as the levels of performance set for any of the above five types of decisions.

In order to establish standards, teachers and administrators must determine the appropriate cut-point for a given decision and a given set of test scores. A **cut-point** is a score at or above which students will be classified one way and below which they will be classified differently. Such a cut-point may separate students who will be

---

[5]Note that the *standards* referred to here are not the *Standards for Educational and Psychological Testing* found in APA 1999. Those *standards* are the minimal features that test developers must include in their tests for the tests to be considered acceptable according to three professional organizations (American Educational Research Association, American Psychological Association, & National Council on Measurement in Education).

admitted into an institution from those who will not, or separate students who are placed into each of the levels of study, or indicate the level at which students are considered to have mastered the content of a course for diagnostic decisions, promotion decisions, or achievement decisions.

In the field of educational measurement, standard setting has been an important issue for several decades (for an excellent collection of articles on this topic, see Cizek 2001). In the language testing field, the ideas involved in standard setting are not commonly discussed (for a recent overview, see Brown & Hudson 2002; for an overview of work on standards for school-age ESL learners, see McKay 2000; for an example study on rater judgments in applying standards, see Alderson, 1993) even though standards are often the basis for making important decisions that may radically affect students' lives and well-being.

One problem with standards is that they often seem to be set rather arbitrarily. As early as 1978, Glass pointed out that "... every attempt to derive a criterion score is either blatantly arbitrary or derives from a set of arbitrary premises" (p. 258). However, such arbitrariness is not necessarily bad, as Popham argued in 1978 (p. 169):

> To have someone snag a performance standard "off the wall," with little or no thinking involved, is truly arbitrary with all the negative connotations that the term deserves. To go about the task of standard setting seriously, relying on decent collateral data, wide-ranging input from concerned parties, and systematic efforts to make sense out of relevant performance and judgmental data is not capriciously arbitrary. Rather, it represents the efforts of human beings to bring their best analytic powers to bear on important decisions.

Whether language teachers like it or not, relatively arbitrary decisions must often be made about their students particularly for purposes of admissions, placement, diagnosis, and achievement. As should be abundantly clear by now, the first two of these types of decisions should typically be made using norm-referenced tests. For admissions decisions and placement, people will be categorized in relationship to each other, and different actions must be taken based on test scores. For diagnostic and achievement decisions, criterion-referenced tests may prove more useful. Until all types of admissions, placement, diagnosis, and achievement decisions are abandoned in human societies, standards will be appropriate and necessary.

Clearly then, standards are here to stay. Because such decisions are important to the lives of the language students involved, testers must use the best available techniques to establish standards. In other words, well-considered (though necessarily imperfect) standards are better than no standards at all.

For example, we could use the well-established contrasting-groups method to establish a cut-point in the following steps:

1. Identify a population of judges who are familiar with the students and sample from that population;
2. Through discussion, the judges collectively define three categories of performance on the test in question: acceptable, borderline, and inadequate;
3. Based on information other than the test scores, the judges identify all students known to them as belonging in acceptable, borderline, or inadequate categories;
4. The test is administered;

5. The distributions of the acceptable and inadequate groups of students are then examined and the standard is set in one of two ways:
   a. Plot the two sets of scores so that they overlap and set the standard at that point where they intersect (see Figure 10.3a);
   b. Calculate the percentage of students classified as acceptable at each test score and set the standard at the score value that classifies 50 percent as acceptable (see Figure 10.3b).

a. Overlapping distributions method

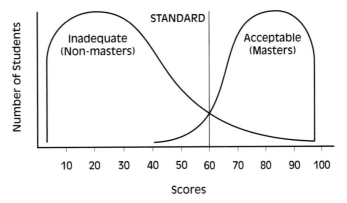

b. Percentage of acceptable performances

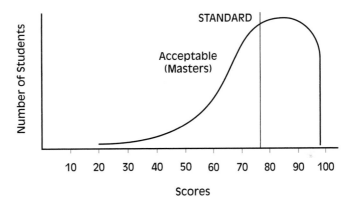

Figure 10.3 Cut-points for contrasting-groups method of standard setting

Conceptually, the contrasting-groups method for standard setting is most closely related to the construct validity strategies that were called intervention and differential-groups studies. Thus, there is a satisfying sense that the use of this method for establishing standards is most closely related to the purpose of the test and therefore supports the validity of the score interpretations. (For discussion of a variety of methods for setting standards, see Brown & Hudson, 2002, pp. 248–268, or Anderson 2003, pp. 139–144.)

Assuming that teachers have used some rational and thoughtful method for setting the standards on a test, they must recognize that no standard will ever be perfect. As such, it is useful to think about how the existing standard on a particular test is related to both test consistency and validity.

Standards and test consistency

Standards are related to test consistency in that teachers can have a relatively high degree of confidence in a decision based on a cut-point on a highly consistent test, whereas they should have much less confidence in a decision and cut-point on a test with low test consistency. The degree of confidence is directly reflected in two of the statistics presented in the previous two chapters. Recall that the standard error of measurement (SEM) and confidence interval (CI) discussed in Chapters 8 and 9 could both be interpreted as bands of confidence around cut-points for NRTs and CRTs, respectively. Also recall that, at least in theory, these were bands of scores within which the students' scores were likely to fall repeatedly (with certain degrees of probability) if they were to take the test over and over again. If a given test is a highly reliable NRT (or dependable CRT), this band of scores, above and below the cut-point, will be relatively narrow. If, on the other hand, the test is not very consistent, the band will be relatively wide.

Remember, the SEM or CI can be used to identify those students who might fall on the other side of a cut-point if they were to take the test again. In other words, students who scored within one SEM below the cut-point might fall above the cut-point if they were to take the test again. Thus, in Chapters 8 and 9, it was argued that additional information should be gathered at least on those students who fall within one SEM (or one CI) of the cut-point in order to help teachers decide on which side of the cut-point each student belongs.

The strategy of using the SEM or CI in decision-making should improve the overall consistency and accuracy of the decisions. This process should probably involve at least the following steps:

1. Set the standard using whatever method is deemed most appropriate in the particular language program.
2. Calculate the SEM or CI, whichever is appropriate for the type of test and decision involved, recognizing that it represents a band of possible decision errors that are normally distributed around the cut-point.
3. Decide whether to consider errors that will work against the student, against the institution, or against both.
4. Isolate those students who scored within one band (for 68 percent confidence) above and/or below the cut-point (depending on Number 3 above). Gather additional information about these students and make decisions on the basis of all available information.
5. At some point, use all available test reliability or dependability information, as well as the SEM and CI, to inspect other possibilities and revise the cut-point for future use.

Standards are also directly related to test validity, in that decisions as to where to put the cut-point will often depend on the purposes of the test.

Validity is not a characteristic of a test. Instead, it should be considered a characteristic of the scores on a test when they are used for a particular purpose. Since validity is also related to the purposes of the test, standards can affect not only the degree to which a set of scores are valid and measuring what they are designed to measure, but also the degree to which the scores have **decision validity,** that is, the degree to which they are being used to make decisions in the way they were intended to be made. Thus testers should not only be concerned with test validity, but also with decision validity.

For instance, let's say some intensive ESL program at an American university administers two forms of a criterion-referenced test at the beginning of each course and again at the end in a counterbalanced design so that no student takes the same form twice. When the tests are administered at the beginning of the course, they are meant to be diagnostic. In addition, the scores are used to decide if any students had been misplaced by the placement test. The cut-points for this decision might vary from course to course, but, let's say, because of the nature of the decision being made, the cut-point typically falls at about the 80 percent or 90 percent level. Such high cut-points would be valid because the program wants to identify only students who had been placed too low for their actual abilities. Students who score this high obviously know the material being covered in the course and should be moved up to the next level of study or exempted from study in that skill area altogether.

If the same tests were administered at the end of the course, the purpose would be entirely different. The decision being made might be whether or not each student should pass the course. Thus the cut-point would probably be set much lower, say at 60 percent or 70 percent, depending on the course. Teachers would also be well advised to use additional information on all students, especially for those students who are close to the cut-point (that is, within one CI below the cut-point).

Hence, decision validity, as I use that term, should also include what Messick (1988, 1994, 1996) refers to as the value implications of test interpretation and social consequences of test use (for an example of a language testing validity study that grapples with the issues of value implications and social consequences, see Guerrero 2000). The **value implications** are the "more political and situational sources of social values bearing on testing" (p. 42). For example, a language test developed by white male structuralists in the 1950s would be based on quite different values from a communicative test developed today by men and women from a variety of backgrounds. As a result, the value implications underlying the development of a test must be considered as they relate to the values of the test users and test takers when the test users are interpreting the scores that result from the test. Related to both test validity and standards, value implications must at least partly be the responsibility of the test users because only the test users know their own values and the values of the test takers, both of which are unavoidably related to the political and pedagogical circumstances surrounding the particular context in which the test is being used and the decision that is to be made on the basis of the scores.

The **social consequences** of test use include both "the appraisal of the potential social consequences of the proposed use and of the actual consequences when used" (p. 42). For example, to require students to take the TOEFL Test of Spoken English

(ETS 2001), which is relatively expensive, in addition to the TOEFL itself before they can enter an American university has certain social consequences: poor students might be excluded from admissions to the university, certain nationalities might therefore be excluded because they come from relatively poor countries, certain departments in the university (who rely on enrollments from particular countries) might be differentially affected by such exclusions, enrollments of international students to the university as a whole might drop, income would therefore be lower, etc. The point is that we do not use tests in a vacuum. There are consequences involved, which we must consider when we are planning, designing, validating, and using tests and test scores. Again, responsibility for the social consequences of test use and test score interpretation are at least partly the responsibility of test users because they are typically more closely linked with those consequences than the test developers are.

One corollary of value implications and social consequences is that language test developers must always be aware that decisions made on the basis of test scores are essentially political. In this sense, the very purpose and validity of a test must also be considered political as well as pedagogical. Consider an end-of-course achievement test on which the rational cut-point from a judgmental and statistical point of view (including reliability and validity) turns out to be 85 percent. Such a cut-point would probably make no sense politically because it is "just too high." In other words, the opinions of experts and statisticians are immaterial if those opinions cause the students to riot in the halls because decisions seem unfair.

Standard setting is also political in another sense: decisions can be made to favor one group or another among the stakeholders (i.e., the interested parties). For instance, in applying the contrasting-groups method, the cut-point could be established as originally described (and illustrated in Figure 10.3a), or it could be fixed at points like those shown in Figures 10.4a and 10.4b. If the purpose for making the decision warrants protecting the institution against mistakes, the cut-point in 10.4a would make most sense. Such a cut-point would protect the institution against **false positives,** or decisions that falsely put students on the "passing" side of the cut-point. Such a strategy might be appropriate for an admissions decision wherein there are more students applying than positions to be had. In that case, a very conservative stance on admissions decisions might make sense because those responsible want as few unqualified students as possible to be mistakenly accepted even if that means that some qualified students will be rejected.

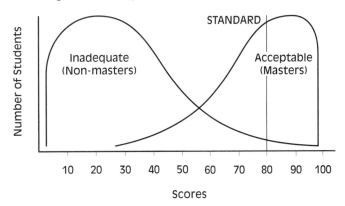

a. Setting standard to protect the institution

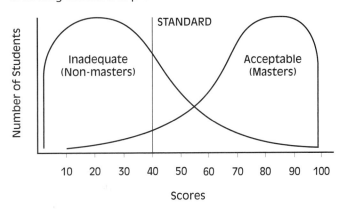

b. Setting standard to protect the students

Figure 10.4 Cut-points for contrasting-groups method methods

If, on the other hand, the purpose in making the decision warrants protecting the students against mistakes, the cut-point in 10.4b might make more sense. Such a cut-point would protect the students against **false negatives,** or decisions that erroneously put students on the "failing" side of the cut-point. This strategy might be appropriate in an end-of-course achievement decision wherein students who fail must repeat the course (an eventuality that even the faculty finds less than pleasing). In that case, the teachers might decide to take a very liberal stance on the pass/fail decisions because they want as few students as possible to be mistakenly failed even if that means that some very weak students will be passed.

In short, teachers may find themselves protecting the interests of the students or protecting the interests of the institution. The way they decide to go will typically depend on the type of decision being made, the gravity of the consequences, and the values of those teachers and administrators who are involved in the decision.

Despite the fact that standard setting is political in nature and difficult, teachers are often faced with setting cut-points and making decisions about students' lives. One thing seems clear from all this discussion. In language program decision-making processes, systematic and open standard setting is preferable to no standards because no standards probably means that the decisions are being made unsystematically, covertly, and perhaps, unfairly.

OTHER ISSUES RELATED TO VALIDITY

Several other issues arise in talking about test validity, standards, politics, etc. They are the washback effect and testing bias. Since no discussion of language testing would be complete without some discussion of these topics and since they are validity-related issues, I will cover them here.

THE WASHBACK EFFECT

Consider the following scenario: you are working in an institution that gets more funding if the number of students reaching a certain **benchmark** (i.e., standard) on the standardized test at the end of the year increases. As a result, at the end of the year, your director will be keeping tabs on how many of your students make the benchmark for funding. Do you think that would affect your teaching? How much would your teaching change? Would you be more likely to teach material that is related to the test? Material that you know will actually be found on the test? This cluster of issues is about **washback,** or roughly speaking, the degree to which a test affects the curriculum that is related to it.

Over the years, several definitions have been offered for the notion of washback. Shohamy, Donitsa-Schmidt, and Ferman (1996) characterized washback as "the connections between testing and learning" (p. 298). Gates (1995) described it simply as "the influence of testing on teaching and learning" (p. 101). Earlier, Shohamy (1992) offered a fairly complete definition of washback: "the utilization of external language tests to affect and drive foreign language learning…this phenomenon is the result of the strong authority of external testing and the major impact it has on the lives of test takers" (p. 513). According to Messick (1996), washback "…a concept prominent in applied linguistics, refers to the extent to which the introduction and use of a test influences language teachers and learners to do things they would not otherwise do that promote or inhibit language learning" (p. 241). Clearly, washback in the language teaching field involves the effects of testing on the teaching and learning processes in the language classroom. As such, the term *washback* would fittingly be used in a sentence like the following: The university entrance examinations in Lalaland seem to have a negative *washback* effect on language teaching in Lalaland high schools.

To add to the confusion of definitions, various authors have also used other terms to refer to that same notion. Alderson and Wall (1993) pointed out that "the phenomenon is referred to as 'backwash' in general education circles, but it has come to be known as 'washback' in British applied linguistics" (p. 115). I have also seen instances of language teaching experts calling the concept *test impact, measurement-driven instruction, curriculum alignment, test feedback,* and even (in jest) *bogwash.*

The question of whether the washback effect exists was first raised by Alderson and Wall (1993), who pointed out that many assertions had been made about washback by a variety of authors, but very little actual empirical research has been done about the existence and nature of washback. Since then a number of studies have surfaced that indicate that washback does indeed exist (Alderson & Hamp-Lyons 1996; Shohamy, Donitsa-Schmidt, & Ferman 1996; Wall 1996; Watanabe (1996a & 1996b). However, most of the studies cited above also indicate that washback is more complicated in terms of the kinds of impact it has than lay people typically think (for excellent summaries see Wall 1997, or Cheng & Curtis 2004; for a recent book of articles on this topic, see Cheng, Watanabe, & Curtis 2004).

Factors affecting the impact of washback

Gates (1995) argued that washback can vary along two dimensions: in terms of *kind* (positive or negative) and in terms of *degree* (from strong to weak) and suggested that "teachers might reasonably want to determine the type of washback that flows from a given test" (p. 101). He also listed seven other variables that may affect the kind and degree of washback: prestige, accuracy, transparency, utility, monopoly, anxiety, and practicality (pp. 102-103). Alderson and Hamp-Lyons (1996) argued that the amount and type of washback depend on the extent to which: the status of the test (and the level of the stakes involved), the degree to which the test is counter to current teaching practices, what teachers and textbook writers think are appropriate test preparation methods, and how much teachers and textbook writers are willing and able to innovate (p. 296). Mehrens and Kaminsky (1989) addressed the differences in washback in high stakes versus low stakes situations. Low stakes situations typically involve classroom testing, which is being used for learning purposes or research and "won't count." For students, high stakes situations usually involve more important decisions like admissions, promotion, placement, or graduation decisions that are directly dependent on test scores, while for schools, high stakes decisions might include potential cuts in programs and funding that may also be directly dependent on score averages. The washback effect is obviously much stronger in high stakes situations than in low stakes situations.

Negative effects of washback

Washback can negatively affect educational processes in a number of ways. Rather than provide a long involved discussion of these suggestions and where they came from (see Brown 1997; Cheng & Curtis 2004), I will summarize these factors (and who pointed them out) in Table 10.6 (Brown 1997, p. 70). Notice that they are organized into categories: teaching factors, course content factors, course characteristic factors, and course time factors.

Table 10.6 Negative aspects of washback

Teaching Factors
1. Teachers narrow the curriculum (Alderson & Hamp-Lyons 1996)
2. Teachers stop teaching new material and turn to reviewing material (Shohamy et al.1996)
3. Teachers replace class textbooks with worksheets identical to previous years' tests (Shohamy et al. 1996)
4. Unnatural teaching (Alderson & Hamp-Lyons 1996)

Course Content Factors
1. Students being taught "examination-*ese*" (Alderson & Hamp-Lyons 1996)
2. Students practicing "test-like" items similar in format to those on the test (Bailey 1996; Shohamy et al. 1996)
3. Students applying test-taking strategies in class (Bailey 1996)
4. Students studying vocabulary and grammar rules [to the exclusion of other aspects of language] (Bailey 1996)

Course Characteristic Factors
1. Students being taught inappropriate language-learning and language-using strategies (Alderson & Hamp-Lyons 1996)
2. Reduced emphasis on skills that require complex thinking or problem-solving (Alderson & Hamp-Lyons 1996)
3. Courses that raise examination scores without providing students with the English they will need in language interaction or in the college or university courses they are entering; also called test score 'pollution' (Alderson & Hamp-Lyons 1996)
4. A tense atmosphere in the class (Shohamy et al 1996)

Course Time Factors
1. Enrolling in, requesting, or demanding additional (unscheduled) test-preparation classes or tutorials (in addition to or in lieu of other language classes) (Alderson & Hamp-Lyons 1996; Bailey 1996)
2. Review sessions added to regular class hours (Shohamy et al. 1996)
3. Skipping language classes to study for the test (Bailey 1996)
4. Lost instructional time (Alderson & Hamp-Lyons 1996)

Promoting positive washback

A number of suggestions have been made over the years for ways to promote positive washback. Again, rather than provide a long involved discussion of these suggestions and where they came from (see Brown 1997; Cheng & Curtis 2004), I will summarize the suggestions (and who made them) in Table 10.7 (Brown 1997, pp. 73-74). Notice that the suggestions are organized in terms of those related to test design, test content, logistics, and interpretation/analysis.

Table 10.7 Suggestions for promoting positive washback

Test Design
1. Sample widely and unpredictably (Hughes 1989)
2. Design tests to be criterion-referenced (Hughes 1989; Wall 1996)
3. Design the test to measure what the programs intend to teach (Bailey 1996)
4. Base the test on sound theoretical principles (Bailey 1996)
5. Base achievement tests on objectives (Hughes 1989)
6. Use direct testing (Hughes 1989; Wall 1996)
7. Foster learner autonomy and self-assessment (Bailey 1996)

Test Content
1. Test the abilities whose development you want to encourage (Hughes 1989)
2. Use more open-ended items (as opposed to selected-response items like multiple choice) (Heyneman & Ransom 1990)
3. Make examinations reflect the full curriculum, not merely a limited aspect of it (Kellaghan & Greaney1992)
4. Assess higher-order cognitive skills to ensure they are taught (Heyneman & Ransom, 1990; Kellaghan & Greaney 1992)
5. Use a variety of examination formats, including written, oral, aural, and practical (Kellaghan & Greaney 1992)
6. Do not limit skills to be tested to academic areas (should also relate to out-of-school tasks) (Kellaghan & Greaney 1992)
7. Use authentic tasks and texts (Bailey 1996; Wall 1996)

Logistics
1. Insure that test-takers, teachers, administrators, curriculum designers understand the purpose of the test (Bailey 1996; Hughes 1989)
2. Make sure language-learning goals are clear (Bailey 1996)
3. Where necessary, provide assistance to teachers to help them understand the tests (Hughes 1989)
4. Provide feedback to teachers and others so meaningful change can be effected (Heyneman & Ransom 1990; Shohamy 1992)
5. Provide detailed and timely feedback to schools on levels of pupils' performance and areas of difficulty in public examinations (Kellaghan & Greaney 1992)
6. Make sure teachers and administrators are involved in different phases of the testing process because they are the people who will have to make changes (Shohamy 1992)
7. Provide detailed score reporting (Bailey 1996)

Interpretation/Analysis
1. Make sure exam results are believable, credible, and fair to test takers and score users (Bailey 1996)
2. Consider factors other than teaching effort in evaluating published examination results and national rankings (Kellaghan & Greaney 1992)
3. Conduct predictive validity studies of public examinations (Kellaghan & Greaney 1992)
4. Improve the professional competence of examination authorities, especially in test design (Kellaghan & Greaney 1992)
5. Insure that each examination board has a research capacity (Kellaghan & Greaney 1992)
6. Have testing authorities work closely with curriculum organizations and with educational administrators (Kellaghan & Greaney 1992)
7. Develop regional professional networks to initiate exchange programs and to share common interests and concerns (Kellaghan & Greaney 1992)

One other issue that you may want to attend to is bias. I referred to this issue in Chapter 3 when discussing Number 9 in Table 3.1, which asks, "Have race, gender and nationality bias been avoided?" ALTE (1990) provides a more formal definition of testing **bias**: "A test or item can be considered to be biased if one particular section of the candidate population is advantaged or disadvantaged by some feature of the test or item which is not relevant to what is being measured" (p. 136).

To understand testing bias, we need to first separate the concepts of fairness and bias. In my experience, **fairness** is defined differently in different cultures. For instance, in Japan, I am told that, even though the entrance examinations may be unreliable and have other problems, they are viewed as fair because they are equally flawed for everyone. In contrast, in North America, I think I am correct in saying that we want our university entrance examinations, like the SAT and ACT, to be reliable so that each of us will be fairly tested. With regard to bias, in testing terms in North American culture, I think it is safe to say that, to be fair, a test must also provide a visible and positive portrayal of all subgroups in proportion to their representation in the population; must refer to members of all subgroups with respect in terms of titles, names, and descriptions; and must provide equal opportunities to be familiar with the topics, situations, vocabulary, etc. on the test (after Hambleton & Rodgers 1995). In contrast, testing bias occurs when one subgroup is advantaged or disadvantaged in comparison to another in performance terms. Such advantages or disadvantages can occur at item or test score levels.

Perhaps this issue of advantaged or disadvantaged groups will become clearer if we consider the legal definition of item bias, which was formulated years ago in the settlement of the 1984 Golden Rule Insurance Co vs. Mathias court case: any item with a raw difference of .15 in item difficulty (p value) [i.e., what I am calling item facility in this book] for whites over blacks was considered a biased item. The "raw difference" is of course the difference index that I explained in Chapter 4. According to this definition, a difference index of more than .15 between subgroups on a test indicates bias. The subgroups that are important to compare will depend on the local situation. For example, in American public school situations, it is important that tests be examined for bias against African-Americans, Asian-Americans, Native-Americans, and Latino-Americans (as compared to the so-called "norm-group" of Whites). Is this a real problem for language testers? As Oller, Kim, and Choe (2000, p. 341) pointed out, "There is a wide-spread socio-educational problem with language testing at its heart: Speakers of minority languages are over-represented in classes for the learning disabled, disordered and educable mentally retarded and under-represented in classes for the gifted."

Clearly, it is possible for a test to be biased purposefully or inadvertently against any group based on ethnicity, geography, nationality, language background, gender, etc. For instance, consider an IQ item where the answer hinges on understanding the differences between the terms rain, snow, sleet, and hail. Such an item might naturally be biased against local students from my home state of Hawaii because many of them have never (mercifully) seen anything resembling snow, sleet, or hail. Nor would such students necessarily understand the fine gradations of difference among these concepts. Thus, answering incorrectly might have nothing to do with the students' IQs, but rather would be a reflection of the fact that they grew up in a tropical paradise.

As mentioned above, this issue is so important that it has often become a legal issue resulting in legal definitions of bias. In order to understand these definitions, we must first recognize that at least two separate levels of bias exist: bias at the item level and bias at the test score level. Based on that distinction, there are at least four ways of defining bias:

1. The first is a legal definition for item bias that first appeared in the settlement for the 1984 *Golden Rule Insurance Co vs. Mathias* court case: any item with a raw difference of .15 in item difficulty (*p* value) for whites over blacks was considered a biased item.
2. The second was also a legal definition for test bias, called the "80% or 4/5 rule" of adverse impact, that was established by the Equal Employment Opportunity Commission of the U.S. government in 1966: the selection rate for any protected minority group must be at least 80% or 4/5ths as high as the selection rate for the largest group or the test will be considered discriminatory.
3. Many of the statistical definitions for bias (at either the item or test score levels) focus on methods that examine the mean differences between one group and the norm group.
4. Other statistical definitions for bias (at either the item or test score levels) focus on methods that examine the effect sizes of differences in means between one group and the norm group.

In addition, we need to realize that test bias does not just emerge from a test or a test item, but instead comes from numerous sources within the testing process including at least the following: (a) administration procedures, (b) test directions, (c) test content, (d) test knowledge selection, (e) testing method, (f) rating/scoring, (g) score interpretation, and (h) norm sample selection. Unfortunately, all eight of these sources of bias are also sources of measurement error (as explained in Chapter 8), so the trick is to separate differences between subgroups that are due to these factors from differences due to true differences in ability with regard to whatever is being tested and from differences due to random fluctuations in performance.

For example, consider an oral interview test where one rater scores primarily for grammar ability while another focuses on pronunciation and a third rater scores on the basis of fluency. Clearly, if the raters' differences in terms of what is important in oral communication are found to be creating bias against some groups of students, testing bias is the issue. Otherwise, the differences between raters may just be a source of measurement error.

Generally, language testers do the best they can to minimize such biases by minimizing the effects of factors like (a) to (h) above, but it is still advisable to investigate the items and scores on any language test for potential bias. The best strategies for avoiding testing bias are to have careful guidelines for test item writers and test designers (e.g., ETS 1998, 2002b), make results public, and constantly be on the lookout for any systematic test score performance differences between groups. For example, Educational Testing Service breaks down and publishes the results for each and every year of TOEFL tests for various groupings (academic level, gender, language background, and nationality) (e.g., ETS 2002a), so those results can be examined by ETS as well as by the general public. In all cases, members of any affected groups should be involved in the process of judging test items at the developmental stage, as well as in examining score results. (see Hambleton & Rodgers 1995; Kunnan 2000; Popham, 1995, pp. 63-76).

REVIEW QUESTIONS

1. What is validity?

2. What are the three basic types of validity?

3. Which type of validity is most typically based on expert opinion?

4. Which type of validity is an experimental demonstration of the existence of an underlying psychological construct?

5. Which type of validity is based on the correlation of the scores on a new test with scores on a previously well-established test of the same construct?

6. What types of validity are appropriate for NRTs, and which for CRTs?

7. What considerations must language programs take into account when using language tests?

8. What are restrictions of range and skewing problems that you should watch out for in performing any correlational analysis?

9. How are test consistency (reliability or dependability) and validity related to standard setting?

10. What is the difference between fairness and bias? How is item bias defined statistically? What are some of the potential sources of bias in a test?

A. Table 10.8 is taken from the validity section of *TOEFL test and score manual* (ETS 1997, p. 35). This validity section marshals arguments for the validity of the TOEFL from a variety of Educational Testing Services sources and other secondary sources. Much more information is provided in that publication than what is given in Table 10.8 so you should not draw any conclusions about the validity of TOEFL without first obtaining and examining the latest version of the entire publication. Nevertheless, for the sake of practicing what you have learned in this chapter, these tables will suffice.

Table 10.8 displays the degree of relationship between total TOEFL scores and university ratings. At four universities, "the students were ranked in four, five, or six categories based on their proficiency in English as determined by university tests or other judgments of their ability to pursue regular academic courses" (ETS 1997, p. 35).

Table 10.8 Correlations of total TOEFL scores with teacher ratings

University	Number of Students	Correlations with Teacher Ratings
A	215	.78
B	91	.87
C	45	.76
D	279	.79

A1. What type of validity argument does this set of correlations represent? Content? Construct? Criterion-related?

A2. Is this approach concurrent or predictive?

A3. **a.** What does this information imply about TOEFL's validity?

b. What is the percent of overlapping variance (coefficient of determination) between the total TOEFL scores and the ratings provided by the universities?

A4. Are you satisfied with the number of subjects used in the study? Typically, TOEFL is administered to hundreds of thousands of students per year. Is this argument convincing to you?

B. Table 10.9 summarizes information that was actually presented in prose form in ETS 1997.

B1. What type of validity argument does this set of correlations represent? Content? Construct? Criterion-related?

B2. Is this approach concurrent or predictive?

B3. **a.** What does this information imply about the TOEFL's validity?

b. What is the percent of overlapping variance between the total TOEFL scores and the various sets of university testscores?

c. Do you find this argument convincing?

B4. Are you satisfied with the number of subjects used in these studies? Why, or why not?

Table 10.9 Summary of a variety of studies reporting correlations between TOEFL total scores and various university level ESL placement procedures

Study	Institution (N)	Criterion Measure	Correlation
Maxwell (1965)	University of California at Berkeley (N = 238)	English Proficiency Test	.87
Upshur (1966)	San Francisco State (N = 50) Indiana University (N = 38) Park College (N = 12)	Michigan Test of English Language Proficiency	.89
ALI (1966)	Georgetown University (N = 104)	American Language Institute Test	.79

C. Table 10.10 is also found in ETS (1997, p. 35). The table presents a comparison of the performances of an experimental group of international students and a group of native speakers. The international students took both the TOEFL and the *Graduate Record Examination* (GRE) Verbal subtest, while the native speakers took only the GRE.

Table 10.10 GRE Verbal score comparisons

	Mean	S	Reliability	SEM
TOEFL	523	69	.95	15
GRE				
Non-natives (N = 186)	274	67	.78	30
Native Speakers (N = 1495)	514	128	.94	32

C1. What type of standardized score is probably being reported for the GRE results (see Chapter 6)?

C2. a. How do these results support the proposition that the GRE Verbal subtest measures English language ability?

b. What kind of validity argument would this support? Content? Construct? Criterion-related?

C3. Would the GRE Verbal subtest be valid for testing international students' verbal ability to pursue graduate studies? Why, or why not?

C4. Why might the standard deviation and reliability on the GRE be lower for international students than for native speakers?

C5. Are you satisfied with the number of subjects used in this study? Why, or why not?

D1. How would you design an argument for the content validity of the TOEFL?

D2. How would you design an argument for the construct validity of the TOEFL?

E. Describe how you would go about setting the standards for a particular type of test in a real or fictitious language program.

LANGUAGE TESTING
IN REALITY

INTRODUCTION

Many of the articles in the field of language testing, indeed some of the chapters in this book, treat tests as though they are somehow isolated entities floating free of any language teaching reality. In most of this book, however, I have tried to stress the importance of looking at tests within the context of real, living language programs. For this reason, a good deal of attention was paid to the differences and similarities between NRTs and CRTs, and these two categories of tests were always discussed in terms of adopting, developing, and adapting sound language tests for making decisions in real language programs. Clearly, the point of view taken in this book is that tests can and should be integral parts of the larger curriculum in a language program. Although tests may be isolated for purposes of study, they should never be treated as though they are somehow divorced from the language teaching and learning processes that are going on in the same context. In this final section of the chapter, I will address the issue of where tests fit into language programs and discuss the place of testing in curriculum planning and implementation.

• THE PLACE OF TESTS IN CURRICULUM PLANNING

Curriculum planning is taken here to be a series of activities that provide a support framework which helps teachers design effective activities and learning situations to promote language learning. The model shown in Figure 11.1 (from Brown 1995a) describes six broad types of activities that are often identified in the curriculum design literature with promoting good teaching and learning: needs analysis, goals and objectives setting, testing (both NRT and CRT), materials development, teaching, and program evaluation. The model is a simplified, yet complete, version of the widely accepted **systems approach** used in educational technology and curriculum design circles. Dick, Carey, and Carey (2000) discuss the systems approach to curriculum in terms of what a system is (p. 2):

> A system is technically a set of interrelated parts, all of which are
> working together toward a defined goal. The parts of the system
> depend on each other for input and output, and the entire system
> uses feedback to determine if its desired goal has been reached. If it
> has not, then the system is modified until it does reach the goal.

A curriculum that has interrelated parts working toward a clearly defined goal with input and output as well as feedback is a system. A quick glance at the curriculum development process described in Figure 11.1 will reveal that it is a systems approach with all the characteristics described in the above quotation.

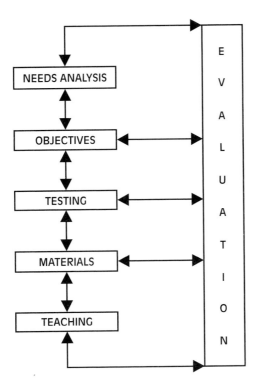

Figure 11.1 Systematic design of language curriculum

Teachers can use the model shown in Figure 11.1 as both a set of stages for developing and implementing a course or program and a set of components that they can monitor for the improvement and maintenance of an already existing course or program. Either way, using this model will encourage a continuing process of curriculum development and maintenance. (For more extensive discussion on the elements of this model, see Brown & Pennington 1991, Brown 1995a, or Brown 2003a.)

Because the topic of this book is language testing, the focus here will be on those issues related to the role of *tests* in language curriculum planning. Once again, examples will be drawn from the English Language Institute (ELI) at the University of Hawaii at Manoa (UHM) to illustrate one way that tests can fit into a program. The discussion will include a brief description of the program as well as information about the various types of tests that have been adopted, developed, or adapted at UHM. The central thesis will be that it is important to get all the tests to fit together into a decision-making matrix.

To help with testing, curriculum developers may want to hire an outside consultant or provide special release time or training for program personnel to learn about language testing. In either case, the rewards for the program should be commensurate with the investment because of the important position that testing holds in the curriculum development process.

In order to use examples from the testing program at UHM, it will be necessary to briefly describe the program itself. After all, tests do not exist in a vacuum but rather are used for decision-making purposes within a specific program.

All ELI courses follow the University of Hawaii's regular schedule for length of term and class hours required. All courses receive three units of credit. They meet either three days per week for 50 minutes, or twice a week for 75 minutes for a total of 15 weeks with an extra week for final examinations each semester. Every effort is made to hold the maximum class size to 20 students. The courses in the ELI are as follows:

ELI 70	Listening Comprehension I
ELI 80	Listening Comprehension II
ELI 72	Reading for Foreign Students
ELI 82	Advanced Reading for Foreign Students
ELI 71	Fundamentals of Writing for Foreign Students
ELI 73	Writing for Foreign Students (3 credits)
ELI 81	Speaking for Foreign Teaching Assistants
ELI 83	Writing for Foreign Graduate Students
ESL 100	Expository Writing: A Guided Approach

FOUR DECISION-MAKING STEPS

As pointed out in Brown (2003b), four decision making steps proved useful in developing our language testing program while I was Director of the ELI from 1986 to 1991. I will cover them chronologically with a particular emphasis on how each step affected the students at UHM. The four steps are as follows:

1. initial screening procedures
2. placement procedures
3. second-week diagnostic procedures and
4. achievement procedures

To accomplish these steps, a number of different tests were used: the ELI Placement Test (ELIPT), the Test of English as a Foreign Language (TOEFL), and the CRTs developed for diagnosis and achievement testing in the individual courses. (For a full report and description of these CRTs, see Brown 1993.) I hope that the strategies we found so useful can be generalized and adapted to various kinds of second and foreign language programs. Procedures similar to these should help teachers integrate their testing procedures into one cogent testing program and help to integrate testing into the overall curriculum.

Initial screening procedures

Each year about 600 new foreign students were admitted to UHM for undergraduate (41%) or graduate (59%) programs. As would be expected from our geographical location, roughly 82% of these students came from Asia with the four largest contingents coming from Hong Kong, the People's Republic of China, Taiwan, and Japan. Before being admitted, students had been screened by the Office of

Admissions and Records. The students' previous academic records, letters of recommendation, and TOEFL scores were all reviewed, and only those students with good academic records *and* total TOEFL scores of 500 or higher were admitted. Applicants exempt from the TOEFL examination and ELI training were those who:

1. Spoke English as a native language;
2. Held a bachelor's or a graduate degree from an accredited university in the United States, Canada (except Quebec), Britain, Australia, or New Zealand;
3. Had SAT verbal scores of 500 or better;
4. Had completed all their education (K-12 or more) in countries listed in no. 2.

This information, including each student's three TOEFL subtest scores and total score, was then sent to the ELI. If students' scores on the TOEFL were above 600, the students were notified that they were exempt from any ELI requirement. Those students who had scored between 500 and 599 on the TOEFL were notified that they would have to take the ELI Placement Test (ELIPT) when they got to UHM. Clearly, the initial screening procedures were designed to narrow the range of English proficiencies with which the ELI would ultimately have to deal. Note, however, that even after these broad screening decisions had been made, any student could request an interview with the Director or Assistant Director, at any time, to appeal our decisions. This allowed us some flexibility and an initial opportunity to spot students who actually did not need ELI training and should therefore be exempted from the ELIPT. Students who fell into this category were typically those who met at least one of the following criteria:

1. They had received an Associate of Arts or Sciences degree from an American community college with a GPA of 3.0 or higher.
2. They had attended school in the United States, Canada (except Quebec), Britain, Australia, or New Zealand for a minimum of 5 years.
3. They had attended English medium schools in any Commonwealth country for a minimum of 10 years.

Falling into any one of the above categories did not mean that the student was automatically exempted, but rather that the student was given an opportunity to present a case for exemption in an interview with the Director or Assistant Director. When we had any doubt, however, we insisted that the student take the ELIPT. Thus, some students may have taken a test that was not necessary, but few students who really needed ELI training were missed.

In the end, most students who scored between 500 and 599 on TOEFL were required to take the ELIPT, because we wanted more information on their language abilities in the three main academic skill areas that our courses dealt with. We were also interested in getting information that was a bit more recent than their TOEFL scores and more directly related to the teaching and learning that were going on in the ELI.

Many teachers may find themselves in a position in which they need to determine how much of a given language their students have learned during their lives. At first, they will only be concerned with knowing about the students' proficiency in general terms without reference to any particular program. This is likely to be the case when students are brand new to a language program and the teachers want to get a general notion of how much of the language they know, as in the admissions decisions at UHM. To do this, teachers will probably need tests that are general in nature, such as the TOEFL in the ELI example. These same teachers may also want to establish guidelines for which types of students are automatically exempt from training, which students need to take the placement test, and which students deserve an interview or further information gathering (because they fall into the gray area were a decision may not be clear-cut).

At the same time they are using such initial screening measures, teachers may be able to get a tentative estimate of the general level of language proficiency of their students. For those familiar with the TOEFL, the TOEFL range for students in the ELI was between 500 (the minimum score for admissions to UHM) and 600 (the point at which students were automatically exempted from ELI training), which gives a general idea of the overall ability parameters involved in the ELI course structure. Such information may help in determining entrance standards (or exit) for a curriculum, in adjusting the level of goals and objectives to the true abilities of the students, or in making comparisons across programs. As a result, initial screening procedures are often based on proficiency tests that are general in nature, but nonetheless important and globally related to curriculum structure.

Placement procedures

As Director of the ELI, my duties included placing the students into levels of study that were as homogeneous as possible in order to facilitate the overall teaching and learning of ESL. To that end, the ELI had quite naturally developed its own placement procedures. These procedures were not based entirely on the placement test results, as is the case in some language programs. In addition to the test scores, we used the information gained from the initial screening, as well as the second-week diagnosis and achievement procedures that came later. Using all this information helped insure that we were being maximally fair to the students and that they were working at the level that would most benefit them.

The English Language Institute Placement Test (ELIPT) was a three-hour test battery made up of six subtests: the Academic Listening Test, Dictation, Reading Comprehension Test, Cloze, Academic Writing Test, and Writing Sample. Placement into the academic listening skills courses was based primarily on the Academic Listening Test and Dictation, while placement into the reading courses was based on the Reading Comprehension Test and Cloze, and placement into the writing courses was based on the Academic Writing Test (multiple-choice proofreading) and Writing Sample (composition task). We had systematically designed our tests so that two subtest scores could be used for each of the three skill areas: one was discrete-point in nature and the other was integrative (see Chapter 2 for more on discrete-point and integrative tests). We felt that having these two types of subtests for each skill area provided us with two different views of the students' abilities in each skill.

However, relying solely on these test scores would have been very irresponsible. We insured a more human touch by doing the placement of students in a face-to-face interview with a member of the ELI faculty. The interviewers had all the information that they might need (including the student's records, TOEFL scores, and ELIPT test scores) when they conducted the interviews. The interviewers were told to base their placement decisions for each skill area on the two subtest scores, but also on other information in the student's records and any information gained by talking to the student. If the faculty member was unsure of the appropriate level for a student, or if the student contested the placement decisions, the ELI Director or Assistant Director took over and made the necessary decisions. The students then registered for the appropriate courses and the semester began.

The interview procedure allowed us to place students more accurately than any test score alone because the placement was based on many sources of information considered together. Indeed, the ELIPT subtest scores (both integrative and discrete-point for each skill) were considered. But more importantly, other factors were taken into account like the length of time the student had studied English, the amount of time since the student had studied it, the amount of time in the United States, their TOEFL subtest scores, their spoken language during the interview, their academic records, and any other information available at the time. All these details helped us to place students in a way that respected them as human beings who were important to us.

Sooner or later, most teachers will find themselves having to make placement decisions. In most language programs, students are grouped according to ability levels. Such grouping is desirable so that teachers can focus in each class on the problems and learning points appropriate for students at a particular level. As discussed in Chapter 1, placement tests can help make such decisions. Such tests are typically norm-referenced and therefore fairly general in purpose, but, unlike proficiency tests, placement tests should be designed (through careful item writing, item analysis and revision—see Chapters 3 and 4) to fit the abilities and levels of the students in the particular program. The purpose of such tests is to show how much ability, knowledge, or skill the students have. The resulting scores are then used to place students into levels of study, or perhaps exempt them entirely.

To do this, teachers will need tests that are general in nature, but designed specifically for the types and levels of their students, as well as for the goals of their program. Teachers may also need to establish guidelines for using as many types of test information as possible along with other types of data. In addition, they might want to conduct placement interviews wherein all available information is marshaled for making the placement decisions. They might also consider further testing or information gathering for those students who fall close to their cut-points say plus or minus one SEM of any division point between levels (see Chapter 8).

The ELI students were placed in each skill on the basis of a complete set of placement procedures. Remember, two placement subtest scores were available for each skill along with considerable additional information. The placement decisions were made on the basis of all this information and the students had recourse to a second interview with the Director or Assistant Director if they wanted it. We felt that our placement decisions were as fair as possible because they were based on a relatively large and varied collection of information sources, and there was a line of appeal that students could follow if they felt that they had not been treated fairly. However, the process of determining whether or not a student has been placed in the proper level did not stop here. The process continued as long as the students were associated with the ELI.

Second-week diagnostic procedures

During the second week of instruction, ELI teachers were required to give a diagnostic test of the skill that they were teaching and to keep a close watch on their students to see if any had been misplaced. When a student was identified who appeared to be in the wrong level, the teacher consulted with the ELI Director and, if necessary, an interview with the student was arranged. In most cases, students who were found to be misplaced were moved to a higher level of study or exempted in the relevant skill area.

The tests that were used in the second week of classes were provided by the ELI. One teacher was given 10 hours per week release time (and the title "Testing Lead Teacher") for the sole purpose of developing and improving these tests. This teacher worked with other lead teachers (one for each skill area) and the various groupings of teachers within the skill areas to create CRTs for each course. The testing lead teacher did not actually write the tests. Rather, the lead teacher's responsibility was to coordinate groups of teachers who actually did the item writing and test production. Then the testing lead teacher took care of duplicating the tests, helping the teachers administer them, scoring the tests, reporting the results to the teachers, analyzing the pre-test and post-test results (for CRT statistics), revising the tests (again, in consultation with the teachers), and starting the whole process over again the next semester.

CRTs in two forms (A and B) were produced for each of the courses. (See Brown 1993 for a description of these CRTs at an earlier stage of development.) These CRTs were designed to measure the specific objectives of each course. Hence they could be administered at the beginning of the courses as diagnostic tests and at the end as achievement tests. The tests were administered in a **counterbalanced design** such that half of the students took form A at the beginning of the course while the other half took form B. At the end of the course, all students took the opposite form. This counterbalancing was done so that students did not see exactly the same test twice.

Many teachers may find themselves using such diagnostic procedures for purposes of checking to see if their placement decisions were correct, but also for purposes of identifying and diagnosing students' strengths and weaknesses in relation to the course objectives. These procedures may be based extensively on test results, but other factors should probably also come into play. Teachers' observations of the students' classroom performances and attitudes may serve as one source of information; an interview with the Director may be another. The point is that procedures should be put in place to help students and their teachers focus their efforts where they will be most effective.

These diagnostic procedures are clearly related to achievement procedures. After all, diagnosis and achievement decisions can be based on two administrations of the same test (preferably in two counterbalanced forms as described above). However, while diagnostic decisions are usually designed to help identify students' strengths and weaknesses at the beginning or during instruction, achievement procedures are typically focused on the degree to which each student has accomplished the course objectives at the end of instruction. In other words, diagnostic procedures are usually made along the way as the students are learning the language, while achievement procedures come into play at the end of the course.

Achievement procedures

In the ELI, the CRT post-tests were administered as part of the achievement procedures. The CRT achievement tests were administered during the students' regularly scheduled final examination periods, which were two hours long. Since the CRTs were designed to last no more than 50 minutes, the remaining hour and ten minutes could be utilized by the teacher to administer a personal final examination if desired. In terms of grading, the results of these achievement tests were initially counted as 10 percent of the students' grades so that the tests would be taken seriously. The students were informed of this at the beginning of the course. Since, early on, the criterion-referenced tests were more or less experimental, we were very careful about treating them as **minimal competency tests** on which students must achieve a certain minimum score in order to pass the course. However, later, when the tests were more fully developed, standards were established for what it meant to succeed in our courses and the tests counted as a higher proportion of the students' grades.

```
┌─────────────────────────────────────────────────────────────────────┐
│                                                                       │
│  English Language Institute                    Moore Hall, Room 570   │
│                                                                       │
│  ELI STUDENT PERFORMANCE REPORT                                       │
│                                                                       │
│  Student's Name: _____    │
│                     (Family name)           (Other names)            │
│                                                                       │
│  ELI _____   Section _____   ☐ Fall  ☐ Spring  ☐ SSI  ☐ SSII  20 ___ │
│                                                                       │
│  ☐ Undergraduate   ☐ Graduate   ☐ Unclassified   ☐ EWC Grantee       │
│                                                                       │
│  Academic Dept.: _____   Academic Advisor: _____    │
│                                                                       │
│                                                                       │
│  _____ (DO NOT WRITE BELOW THIS LINE!!!) _____    │
│                                                                       │
│  1. Hours Absent (circle)         0  1  2  3  4  5  ☐ More than 5    │
│                                                                       │
│  2. Class Participation     Very Little   1 2 3 4 5 6 7   Very Much  │
│                                                                       │
│  3. Class Motivation        Very Poor     1 2 3 4 5 6 7   Excellent  │
│                                                                       │
│  4. Overall Improvement     Very Little   1 2 3 4 5 6 7   Very Much  │
│     in this Skill Area                                                │
│                                                                       │
│  5. Mastery of Course    50% or  60% 65% 70% 75% 80% 85% 90% 95% 100%│
│     Objectives (approx.)  lower                                       │
│                                                                       │
│  6. Recommended Action for Next Semester                              │
│        ☐ EXEMPT in this skill area      ☐ ENROLL in _____    │
│                                                                       │
│  7. Course Grade - ELI Courses          Course Grade - ESL Courses    │
│                                                                       │
│     ☐ No credit   ☐ Credit   ☐ Incomplete   (A B C D F or I) = ____  │
│                                                                       │
│  8. Remarks                                                           │
│                                                                       │
│                                                                       │
│                                        _____    │
│                                             ELI Instructor            │
└─────────────────────────────────────────────────────────────────────┘
```

Figure 11.2 ELI student performance report

Again, the administration and scoring of these tests was coordinated by the testing lead teacher. In addition to the tests, our achievement procedures included the requirement that each teacher fill out an evaluation report form (see Figure 11.2) for each student. Since most of our courses were taken on a credit/no credit basis, these evaluation reports served much the same function as grades in that they were statements of the students' overall achievement in the course. Unlike grades, these reports were fairly detailed and gave a prose description of each student's performance. In addition, the teachers were asked to state specifically what level of ELI course the students should take in the next semester. In some cases, the teacher might suggest that a student skip a level or be exempt from any further study in that skill area. In such a case, the teacher petitioned the ELI Director and, if the petition was approved, the teacher advised the student about how to proceed.

One copy of the student performance report was kept on file in the ELI, and another was sent to the student's academic department so that the student's academic advisor was apprised of the student's progress and remaining ELI requirements. In this way, students who no longer fit in the particular course level to which we had initially assigned them could be identified and adjustments in their placement could be made— even after they have studied for a full semester or more.

Most teachers will probably agree that they would like to foster achievement, particularly in the form of language learning, in their course or program. In order to find out if their efforts have been successful and to help maximize the possibilities for student learning, achievement procedures like our tests and performance reports may prove useful. Remember that the tests used to monitor such achievement should be developed to measure the very specific objectives of a given course or program and that they must be flexible in the sense that they can readily be made to change in response to what is learned from them in terms of the tests themselves or other curriculum elements. In other words, carefully designed achievement procedures are most useful to a language program when they are flexible and responsive for affecting curriculum changes and continually analyzing those changes with reference to the program realities.

Testing as an integrated system

In the system described here for the ELI at UHM, the vast majority of the students served by the initial screening, placement, second-week diagnostic, and achievement procedures were correctly classified and placed and were systematically learning a substantial amount within our program. We felt confident that most of our students were being helped with their language learning needs. Nonetheless, decisions are made by human beings. Since humans are known to make mistakes and since incorrect decisions can cost the students dearly in the form of extra tuition or unnecessary time spent studying ESL, it is always necessary to base decisions on the best and most varied information available, and continue to maintain avenues for double-checking those decisions and for appeal on the part of the students.

Nevertheless, testing, though an essential component of any sound language curriculum, is only *part* of the curriculum. Likewise, test results should form part of the basis for any decision, but only part. Other sources of information may prove equally important. For instance, teachers might want to consider admissions scores, letters of recommendation, interviews, student evaluation reports, transcripts of academic work at other institutions, teacher judgments, or any other available sources. However, all sources of information will be most useful if they are systematically sorted and integrated into a regular systematic testing program like the initial screening, placement, second-week diagnostic, and achievement procedures recently established for decision making in the University of Hawaii ELI.

Multiple opportunities exist for cross-verifying and changing decisions, and these opportunities should be provided at various points of time within the curriculum process. Above all else, no decision should be made on the basis of a single piece of information. Even a tried-and-true test that has proven reliable and valid for years generates some error variation. A second, different source of information minimizes the chances that such error will influence the reliability of the related decisions.

Certainly, all the decision-making procedures described above will take a great deal of effort on the part of the administrators and teachers, but the benefits gained from effective and humane decision-making procedures accrue to all participants in a program—students, teachers, and administrators alike.

REVIEW QUESTIONS

1. What are the components of language curriculum development? And, how is testing related to each of those components?

2. What is the purpose in the ELI at UHM of each of the following types of information gathering procedures?

   a. initial screening procedures

   b. placement procedures

   c. second week diagnostic procedures

   d. achievement procedures

APPLICATION EXERCISES

A1. Which of the components of language curriculum development outlined in this chapter are well defined in your language program (or one that you know about)? Which are not well defined?

A2. What tests are used in your program (or one that you know about) and how are they related to the existing components of language curriculum?

B1. What are the equivalents in your language program (or one that you know about) for each of the following information gathering procedures:

   a. initial screening procedures
   b. placement procedures
   c. first week diagnostic procedures
   d. achievement procedures

B2. If any of these four procedures does not exist in your program, should they be instituted? Why? Or why not?

REVIEW QUESTIONS ANSWER KEY

Chapter 1

1. The interpretation of CRT scores is considered absolute because a student's score on a particular objective or language point indicates the percent of the knowledge or skill that the student has learned.
   Another possible answer: CRT
   The interpretation of NRT scores is considered relative because each student's score is interpreted relative to the scores of all other students who took the test.
   Another possible answer: NRT

2. NRTs spread students out along a continuum of general abilities or proficiencies.
   Another possible answer: NRT

3. CRTs measure the amount of learning that a student has accomplished on the material that was taught. If all the students learned 100% of the material, they would all score 100% on the test.
   Another possible answer: CRT

4. Students may know the general format of the questions on an NRT, but they will typically not know before the test what specific content or skills will be covered by those questions.
   Another possible answer: NRT

5. CRTs can typically consist of a series of short, well-defined subtests with similar item contents.
   Another possible answer: CRT

6. Placement test

7. Diagnostic test

8. Achievement test

9. Proficiency test

10. It would be difficult, if not impossible, because of differences in testing purpose, ranges of ability, and variety of content.

Chapter 2

1. Theoretical issues include language teaching methodology issues, the distinction between competence and performance, and the difference between discrete-point and integrative tests. Practical issues include fairness issues, cost issues, and logistical issues.
   Theoretical issues have to do with what tests should look like and what they should do. Practical issues have to do with physically putting tests into place in a program.

2. Answer according to your own teaching philosophy.

3. Task-based testing is a specific type of performance testing. In general, performance testing evaluates the actual use of language in concrete situations.

Task-based testing evaluates students' abilities to accomplish particular tasks or task types in which target language communication is essential.

They are communicative because the examinees must perform meaningful tasks, the tasks must be as authentic as possible, and success or failure in the outcome of the tasks must be rated by qualified judges.

4. Chomsky defines competence as the speaker-hearer's knowledge of his language and performance as the actual use of language in concrete situations.

One can be competent on a test in his/her knowledge of a language, but still demonstrate imperfect performance.

5. Discrete-point tests measure the small bits and pieces of a language (a multiple-choice test measuring students' knowledge of particular structures). Integrative tests are typically designed to use several skills at one time (dictation or cloze tests).

Answer part 2 according to your own teaching philosophy.

6. Characteristics: 1) meaningful communication, 2) authentic situation, 3) unpredictable language input, 4) creative language output, and 5) includes all language skills (reading, writing, listening, & speaking)

Components: 1) grammatical competence, 2) sociolinguistic competence, 3) discourse competence, and 4) strategic competence

7. The aim in maximizing objectivity is to give each student an equal chance to do well. Some of the elements of a language course, such as the communicative components, may not be testable using most objective test types.

In these cases, some objectivity may be sacrificed in order to set up testing situations, such as role plays, where teachers will have to decide how the performance of each student will be scored.

8. Ease of construction, ease of test administration, and ease of test scoring.

All three are equally important, though certain trade-offs are often necessary.

The easiest types of tests to construct initially (composition, dictation, translation) are usually the most difficult to score and least objective, while those test types which are more difficult to construct initially (multiple-choice, true-false, matching) are usually the easiest to score and most objective.

9. The theoretical orientation, the practical orientation, and test characteristics (see Table 2.4).

Answer part 2 according to your own situation.

10. Establishing purposes of test, evaluating the test itself, arranging the physical needs, making pre-administration arrangements, administering the test, scoring, interpreting, record keeping, test analyses, and ongoing research (see Table 2.5).

Answer part 2 according to your own situation.

11. An address is made up of a column letter(s) and a row number, and each cell has its own distinct address that is different from all the other cells' addresses, e.g., the cell in the upper left corner of the spreadsheet is labeled A1.

Cells are squares made by the intersections of the rows and columns in a spreadsheet. Excel™ has 65,536 rows and 230 columns.

Chapter 3

1. The smallest unit that produces distinctive and meaningful information or feedback on a test when it is scored or rated.

2. A test is made up of test items. Some items, like multiple-choice or true-false items, form the individual test questions. Other items are built into more integrative types of language tests such as dictations, interviews, role plays, or compositions.

3. The item in a cloze test is the nth blank in a text.

    In a dictation, items are typically each word which is scored according to the test objectives, which can include word elements like spelling, handwriting, etc.

    Composition items also are determined by test objectives and can include written language elements such as grammar, sentence and paragraph construction, spelling, etc., or the item may be determined by the content or subject of the composition.

4. The degree to which each item is properly written so that it measures all and only the desired content.

5. To insure that the students answer the items correctly only if they know the concept or skill being tested or have the skill involved.

6. Receptive response items require the student to select a response rather than actually produce one. Productive response items require the students to actually produce responses rather than just select them receptively. Personal response items encourage the students to produce responses that hold personal meaning.

Chapter 4

1. *IF* is used to examine the percentage of students who correctly answer a given item. To calculate *IF*, add up the number of students who correctly answered a particular item and divide that sum by the total number of students who took the test.

    This value is the percentage of correct answers for a given item.

2. *ID* indicates the degree to which an item separates the students who performed well from those who did poorly on the test as a whole.

    First, line up the students' names, their individual item responses, and total scores in descending order based on the total scores. Divide the students into three groups to determine the upper and lower groups of scores. Separately calculate the *IF* for the lower and upper group. Then subtract the *IF* for the lower group from the *IF* for the upper group on each item.

    This gives you an index of the contrasting performance of those students who scored "high" on the whole test with those who scored "low." Those items that have a high ID are performing most like the total test scores and will probably be the best items for testing those abilities for NRT purposes.

3. (a) Pilot a relatively large number of test items on a group of students similar to the group that will ultimately be assessed with the test; (b) Analyze the items using format analysis and statistical techniques; (c) Select the best items to make up a shorter, more effective revised version of the test.

A difference between NRTs and CRTs is that NRTs are constructed to produce normal distributions, while CRTs do not necessarily do so. The item selection process for developing NRTs is designed to retain items that are well-centered (with *IF*s of .30 to .70) and spread students out efficiently (with *ID*s as high as you can get). In contrast, CRTs are designed to measure student achievement so the *DI* and/or *B*-index item analysis statistics are used instead of *ID*.

4. Item quality analysis determines the degree to which each item is measuring the content that it was designed to measure and the degree to which that content should be measured at all.

   From a teacher's perspective, content congruence may be more important. Teachers would be more interested in content applicability.

5. *DI* indicates the degree to which an item is reflecting gain in knowledge or skill. The *IF* for the pre-test results (or non-masters) is subtracted from the *IF* for post-test results (or masters) to calculate the difference index.

6. The difference index uses the intervention pre-test/post-test strategy and subtracts the pre-test results from the post-test results. The *B*-index uses differential group strategies and avoids the problem of two administrations of the CRT by comparing the *IF*s of those students who passed a test with the *IF*s of those who failed it.

7. *DI* = *IF* post-test – *IF* pre-test. Indicates the percentage of increase or decrease in knowledge of a concept or skill after instruction.

   B-Index = *IF* pass – *IF* fail. Indicates the degree to which students who passed the test outperformed the students who failed the test on each item.

8. Calculating difference indexes (comparing pre-test and post-test results) would provide additional information about how sensitive each item was to instruction. Calculating *B*-indexes (for the post-test results) would help teachers understand how effective each item was for deciding who passed the test and who failed.

9. NRT item statistics like item facility and item discrimination analyses are used to determine which items were too easy or too difficult to demonstrate a spread of scores. Criterion-referenced item analysis techniques include the difference index and the *B*-index to help determine which subsets of CRT items are most closely related to the instruction and learning in a course and/or that subset most closely related to the distinction between students who passed or failed the test.

10. Answer according to your own experience.

Chapter 5

1. The number of occurrences (or) frequencies of the score values arranged from high to low scores is called a frequency distribution.

   Knowing the percent of other examinees falling below or above each student is an integral part of interpreting NRT scores.

2. Nominal, ordinal, and continuous scales.

   Nominal scales are used for categorizing and naming groups. Ordinal scales order or rank the data. Continuous scales show the distances between the points in the rankings.

3. Central tendency describes the most typical behavior of a group.

Four statistics are used for estimating central tendency: the mean, the mode, the median, and the midpoint.

The most often reported is the mean.

4. Dispersion is how the individual performances vary from the central tendency.

Range, high and low, standard deviation, and variance.

5. Both are important because the user of the test results must be able to visualize the middle (or typical) behavior of the group as well as the performances of those students who varied away from the typical behavior.

6. *Minimum Score to Maximum Score* axis is the ordinate and *Number at Each Score* is the abscissa.

Chapter 6

1. 1 chance out of 52.

1

52

1/52

The same.

The same for *any* queen. 1/13 to pick *a* queen.

2-4. Possible example:

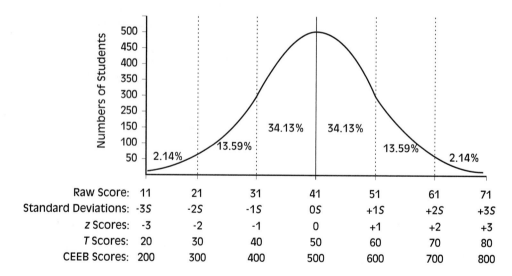

Raw Score:	11	21	31	41	51	61	71
Standard Deviations:	-3S	-2S	-1S	0S	+1S	+2S	+3S
z Scores:	-3	-2	-1	0	+1	+2	+3
T Scores:	20	30	40	50	60	70	80
CEEB Scores:	200	300	400	500	600	700	800

Where raw score:

$M = 41$

$S = 10$

$N = 3541$

5. 34.13% x 2 = 68.26%

6. 15.73 or 15.87 (depending on how you calculate)

    84.13%

    50%

7. 84.13

    15.9

    93.3

8. Positively skewed distribution

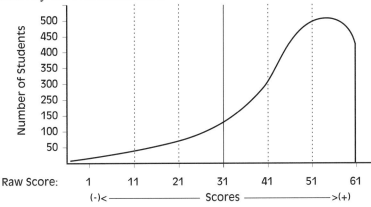

Negatively skewed distribution

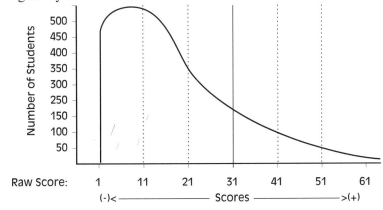

Skewed distributions indicate a problem in NRTs.

Skewed distributions are a positive indicator in CRTs.

On a pre-test, before the students have studied the material in a course, a positively skewed distribution would indicate that most of the students do not know the material and therefore need to take the course. On the post-test, a negatively skewed distribution would indicate that most of the students had learned the material well.

9. Counterbalancing is a way around the problem of practice effect, which occurs when the scores on a second administration are higher because the students have already experienced, or "practiced," the same test on a previous occasion. To do counterbalancing, testers need to develop two parallel forms of the CRT so that they are very similar. During the pre-test, half of the students take Form A and half take Form B. After instruction, the first half then takes Form B and the second half takes Form A. Counterbalancing insures that no student takes exactly the same test twice. Hence, the practice effect is minimized.

10. Yes.

When a pattern for a set of data that takes the shape of a bell-shaped curve. The data will tend to be concentrated near the center and decrease symmetrically on both sides.

Normal distribution indicates the percents of students who will score within certain score ranges on a measure, what percentiles mean in terms of exactly where an individual's score falls in the normal distribution, and what happens when departures from the normal distribution occur (that is, when distributions are *not* normal) and what language testers do when things go wrong and deviate from normality.

Be sure that the sample is large enough. Using item analyses, examine test items for the purpose of revising the test. Investigate any variance problems.

Chapter 7

1. The examination of how the scores on two tests go together with regard to dispersing the students.

The degree to which two sets of scores covary is estimated statistically by calculating a correlation coefficient.

Two sets of scores that vary together.

2. +1.0 to –1.0.   Zero

3. The design requirement is that the two sets of numbers must both be continuous scales, rather than ordinal or nominal scales.

Independence, normally distributions, and linearity.

Independence requires that each pair of scores be unrelated to all other pairs of scores. Normal distributions require that neither of the two distributions can be skewed.

Linearity means that the relationship between the two sets of scores must be linear.

4. A linear relationship is one wherein the relationship between the two sets of scores in correlational analysis can be represented by a straight line on a scatterplot.

Curvilinear relationships form one or more curves when plotted out.

5. When its correlation coefficient indicates that the correlation is due to factors other than chance with the appropriate degree of certainty.

a) Table the data and determine correlation. b) Determine whether chance is directional or non-directional. c) Determine the degree of certainty. d) Find the number of pairs of scores involved in the calculations, minus 2 (N-2) on the Critical Values of the Pearson Product-moment Correlation Coefficient chart. e) The value that is in the place where that row and column intersect is the critical value that the observed correlation must exceed (regardless of its sign, + or –) to be considered statistically significant, or due to factors other than chance with the appropriate degree of certainty (that is, 95 percent or 99 percent).

There is less than a 5 percent probability that this correlation coefficient occurred by chance alone.

6. Yes. About 5 percent of correlation coefficients will be significant at $P < .05$ even if based on sets of random numbers.

7. No. Meaningfulness is not probabilistic; rather, meaningfulness requires a judgment about the degree to which a coefficient (already shown to be significant) is also interesting.

8. Square the value of the correlation coefficient (r_{xy}).
It directly represents the proportion, or percent, of overlapping variance between two sets of scores.

9. The point-biserial correlation coefficient is used to compare a nominal scale with a continuous scale in terms of the degree of relationship.
It is commonly used to estimate the item discrimination through item to whole-test correlations.

Chapter 8

1. Variables in the environment like noise, heat, etc.; the adequacy of administration procedures; factors like health and motivation in the examinees themselves; the nature and correctness of scoring procedures.
Both are general sources of score variance. Meaningful variance on a test is variance that is directly attributable to the testing purposes. Measurement error is variance due to other extraneous sources.

2. CRTs won't necessarily produce a normal distribution, so statistics used on NRTs, which assume normality, will not accurately estimate reliability when used on CRTs.

3. Test-retest, equivalent forms, and internal-consistency strategies.
Test-retest reliability provides an estimate of the stability of a test over time. Equivalent forms reliability provides an estimate of the consistency of scores across forms rather than over time. Internal-consistency reliability strategies estimate the consistency of a test using only information available in one administration of a single test.

4. Interrater and intrarater reliability are two types of reliability necessary where raters make judgments and give scores for the language produced by students.
They are often appropriate when testing students' productive skills (speaking and writing) as in composition, oral interviews, role plays, etc.

5. Intrarater reliability (or rater on two occasions) is similar to test-retest reliability because you are calculating a correlation coefficient between the two sets of scores from one test in two administrations.
Interrater reliability (two raters) is similar to equivalent forms because the data are based on two different tests.

6. SEM is a statistical calculation of reliability used to interpret individual test scores and give an indication of how accurate the estimate of an individual's true test score might be.
A test that has a small SEM is more consistent than one with a large SEM.

7. Meaningful variance and measurable error.
Make sure that the test is as long as (is) reasonable, is well-designed and carefully written, assesses relatively homogeneous material, has items that discriminate well, is normally distributed, and is administered to a group of students whose abilities are as widely dispersed as logically possible within the context.

Chapter 9

1. Threshold loss agreement, squared-error loss agreement, and domain score dependability.

2. Agreement coefficient and Kappa coefficient

3. The phi (lambda) is presented for estimating squared-error loss agreement.
It measures the degree of mastery and non-mastery along the score continuum based on a cut-point., while taking into account the distances of students' scores from that cut-point.

4. Phi dependability index

5. The CI can be used to estimate a band of error around each student's score; it functions in a manner analogous to the standard error of measurement (SEM) for NRTs.

6. Meaningful variance and measurement error.

7. To maximize the possibility that a test designed for CRT purposes will be dependable, make sure that it is as long as is reasonable, is well-designed and carefully written, assesses relatively homogeneous material, has items that produce high difference indexes, and is clearly related to the instructional objectives of the course or program in which it is used.

Chapter 10

1. Test validity is the degree to which a test measures what it claims, or purports, to be measuring.

2. Content validity, construct validity, and criterion-related validity.

3. Content validity

4. Construct validity

5. Criterion-related validity

6. All three are appropriate for NRTs, while only content and construct validities are appropriate for CRTs.

7. Standard setting and washback affects

8. A narrow range of abilities or skewing can have dramatic effects on the analysis, thereby possibly producing misleading results. Descriptive statistics should always be examined whenever such analyses are conducted.

9. Standards are related to test consistency in that teachers can have a relatively high degree of confidence in a decision based on a cut-point on a highly consistent test, whereas they should have much less confidence in a decision and cut-point on a test with low test consistency. Standards are also directly related to test validity, in that decisions as to where to put the cut-point will often depend on the purposes of the test.

10. To be fair, a test must provide a visible and positive portrayal of all subgroups in proportion to their representation in the population; must refer to members of all subgroups with respect in terms of titles, names, and descriptions; and must provide equal opportunities to be familiar with the topics, situations, vocabulary, etc on the test. A test is considered bias if one particular section of the candidate population is advantaged or disadvantaged by some feature of the test or item which is not relevant to what is being measured.

A difference index of more than .15 between subgroups on a test indicates bias.

Bias comes from numerous sources within the testing process including at least the following: (a) administration procedures, (b) test directions, (c) test content, (d) test knowledge selection, (e) testing method, (f) rating/scoring, (g) score interpretation, and (h) norm sample selection.

Chapter 11

1. Tests should be integral parts of the larger curriculum in a language program and exist in the same context as the language teaching and learning processes. Decisions taken based on test results affect all of the above components.
Evaluation, teaching, materials, testing, objectives, needs analysis.

2. a. Before being admitted, students had been screened by the Office of Admissions and Records. The students' previous academic records, letters of recommendation, and TOEFL scores were all reviewed, and only those students with good academic records *and* total TOEFL scores of 500 or higher were admitted.

   b. Once admitted, students were placed into levels of study that were as homogeneous as possible in order to facilitate the overall teaching and learning of ESL

   c. During the second week of instruction, ELI teachers were required to give a diagnostic test of the skill that they were teaching and to keep a close watch on their students to see if any had been misplaced.

   d. CRT post-tests were administered during the students' regularly scheduled final examination periods as part of the achievement procedures.

Chapter 1

Answers for Chapter 1 are too specific to your situation for an answer key to be provided. Please compare your answers to material presented in the chapter.

Chapter 2

Answers for Chapter 2 are too specific to your situation for an answer key to be provided. Please compare your answers to material presented in the chapter.

Chapter 3

A) The answers for A will be too specific to the test you choose for an answer key to be provided. Please compare your answers to material presented in the chapter.

B) Count the number of times you laugh while reading the *ESL/EFL Teacher Certification Test;* then, divide the result by 10 and multiply times the barometric pressure on the day you take the test. If your score is over 110%, you pass.

Chapter 4

A) All the answers that you need are in the following screen:
Application Answers for Item Statistics (from Screen 4.8)

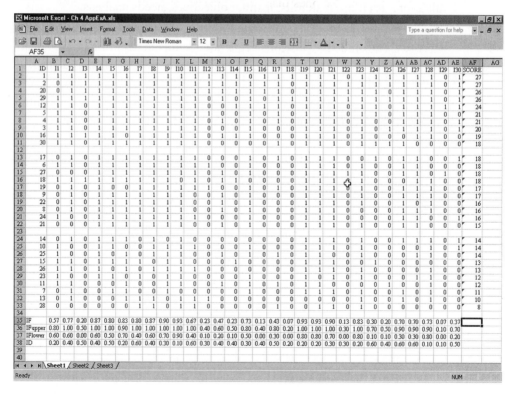

ID	I1	I2	I3	I4	I5	I6	I7	I8	I9	I10	I11	I12	I13	I14	I15	I16	I17	I18	I19	I20	I21	I22	I23	I24	I25	I26	I27	I28	I29	I30	SCORE
1	1	1	1	1	1	1	1	1	1	1	1	1	1	1	0	1	1	1	1	1	1	1	0	1	1	1	1	1	0	1	27
2	0	1	1	1	1	1	1	1	1	1	1	1	1	1	1	1	0	1	1	1	1	1	1	1	1	1	1	1	0	1	27
20	0	1	1	1	1	1	1	1	1	1	1	1	1	1	1	1	0	1	1	1	1	1	1	0	1	1	1	1	0	1	26
29	1	1	1	1	1	1	1	1	1	1	1	0	1	0	1	0	1	1	1	1	1	1	1	1	1	1	1	1	0	1	26
12	1	1	1	0	1	1	1	1	1	1	1	0	0	1	1	1	1	0	1	1	1	0	1	1	1	1	1	1	1	1	24
5	1	1	0	1	1	1	1	1	1	1	1	1	0	1	0	0	1	0	1	1	1	1	1	1	1	1	1	1	0	0	21
4	1	1	1	1	1	1	1	1	1	1	0	1	0	1	0	1	0	1	1	1	0	1	1	0	1	1	1	1	0	1	21
3	1	1	0	1	1	1	1	1	1	1	0	0	0	1	0	0	0	1	1	1	0	1	1	1	1	1	1	0	1	20	
16	1	1	1	1	1	1	0	1	1	1	1	0	1	1	1	0	0	0	1	0	1	0	0	0	1	1	0	0	19	
30	1	1	0	1	1	1	1	1	1	1	0	0	0	0	0	1	0	1	0	1	1	1	1	1	0	0	0	0	18	
17	0	1	0	1	1	1	1	1	1	1	0	0	0	1	0	1	0	1	1	0	0	1	0	1	0	0	1	18		
6	1	1	0	1	1	1	1	1	1	1	1	0	0	1	0	0	0	1	1	1	0	1	0	0	1	1	0	0	18	
27	0	0	0	1	1	1	1	1	1	1	1	0	0	0	0	1	1	1	1	0	0	1	1	0	1	0	1	0	18	
18	1	1	1	1	1	1	1	1	1	0	1	0	1	1	0	0	0	1	0	0	0	1	1	0	0	18			
19	0	1	0	1	0	0	1	1	1	1	1	0	0	1	0	1	1	1	1	0	0	1	1	1	0	0	17		
9	0	1	0	1	1	1	1	1	1	0	0	1	0	1	0	1	0	0	0	1	0	1	1	0	0	17			
22	0	1	0	1	1	1	1	1	1	0	0	1	0	1	0	1	1	1	0	1	0	1	0	0	0	16			
8	0	1	0	1	1	1	1	1	0	1	0	1	0	1	0	0	0	1	1	0	0	1	1	1	0	16			
24	1	0	0	1	1	1	1	1	1	1	0	0	1	0	1	1	0	0	0	1	1	1	0	0	16				
21	0	0	0	1	1	1	1	1	1	1	0	1	0	1	0	0	0	1	0	1	1	0	0	0	15				
14	0	1	0	1	1	1	0	1	0	1	0	0	0	0	0	0	1	1	0	0	1	1	1	0	14				
10	1	0	0	1	0	1	1	1	1	1	1	0	1	1	1	0	0	0	0	0	0	1	1	14					
25	1	0	0	1	0	1	0	1	1	1	0	0	1	0	1	0	1	1	0	0	1	1	0	14					
15	1	1	0	1	1	1	0	0	1	0	0	1	0	0	0	1	0	0	0	0	0	13						
26	1	1	0	1	0	1	0	1	1	1	0	0	0	0	0	1	1	1	0	0	1	0	13					
23	1	0	0	1	1	0	1	0	1	1	0	0	0	1	0	0	1	0	1	0	0	12						
11	1	1	0	0	0	1	0	1	0	1	0	0	0	0	1	0	1	0	0	0	12							
7	0	1	0	0	1	1	0	0	1	0	0	0	0	1	0	0	1	1	0	1	0	1	0	11					
13	0	1	0	0	0	0	1	1	0	1	0	0	0	0	0	0	1	0	0	1	0	1	0	10					
28	0	0	0	0	0	0	1	1	0	1	1	0	0	0	0	1	0	0	1	1	0	1	0	0	0	0	0	8			
IF	0.57	0.77	0.20	0.87	0.80	0.83	0.80	0.87	0.90	0.93	0.67	0.23	0.47	0.23	0.73	0.13	0.43	0.07	0.93	0.93	0.90	0.13	0.83	0.30	0.20	0.70	0.70	0.73	0.07	0.37	
IFupper	0.80	1.00	0.50	1.00	1.00	0.90	1.00	1.00	1.00	1.00	1.00	0.40	0.60	0.50	0.80	0.40	0.80	0.20	1.00	1.00	1.00	0.30	1.00	0.70	0.50	0.90	0.90	0.90	0.10	0.70	
IFlower	0.60	0.60	0.00	0.60	0.50	0.70	0.40	0.60	0.70	0.90	0.40	0.10	0.20	0.10	0.50	0.00	0.30	0.00	0.80	0.80	0.70	0.00	0.80	0.10	0.10	0.30	0.30	0.80	0.00	0.20	
ID	0.20	0.40	0.50	0.40	0.50	0.20	0.60	0.40	0.30	0.10	0.60	0.30	0.40	0.40	0.30	0.40	0.50	0.20	0.20	0.20	0.30	0.30	0.20	0.60	0.40	0.60	0.60	0.10	0.10	0.50	

B) You should probably begin by noticing that the question numbers are in the first column and that there is some kind of grouping going on as indicated by the second column HIGH and LOW labels. Next, you will want to look for the item facility values. They are listed in the third column under Difficulty. The output then gives the number of students in the HIGH and LOW groups who chose each of the four options, A–D. Based on my knowledge of the test and of the numbers of students tested, I can tell you that there was no option E and that the HIGH and LOW groups are not the upper and lower thirds but rather the upper half and lower half. Finally, you probably looked for the item discrimination index and ended up guessing that it was in the last column labeled correlation. This last column presents the point-biserial correlation coefficient (this statistic is explained much more fully in Chapter 7). As I mentioned briefly in the chapter, the point-biserial correlation coefficient functions much the same as the item discrimination index.

My top five choices for items to keep are numbers 7, 9, 10, 12, and 13. They are generally the best discriminators and all but one fall within the range of .30 to .70 in item facility. Item 12 is outside that range but is such a good discriminator that I decided to keep it as a counter weight to number 10 which is fairly difficult. In the process of choosing these five items, I also considered number 6, but was disturbed by the fact that it was so easy and the fact that almost as many people in the LOW group answered correctly as in the HIGH group.

C) In the case of the items in Screen 4.6, the easiest approach to choosing 15 out of the 20 items solely on the basis of the difference index would be to eliminate the worst five items. The lowest *DI*s are clearly items 45, 46, 52, 56, and 58. The remaining items would therefore be the ones that I would select under these conditions. The highest of the rejected items, at .082, is considerably lower than the lowest of the remaining selected items, at .131, so this serves as a logical breaking point for making this kind of selection.

However, you must also think about what the *DI*s in the selected items mean in terms of percentage of gain among your students. In this case, you must decide whether you are willing to accept items that show as little as a 13.1 percent gain in the number of students answering the item correctly. Perhaps, items that are as low as 13 percent should be revised to fit the course objectives better, or perhaps the particular objectives involved should be taught better or practiced more thoroughly. Nevertheless, before making any selections on real items, you would want to insist on examining the items themselves so that format and content analyses could be brought into the selection process along with the *DI*s shown in Screen 4.6.

D) The *B*-indexes for the item data given in Screen 4.9 are as follows:

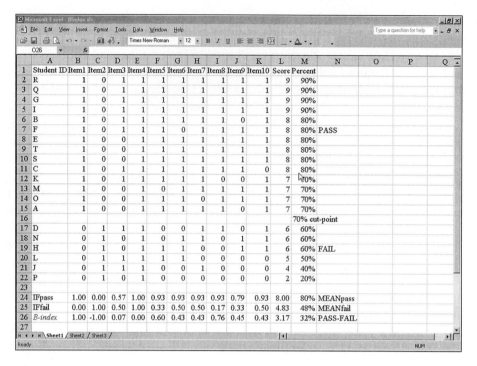

Those items which performed very poorly in Screen 4.9 were numbers 2, 3, and 4 (i.e., those items that helped least with the pass-fail decision at the 70 percent cut-point). The actual choices from among the remaining "good" items might differ somewhat depending on which set of results was used, on the number of items that were ultimately needed, and on the purpose and quality of the items being analyzed.

Chapter 5

A1) Three

A2) a. 51.3   **b.** 9.01   **c.** 207

A3) a. Cloze   **b.** Total TOEFL

A4) a. Writing Sample

     b. Possibly because only some of the students who took the other tests were required to do the Writing Sample.

A5) a. Total TOEFL

     b. Total TOEFL, but this is a standardized score (see next chapter) so it may turn out that one of the other tests had the widest dispersion in terms of raw scores (the actual number of items answered correctly by each student).

A6) It would always be nice to also have the low-high scores and the range plus a graph of each set of scores. However, this is not always feasible and the information that is presented in this table is adequate to visualize how the students performed on each of the subtests.

B1) TEST A:

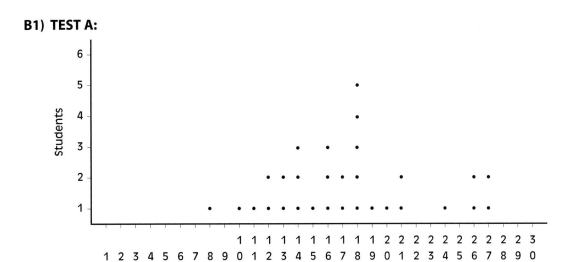

TEST B:

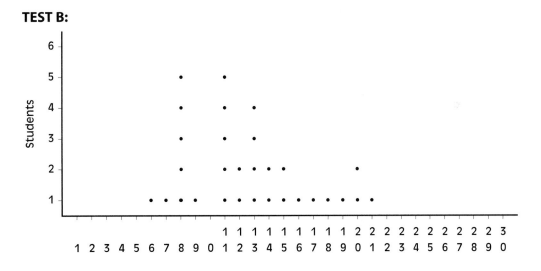

TEST C:

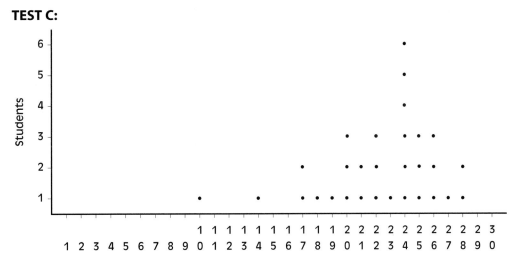

TEST D:

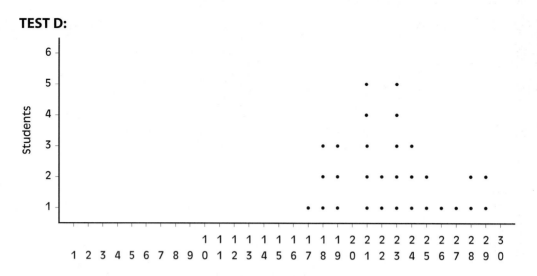

B2) SRI LANKAN HIGH SCHOOL CLOZE TEST RESULTS

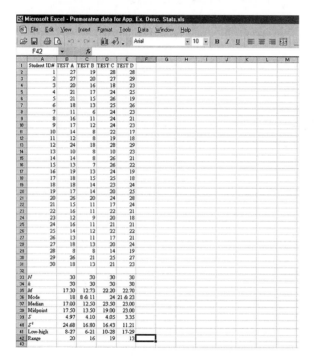

	Student ID#	TEST A	TEST B	TEST C	TEST D
2	1	27	19	28	28
3	2	27	20	27	29
4	3	20	16	18	23
5	4	21	17	24	25
6	5	21	15	26	19
7	6	18	13	25	26
8	7	11	6	24	23
9	8	16	11	24	21
10	9	17	12	24	23
11	10	14	8	22	17
12	11	12	8	19	18
13	12	24	18	28	29
14	13	10	8	10	23
15	14	14	8	26	21
16	15	13	7	26	22
17	16	19	13	24	19
18	17	18	15	25	18
19	18	18	14	23	24
20	19	17	14	20	25
21	20	26	20	24	28
22	21	15	11	17	24
23	22	16	11	22	21
24	23	12	9	20	18
25	24	16	11	21	21
26	25	14	12	22	22
27	26	13	11	17	21
28	27	18	13	20	24
29	28	8	8	14	19
30	29	26	21	25	27
31	30	18	13	21	23
32					
33	N	30	30	30	30
34	k	30	30	30	30
35	M	17.30	12.73	22.20	22.70
36	Mode	18	8 & 11	24	21 & 23
37	Median	17.00	12.50	23.50	23.00
38	Midpoint	17.50	13.50	19.00	23.00
39	S	4.97	4.10	4.05	3.35
40	S^2	24.68	16.80	16.43	11.21
41	Low-high	8-27	6-21	10-28	17-29
42	Range	20	16	19	13

Chapter 6

A1) About the 16th percentile (or to be precise, $15.73 = 2.14 + 13.59$) because a student at 85 would be -1 standard deviations below the mean.

A2) About 82 percent (or to be precise, $81.85\% = 34.13 + 34.13 + 13.59$).

A3) About 5 standard deviations ($177 - 100 = 77$; $77 \div 15 = 5.13 \approx 5$). No, this score would not necessarily mean that Iliana is intelligent. You have no idea what type of measure is involved so you simply cannot draw any conclusions except that, whatever the scale, Iliana is unusually high on it.

A4) $z = 5.13 \approx 5$; $T = 101.3 \approx 100$; CEEB $= 1013 \approx 1000$.

Student	Raw Score	z score	T score	CEEB score
A	64	+2	70	700
B	50	0	50	500
C	43	−1.0	40	400
D	39.5	−1.5	35	350
ETC.				

C1) **a.** z scores = Test C
    b. T scores = Test B
    c. CEEB scores = Test A

C2) **a.** the largest standard deviation = Test A
    b. the lowest mean = Test C
    c. the largest number of items = Test A
    d. a negatively-skewed distribution = Test B

C3) In Test C:
    a. a raw score of 11 equals a z score of 0.
    b. a raw score of 7 equals a T score of 40.
    c. a raw score of 19 equals a CEEB score of 700.

D) Raw scores and standardized scores

Students	Score	z	T	CEEB
Shenan	77	2.00	70.0	700
Robert	75	1.50	65.0	650
Randy	72	.75	57.5	575
Mitsuko	72	.75	57.5	575
Millie	70	.25	52.5	525
Kimi	70	.25	52.5	525
Kazumoto	69	.00	50.0	500
Kako	69	.00	50.0	500
Joji	69	.00	50.0	500
Jeanne	69	.00	50.0	500
Issaku	68	−.25	47.5	475
Iliana	68	−.25	47.5	475
Dean	67	−.50	45.0	450
Corky	64	−1.25	37.5	375
Bill	64	−1.25	37.5	375
Archie	61	−2.00	30.0	300

E) You are entirely on your own for this one.

Chapter 7

A) Pearson r (from Screen 7.8 Data) = .7838552 ≈ .78

B) With $(N - 2) = (16 - 2) = 14$, $r = .78$ would be significant at $p < .01$ for either a directional ($r_{critical}$ = .5742) or non-directional ($r_{critical}$ = .6226) decision (see Table 7.5). As for meaningfulness, it would be useful to square the correlation of .78 and examine the coefficient of determination, which in this case, equals .6084 ≈ .61 and means that about 61 percent of the variance of each of the two measures is overlapping with the other measure. Whether or not that is meaningful will depend on the nature of the variables and their relationship.

C) The answers that you should have obtained are the following:

	A	B	C	D	E	F
1	STUDENT	I1	I2	I3	I4	Total Score
2	Robert	1	0	1	0	100
3	Mitsuko	1	0	1	0	90
4	Randy	1	0	1	0	80
5	Bill	0	1	1	0	60
6	Kazumoto	0	1	1	0	50
7	Archie	0	1	1	0	40
8						
9	r_{pbi}	0.93	-0.93	0.00	0.00	

Chapter 8

Here are the answers worked out by hand using the formulas (answers using a spreadsheet are given below):

A1) $\alpha = 2\left(1 - \dfrac{S^2_{odd} + S^2_{even}}{S^2_t}\right) = 2\left(1 - \dfrac{2.11^2 + 2.39^2}{4.18^2}\right) = 2\left(1 - \dfrac{4.4521 + 5.7121}{17.4724}\right)$

$= 2\left(1 - \dfrac{10.1642}{17.4724}\right) = 2(1 - .5817289) = 2(.4182711) = .8365422 ≈ .84$

A2) $K - R21 = \dfrac{k}{k - 1}\left(1 - \dfrac{M(k - M)}{kS^2}\right) = \dfrac{20}{19}\left(1 - \dfrac{10.5(20 - 10.5)}{20 \times 4.18^2}\right)$

$$= 1.0526\left(1 - \dfrac{99.75}{349.448}\right) = 1.0526(1 - .2855) = 1.0526(.7145) = .7521 \approx .75$$

A3) $K - R20 = \dfrac{k}{k - 1}\left(1 - \dfrac{\Sigma S_i^2}{\Sigma S_t^2}\right) = \dfrac{20}{19}\left(1 - \dfrac{3.50}{4.18^2}\right) = 1.0526\left(1 - \dfrac{3.50}{17.4724}\right)$

$$= 1.0526(1 - .2003) = 1.0526(.7997) = .8418 \approx .84$$

A4) Split-half correlation $r = .7208$
Full-test reliability
(Adjusted by Spearman-Brown) =

$$r_{xx} = \dfrac{(n)r}{(n - 1)r + 1} = \dfrac{(2).7208}{(2 - 1).7208 + 1} = \dfrac{(2).7208}{.7208 + 1} = \dfrac{1.4416}{1.7208} = .8377 \approx .84$$

B) These estimates indicate that the test is about 84 percent consistent and about 16 percent inconsistent when interpreted as an NRT. Put another way, about 84 percent of the variation in scores is reliable and about 16 percent is random.

C) $SEM = S\sqrt{1 - r_{xx}} = 4.18\sqrt{1 - .84} = 4.18\sqrt{.16} = 4.18 \times .40 = 1.672$

D) The best strategy would be to calculate the correlation coefficient between the two sets of scores. This procedure is called interrater reliability. Unless you are only interested in the reliability of single ratings, the results of the interrater correlations should be adjusted using the Spearman-Brown Prophecy formula to reflect the actual number of ratings used for each student's work.

Here are the answers worked out in a spreadsheet program (note that small differences among the hand-calculated formula approach, the spreadsheet approach, and your results are to be expected, due to rounding):

	A	B	C	D	E	F	G	H	I	J	K	L	M	N	O	P	Q	R	S	T	U	V	W	X	Y
1	ID#	I2	I3	I4	I5	I7	I8	I11	I12	I13	I14	I15	I16	I17	I21	I22	I24	I25	I26	I27	I30	Total	Odd	Even	
2	2	1	1	1	1	1	1	1	1	1	1	1	1	1	1	1	1	1	1	1	1	20	10	10	
3	20	1	1	1	1	1	1	1	1	1	1	1	1	1	1	1	1	0	1	1	1	19	9	10	
4	1	1	1	1	1	1	1	1	1	0	1	1	1	0	1	1	1	1	1	1	1	18	8	10	
5	29	1	1	1	1	1	1	0	1	0	1	0	1	1	1	1	1	1	1	1	1	17	10	7	
6	12	1	0	1	1	1	1	0	0	1	1	1	1	0	1	0	1	1	1	1	1	15	7	8	
7	17	1	0	1	1	1	1	0	0	0	1	0	1	1	0	1	0	1	1	1	1	13	7	6	
8	4	1	0	1	1	1	1	0	1	0	1	0	1	1	0	0	0	1	1	1	1	13	8	5	
9	5	1	0	1	1	1	1	1	0	0	1	0	1	1	0	1	0	1	0	1	1	13	7	6	
10	16	1	1	1	1	1	1	0	1	1	1	0	0	1	0	0	1	0	0	1	0	12	7	5	
11	3	1	0	1	1	1	1	1	0	0	1	0	1	1	0	0	0	1	1	1	1	12	7	5	
12	18	1	1	1	1	1	1	0	1	1	0	0	1	0	0	0	0	0	1	1	0	11	6	5	
13	19	1	0	1	0	1	1	1	1	0	1	0	0	1	1	0	0	1	1	1	0	11	7	4	
14	27	0	0	1	1	1	1	1	0	1	0	1	0	0	1	1	0	0	1	1	0	11	7	4	
15	30	1	1	1	1	1	1	1	1	0	0	0	0	1	0	1	0	0	1	0	0	11	6	5	
16	6	1	0	1	1	1	1	1	1	0	0	1	0	0	1	0	0	0	1	1	0	11	6	5	
17	8	1	0	1	1	1	1	1	0	0	1	0	1	0	0	0	0	0	1	1	0	10	6	4	
18	24	0	0	1	1	1	1	1	1	0	0	1	0	0	1	0	0	0	1	0	1	10	5	5	
19	9	1	0	1	1	1	1	0	0	0	1	0	1	1	0	0	0	1	1	0	0	10	6	4	
20	21	0	0	1	1	1	1	1	0	0	0	1	0	1	1	0	0	0	1	1	0	9	5	4	
21	22	1	0	1	1	1	1	0	0	1	0	1	0	0	1	0	0	0	1	1	0	9	5	4	
22	14	1	0	1	1	0	1	0	0	0	0	0	0	0	1	0	0	0	1	1	1	8	3	5	
23	15	1	0	1	1	0	1	0	0	0	1	0	0	0	1	0	1	0	0	0	0	7	3	4	
24	10	0	0	1	1	0	1	1	0	0	0	1	0	1	0	0	0	0	0	0	1	7	3	4	
25	23	0	0	1	1	1	0	0	0	0	0	1	0	0	1	0	0	0	0	1	0	6	4	2	
26	13	1	0	0	0	1	1	1	1	0	0	0	0	0	0	0	0	0	1	0	0	6	3	3	
27	25	0	0	1	0	0	1	0	0	1	0	1	0	1	0	0	0	0	0	1	0	6	5	1	
28	28	0	0	0	0	1	1	1	0	0	0	0	0	0	1	0	0	0	0	0	1	5	3	2	
29	7	1	0	0	0	1	0	0	0	0	0	0	0	1	0	0	1	0	0	1	0	5	2	3	
30	26	1	0	0	0	0	1	1	0	0	0	0	0	1	0	0	0	0	1	0	0	5	3	2	
31	11	1	0	0	0	0	0	0	0	0	1	0	1	0	1	0	0	0	0	0	1	5	5	0	
32	IF	0.7667	0.2000	0.8667	0.8000	0.8000	0.8667	0.6667	0.2333	0.4667	0.2333	0.7333	0.1333	0.4333	0.9000	0.1333	0.3000	0.2000	0.7000	0.7000	0.3667	10.50	5.77	4.73	Mean
33	1-IF	0.2333	0.8000	0.1333	0.2000	0.2000	0.1333	0.3333	0.7667	0.5333	0.7667	0.2667	0.8667	0.5667	0.1000	0.8667	0.7000	0.8000	0.3000	0.3000	0.6333	4.18	2.11	2.39	SD
34	IV	0.1789	0.1600	0.1156	0.1600	0.1600	0.1156	0.2222	0.1789	0.2489	0.1789	0.1956	0.1156	0.2456	0.0900	0.1156	0.2100	0.1600	0.2100	0.2100	0.2322	17.45	4.45	5.73	SD²

Summary statistics:

Σσ2 =	3.50	0.8339	=Cronbach alpha
k =	20	0.7518	=K-R21
k-1 =	19	0.8415	=K-R20
k/k-1 =	1.0526	0.8378	=Split-half(adj)
r_split-half =		1.6631	=SEM(K-R20)

Chapter 9

A1) $p_o = \dfrac{A + D}{N} = \dfrac{51 + 24}{100} = \dfrac{75}{100} = .75$

A2) $p_{chance} = \dfrac{[(A + B)(A + C)+(C + D)(B + D)]}{N^2} = \dfrac{[(61)(73) + (39)(27)]}{10000}$

$= \dfrac{[4453 + 1053]}{10000} = \dfrac{5506}{10000} = .5506 \approx .55$

$k = \dfrac{(p_o - p_{chance})}{(1 - p_{chance})} = \dfrac{.75 - .55}{1 - .55} = \dfrac{.20}{.45} = .4444 \approx .44$

B1) agreement coefficient (using Table 9.1) =

$z = \dfrac{(c - .5 - M)}{S} = \dfrac{(24 - .5 - 22.70)}{3.55} = \dfrac{.80}{3.35} = .2388 \approx .24$

$K - R20 = .6471832 \approx .65$

Based on z of .24 (remember, we find the closest table value without regard to the sign, .20 in this case) and K-R20 of .65, Table 9.1 shows a value somewhere between .71 and .75. Let's call it .73.

B2) Following the same steps as B1 above (but using Table 9.2) yields a kappa coefficient somewhere between .41 and .49, or approximately .45.

B3) phi(lambda) dependability index =

$$\Phi(\lambda) = \Phi(.80) = 1 - \frac{1}{k-1}\left[\frac{M_p(1-M_p) - S_p^2}{(M_p - \lambda)^2 + S_p^2}\right]$$

$$= 1 - \frac{1}{30-1}\left[\frac{.7566667(1-.7566667) - .1116667}{(.7566667 - .80)^2 + .1116667}\right]$$

$$= 1 - \frac{1}{29}\left[\frac{.1841222 - .0124552}{.0018777 + .0124552}\right] = 1 - .0344828\left[\frac{.1716528}{.0143471}\right]$$

$$= 1 - (.0344828 \times 11.977129) = 1 - .4132562 = .587438 \approx .59$$

B4) Based on statistics in Table 9.3, phi dependability index =

$$\Phi = \frac{\dfrac{nS_p^2}{n-1}[K - R20]}{\dfrac{nS_p^2}{n-1}[K-R20] + \dfrac{M_p(1-M_p) - S_p^2}{k-1}}$$

$$= \frac{\dfrac{30(.1116033)^2}{30-1}[.6471832]}{\dfrac{30(.1116033)^2}{30-1}[.6471832] + \dfrac{.7566667(1-.7566667) - .1116667}{30-1}}$$

$$= \frac{\dfrac{.3736560}{29}[.6471832]}{\dfrac{.3736560}{29}[.6471832] + \dfrac{.1716528}{29}} = \frac{.0083386}{.0083386 + .005919}$$

$$= \frac{.0083386}{.0142576} = .5848529 \approx .58$$

B5) $CI = \sqrt{\dfrac{M_p(1-M_p) - S_p^2}{k-1}} = \sqrt{\dfrac{.7566667(1-.7566667) - .1116667}{30-1}} = \sqrt{\dfrac{.1716528}{29}}$

$$= \sqrt{.005919} = .076935 \approx .077$$

Naturally, your results should be very similar if you used the spreadsheet (taking into account any rounding that you did differently).

Chapter 10

A1) Criterion-related validity—because the argument is based on the degree of correlation between the scores on the test and a criterion measure (university ratings).

A2) Predictive—because the correlations show the degree of relationship between the scores and future performance as judged at various universities.

A3) a. It could be inferred that this information indicates that the TOEFL is valid for predicting overall performance in university academic English as judged by various universities. Of course, such results are open to a variety of interpretations.

  b. The coefficients of determination range from a low of .5776 ($r^2 = .76^2 = .5776$) to a high of .7569 (for $r^2 = .87^2 = .7569$). As part of the overall pattern of validity evidence, these coefficients seem to me to form a fairly convincing argument. Has the population of students changed at all? Has the test changed substantially?

A4) You must decide for yourself the answers to these questions and the implications of those answers.

B1) Criterion-related—because the argument is based on the degree of correlation between the scores on the test and a criterion measure (university placement procedures).

B2) Probably concurrent—though it is hard to know from this table alone whether the two sets of tests were administered at about the same time. In well-designed studies, they would be administered at roughly the same time, so let's give them the benefit of the doubt.

B3) a. It could be inferred that this information is valid for making placement decisions in ESL programs. It would be safer to look at these correlations as indicating that TOEFL scores are fairly highly correlated with other large scale NRTs at various universities and are therefore related to overall ESL proficiency to a reasonably high degree.

  b. The coefficients of determination range from a low of .6241 (for $r^2 = .79^2 = .6241$) to a high of .7921 (for $r^2 = .89^2 = .7921$). Again, as part of the overall pattern of validity evidence, this seems to add fairly convincing evidence. What do you think?

B4) You must again decide for yourself the answers to these questions and the implications of those answers.

C1) CEEB

C2) a. Students who are strong in the construct of concern (English language ability, i.e., native speakers) score much higher than students who are not so strong (i.e., non-natives).

  b. Construct validity—this is a differential groups type of study.

C3) You must once again decide for yourself the answers to these questions and the implications of those answers.

C4) The standard deviation and reliability are probably lower for the non-natives than for the natives because the GRE was designed for natives, which means that the scores for the non-natives are uniformly low and fairly homogeneous (i.e., they do not vary as much as the scores for the natives).

C5) You must once again decide for yourself the answers to these questions and the implications of those answers.

D1) Personally, I would set up the test items for review by a panel of experts with some sort of rating scale for each question so that the judges can decide the degree to which each item is measuring overall ESL proficiency (like that shown in Table 10.1).

D2) One last time, this is the type of question that you should answer for yourself based on the evidence presented. I could tell you what I believe, but it is more important for you to decide for yourself what you think. It would also be wise to form no opinion at all until you have reviewed all the latest available information on the validity of the TOEFL. Remember the information presented here was only part of a larger pattern of information that ETS marshalled in ETS 1977 to defend the validity of the test.

E1) The answer to this standards setting question will depend on the method that you have chosen and the nature of the language program and decision that you have in mind. However, the steps listed should include at least those given in the body of the chapter plus some application of the SEM or CI discussed in Chapters 8 and 9, and recognition of the values implications, social consequences, and political considerations involved in standards setting and the decisions that accompany those standards.

Chapter 11

Answers for Chapter 11 will be too specific to your situation for an answer key to be provided. Please compare your answers to material presented in the chapter.

A

abscissa – the horizontal line, or *X* **axis,** of a two-axis graph, which is found in three forms: a **histogram,** a **bar graph,** or a **frequency polygon;** the vertical line is called the **ordinate,** or *Y* **axis**

achievement decisions – decisions about the amount of learning that students have mastered or accomplished, typically administered at the end of a term, syllabus or textbook; decisions may take the form of deciding which students will be advanced to the next level of study, determining which students should graduate, or grading the students

achievement tests – tests designed specifically in reference to a particular course of study to determine how effectively students have mastered the instructional objectives; typically administered at the end of a course, most achievement tests will be directly based on teaching objectives and will therefore be criterion-referenced

address – the name of each cell in a **spreadsheet** consisting of column letter(s) and row number(s); the cell in the upper left corner of the spreadsheet is labeled A1, and the address of the next cell is B1

agreement – a term used exclusively for estimates of the consistency of **criterion-referenced tests** in the way the term **reliability** is used for **norm-referenced tests**

agreement coefficient (P_o) – a **reliability** statistic that provides an estimate of the proportion of students who have been consistently classified as **masters** and **nonmasters** on two administrations of a **criterion-referenced test;** using a predetermined **cut-point,** the students are classified on the basis of their scores into the master and non-master groups on each test administration

analytical approach – a scoring approach in which the teachers rate various aspects of each student's language production separately, in contrast to a task scored using a **holistic approach**

B

bias – a situation where one subgroup is advantaged or disadvantaged in comparison to another by some feature of the test or item that is not relevant to what is being measured

bar graph – a graph normally used to display the **frequency** values of a set of scores by assigning two bars, each side-by-side

benchmark – a **standard** set by which to measure progress

bimodal – a statistic of **central tendency** that describes the two points where scores occur most frequently, as in two peaks of a bell curve

B-index – an **item** statistic that compares the *IF*s of those students who passed a test with the *IF*s of those who failed it

C

CEEB scores (College Entrance Examination Board) – a variation of the *z* **score** used for reporting U.S. standardized tests scores (e.g., SAT, GRE, TOEFL); calculated by multiplying the *z* score by 100 and adding 500

ceiling effect – the result of a distribution of test scores that is **negatively skewed,** with most of the students having scored well, so that the related statistics may be impossible to interpret

cells – squares made by the intersections of the rows and columns in a **spreadsheet** used to store data, such as a numbers, names, or dates

central tendency – the central point in the distribution of data that describes the most typical behavior of a group; can be determined by four different estimates: the **mean, mode, median,** and **midpoint**

coefficient of determination (r_{xy}^2) – a statistical tool used to make judgments of meaningfulness, calculated by squaring the correlation coefficient, r_{xy}; the result is a coefficient that directly represents the proportion of overlapping variance between two sets of scores

communicative movement – an approach in language testing formed in the 1980s based on the idea that language is unpredictable; involves assessment based on performance criteria; typical tests would include role plays, problem-solving, group tests, and task-based tests and consist of language that is meaningful and as authentic as possible

concurrent validity – a type of **criterion-related validity** where both measures are administered at about the same time

conferences – any assessment procedure that involves students visiting the teacher's office for brief meetings, during which the teacher can assess students' language abilities and/or give students feedback on their work

confidence interval (CI) – a statistical calculation of **reliability** used to estimate a band around each student's score, within which they would probably score within a certain probability if they were to take the test again; the CI functions for **criterion-referenced tests** in a manner analogous to the **standard error of measurement** for **norm-referenced tests**

conservative estimate – an estimate of correlation that errs on the low side rather than the high side if it is not 100% accurate

content applicability – the degree to which the content is appropriate for a given course or program

content congruence – the degree to which an **item** is measuring what it was designed to assess

content validity – the degree to which a test is a representative sample of the content the test was designed to measure

continuous scale – a scale that orders a named group of **data,** but also provides additional information; can also show the distances between the points in the rankings

correct answer – the choice that will be counted correct in a **multiple-choice item**

correlation analysis – a family of statistical analyses that determines the degree of relationship between two sets of numbers and indicates whether that relationship is significant, as well as meaningful

correlation coefficient – a numerical value representing the degree to which two variables are related; can range from +1.0 to −1.0, with zero representing no relationship

correlation matrix – a chart formation useful in efficiently presenting a large number of **correlation coefficients**

counterbalanced design – a test administration design where at the beginning of a course one half of a group takes Form A, while the other half takes Form B; at the end of the course, all students take the opposite form, so that they do not see exactly the same test twice

covary – the degree to which two sets of scores vary together, estimated statistically by calculating a **correlation coefficient**

criterion measure – a well-respected, valid test used as the criterion by which to compare another test to determine **criterion-related validity**

criterion-referenced test (CRT) – a type of test produced to measure well-defined instructional objectives and assesses achievement or performance against a predetermined **cut-point** rather than **normal**

distribution; measures what has been mastered in a course of study and test results can be reported in descriptive **scales** as well as numerical scores

criterion-related validity – a demonstration of validity by showing that scores on a test being validated correlate highly with some other, well-respected measure of the same construct

critical correlation – the degree to which any given results could have occurred by chance alone

Cronbach alpha coefficient (α) – an equation used to measure **internal-consistency** and **reliability,** often used as an alternative procedure for calculating the **split-half reliability**

cross-product – the mathematical result of multiplying the **deviation** from the **mean** of one set of data by the deviation from the mean of a second set of data when calculating the **correlation coefficient**

cumulative frequency – the number of students who scored at or below a particular score in a frequency distribution

cumulative percentage – a percentage of the total number of students who scored at or below a particular score in a **frequency distribution;** particularly important for interpreting **norm-referenced test** results

curriculum planning – a series of activities that provide a framework to help teachers design effective activities and learning situations to promote language learning

curvilinear – relationships that form a curve when plotted out

cut-point – a predetermined score, at or above which students will be classified one way and below which they will be classified differently

D

data – sets of numbers and other information, used as the basis for statistical analysis

decision consistency – a **reliability** strategy used to gauge the degree to which decisions that classify students as masters or non-masters are consistent; developed specifically for **criterion-referenced test** consistency estimation and not dependent on a high **standard deviation**

decision validity – the degree to which scores are used to make decisions as they were intended to be made

dependability – a term used exclusively for estimates of the consistency of **criterion-referenced tests** in the way the term **reliability** is used for **norm-referenced tests**

descriptive statistics – numerical representations of how a group performed on a test, two aspects of which are called **central tendency** and **dispersion**

deviation – a statistic that represents the differences of all scores from the **mean**

diagnostic decisions – decisions made at the beginning or middle of the term aimed at fostering achievement by promoting strengths and eliminating the weaknesses of individual students

diagnostic tests – tests designed to determine the degree to which the specific instructional objectives of the course have already been accomplished and to effect **diagnostic decisions;** usually **criterion-referenced** in nature

(the) diagonal – the line descending diagonally across a table dividing the correlations above and to the right of the diagonal from the numbers below and to the left of the diagonal, when a set of numbers correlates perfectly with itself

difference index (DI) – indicates the degree to which a **criterion-referenced test** item is reflecting gain in knowledge or skill

differential group strategy – a strategy used for comparing the performance on a

criterion-referenced test item using two groups of students by comparing the *IF* of each: one group has the knowledge or skills that are assessed on the test **(masters)** and another group lacks them **(non-masters)**

differential-groups studies – studies designed to compare the performances of two groups on a test, that demonstrate how the test scores differentiate between groups: one group has the knowledge or skills that are assessed on the test **(masters)** and another group lacks them **(non-masters)**

directional decision – a decision used to determine the **critical correlation** where sound logical or theoretical reasons exist for expecting the correlation to be either positive or negative

discrete-point tests – tests constructed to measure students' knowledge of different structures by assessing independent bits of language

dispersion – how individual scores vary around the **central tendency;** four indicators of dispersion are the **range, high** and **low, standard deviation,** and **variance**

distracters – those choices that will be counted as incorrect in a **multiple-choice item;** they should distract or divert the students' attention away from the correct answer

distribution – a spread or pattern for a set of **data,** with data in **normal distribution** concentrated near the center and decreasing symmetrically on both sides

domain-referenced test (DRT) – a type of **criterion-referenced test (CRT)** whose items are sampled from a general, but well-defined, domain of behaviors, rather than from individual course objectives as in **objectives-referenced tests**

E

equivalent-form reliability – one of three basic **reliability** strategies where two differ-

ent forms of the same test are administered to a single group of students; the scores are then correlated, the results of which provides an estimate of the consistency of scores across forms; also called **parallel-forms reliability**

error variance – one of two general sources of variance, due to extraneous sources, e.g., personal problems, scoring procedures, test item problems, etc.

expected outcomes – represent those events for which a person is trying to determine the probability

F

fairness – the degree to which a test is impartial and free from **bias**

false negatives – decisions that erroneously put students on the "failing" side of the **cut-point**

false positives – decisions that falsely put students on the "passing" side of the **cut-point**

fill-in items – test items wherein a word or phrase is replaced by a blank in a sentence or longer text; students must fill in that missing word or phrase

frequency – a tally procedure used to indicate how often a particular event occurs or how often a certain characteristic appears

frequency distribution – the frequencies of the score values arranged sequentially with obtained scores arranged on the *X* **axis** and frequency arranged on the *Y* **axis** to demonstrate the number of times a score has occurred

frequency polygon graph – a form of visual representation that allows the frequencies of a set of scores to be displayed by assigning dots for score values to the *X* **axis** and putting the possible frequency values on the *Y* **axis**

G

general description – an element of **item specification** that gives a brief general description of the knowledge or skills being measured by the item

H

high score – the highest score within a range; used to indicate where on the scale the spread of scores is located

histogram – a form of visual representation that allows the frequencies of a set of scores to be displayed by assigning an X for score values to the **X axis** and putting the possible frequency values on the **Y axis**

holistic approach – a scoring approach in which the teachers use a single general scale, often descriptive, to give a single global rating for a student's language production, in contrast to using an **analytic approach**

I

independence – when each pair of scores is unrelated to all other pairs; one of three assumptions underlying the **Pearson product-moment correlation coefficient**

instructed – students who have received instruction after a **pre-test** and can be tested again to measure what they learned through a **post-test**

instructional value – information gained as a useful side-effect of teaching to a test, e.g., the effectiveness of the needs analysis objectives, tests themselves, materials, teaching, students study habits, etc.

integrative movement – an approach to language testing with roots in the argument that language should be tested within a context

integrative tests – tests designed for students to use several skills at once in the larger, more natural context of extended text, e.g., dictation, cloze test, and writing samples

internal-consistency reliability – a method of measure used to estimate the extent of which the scores of individual or group items on a test correlate with each other

interrater reliability – a method of estimating the consensus of judgments calculating a **correlation coefficient** of two or more independent raters of a student's performance

intervention strategy – strategy used for comparing the performance on a **criterion-referenced test** item of those students who have studied the content with those who have not; first a **pre-test** is given to **uninstructed** students. The next step is to intervene with whatever instruction is appropriate and then test the **instructed** students on a **post-test;** allows the test developer to do an item-by-item comparison of the two sets of *IF* results

intervention studies – studies used to compare the performance of one group of students before and after some type of intervention; show how those test scores differentiate through pre- and post-testing

intrarater reliability – a method of estimating the consistency of judgments by calculating a **correlation coefficient** of two sets of scores produced by the same rater for the same group of students

item – the smallest unit that produces distinctive and meaningful information or feedback on a test when it is scored or rated

item analysis – the statistical, systematic evaluation of the effectiveness of the individual items on a test for purposes of revising and improving the test; three types of analyses for **norm-referenced tests** are: **item format analysis, item facility analysis,** and **item discrimination** analysis; three concerns for **criterion-referenced tests** are: **item quality analysis, item difference index,** and *B*-index

item content analysis – analysis to determine the degree to which each item is measuring the content that it was designed to measure

item discrimination (*ID*) – a statistic that indicates the degree to which an item separates the students who performed well from those who did poorly on the test as a whole

item facility (*IF*) (also called item difficulty, item easiness) – a statistic used to examine the percentage of students who correctly answer a given item

item format – the degree to which each item is properly written so that it measures all and only the desired content

item format analysis – analysis to assist in the writing or critiquing of an **item format** to insure that students answer the items correctly only if they know the concept or skill being tested, not because of a poorly designed item

item quality analysis – analysis to determine the degree to which test items are valid for the overall purposes and content of the course or program involved; includes **item content analysis**

item specification – clear item descriptions for the purpose of test writing, include a **general description,** a **sample item, stimulus attributes, response attributes,** and **specification supplements**

item stems – the main part of a **multiple-choice item** that contains a sentence or question to be completed or answered by selecting the correct **option**

item variance (ΣS_i^2) – a statistical variable that is equal to the proportion of students who answered correctly times the proportion who answered incorrectly

K

kappa coefficient (*k*) – a **reliability** statistic that provides an estimate of the classification agreement that occurs beyond what would be expected by chance alone; developed to adjust for the problem of a chance lower limit by adjusting to the proportion

of consistency in classifications beyond that which would occur by chance alone and is interpreted as a percentage of **agreement** (p_o)

Kuder-Richardson formula 20 (K-R20) – an internal-consistency reliability statistic that avoids the problem of underestimating the reliability of certain language tests and more accurate than the **K-R21**

Kuder-Richardson formula 21 (K-R21) – an **internal-consistency reliability** statistic for reporting variations of internal-consistency reliability

kurtosis – the degree of peaking in a distribution curve of data

L

language testing functions – four basic kinds of decisions: **proficiency, placement, achievement,** and **diagnostic;** define the four types of tests identified in language testing

leptokurtic – a non-normal **distribution** of **data** forming a very steep peak; indicates something unusual about the **sample**

linear – where the relationship between the two sets of scores is in **correlation** and can be represented by a straight line on a **scatterplot;** one of three assumptions underlying the **Pearson product-moment correlation coefficient**

low score – the lowest score within a range; used to indicate where on the scale the spread of scores is located

M

marginals – numbers or totals appearing in the margins of diagrams that describe the calculation of **agreement coefficient**

masters – a group that has the knowledge or skills that are assessed on a test

matching items – test items where students are given two columns of information and must match the **premises** in the left-hand column with the correct **option** listed in the right-hand column

matching item premise – the list of information in the left-hand column provided in a **matching item** that must be matched with the correct **option** listed in the right-hand column

mean – a statistic of **central tendency** that is the equivalent to the arithmetic average obtained by totaling the scores and then dividing the sum by the number of scores

meaningful variance – variance that is directly attributable to the purposes of the test purposes

meaningfulness – a judgment about the degree to which a coefficient already shown to be significant is also relevant and informative

measurement error – a source of variance, due to extraneous sources, e.g., personal problems, scoring procedures, test item problems, etc.

median – a statistic of **central tendency** that describes the point below which 50 percent of the scores fall and above which 50 percent fall

midpoint – a set of scores that point is halfway between the highest score and the lowest score on the test

minimal competency tests – tests on which students must achieve a certain minimum score in order to pass a course

missing data – a situation where a piece of data from one of two sets is missing, therefore requiring the data to be dropped from the calculation

mode – a statistic of **central tendency** that describes the point where scores occur most frequently, as in the peak of a bell curve; some distributions have two or three modes called **bimodal** or **trimodal** respectively

movements – trends or developments in language testing identified such as the prescientific movement, the **psychometric/ structuralist movement,** the **integrative/ sociolinguistic movement** and the **communicative movement**

multiple-choice items – test items where the student must choose the correct answer from a group of options; consists of an **item stem,** or the statement or question to be answered, a **correct answer,** the choice that will be counted correct, and the **distracters,** those choices that will be counted as incorrect; the term **options** refers collectively to all the alternative choices including the correct answer and the distracters

N

negatively skewed – a **distribution** pattern of scores where the majority of scores are together at the high end of the scale

nominal scale – a **scale** used for categorizing and naming groups, typically gender, nationality, native language, educational background, socio-economic status, and level of language study

non-directional decision – a decision used to determine the **critical correlation** where there is no sound logical or theoretical reason to expect the correlation to be either a positive or negative value and expectations before calculating the coefficient are related to the probabilities of a coefficient occurring by chance alone

non-masters – a group that lacks the knowledge or skills that are assessed on a test

normal distribution – a **frequency** distribution of test scores that takes the shape of a bell-shaped curve, concentrated near the center and decreasing symmetrically on both sides; two characteristics are **central tendency** and **dispersion**

norm-referenced test (NRT) – a type of test where a student's test scores are interpreted relative to all the other students' scores, usually with reference to **normal distribution**

O

objectives-referenced test (ORT) – a type of **criterion-referenced test;** items are sampled from individual course objectives rather than a domain of behaviors as in **domain-referenced tests**

observed correlation – any calculated **correlation coefficient** used to determine the probability that a correlation coefficient occurred by chance

options – refers collectively to all the alternative choices of a **multiple-choice test** question presented to the students including the correct answer and the distracters; also the choices provided to match with **premises** in **matching items**

ordinal scale – a scale that names and orders, or ranks a group of observations

ordinate – the vertical line or *Y* **axis** of a two-axis graph; found in three forms: a **histogram,** a **bar graph,** or a **frequency polygon;** the horizontal line is called the **abscissa,** or *X* **axis**

outlier – an extreme score that does not belong to the group and may skew data

P

parallel-forms reliability – one of three basic **reliability** strategies where two different forms of the same test are administered to a single group of students, then scores from both tests are correlated, the results of which provides an estimate of the consistency of scores across forms; also called **equivalent-form reliability**

partial credit – entails giving some credit for answers that are not 100 percent correct

Pearson product-moment correlation coefficient (Pearson's *r*) – the statistic used for determining the **correlation** of two sets of continuous scale **data**

peer-assessment – any items wherein students are asked to rate each other's knowledge, skills, or performances

percentage – a rate or proportion per 100; the proportion that each student has learned without reference to the performances of the other student; proportion of questions the students answered correctly

percentile – the proportion of students who scored above and below a particular student, e.g., a student with a percentile score of 70 performed better than 70 out of 100 students but worse than 30 out of 100

percentile scores – how a given student's score relates to the test scores of the entire group of students

percents – refer to the result of 100 times the proportion that results from dividing a subgroup of data points by the total number of data points

performance assessment – a **communicative** test that measures the ability of a student to successfully complete a task or function involving the unpredictability of language, useful functions, and meaningful and authentic language; typical test types include role plays, problem-solving, group tests, and task-based tests

personal response items – students' production of responses that hold personal meaning; personal response item formats include **self-assessments, conferences,** and **portfolios**

phi dependability index (Φ) – a general-purpose estimate of the **domain-referenced** dependability of a test; used to estimate the overall dependability of the scores without reference to a cut-score; this interpretation assumes that the items are sampled from a well-defined domain and gives no information about the reliability of the individual objectives-based subtests

phi(lambda) dependability index (Φ(λ)) – a **squared-error loss agreement** index that can be estimated using a single test administration

placement decisions – decisions in which the goal is to group students of similar ability levels together, resulting in classes that have students with relatively homogeneous ability levels

placement test – a test specifically related to a given program, particularly in terms of the relatively narrow range of abilities assessed and the content of the curriculum, for the purpose of efficiently separating the students into level groupings within that program

platykurtic – a non-normal distribution of **data** forming a flat peak, indicating something unusual about the **sample**

point-biserial correlation coefficient (r_{pbi}) – a statistic used to estimate the degree of relationship between a **nominal scale** and a **continuous one**

population – the largest group of people represented to be studied or observed; often too large to allow examination of the total group, a representation or **sample** may be selected

portfolios – any procedure that requires students to collect samples of their second language use (e.g., compositions, cassette recordings, video clips, etc.) into a box or folder for examination at some time in the future by peers, parents, teachers, etc.

positively skewed – a distribution pattern of scores where the majority of scores are together at the low end of the scale

possible outcomes – the number of potentially different events that might occur as the events unfold

post-test – a test given to students at the end of a course of study to assess their achievement

practical issues – issues that have to do with physically putting tests into place in a program, including costs, logistics, scoring, fairness, etc.

pragmatics – ways that linguistic and extra-linguistic elements of language are interrelated and relevant to human experience

predictive validity – a type of **criterion-related validity** where the two sets of numbers from the measures are collected at different times

prescientific movement – an approach to language testing associated with the grammar-translation approaches to language teaching; characterized by translation and essay tests developed by classroom teachers who develop and score their own tests

pre-test – a test given to students before beginning a course of study to assess their current level of knowledge

probability – a theory used to predict the chance of a particular outcome through calculation; the ratio of the **expected outcomes** to the **possible outcomes** ranging from 0 to 1.0; commonly discussed in percentage terms

productive response items – test items that require the students to produce responses rather than select them receptively; include **fill-in, short-response,** and **task-based** items

proficiency decisions – decisions based on the students' general levels of language proficiency; often used as a prerequisite to entry or exit from some type of institution; often based on proficiency tests specifically designed for such decisions

proficiency tests – tests designed to assess the general knowledge or skills commonly required or as a prerequisite to entry into (or exemption from) a group of similar institutions, e.g., *Test of English as a Foreign Language* (TOEFL)

program fair tests – the impartial assessment of tests to assure that the objectives of the test(s) involve appropriately match the curriculum goals and objectives of the programs involved

psychological construct – an attribute, proficiency, ability, or skill defined in psychological theories; forms the basis for understanding **construct validity**

psychometric-structuralist movement – language testing influenced by behavioral psychology that typically sets out to measure the discrete structural points taught in the audio-lingual tradition; tests are usually in multiple-choice format, easy to administer and score, and are carefully constructed to be objective, reliable, and valid

R

range – the number of points between the highest score on a measure and the lowest score plus one

raw scores – the actual numbers of items answered correctly on a test

receptive response items – test items that require the student to select a response rather than produce one; include **true-false, multiple-choice,** and **matching items**

reliability coefficient ($r_{xx'}$) – a numerical value similar to a correlation coefficient in that it can go as high as +1.00 for a perfectly reliable test but can only go as low as 0.00 because a test cannot logically have less than zero reliability

response attributes – an element of **item specification** that provides a clear description of the types of either options from which students will be expected to select their receptive language choices (responses) or standards by which their productive language responses will be judged

S

sample – subset selected, randomly or otherwise, to represent a **population**

sample item – an element of **item specification** that provides an example item to demonstrate the desirable item characteristics

scales – the way quantifiable data are defined as countable or measurable; three scales used to represent different ways of observing, organizing, and quantify language data are the **nominal, ordinal,** and **continuous** scales

scatterplot – a form of visual representation that allows for representing two sets of scores at the same time and examining their relationship; increments for one set is marked along the **X axis** and the other along the **Y axis** and a mark is then plotted at the point where the coordinates meet

self-assessment – any items wherein students are asked to rate their own knowledge, skills, or performances; indicates to the teacher how the students view their own language abilities/development

short-response items – test items that the students can answer in a few phrases or sentences

skewed – a distribution pattern of scores that does not have the prototypical symmetrical "bell" shape

social consequences – ramifications of a test on a social or cultural level; includes both potential consequences of proposed use and actual consequences when used

Spearman-Brown prophecy formula – an equation used to adjust the half-test correlation resulting from the **split-half** method to estimate the full-test reliability

specification supplement – an element of **item specification** providing some items that are necessary for clarifying **general description, sample item, stimulus attributes, response attributes**

split-half method – an internal-consistency strategy where equivalent forms of a test are created from the single test being analyzed by dividing it into two equal parts and each part is scored separately as though they were two different forms; then a **correlation coefficient** is calculated for the two sets of scores and adjusted to provide a coefficient that represents the full-test reliability; this adjustment of the half-test correlation to estimate the full-test reliability is accomplished by using the **Spearman-Brown prophecy formula**

spreadsheet program – a flexible computer tool that allows one to enter rows and columns of numbers, then manipulate, analyze, and present them in any way; *Excel*^{TM} (Microsoft, 2003) is the spreadsheet program that most people use today

squared-error loss agreement – a **reliability** strategy developed specifically for **CRT** consistency that does not depend on a high standard deviation; measures the degree of **mastery** and **non-mastery** along the score continuum based on a **cut-point**

standard – a criterion level or cut-point against which each student's performance is judged; used for one of five types of decisions: **admissions, placement, diagnostics, advancement** and **certification**

standard deviation (SD) – a statistic used to summarize the variation or **distribution** of scores around the **mean;** an averaging process generally considered a strong estimate of the dispersion of scores widely used in language testing

standard error of measure (SEM) – a statistical calculation of **reliability** used to interpret individual student scores to give an indication of how accurate an individual's true test score might be; based on the percentages in the **normal distribution,** it can also be used to estimate the probability with which the tester expects those scores to fall within one SEM of where it is

standard scores – represent a student's score in relation to how far the score varies from the test **mean** in terms of **standard deviation** units; the three most commonly reported types of standard scores are *z, T,* and **CEEB** scores

standard setting – the process of deciding where and how to make **cut-points**

statistically significant – the probability of a type I error of generalizing a statistic from a sample to its population; a **correlation coefficient** indicating correlation is due to factors other than chance with the appropriate degree of certainty

stimulus attributes – an element of **item specification** that provides a clear description of the stimulus material or the material to which they will be expected to react to through the **response attributes**

systems approach – an approach to curriculum design that is based on a set of interrelated parts, all of which are working together toward a defined goal

T

T **score** – a standard score useful for reporting test results transformed from *z* **scores**

task items – test items that require students to perform a task in the language that is being tested; includes communicative tasks, problem-solving tasks, portfolios, or writing tasks

task-based assessment – a **performance assessed** test that elicits and evaluates students' abilities to accomplish particular tasks or task types in which target language communication is essential

test reliability – the extent to which the test results can be considered consistent or stable

test variance – an intermediary step in the calculation of the **standard deviation**; the square of the standard deviation

test-retest reliability – one of three basic reliability strategies, most appropriate for estimating the stability of a test over time, where a test is administered twice to the same group, with a reasonable interval of time between testing sessions, then scores from both tests are correlated

testwiseness – the ability to easily comprehend almost any test directions, knowledge of guessing strategies, or strategies for maximizing the speed of task performance

theoretical issues – issues about how tests should be designed and how they should perform, with dialogue often based in the beliefs of various theories of pedagogy, teaching methodologies, relative skill importance, and coordinating teaching and testing methods within a program

threshold loss agreement – a reliability strategy that does not depend on a high **standard deviation**, developed specifically for **criterion-referenced test** consistency estimation; includes two statistics, **agreement coefficient** and **kappa coefficient,** both of which measure the consistency of **master/non-master** classifications; generally requires the administration of a test on two occasions; sometimes called **decision consistency**

trimodal – a statistic of **central tendency** that describes the three points where scores occur most frequently, as in three peaks of a bell curve

true-false items – test items typically written as statements and students must decide whether the statements are true or false

U

uninstructed – students before instruction in a **pre-test**

V

validity coefficient – a statistic used to indicate the relationship between the two sets of scores; also called **correlation coefficient**

validity – the degree to which a test measures what it claims, or purports, to be measuring

value implications – the concept that indicates the political and situational implications of social values and their affect on testing

variance (S^2) – a **descriptive** statistic for **dispersion**, equal to the squared value of the **standard deviation**

W

washback – the degree to which a test affects the curriculum that is related to it

weighted scores – scores that are based on the assignment of more or less value for different questions or sections of a test

X

X axis – the horizontal line or **abscissa** of a two-axis graph, which is found in three forms: a **histogram,** a **bar graph,** or a **frequency polygon;** the vertical line is called the **ordinate,** or Y **axis**

Y

Y axis – the vertical line or **ordinate** of a two-axis graph, which is found in three forms: a **histogram,** a **bar graph,** or a **frequency polygon;** the horizontal line is called the **abscissa,** or X **axis**

Z

z score – a **standard score** that is a direct indication of the distance that a given raw score is from the mean in standard deviation units; determined by subtracting the **mean score** from the **raw score,** then dividing the result by the **standard deviation**

ACTFL. (1986). *ACTFL proficiency guidelines (Revised).* Hastings-on-Hudson, NY: American Council on the Teaching of Foreign Languages.

ACTFL. (2004). *ACTFL proficiency guidelines (Revised).* Hastings-on-Hudson, NY: American Council on the Teaching of Foreign Languages. Retrieved January 1, 2004 from the World Wide Web: http://www.sil.org/lingualinks/LANGUAGELEARNING/OtherResources/ACTFLProficiencyGuidelines/ACTFLProficiency Guidelines.htm

Alderson, J.C. (1993). Judgments in language testing. In D. Douglas and C. Chapelle (Eds.) *A New Decade of Language Testing Research* (pp. 46-57). Washington, DC: TESOL.

Alderson, J.C., & Hamp-Lyons, L. (1996). TOEFL preparation courses: A study of washback. *Language Testing, 13,* 280-297.

Alderson, J.C., & Wall, D. (1993). Does washback exist? *Applied Linguistics, 14,* 115-129.

Alderson, J.C., Clapham, C., & Wall, D. (1995). *Language test construction and evaluation.* Cambridge: Cambridge University.

Alderson, J.C., Krahnke, K.J. & Stansfield, C.W. (1987). *Reviews of English Language Proficiency Tests.* Washington, DC: TESOL.

ALI. (1966). *A report on the results of English testing during the 1966 pre-university workshop at the American Language Institute.* Unpublished ms. Washington, DC: American Language Institute, Georgetown University.

Allison, D. (1999). *Language Testing and Evaluation.* Singapore: Singapore University.

ALTE. (1998). *Multilingual Glossary of Language Testing Terms.* Cambridge: Cambridge University.

Anderson, L.W. (2003). *Classroom Assessment: Enhancing the Quality of Teacher Decision Making.* Mahwah, NJ: Lawrence Erlbaum Associates.

APA. (1999). *Standards for educational and psychological testing.* Washington, DC: American Psychological Association.

APA. (2001). *Publication manual of the American Psychological Association* (5th ed.). Washington, DC: American Psychological Association.

Bachman, L. & Savignon. S. (1986). The evaluation of communicative language proficiency: a critique of the ACTFL oral interview. *Modern Language Journal,* 70, 380-397.

Bachman, L.F. & Palmer, A.S. (1996). *Language testing in practice.* Oxford: Oxford University.

Bachman, L.F. (1987). The development and use of criterion-referenced tests of language proficiency in language program evaluation. In A. Wangsotorn, K. Prapphal, A. Maurice and B. Kenny (Eds.), *Trends in language programme evaluation.* Bangkok: Chulalongkorn University.

Bachman, L.F. (1989). The development and use of criterion-referenced tests of language proficiency in language program evaluation. In K. Johnson (Ed.), *Program design and evaluation in language teaching* (pp. 242-258). London: Cambridge University.

Bachman, L.F. (1990). *Fundamental considerations in language testing.* Oxford: Oxford University Press.

Bachman, L.F., Lynch, B.K., & Mason, M. (1995). Investigating variability in tasks and rater judgments in a performance test of foreign language speaking. *Language Testing, 12*(2), 239-257.

Bailey, K.M. (1996). Working for washback: A review of the washback concept in language testing. *Language Testing, 13,* 257-279.

Bailey, K.M. (1998). *Learning about Language Assessment: Dilemmas, Decisions, and Directions.* New York: Heinle & Heinle.

Barnwell, D.P. (1996). *A history of foreign language testing in the United States: From its beginnings to the present.* Tempe, AZ: Bilingual Press.

Beretta, A. (1986). Program-fair language teaching evaluation. *TESOL Quarterly,* 20(3), 431-444.

Berk, R.A. (1984). Selecting the index of reliability. In R.A. Berk (Ed.) *A guide to criterion-referenced test construction.* Baltimore: Johns Hopkins University Press.

Brennan, R.L. (1980). Applications of generalizability theory. In R.A. Berk (Ed.) *Criterion-referenced measurement: the state of the art.* Baltimore: Johns Hopkins University Press.

Brennan, R.L. (1984). Estimating the dependability of the scores. In R.A. Berk (Ed.) *A guide to criterion-referenced test construction.* Baltimore: Johns Hopkins University Press.

Brennan, R.L. (2001). *Generalizability theory.* New York: Springer-Verlag.

Brière, E.J. (1979). Testing communicative language proficiency. In R. Silverstein (Ed.) *Proceedings of the third international conference on frontiers in language proficiency and dominance testing.* Occasional papers on linguistics, No. 6. Carbondale, IL: Southern Illinois University.

Brown, J.D. (1981). Newly placed versus continuing students: comparing proficiency. In J.C. Fisher, M.A. Clarke & J. Schachter (Eds.) *On TESOL '80 building bridges: research and practice in teaching English as a second language.* Washington, DC: TESOL.

Brown, J.D. (1984a). Criterion-referenced language tests: what, how and why? *Gulf Area TESOL Bi-annual,* 1, 32-34.

Brown, J.D. (1984b). A norm-referenced engineering reading test. In A.K. Pugh & J.M. Ulijn (Eds.) *Reading for professional purposes: studies and practices in native and foreign languages.* London: Heinemann Educational Books.

Brown, J.D. (1988a). *Understanding research in second language learning: A teacher's guide to statistics and research design.* London: Cambridge University.

Brown, J.D. (1988b). Components of engineering-English reading ability. *System,* 16, 193-200.

Brown, J.D. (1989a). Improving ESL placement tests using two perspectives. *TESOL Quarterly,* 23.

Brown, J.D. (1990a). Short-cut estimates of criterion-referenced test consistency. *Language Testing, 7*(1), 77-97.

Brown, J.D. (1990b). Where do tests fit into language programs? *JALT Journal, 12,* 121-140.

Brown, J.D. (1992). Classroom-centered language testing. *TESOL Journal,* 1, 12-15.

Brown, J.D. (1993). A comprehensive criterion-referenced language testing project. In D. Douglas and C. Chapelle (Eds.) *A New Decade of Language Testing Research* (pp. 163-184). Washington, DC: TESOL.

Brown, J.D. (1995a). *The elements of language curriculum: A systematic approach to program development.* Boston, MA: Heinle & Heinle.

Brown, J.D. (1995b). Differences between norm-referenced and criterion-referenced tests. In J.D. Brown & S. O. Yamashita (Eds.), *Language testing in Japan* (pp. 12-19). Tokyo: Japanese Association for Language Teaching.

Brown, J.D. (1996a). *Testing in language programs.* Upper Saddle River, NJ: Prentice-Hall.

Brown, J.D. (1996b). English language entrance examinations in Japan: Problems and solutions. In G. van Troyer (Ed.) *JALT '95: Curriculum and evaluation* (pp. 272-283). Tokyo: Japan Association for Language Teaching.

Brown, J.D. (1996c). Fluency development. In G. van Troyer (Ed.) *JALT '95: Curriculum and evaluation* (pp. 174-179). Tokyo: Japan Association for Language Teaching.

Brown, J.D. (1997). Do tests washback on the language classroom? *TESOLANZ Journal, 5,* 63-80.

Brown, J.D. (Ed.) (1998). *New ways of classroom assessment.* Arlington, VA: TESOL.

Brown, J.D. (1999a). The roles and responsibilities of assessment in foreign language education. *JLTA Journal, 2,* 1-21.

Brown, J.D. (1999b). Relative importance of persons, items, subtests and languages to TOEFL test variance. *Language Testing, 16*(2), 216-237.

Brown, J.D. (2001). *Using surveys in language programs.* Cambridge: Cambridge University Press.

Brown, J.D. (2002). Do cloze tests work? Or, is it just an illusion? *Second Language Studies, 21*(1), 79-125.

Brown, J.D. (2003a). The many facets of language curriculum development. *ELT in a globalized world: Innovations and applications—Selected papers from the 5th CULI International Conference, 2003* (pp. 1-18). Bangkok: CULI, Chulalongkorn University.

Brown, J.D. (2003b). Creating a complete language-testing program. In C. A. Coombe & N. J. Hubley (eds.), *Assessment Practices* (pp. 9-23). Washington, DC: TESOL.

Brown, J.D. (avec contributions de LAIRDIL). (1995). *Aspects of fluency and accuracy (Conférence nº 4).* Toulouse, France: Laboratoire Inter-Universitaire de Recherche en Didactique des Langues.

Brown, J.D. (translated by M. Wada). (1999). *Gengo tesuto no kisochishi (Literally: Basic knowledge of language testing).* Tokyo: Taishukan Shoten.

Brown, J.D. & Bailey, K.M. (1984). A categorical instrument for scoring second language writing skills. *Language Learning, 34,* 21-42.

Brown, J.D. & Hudson, T. (2002). *Criterion-referenced language testing.* Cambridge: Cambridge University Press.

Brown, J.D. & Pennington, M.C. (1991). Unifying curriculum processes and curriculum outcomes: the key to excellence in language education. In M.C. Pennington (Ed.) Building Better English Language Programs: Perspectives on evaluation in ESL. Washington, DC: NAFSA.

Brown, J.D. & Rodgers, T. (2002). *Doing applied linguistics research.* Oxford: Oxford University Press.

Brown, J.D. & Ross, J. A. (1996). Decision dependability of item types, sections, tests, and the overall TOEFL test battery. In M. Milanovic & N. Saville (Eds.), *Performance Testing , Cognition and Assessment* (pp. 231-265). Cambridge: Cambridge University.

Brown, J.D. & Yamashita, S.O. (1995a). English language entrance examinations at Japanese universities: What do we know about them? *JALT Journal, 17*(1), 7-30.

Brown, J.D. & Yamashita, S.O. (1995b). English language entrance examinations at Japanese universities: 1993 and 1994. In J.D. Brown & S.O. Yamashita (Eds.) *Language Testing in Japan* (pp. 86-100). Tokyo: Japan Association for Language Teaching.

Brown, J.D., Cook, H.G, Lockhart, C. & Ramos, T. (1991). Southeast Asian Languages Proficiency Examinations. In S. Anivan (Ed.) *Current developments in language testing* (pp. 210-226). Singapore: SEAMEO Regional Language Centre.

Brown, J.D., Cunha, M.I.A., & Frota, S. de F.N. (2001). The development and validation of a Portuguese version of the Motivated Strategies for Learning Questionnarie. In Z. Dörnyei & R. Schmidt (Eds.), *Motivation and second language acquisition* (pp. 257-280). Honolulu, HI: Second Language Teaching & Curriculum Center, University of Hawai'i Press.

Brown, J.D., Hudson, T., Norris, J.M., & Bonk, W. (2002). *Investigating second language performance assessments.* Honolulu, HI: Second Language Teaching & Curriculum Center, University of Hawai'i Press.

Canale, M. & M. Swain. (1980). Theoretical bases of communicative approaches to second language teaching and testing. *Applied Linguistics, 1,* 1-47.

Canale, M. & M. Swain. (1981). A theoretical framework for communicative competence. In A. Palmer, P.J.M. Groot, & G.A. Trosper (Eds.) *The construct validation of tests of communicative competence.* Washington, DC: TESOL.

Canale, M. (1983a). On some dimensions of language proficiency. In J.W. Oller Jr. (Ed.) *Issues in language testing.* Cambridge, MA: Newbury House.

Canale, M. (1983b). From communicative competence to communicative language pedagogy. In R.C. Richards & R.W. Schmidt (Eds.), *Language and communication.* London: Longman.

Candlin, C.N. (1986). Explaining communicative competence limits of testability? In C. W. Stansfield (Ed.), *Toward communicative competence testing: Proceedings of the Second TOEFL Invitational Conference.* Princeton, NJ: Educational Testing Service.

Carroll, J.B. (1972). Fundamental considerations in testing for English language proficiency of foreign students. In H.B. Allen & R.N. Campbell *Teaching English as a second language: A book of readings* (2nd ed.). New York: McGraw-Hill.

Cartier, F. (1968). Criterion-referenced testing of language skills. *TESOL Quarterly, 2,* 27-32.

Cheng, L. and Curtis, A. (2004). Washback or backwash: A review of the Impact of Testing on Teaching and Learning. In L. Cheng, Y. Watanabe, A. Curtis (eds.). *Washback in Language Testing: Research Contexts and Methods* (pp. 3-17). Mahwah, NJ: Lawrence Erlbaum Associates.

Cheng, L. and Watanabe, Y. with Curtis, A. (eds.). (2004). *Washback in Language Testing: Research Contexts and Methods.* Mahwah, NJ: Lawrence Erlbaum Associates.

Childs, M. (1995). Good and Bad Uses of TOEIC by Japanese Companies, In J.D. Brown & S.O. Yamashita (Eds.). *Language testing in Japan* (pp. 66-75). Tokyo: Japan Association for Language Teaching.

Chomsky, N. (1965). *Aspects of the theory of syntax.* Cambridge, MA: M.I.T Press.

Cizek, G. J. (Ed.). (2001). *Setting performance standards: Concepts, methods, and perspectives.* Mahwah, NJ: Lawrence Erlbaum Associates.

Cook, H. G. (1990). Tailoring ESL reading placement tests with criterion-referenced items. Unpublished M.A. theses. Honolulu, HI: University of Hawaii at Manoa.

Cziko, G. A. (1982). Improving the psychometric, criterion-referenced, and practical qualities of integrative language tests. *TESOL Quarterly, 16,* 367-379.

Cziko, G.A. (1983). Psychometric and edumetric approaches to language testing. In J.W. Oller, Jr. (Ed.) *Issues in language testing research.* Cambridge, MA: Newbury House.

Davidson, F. & Lynch, B.K. (1993). Criterion-referenced language test development: A prolegomenon. In A. Huhta, K. Sajavaara, & S. Takala (Eds.). *Language testing: New openings* (pp. 73-89). Jyväsklyä, Finland: Institute for Educational Research, University of Jyväsklyä.

Davidson, F. & Lynch, B.K. (2002). *Testcraft: A teacher's guide to writing and using language test specifications.* New Haven, CT: Yale University.

Delamere, T. (1985). Notional-functional syllabi and criterion-referenced tests: The missing link. *System, 13,* 43-47.

Dick, W., Carey, J.O., & L. Carey. (2000). *The systematic design of instruction* (5th ed.). Upper Saddle River, NJ: Pearson Educational.

Douglas, D. (2000). *Assessing languages for specific purposes.* Cambridge: Cambridge University.

Ebel, R.L. (1979). *Essentials of educational measurement* (3rd ed.). Englewood Cliffs, NJ: Prentice-Hall.

Erickson, M. & J. Molloy. (1983). ESP test development project for engineering students. In J.W. Oller, Jr. (Ed.) *Issues in language testing research.* Cambridge, MA: Newbury House.

ETS. (1968). *Modern Language Association Foreign Language Proficiency Tests for Teachers and Advanced Students.* Princeton, NJ: Educational Testing Service.

ETS. (1996). *TOEFL Test of Written English Guide.* Princeton, NJ: Educational Testing Service.

ETS. (1997). *TOEFL test and score manual (1997 edition).* Princeton, NJ: Educational Testing Service.

ETS. (1998). *Overview: ETS fairness review.* Princeton, NJ: Educational Testing Service.

ETS. (2000). *Computer-based TOEFL score user guide (2000-2001 edition).* Princeton, NJ: Educational Testing Service.

ETS. (2001). *TSE and SPEAK score user's guide (2001-2002 edition).* Princeton, NJ: Educational Testing Service.

ETS. (2002a). *TOEFL test and score data summary (2002-2003 edition).* Princeton, NJ: Educational Testing Service.

ETS. (2002b). *ETS standards for quality and fairness.* Princeton, NJ: Educational Testing Service.

ETS. (2003). *Test of English as a foreign language.* Princeton, NJ: Educational Testing Service.

ETS. (2004). *TOEFL Concordance Tables.* Princeton, NJ: Educational Testing Service. Retrieved [January 1, 2004] from the World Wide Web: http://www.toefl.org/educator/edconcords1.html

Farhady, H. (1982). Measures of language proficiency from the learner's perspective. *TESOL Quarterly, 16,* 43-59.

Fisher, R.A. & F. Yates. (1963). *Statistical tables for biological, agricultural and medical research.* London: Longman.

Gardner, D. (1996). Self-assessment for self-access learners. *TESOL Journal, 5*(3), 18-23.

Gates, S. (1995). Exploiting washback from standardized tests. In J.D. Brown & S. O. Yamashita (Eds.), *Language testing in Japan* (pp. 101-106). Tokyo: Japanese Association for Language Teaching.

Genessee, F. & Upshur, J.A. (1996). *Classroom evaluation in second language education.* Cambridge: Cambridge University.

Glaser, R. (1963). Instructional technology and the measurement of learning outcomes: Some questions. *American Psychologist, 18,* 519- 521.

Glass, E.V. (1978). Standards and criteria. *Journal of Educational Measurement, 15,* 237-261.

Griffee, D. T. (1995). Criterion-referenced test construction and evaluation. In J.D. Brown & S. O. Yamashita (Eds.), Language testing in Japan (pp. 20-28). Tokyo: Japanese Association for Language Teaching.

Guerrero, M.D. (2000). The unified validity of the Four Skills Exam: Applying Messick's framework. *Language Testing, 17*(4), 397-421.

Halliday, M.A.K. (1979). *Language as social semiotic.* London: Arnold.

Hambleton, R., & Rodgers, J. (1995). Item bias review. *Practical Assessment, Research & Evaluation, 4*(6). Retrieved January 1, 2004 from http://pareonline.net/getvn.asp?v=4&n=6.

Harris D.P. & L.A. Palmer. (1970). *Comprehensive English language test for speakers of English as a second language.* New York: McGraw-Hill.

Hatch, E. & A. Lazaraton. (1991). *The research manual: design and statistics for applied linguistics.* Cambridge, MA: Newbury House.

Henning, G. (1987). *A guide to language testing: development, evaluation, research.* Cambridge, MA: Newbury House.

Heyneman, S. P., & Ransom, A. W. (1990). Using examinations and testing to improve educational quality. *Educational Policy,* 177-192.

Hinofotis, F.B. (1981). Perspectives on language testing: past, present and future. *Nagoya Gakuin Daigaku Gaikokugo Kyoiku Kiyo, 4,* 51-59.

Hudson, T. & B. Lynch (1984). A criterion-referenced approach to ESL achievement testing. *Language Testing, 1,* 171-201.

Hudson, T. D. (1989a). Mastery decisions in program evaluation. In K. Johnson (Ed.). *Program design and evaluation in language teaching* (pp. 259-269). London: Cambridge University.

Hudson, T. D. (1989b). Measurement approaches in the development of functional ability level language tests: norm-referenced, criterion-referenced, and item response theory decisions. Unpublished PhD dissertation. University of California at Los Angeles.

Huff, D. & I. Geis (1993). *How to lie with statistics.* New York: W.W. Norton.

Hughes, A. (1989). *Testing for language teachers.* Cambridge: Cambridge University Press.

Hymes, D.H. (1967a). Models of interaction of language and social setting. *Journal of Social Issues, 33,* 8-28.

Hymes, D.H. (1967b). Modes of interaction of language and social life. In J. MacNamara (Ed.), *Problems of bilingualism, Journal of Social Issues, 23,* 8-28.

Hymes, D.H. (1972). On communicative competence. In J. Pride & J Holmes (Eds.), S*ociolinguistics: Selected readings* (pp. 269-293). Harmondsworth, UK: Penguin.

Jacobs, H.L., S.A. Zinkgraf, D.R. Wormuth, V.F. Hartfiel & J.B. Hughey. (1981). *Testing ESL composition: a practical approach.* Rowley, MA: Newbury House.

Johnson, J. (1998). Peer assessment: So how did you like my presentation? In J.D. Brown (Ed.), *New ways of classroom assessment* (pp. 67-69). Alexandria, VA: TESOL.

Kellaghan, T. & Greaney, V. (1992). *Using examinations to improve education: A study of fourteen African countries.* Washington, DC: The World Bank.

Keppel, G. (2002). *Introduction to design and analysis: A student's guide* (8th ed.). New York: W.H. Freeman.

Kondo-Brown, K., & Brown, J.D. (2004). *The Japanese Placement Tests at the University of Hawai'i: Applying item response theory* (NFLRC NetWork #20) [HTML document]. Honolulu: University of Hawai'i, Second Language Teaching & Curriculum Center. Accessed January 1, 2004 from the World Wide Web: http://www.LLL.hawaii.edu/nflrc/NetWorks/NW20/

Kuder, G.F. & M.W. Richardson. (1937). The theory of estimation of test reliability. *Psychometrika, 2,* 151-160.

Kunnan, A.J. (1992). An investigation of a criterion-referenced test using G-theory, and factor and cluster analysis. *Language Testing, 9*(1), 30-49.

Kunnan, A.J. (1995). *Test taker characteristics and test performance: A structural modeling approach.* Cambridge: Cambridge University.

Kunnan, A.J. (2000) *Fairness and validation in language assessment.* Cambridge: Cambridge University.

Lado, R. (1961). *Language testing: The construction and use of foreign language tests.* London: Longmans.

Lynch, B.K. & Davidson, F. (1994). Criterion-referenced language test development: Lining curricula, teachers, and tests. *TESOL Quarterly, 28,* 727-743.

Lynch, B.K. & Davidson, F. (1997). Criterion referenced testing. In C. Clapham & D. Corson (Eds.), *Encyclopedia of language and education: Volume 7 Language testing and assessment* (pp. 263-273). Dordrecht, The Netherlands: Kluwer Academic.

Maxwell, A. (1965). A comparison of two English as a foreign language tests. Unpublished ms. Davis, CA: University of California (Davis).

McKay, P. (2000). On ESL standards for school-age learners. *Language Testing, 17*(2), 185-214.

McNamara, M. J., & Deane, D. (1995). Self-assessment activities: Toward autonomy in language learning. *TESOL Journal, 5*(1), 17-21.

McNamara, T. (1996). *Measuring second language performance.* London: Longman.

Mehrens, W. A., & Kaminsky, J. (1989). Methods for improving standardized test scores: Fruitful, fruitless, or fraudulent? *Educational Measurement: Issues and Practice, 8,* 14-22.

Mendelsohn, D. (1992). Instruments for feedback in oral communication. *TESOL Journal, 1*(2), 25-30.

Messick, S. (1988). The once and future issues of validity: assessing the meaning of consequences of measurement. In H. Wainer and H.I Braun *Test validity.* Hillsdale, NJ: Lawrence Erlbaum.

Messick, S. (1994). The interplay of evidence and consequences in the validation of performance assessments. *Educational Researcher, 23*(2), 13-23.

Messick, S. (1996). Validity and washback in language testing. *Language Testing, 13,* 241-256.

Microsoft (2003). *Excel™*. Redman, WA: Microsoft.

Murphey, T. (l995). Tests: Learning through negotiated interaction. *TESOL Journal, 4,* 12-16.

Norris, J. (1996). Performance and portfolio assessment (1985-1995): An extended annotated bibliography of sources useful for language teachers (NetWork #4) [HTML document]. Honolulu: University of Hawai'i, Second Language Teaching & Curriculum Center. Retrieved [January 1, 2004] from the World Wide Web: http://www.nflrc.hawaii.edu/NetWorks/NW04/

Norris, J. M. (2002). *Language Testing: Special Issue – Interpretations, intended uses, and designs in task-based language assessment.* London: Arnold

Norris, J.M., J.D. Brown, T. Hudson, & J. Yoshioka, J. (1998). *Designing second language performance assessments* (Technical Report #18). Honolulu, HI: University of Hawai'i, Second Language Teaching & Curriculum Center.

O'Malley, J. M., & Valdez Pierce, L. (1996). *Authentic assessment for English language learners: Practical approaches for teachers.* Reading, MA: Addison-Wesley.

Oller, J.W. Jr. (1979). *Language tests at school: a pragmatic approach.* London: Longman.

Oller, J.W. Jr., Kim, K., Choe, Y. (2000). Testing verbal (language) and non-verbal abilities in language minorities: A socio-educational problem in historical perspective. *Language Testing, 17*(3), 341-360.

Oscarson, M. (1997). Self-assessment of foreign and second language proficiency. In C. Clapham & D. Corson (Eds.), *Encyclopedia of language and education: Volume 7 Language testing and assessment* (pp. 175-187). Dordrecht, The Netherlands: Kluwer Academic.

Plake, B.S. & Impara, J.C. (Eds.). (2001). *The fourteenth mental measurements yearbook.* Lincoln, NE: Buros Institute.

Plake, B.S., Impara, J.C., & Spies, R.A. (Eds.). (2003). *The fifteenth mental measurements yearbook.* Lincoln, NE: Buros Institute.

Popham, W.J. & T.R. Husek. (1969). Implications of criterion-referenced measurement. *Journal of Educational Measurement, 6,* 1-9.

Popham, W.J. (1978). *Criterion-referenced measurement.* Englewood Cliffs, NJ: Prentice-Hall.

Popham, W.J. (1995). Classroom assessment: What teachers need to know. Boston: Allyn and Bacon.

Premaratne, G.K. (1987). A close study of the cloze procedure: a comparison of three cloze types used in ESL testing. Unpublished MA thesis, University of Hawaii at Manoa.

Rietveld, T., & van Hout, R. (1993). *Statistical techniques for the study of language and language behaviour.* Berlin: Mouton de Gruyter.

Sasaki, M. (1996). *Second language proficiency, foreign language aptitude, and intelligence: Quantitative and qualitative analyses.* New York: Peter Lang.

Savignon, S.J. (1972). *Communicative competence: an experiment in foreign-language teaching.* Philadelphia: Center for Curriculum Development.

Savignon, S.J. (1985). Evaluation of communicative competence: the ACTFL provisional proficiency guidelines. *Modern Language Journal, 69,* 129-142.

Shavelson, R. J., & Webb, N. M. (1991). *Generalizability theory: A primer.* Newbury Park, CA: Sage.

Shohamy, E. (1992). Beyond performance testing: A diagnostic feedback testing model for assessing foreign language learning. *Modern Language Journal, 76*(4), 513-521.

Shohamy, E., Donitsa-Schmidt, S., & Ferman, I. (1996). Test impact revisited: Washback effect over time. *Language Testing, 13,* 298-317.

Spolsky, B. (1978). Introduction: linguists and language testers. In B. Spolsky (Ed.) *Advances in language testing series: 2.* Arlington, VA: Center for Applied Linguistics.

Spolsky, B. (1995). *Measured words: The development of objective language testing.* Oxford: Oxford University.

Stansfield, C. W., & Kenyon, D. M. (1992). Research of the comparability of the oral proficiency interview and the simulated oral proficiency interview. *System, 20,* 347-364.

Subkoviak, M.J. (1988). A practitioner's guide to computation and interpretation of reliability indices for mastery tests. *Journal of Educational Measurement, 25,* 47-55.

University of Michigan. (1961). *Michigan test of English language proficiency: Form A.* Ann Arbor, MI: University of Michigan Press.

Upshur, J.A. (1966). Comparison of performance on "Test of English as a Foreign Language" and "Michigan Test of English Language Proficiency." Unpublished ms. Ann Arbor, MI: University of Michigan.

Wall, D. (1996). Introducing new tests into traditional systems: Insights from general education and from innovation theory. *Language Testing, 13,* 234-354.

Wall, D. (1997). Impact and washback in language testing. In C. Clapham & D. Corson (Eds.), *Encyclopedia of language and education: Volume 7 Language testing and assessment* (pp. 291-302). Dordrecht, The Netherlands: Kluwer Academic.

Watanabe, Y. (1996a). Does grammar translation come from the entrance examination? Preliminary findings from classroom-based research. *Language Testing, 13,* 318-333.

Watanabe, Y. (1996b). Investigating washback in Japanese EFL classrooms: Problems and methodology. *Australian Review of Applied Linguistics, 13,* 208-239.

Widdowson, H.G. (1978). *Teaching language as communication.* Oxford: Oxford University Press.